Adventure Guide to the

Inside
Passage
& Coastal Alaska

4th Edition

Adventure Guide to the

Inside
Passage
& Coastal Alaska

4th Edition

Ed & Lynn Readicker-Henderson

HUNTER

HUNTER PUBLISHING, INC,
130 Campus Drive, Edison, NJ 08818
☎ 732-225-1900; 800-255-0343; Fax 732-417-1744
comments@hunterpublishing.com

Ulysses Travel Publications
4176 Saint-Denis, Montréal, Québec
Canada H2W 2M5
☎ 514-843-9447; Fax 514-843-9448

Windsor Books
The Boundary, Wheatley Road, Garsington
Oxford, OX44 9EJ England
☎ 01865-361122; Fax 01865-361133

ISBN 1-58843-288-2

© 2002 Hunter Publishing, Inc.

*This and other Hunter travel guides are also
available as e-books in a variety of digital formats
through our on-line partners, including netlibrary.com, Amazon.com,
BarnesandNoble.com, publicationsunbound.com and eBooks.com.*

Cover photo © Estock Photo. Sea lions on channel marker.
Back photo & interior images © Lynn & Ed Readicker-Henderson
Index by Elite Indexing
Cartoons by Joe Kohl

Maps by Kim André © 2002 Hunter Publishing, Inc.
(Base maps provided by Lynn Readicker-Henderson)

1   2   3   4

www.hunterpublishing.com

Hunter's full range of guides to all corners of the globe is featured on our exciting website. You'll find guidebooks to suit every type of traveler, no matter what their budget, lifestyle, or idea of fun.

Adventure Guides – There are now over 40 titles in this series, covering destinations from Costa Rica and the Yucatán to Tampa Bay & Florida's West Coast, New Hampshire and the Alaska Highway. Complete information on what to do, as well as where to stay and eat, *Adventure Guides* are tailor-made for the active traveler, with a focus on hiking, biking, canoeing, horseback riding, trekking, skiing, watersports, and all other kinds of fun.

Alive Guides – This ever-popular line of books takes a unique look at the best each destination offers: fine dining, jazz clubs, first-class class hotels and resorts. In-margin icons direct the reader at a glance. Top-sellers include *The Cayman Islands, St. Martin & St. Barts,* and *Aruba, Bonaire & Curaçao.*

Our ***Hunter-Rivages Hotels of Character & Charm*** books are top sellers, with titles covering France, Spain, Italy, Paris and Portugal. Originating in Paris, they set the standard for excellence with their fabulous color photos, superb maps and candid descriptions of the most remarkable hotels of Europe.

Our ***Romantic Weekends*** guidebooks provide a series of escapes for couples of all ages and lifestyles. Unlike most "romantic" travel books, ours cover more than charming hotels and delightful restaurants, with a host of activities that you and your partner will remember forever.

One-of-a-kind travel books available from Hunter include *Best Dives of the Western Hemisphere; The Jewish Travel Guide; Golf Resorts; Cruising Alaska* and many more.

Full descriptions are given for each book, along with reviewers' comments and a cover image. You can also view the table of contents and sample pages. Books may be purchased on-line via our secure transaction facility.

Acknowledgments

This book started when John and Sylvia, of Wrangell's Alaska Vistas, reminded us that it was time to go back to the Stikine River, the most beautiful spot on earth. Without them, none of this ever would have happened. As always, many thanks to Kathy Day, of Kathy Day Public Relations, who knows everybody and everything, and has been vital to every one of these books we've written. David Trainer and Leslie Hall kept things going when we would have let them drop. Buckwheat, John Beiler, and especially Marie Oboscky made the research sheer heaven. Thanks to Andrea Petzel for her salmon expertise. We wish a peaceful road for all of you.

Contents

▤ Maps

Introduction

Alaska has over 45,000 miles of coastline – more than the rest of the United States combined. With so much shoreline, the best way to see the state is by ship. More than three-quarters of a million people visit Alaska by cruise ship every year. But from those big cruise ships, you're not going to see much. That leaves you with two good options for seeing the real Alaska: you can take a boutique cruise – jump on one of the small ships that travel the Inside Passage and get pampered in the rain forest; or you can go for the more flexible option, one that Alaskans use, and ride the Alaska Marine Highway ferry system. From Bellingham, Washington up the Inside Passage, through Southcentral Alaska and Prince William Sound, and as far west as Dutch Harbor in the Aleutians, the Alaska Marine Highway is Alaska's coastal road system. Most communities along the ferry route are not connected to the state's interior – there are few automobile roads that reach to the coast – so the AMH serves as an invaluable lifeline.

For the traveler, a ship along Alaska's coast is the ideal way to see some of the very best the state has to offer. The cruise ships hit the towns; the ferry does that and travels through hundreds of tiny bays and inlets, around islands so thick with trees and brush that the forests look like a single solid mass. Past glaciers and icefields, ships follows the whale migration route, and it's not unusual to look out from the deck and see the long back of a humpback whale pacing the boat. Dall's porpoise, harbor seals, and Steller's sea lions are only some of the many animal attractions.

When you travel on the Alaska Marine Highway you get exactly the same view the cruise ship passengers get – for a fraction of the price. Better, the big cruise ships park in towns during daylight hours and travel only at night. The Alaska Marine Highway is always running, and it not only goes to all the same places the cruise ships do, it goes to a lot of places the cruise lines have never heard of.

The towns along Alaska's coast are small – Juneau, the state capital and the largest ferry port, has only about 35,000 people. The towns are manageable for the traveler, and Alaskans along the coast are always hospitable to new people, anxious to distract themselves from island fever. Lodging runs from rustic cabins set deep in the woods to four-star hotels. Along the coast, you can be as rough or sybaritic as you wish.

The coast of Alaska has something for everyone: beautiful scenery, vital culture, thriving industry, and history ranging from the early natives to travelers from Russia, Europe, and the Americas. The coast has always been the center of activity in the state. You're entering the best part of Alaska, mingling with both locals and those from Down South in a casual atmosphere. You can kick back and leave the driving to the captain.

Traveling Alaska by ship opens up more of the state than all of the north's road systems combined. The landscape is always varied, always beautiful, and there's always something new and spectacular to see.

When a whale comes up to breathe, you can hear it exhale from more than a mile away. Year after year the whales head from their winter homes in Hawaii to their summer grounds in Alaska. You can travel the same waters as the whales and find out why they keep coming to the coast, the true heart of Alaska.

■ Who We Are, What We Do & What You're in For

Okay, so why should you trust your vacation to us? We've been writing about coastal Alaska for nearly a dozen years; over that time, we've been lucky enough to get to see and do just about everything in the state. This book brings you the places and things that we think you're going to love.

However, let's admit to a couple biases right up front: you go to the North to see the wild, to be outside, to see the best that nature has to offer. You don't go up there to eat or sleep at the exact same places you can find at home. Chain stores, in all their many permutations, make for mediocre experiences. We believe that you get the best trip when you deal with the people who live, work, and make a place their home. If you're planning to spend your trip eating two meals a day at McDonald's, this book isn't for you.

We also believe the best travelers, the happiest travelers, are the ones who know what they're looking at. That's why we spend so much time on history and culture. It ain't just like it is back home.

And we hope it never is.

Thanks for traveling with us.

■ How This Book is Organized

After the introductory material, where we fill you in on the life and cultures of the North, and how to get the most out of your trip, the book follows a pretty simple route.

The towns are listed in order if you were traveling from south to north and west to east; in other words, the book follows the sweep of the coastline, starting with Bellingham down in Washington State, moving north through the islands of Canada, into the Southeastern panhandle, then into Prince William Sound, on to Kenai, and finally out to the Aleutians.

Each stop is organized in the same way: first comes the area's history and a section of basic information – Internet, tourist info, etc. Turn here first for the questions you're going to have when you hit town. Then we give the "quick stop," the "don't miss" and the "best freebie" in each town. The quick stop is designed for cruise ship passengers or anybody else who comes to a town with less than a day to spend. "Don't miss" items offer the very best the town has to offer, and the "best freebie" is, well, you guessed it, the best free thing to do. From there, on to stuff around the town, adventures, and restaurants and hotels. Obviously, in some towns, these get kind of compressed – there's not a lot of need for separate sections in villages like Kake that have one hotel.

Throughout the book, there are scattered suggestions for extra reading, and authors' picks – the stuff that we think is absolutely the best Alaska has to offer.

The Land

The word Alaska comes from the Aleutian word *alakshak*, "land that is not an island." Maybe the Aleuts were just trying to misdirect the Russians, get them inland and away from the island paradise that the Aleuts themselves called home.

Alaska's coast includes climatic and geographic extremes, from the lush temperate rainforests of Southeast Alaska to the barren rocky islands and towering volcanoes of the Aleutians.

Southeast Alaska, also known as the **Alexander Archipelago,** is roughly 520 miles long by 125 miles wide. **Southeast, Southcentral** on the mainland, and the **Prince William Sound** areas are dominated by vibrant rainforest punctuated by mountains rising almost directly from the sea. Most of the mountain peaks are in the 2,000-4,000-foot range, with the lower peaks usually topped by alpine meadows and the higher peaks snow-covered year-round.

The land along the **Alaska Peninsula** and into the **Aleutians** is a strange mixture of barren and lush. The gray rocks of the islands rise almost vertically from the sea and are capped by rich green vegetation. Other islands are more gradually shaped, but the vegetation is lower, stunted by the extremely harsh weather. The peninsula has none of the dense forests that characterize Southeast and Southcentral. Surrounded by water as deep as 25,000 feet and suffering from weather that can be foggy in one spot, pouring rain two feet over, and sunny a dozen feet ahead, the Aleutians today are as wild as they were when the first settlers reached them, crossing the Bering Land Bridge.

■ Rivers, Lakes & Streams

Flowing out of 20,000 mountain lakes in Southeast are more than 40,000 miles of river and stream, weaving through the thick patches of Sitka spruce, Western hemlock, and devil's club. All this water comes from Southeast's amazing weather. It rains. All the time.

SUNNY DELIGHT

Some parts of Baranof Island receive more than 400 inches of rain a year; Stewart/Hyder has the third greatest recorded snowfall of any spot on earth, with more than 1,100 inches in a single year. The saying goes, "If you can see the mountains, it's about to rain. If you can't see the mountains, it is raining." To see a mountaintop in Southeast is a rare occasion, and a sunny day should be enjoyed to the fullest. The state government in Juneau has actually shut down on sunny summer days so that employees can get outside and enjoy the respite from rain. The proper coast term for a sunny day is "cloud impaired."

■ Ice

While rain shapes modern life in coastal Alaska, it was ice that shaped the land itself. At least 10,000 years ago the entire coastal area was covered with thick sheets of glacial ice – there was once more than 2,000 feet of ice where Anchorage now sits, and at least double that on top of most of Southeast. As the glaciers retreated, they dragged millions of pounds of rock and gravel with them, carving the land as they went. In Southeast, you can judge the height of mountains by using the mile rule – the glacier that once covered Southeast was roughly a mile thick; mountains lower than that are smooth and rounded; over that 4,500-foot or so mark, mountain tops are sharp and craggy.

The dramatically deep valleys you can see are largely a result of glacial retreat. Many of the canals and channels are actually "drowned" fjords, which filled with sea water as the land levels fluctuated. Glaciers remain one of the main attractions of the region.

■ Volcanoes

The entire coast is ringed by volcanoes. **Mt. Edgecumbe**, across Sitka Sound from the town of Sitka, is a perfect volcanic cone, as delicately shaped as Japan's Mt. Fuji, and there are still hot springs – Tenakee, Goddard, White Sulfur – bubbling up from geothermal activity. Although there are no longer active volcanoes in Southeast, eruptions in the Alaska Peninsula and the Aleutians are common, and frequently the ferry makes a run past a smoking cone.

Active volcanoes dot the Southcentral landscape. Augustine erupted in 1986, and in 1993, an eruption of Redoubt shut down transportation in Southcentral's skies for days as the ash cloud billowed. But these events are the exception, not the rule for Southcentral.

It is on the **Alaska Peninsula** and the **Aleutians** that the volcanoes begin to dominate. **Katmai**, the "Valley of 10,000 Smokes," saw the largest volcanic eruption ever recorded when, in 1912, a virtually unknown volcano, **Novarupta**, exploded. Prior to that, the landscape had been lush and full of wildlife. The eruption dumped 700 feet of ash in some places, and Katmai remains one of the most active volcanic regions in the world.

■ Earthquakes

Southeast is also mostly safe from earthquakes; their fury is largely felt in Southcentral. From Yakutat to Kodiak, this is a prime earthquake zone, forever made famous by a single event. On Good Friday, 1964, a tremor measuring 8.4 on the Richter Scale hit Anchorage. Tidal waves nearly wiped out every city along the Southcentral coast.

But things are usually more calm in Southcentral. Prince William Sound, now infamous because of the *Exxon Valdez* oil spill, is sheltered, quiet water, studded with hundreds of tiny islands covered by the same kind of rainforest as Southeast.

The Cultures

■ Southcentral & The Aleutians

 The dominant group in the western Gulf of Alaska and the Aleutians is the **Aleut Indians**. The Aleuts came over the Bering Land Bridge, liked what they saw right there at its base, and stayed, making a living from the rich seas and harsh lands of western Alaska. For linguistic purposes, Aleuts are split into western, central, and eastern branches, but the language differences are dialectical and, unlike the **Koniags** (the other coastal Eskimo group), an Aleut from Attu can understand one from Chignik.

NOT EVERY INDIAN IS AN ALEUT

When the Russians first arrived in the area, they applied the term "Aleut" indiscriminately to every native they found. Because of this usage, which survives to modern times, the coastal Koniag Eskimos were also lumped into the "Aleut" category, despite the fact they were from quite a different group, and spoke an entirely different language. Physical differences are less marked. Athabaskan Indians also inhabited large parts of Southcentral, though they were not dominant along the coast.

Before the arrival of the Russians, Aleut culture thrived. They hunted from **baidarka** (kayaks) for whale, seal, sea lion, and otter, using tools made from bone and stone. Their clothing was made from animal intestines, which made it waterproof.

Aleut dwellings were communal and usually subterranean, covered with the excellent insulation of growing grass. Some of these underground houses are said to have been as large as 250 feet long. The houses had hatches in the ceiling to allow light in and smoke out; the ceiling was often held in place by rafters of whalebone, instead of scarce timber. Windows were made of translucent panes of otter intestine. In the hierarchy of society, the back of the house was always reserved for the most respected member of the dwelling. The Russians weren't very impressed with all this: "What is more revolting than all else is the filth around their huts, for the islanders do not go far away to do anything – and this gives one a very bad impression of their tidiness."

But while the Russians were out shivering in wool and living in houses entirely unadapted to local conditions, the Aleuts and Koniags were pretty comfy. In addition to clothes made of intestines, the Aleuts had developed highly decorated and very practical garments. **Parkas** were made of sea otter skin or bird skin – the feathers were worn on the inside, and so the down coat was invented. It took about 40 tufted puffins to make one parka, but cormorants were preferred for style and comfort. Aleut men wore **wooden hats**, shaped somewhat like a limpet shell, heavily decorated to show status and place in the community. The hats were especially important during visits to other villages. They also shielded the eyes to prevent the social gaffe of looking directly into someone's eyes (even the Russians noted how incredibly polite the Aleuts were, and how well their society ran). The Aleuts also wore complicated tattoos and **labrets**, small decorated ivory pieces stuck into the lips and cheeks.

In the eastern and central Aleutians, burial was usually by mummification. The deceased was buried with everything needed for the next life, from a baidarka and tools to mats and eating utensils.

According to G.I. Davydov, who traveled the coast in 1802-1807 (an excellent translation of his voyage account is available from the Limestone Press), the coastal natives were fond of games, fairly indifferent to suffering, and extremely curious, always on the lookout for something new and diverting.

How badly the Aleuts fared when the Russians arrived is recounted elsewhere in this book. Davydov mentions that as of his trip, nobody had bothered to be interested enough in the locals to even make a collection of simple artifacts.

Here, suffice it to say that on August 21, 1732, when the Russian ship SV *Gavrill* headed for the "large country" they'd heard about (in an expedition that, incidentally, established that there was water dividing Alaska and Asia, fueling hopes for a Northwest Passage), the Aleut world came to a crashing end.

There are very, very few full-blooded Aleuts left. The population was nearly destroyed by the Russian and U.S. exploitation of their hunting grounds, and it has been a long, slow road back. The Aleuts are back, however. The native corporations are helping the increasingly organized villages take care of business and fend off the outside world. With so much land in some of the richest fishing ports in the world, many of the villages are thriving – the village of Sand Point has one of the highest per capita incomes in the U.S.

Cook's First Contact

By the time Captain James Cook first reached Aleut lands, he had already established himself as one of the greatest travelers the world will ever know. Alaska was his third and final voyage – when he wrote the passage below, he was only months from his final fate of being killed and eaten in the Sandwich Islands (Hawaii). But he had already charted the coasts of Australia (think of having to get through the Great Barrier Reef in a sailing ship, with no charts – the man was a sailing genius) and New Zealand; circumnavigated the globe twice; eliminated on his ships the horror of scurvy by the simple expedient of making his men eat sauerkraut – he didn't know what vitamin C was, but he knew sauerkraut kept the sailors healthy. He had been everywhere, done everything. This is what he wrote of his first sighting of locals in Prince William Sound:

"Men Women and Children were all Cloathed alike, in a kind of frocks made from the Skins of different animals, such as the Sea-Beaver [otter], Racoons, Martins Hares squirrels & all of which they wore with the fur side out. Some of the Women wore a bear skin over this dress and most of the men wore... a leather pelt, or rather a shirt made of the skin of large guts, probably those of the whale, they are made to draw tight round the neck, the sleeves reach as low as the wrist round which they are tied with a string."

Much better than Cook's own woolen greatcoat. Cook also commented that "the Men had Mittens made of the skins of bear paws, and high-crowned conical straw caps; also others made of wood resembling a seal's head."

He commented on the fact that the women tattooed or stained their chins to imitate a beard, and that both men and women had labrets. Some also had bones through the nose.

Cook took his notes, drew the coastline, and moved a few days closer to his end in Hawaii.

■ Southeast

Although smaller tribes of Indians abounded in the Alexander Archipelago – Tsimshian, Nootka, Samish, Bella Coola – Southeast Alaska was dominated by two groups of Indians, the **Tlingit** and the **Haida**.

"TLINGIT"

It's pronounced KLINK-it by Americans. The actual native pronunciation of the word is closer to Khling-GET, but the sounds involved are unfamiliar to English speakers and the odds of saying it correctly are about zero. If you want to give it a try, aspirate the first "K," like you've got a little peanut butter on the roof of your mouth. The "G" sound is aspirated much more harshly. Over the past few years, the movement in Southeast has been toward at least giving proper pronunciation a shot.

As a general rule, the Haida occupied the southern reaches, from the Queen Charlotte Islands to the Ketchikan area, while the Tlingit lived on the islands farther north, as well as the inland areas of Alaska, Yukon, and British Columbia.

Culturally, the Tlingit and the Haida are remarkably similar. Blessed with living in a naturally rich area, they dined well on deer, bear, seal, otter, duck, and five varieties of salmon. Bushes hung low with fat berries ripe for picking. Survival was never a problem – there was no word in the Tlingit language for starvation, but there was the traditional saying: "when the tide's out, the table's set," reflecting the rich variety of sea life in the local diet.

These cultures were all remarkably familiar with the sea. It takes only a few minutes of hiking in Alaskan forests to realize there has to be an easier way to get from place to place – the Natives found the answer in the water. All early explorers noted their comfort in boats – remember, these people hunted whales out of kayaks. The world, to the coastal Natives, was rather like a modern nautical chart: endlessly detailed knowledge of the ocean, but the land behind was a big blank. Their houses faced the water, their lives were spent on the water. In a way, modern Alaskan life is still much the same.

Making use of time that most cultures had to spend searching for food, the cultures of the Tlingit and Haida developed in some amazingly complex ways.

Community Structure

Southeastern society was extremely hierarchical. Villages were headed by a chief (in the case of the Haida, up to four chiefs oversaw a single village). Everyone in the community had a particular rank in life, almost like a caste. There was free mixing among the ranks in daily life, but there was little intermarriage between the low and high strata of society. Chieftainship was hereditary, usually passed from the current chief to a nephew. But being chief had few material benefits. Chiefs had no power to order the villagers to work on their behalf and, indeed, paid more for services because of their high rank.

Until European contact (and, some historians maintain, until well after), both the Tlingit and the Haida kept slaves, although only the higher ranks were allowed slave ownership. Slaves were usually obtained from captives of the many battles that raged among the villages; however, if you were born to a slave family, you would remain a slave.

The battles tended to be fought over trade routes. Trade in Southeast was rich long before the coming of the Europeans (who continued fighting over exactly the same trade routes). Again, the Tlingit controlled the northern routes, the Haida the southern.

Home life revolved around communal dwellings. Haida structures averaged 100 feet by 75 feet. Inside, there was little "furniture." Possessions were kept in bentwood boxes, decorated with totemic designs. Cooking was done in containers made of spruce-fiber; most food was boiled. Clothes were also often made of plant fibers, including cedar tree bark and spruce root. Special occasion wardrobes were made of otter, seal, and marten fur.

Within the hierarchical structure, a village was further organized around a dual structure of **clan** and **totem**. Clan was extended family. Totem was a little more complicated, and assured a genetically mixed village. One could not marry within one's own totem. Totems were distinguished by an animal sign: bear, eagle, raven, and whale are the most commonly seen in totemic design. Children became part of the same totem as their mother.

Totemic design defines the highly geometric, starkly black and red art that the natives used to decorate their homes, canoes, and blankets. It's a kind of cubism, flattening out drawings of animals, with an iconography of every gesture and posture. The art of the coastal Indians is as sophisticated as the most detailed architectural drawing, while simultaneously looking as modern and spontaneous as a Picasso.

Jonathan Raban, in his book *Passage to Juneau* describes coastal art: "The most arresting formal feature of coastal Indian art, its habit of dismembering creatures and scattering their parts into different quarters of a large design, perfectly mimicked the way in which a slight ripple will smash a reflection into an abstract of fragmentary images." They were just painting things the way they saw them from their boats.

CAPTAIN GEORGE VANCOUVER

Captain George Vancouver, who learned sailing from Captain Cook, found himself working his ship through the Inside Passage a few years after Cook died. Vancouver was still looking for that 18th-century bugaboo, the Northwest Passage, a short route from Europe to Asia. Of course he didn't find it, but here are his notes on the Tlingit: "The behaviour of these people was so totally unlike the context of any we had yet met with as to induce an opinion in Mr. Whidbey and his party, that these Indians were a part of that tribe who had attacked the yawl [a few days earlier, one of Vancouver's boats had been attacked], & that the very extraordinary exhibition they had made ['each bearing a green bough and singing and dancing in a most savage and uncouth manner'] was a supplication for mercy and forgiveness."

A few days later Vancouver's party "met another small party of natives, consisting of seven men only.... After they had put on their warm garments, they advanced to meet the boat; one of them was armed with a musket, and another with a pistol; these they cocked, while the other five, each provided with a bow, and plenty of arrows, had them ready for immediate service."

In other words, news of the Europeans had spread from the north long before the arrival of Vancouver's ships, and the news wasn't good.

■ Totem Poles

Contrary to popular opinion, totem poles were never objects of worship. They were a heraldic emblem, as well as a method of storytelling, a means of keeping a community memory. Although the poles used common elements and figures, any attempt to "read" a totem is possible only if you know the family and the story the pole commemorates. Usually this is only possible if there were written records of the pole raising, or if a member of the family that commissioned the pole is still around. Pole stories are also considered a kind of intellectual property; unless the family has given you the right to tell a story, it's none of your business. We'll describe poles in this book, but we won't give you the story line.

Poles were usually erected after a family achieved some measure of economic success. Part of the fun was showing off. The largest poles were reserved for chiefs of extended family groups and those of high social ranks. Totem pole carvers were among the highest-status residents. They were tested on their knowledge of religion and mythology, as well as their carving experience, before being retained to carve a pole. They were welcomed in every village, enjoyed unrestricted freedom to travel, and were often wealthier and more famous than tribal chiefs. The downside of being a carver was that, if you made a mistake, you could be put to death.

Totem poles always tell a story.

Carvers were apprenticed when young, and they were expected to have the spiritual abilities of a shaman. Although the poles were not religious in nature, their importance to the community required a great deal of sensitivity and stamina: larger memorial poles could take over a year to carve.

Poles were invariably carved of cedar wood; larger poles were often hollowed first to make them more manageable. Tools, before European contact, were made of stone or bone. In the farther northern reaches of the pole-carving cultures, hammered copper was used.

Poles were not brightly colored. Because of the nature of cedar wood, which must be able to "breathe," painting the pole was the first step to destroying it. Native carvers used simple pigments made of plant materials, charcoal, and some oxides. Few colors other than black, red, and blue were used, and poles were seldom entirely painted. Instead, the colors were used as accents, and many poles were not painted at all. The very best place to see a traditional pole is at **Saxman** (page 151) or the **Totem Heritage Center**, both in Ketchikan (page 153).

Poles fall into seven basic types.

- **Memorial poles** were erected to honor a deceased chief. These were heraldic in nature and were considered the finest of all poles. Very few examples remain in a well-preserved state.

- **Grave figures** are the most numerous of poles. Smaller than memorial poles, they showed the totemic figure of the deceased, identifying the grave site as that of a certain branch of a clan.

- **House posts** and **pillars** were probably the first type of pole developed, springing from the design of the long houses used along the Pacific Coast. The houses in this area were heavily decorated inside and out, and the posts and pillars were part of the adornments. Most of these disappeared with the houses, but they were once probably more numerous than the grave poles. The only limit to the use of house posts was the wealth of the owner and the space available.

- Similar to the house post was the **house front**, or **portal pole**. This was purely a measure of status, fronting a house to show who lived there by incorporating the family's crest or totemic figures.

- **Welcoming poles** were erected by the waterfront. These were usually unpainted, and in old pictures of villages in Southeast you'll see these standing in pairs. They were often constructed just for the occasion of a potlatch, or a large tribal gathering.

- **Mortuary poles** are related to the grave figures, but are considerably rarer. Only the Haida made general use of these poles, which were erected at a memorial potlatch.

- There were **special poles** that didn't fit into the above categories. These could tell stories of a successful hunt, but more often they were erected by chiefs out for revenge. The poles were designed to ridicule a specific person or group; considering the cost and difficulties of creating a pole, it's easy to imagine just how mad you'd have to be to put up a ridicule pole.

Poles were a vital part of coastal culture. A single village might have a hundred poles, and the raising of one was always a cause for celebration. A singer was hired to relate the history of the family and to narrate their accomplishments. The singer also hired and trained dancers to perform at the pole raising. Despite stories to the contrary, slaves were not sacrificed to the pole, nor buried beneath the base. Only a single skeleton has ever been found under a pole.

POTLATCH

Pole raising often coincided with a potlatch. This term is a corruption of the Nootka word *patshatl*, meaning gift. Potlatches are famous in story as an opportunity for a family to give away all its possessions, showing its wealth, but they were a lot more complicated than that. A potlatch was given only with extreme protocol. Guests arrived on the shore in order, according to their status and rank. They were greeted by their hosts with great display. Then the feasting, which could last for several days, began. The pole raising was the height of the celebration. After the pole's story was told, the singing and the dancing finished, the gift-giving began. Gifts were carefully selected. An improper gift could be given as a purposeful insult and could lead to war. The generous spirit of the potlatch was not well understood by Europeans and the qualities of the poles were not generally appreciated. In 1884, Canadian law forbade potlatch ceremonies. This was merely another nail in the coffin for local villages.

Despite the joy at their raising, poles were not necessarily meant to last; when their function was done, poles were allowed to fall into disrepair. The settlement of Alaska by Europeans forced many native villages to move, and the poles were left behind to rot. When hiking in remote areas, one sometimes encounters a moss-covered tree with a face – it's an old pole, turning into forest mulch. At Saxman, near Ketchikan, there's a good example of this, with a forest trail and two downed poles rotting in the forest.

Archeologists and anthropologists have done a remarkable job finding and preserving poles, but taken out of context they lose some of their beauty and become nothing more than museum pieces. Many such pieces suffer from the fact that early European efforts to preserve poles involved painting them, and so hastened their destruction.

There are also certain other issues at stake: for instance, on Chief Shakes' Island, in Wrangell, there is a reproduction of a shame pole. In the normal course of events, the original pole would have disintegrated, and with it the memory of the disgrace. But now the pole has been recarved, and the family involved is, not surprisingly, not amused.

After decades of neglect, totem carving is making a comeback. There are trained carvers working in several communities, and the tradition is being revitalized with the incorporation of modern elements into standard designs. Talk to the carvers in Sitka, and take a look at the poles in Ketchikan at the Westmark: they show that, once again, totem carving is becoming an essential part of the native culture.

■ Tlingit Legends

The Raven

One of the most common figures on totems is the raven. As we'll discuss in more detail later, in the *Wildlife* section, the raven was an important bird to the Tlingits. It had the place of the wolf in Southwest Native culture: the trickster, the shaman. There are hundreds of stories of the exploits of Raven. Here are a couple good ones.

According to the Tlingits, the raven is credited with stealing sunlight. At the time the world was created, it was all dark. The raven set out to obtain light, which was held jealously by a rich man. The raven seduced the rich man's daughter, and the resulting child was doted upon by the grandfather. The child began asking for larger and larger things. The stars were put into the sky at his request. Finally, the child made a grab for the sunlight, changed into a raven form, and delivered the sun to his father.

In the earliest times, according to the legends, the raven was white. He earned his blackness when a scheme backfired. Escaping from a hut as he tried to steal water, he got stuck in the smoke hole. The smoke hole spirits held him there until his color had changed, and only then did they release him.

There is also a raven story that is analogous to that of the biblical flood. The raven became curious about what was under the sea, so he had the Woman Under the Earth raise the waters so he could get a good look. The waters were raised slowly, so that the people could escape in their canoes.

The Mosquito

Although the raven was the hero of most of their stories, the Tlingits were highly practical people as well. Their legends include this story about the first mosquito.

The sister to the chief was told she would never have children. Soon thereafter, however, she found herself pregnant. The fetus grew at an unnatural speed and was born after mere weeks. When he arrived, the child was covered with hair and had sharp teeth. His evil nature was proven when he was found killing animals for pleasure, not out of necessity. But, because he was the chief's nephew, nothing could be done. Finally, the chief himself got worried and fought the demon-child. The chief cut the demon with his knife, but no blood came out. Determined to rid his village of the evil, the chief began to wrestle with the demon. All night they wrestled.

At the end of the battle, the chief managed to throw the demon into the fire, but the demon wasn't dead yet. From the fire came a voice declaring that the demon would drink the chief's blood for a thousand years. Ashes rose from the fire, and each ash became a mosquito. At night, by your campfire, you may wonder how many of the thousand years are left!

The Bear

And finally, while we're doing legends, here's one about bears: Long ago, some girls were out gathering berries. The girls should have been singing to tell the bears they were there, but one of them just kept talking. The bears wondered if she was making fun of them, and they started to watch the girls. The girls headed home, but the talkative one slipped in some bear scat, and she dropped her berries. She got mad, and she started to complain. The bears, watching, again wondered if she was talking about them.

Two young men suddenly appeared out of the forest. One of them offered to help the girl find more berries, so she followed them into the forest, but she noticed that they were both wearing bear robes. After a while, they arrived at a large house, high up on the side of a mountain. Inside, there was a small fire, and everybody around it was wearing bear robes. Grandmother Mouse ran up to the girl and said she had been taken into the bear den, and was going to be made into a bear. Finally, the girl had the sense to shut up and be afraid. Already the hair on her robe was growing longer, more like a bear's. But then one of the young bears, the son of the chief, went up to her and said, "You can live if you become my wife. Otherwise, you'll die."

She married the bear, and she lived as a bear, taking care of the fire. She noticed that whenever the bears went out, they put on their robes and became animals. The next winter, when she gave birth to twins, the babies were half human and half bear.

One day her brothers came looking for her. She rolled a snowball down the mountain to show them where she was, and they climbed up to the house. The bear husband met her brothers, knowing they would kill him. But first he taught them the songs that hunters must use over his body to ensure their good luck in the hunt. The young men killed the bear, using smoke to get him out of the cave. They speared him, but they didn't harm the children.

The children grew to become great bear hunters, leading others to the bear dens and teaching the ritual songs. Later, after their mother died, they put on their bear coats again, and went back to live with the bears.

Wildlife

The natives of Alaska lived in one of the richest, most biologically diverse regions of the world. Humpback whales, minke whales, fin whales, killer whales, Dall's and harbor porpoise, seals, sea lions, bear, moose, deer, river and sea otters all abound. The list goes on and on, and it includes the ubiquitous bald eagle.

In the towns along the coast or on easy side trips, you've got an excellent chance of seeing moose, black bears, grizzly bears, Dall's sheep, mountain goats, wolves, foxes, moose, beavers, deer, elk, and caribou, not to mention a host of smaller mammals. The streams and lakes are teeming with fish: king salmon, sockeye, Dolly Varden, grayling, char, and trout. In the sky, there are more than 400 species of birds: sandhill cranes, endless varieties of ducks and geese, the ever-present raven (bigger than the common crows, and also a more graceful flier), the near-legendary yellow-bellied sapsucker. Any time you stop for a picnic a magpie or a Steller's blue jay is likely to land on the table and steal some food. Bald eagles are such a common sight in along the coast that the locals don't usually even notice them.

■ When & Where to See Wildlife

What you will see of this amazing variety is largely a matter of luck, partly a matter of timing, and partly a matter of looking in the right places, being able to see the moose hiding in the brush, spotting the eagle in the top of the tree. But keep in mind that no matter where an animal is supposed to be, it's always going to be where it wants to be. A simple example is that of the moose in a marsh: we had sighted more than 50 moose in a wide variety of other places before we finally saw one in a marsh.

Traditional wisdom says that the bigger animals come out in the early morning and late evening. In the far north, in the summer time, there really is no morning or evening, but 5-8 AM and 7-10 PM can be prime animal-spotting hours.

Traditional wisdom also says to keep a close eye out by water, where the animals go to feed. Keep your eyes open: the banks of ponds, streams, and lakes are great places to see bears. The best place to see the animals is from the comfort of your own car or boat.

Small towns such as Homer and Cordova (where moose keep blocking the airport runway) suffer from wandering moose as a road hazard. In a confrontation with a moose, you will lose.

■ Rules of the Wild

Never follow an animal. If you do, you are doing several dangerous things:

- You are endangering the animal's survival by taking it from its food source, possibly from its young, and making it burn valuable calories. This is a crime, subject to arrest and fines – if you see someone hassling wildlife, make a note of their license plate or boat numbers and report them at the next ranger station.

- You are endangering yourself. Every year people are attacked by moose. Invariably, the moose wins. Bear attack stories are largely lies, but real bear attacks are usually caused by the person doing something they shouldn't have been doing.

- You are depriving others of the chance to see the animal.

Never forget that these animals are wild and interested only in their own survival. When you spot an animal, remember that you are invading the animal's home, and that its rights are foremost. The more calm and quiet you are, the more likely it is that the animal will look you over for a moment and then go back about its business, leaving you plenty of time for photos.

OBSERVING WILDLIFE BY CAR OR BOAT

If you see wildlife while driving, pull your car slowly to the side of the road. A Canadian Park Ranger told us that the biggest danger on the Alaska Highway are people who do not follow this advice, thus causing accidents. Pile-ups on the road south of Anchorage, in the Kenai, are common as people stop on blind curves to gawk at the mountains goats. In Petersburg, deer in the road cause accidents; in Homer, it's moose. Get the car off the road, and then shut off the engine. Make no sudden moves or sounds. Same thing in a boat – while you don't have to worry so much about collisions, if you shut the engine off – or at least cut back to bare steerage – and stay quiet yourself, the animal is more likely to stick around.

Here are the basic rules:

- Keep at least 100 yards away from the animal. It might come up a lot closer to you, but that's its business.
- In any kind of craft – or even if you're walking – don't approach head on. That can easily be seen as a threat. Come up to the 100-yard distance from an angle.
- Don't watch any animal for more than a half-hour. Let them get back to what they're supposed to be doing – making a living. Whether it looks like they're paying attention to you or not, they do know that you're there.

Never feed an animal (except the mosquitoes; there isn't much that can be done about that), and keep all food at your campsite in scent-proof containers, to discourage the curious. At all times, treat animals with respect; they, in turn, will treat you to a look at the beauty and the power of nature.

To keep track of Alaska's wildlife and the threats it faces, join the **Alaska Wildlife Alliance**, P.O. Box 202022, Anchorage, AK 99520. They've been fighting the good fight for more than 20 years.

📖 The Alaska Department of Fish and Game produces an excellent brochure, ***Southeast Alaska: Guidelines for Wildlife Viewing***. Its most valuable chapter explains how to tell when you're too close to an animal and need to back off. Bothering animals is against state law, punishable by up to six months in jail and a $1,000 fine. Help the Fish and Game people protect the wildlife by reporting violators, especially boats that chase down whales. Get the number of the vessel, take a picture, and make them pay for disrupting wildlife. See page 69 for Fish and Game contact info.

Marine Life

■ Whales

Spend some time along the Alaskan coast, and you're going to see whales. They might be the little beluga whales, the stately humpback, or the incredible, giant fin whales, but spend time on the water, and sooner or later you're going to come across something.

Your best bets are around Haines, Skagway, and the Kenai Peninsula. If you're serious about whale watching, take the ferry (passengers on the big cruise ships don't see whales as often; the ships are too high, too noisy, and usually traveling only after dark) and get the camera ready. Whales are as common as dogs to Alaskans (a ferry was once stopped for several hours because the entire channel was full of whales and the ship couldn't get through), but nobody ever gets tired of seeing a breaching humpback.

There are roughly 500 humpbacks that summer in Alaskan waters between the months of April and November. There are some whales that hang out year-round, but it rarely seems to be the same whales each year. Scientists are still working on which ones stay and why.

Humpbacks

Humpbacks are most commonly seen in Southeast. Humpback whales grow to 50 feet, but most are closer to 40. They are distinguished by the way they swim and their shape at the waterline: their back forms a right angle as they dive. Whales do not generally show their tails above water unless they are sounding or diving deep – when you see the tail, that's usually the last you'll see of the whale for a while.

 DID YOU KNOW? *Humpback tails are as distinctive as human fingerprints, and scientists use the patterns on their huge, broad tails as means of identification.*

Another thing that can be used to ID a humpback is the pattern of the barnacles that have grown on it. There is a species of barnacle that only grows on humpbacks; a full-grown whale may be carrying upwards of 500 pounds of these critters, and scientists can compare photos of growth patterns to help sort out which whale is which. As an interesting side note, of course, the whales aren't that happy to be dragging around all this deadweight of barnacles, so there's a biological war going on: the barnacles have to take hold quickly, and the whale, just as quickly, sloughs off skin, trying to get rid of the barnacles. Some scientists say humpbacks shedding skin more than two hundred times faster than humans do.

Whale Song

One of the main points of study with humpbacks is their song. Scientists all over the Alaskan coast drop hydrophones in the water to record whale song, which has definite rhythms and repetitions. Whales have been known to stop a song when leaving Alaska for the warmer waters of the south, and then pick it up on exactly the same note when they return the following year.

Breaching

The premier animal sighting in Alaska is a breaching whale. Humpbacks come all the way out of the water – it's amazingly slow, the whale just keeps moving up and up and up before falling back down on its side. Whales like to flop back and forth, beating the water with their flukes. Some of the reasons for this behavior are unknown, but often it's seen when the animals are feeding. Breach behavior is also thought to be simply for the fun of it, and sometimes as a sign of agitation. There are less scrupulous whale-watching tour operators who will take out a dozen small boats, surround a group of whales from a legal distance, and thrill their clients with the whales coming up out of the water – which the whales do because they're seriously pissed off and feel threatened.

Feeding

Humpbacks only feed in Alaska – they fast during the winter months in Hawaii. In Alaska's rich waters, sometimes the whales create a "bubble net" by swimming around a school of krill and trapping them in their exhalation. They then lunge up through the krill, mouths open, scooping up tons of krill and sea water. The water gets squeezed out through the baleen, long spiny plates that take the place of teeth in many species of whales.

This is, to say the least, amazing to watch. The whales do this in groups, so suddenly you can see five or six whale mouths suddenly surging above the water, the bright pinks of their tongues visible as they come up to chomp down on whatever got caught in the bubble net. You won't forget seeing this. More common is to see lunge feeding – one whale will come up out of the water a few feet, having just sucked up everything in its path. Kind of like bubble net feeding when you're alone.

There are a couple of other behaviors that humpbacks do that nobody's quite sure about. They sometimes lay on their back and slap their flippers on the water as hard as they can. We saw one do a front flip, for no apparent reason. They're whales. Who's going to tell them what to do?

WATCHABLE WILDLIFE *When watching the sea, look for the spout, the whale's breath, which is visible from quite a distance – up to eight miles. It looks like a small palm tree of water and, from a distance, is much easier to spot than the body of the whale.*

BALEEN

Humpbacks are a type of baleen whale, which means they eat fairly small stuff – nothing bigger than, say a shrimp or so – and do so by scooping up a mouthful of water and then squeezing the water out through baleen plates, which catch the good stuff and leave it behind. Baleen is made of the same stuff as your fingernails and hair, and you'll see chunks of it on sale in gift shops. Humpbacks have fairly small baleen plates – a couple feet at most. The big pieces of baleen you see probably came from pilot or right whales. There's a theory afoot that smaller baleen points to higher on the evolutionary scale. The blue whale, biggest beast in the sea, has the smallest baleen.

Other Whales

Minke whales, also common along the coast, have an almost invisible spout, and they don't stay on the surface for very long when they breathe, making them very difficult to spot; they're also likely to stay up only for a couple of breaths at most. Minkes are often mistaken for large porpoises, very small humpbacks or, occasionally, orca. The smallest of the rorqual, or toothed whales, minke whales run up to 31 feet for females, 27 feet for males, weighing up to perhaps 10 tons. They are characterized by a triangular snout. Their body color is black above and white below, and many have a band of white in the middle of their flippers. Their dorsal fin is considerably back of the center, giving them an oddly sleek, racy look. Minke are not particularly endangered: there are estimated to be more than 500,000 of them. They mostly travel alone.

The other big species of whale you might spot is the **fin whale,** but you'll have to be pretty far west, into the Aleutians, to see one. Fin whales are giants of the sea, with some approaching 80 feet in length. They are dark gray to brownish-black on the sides and white on the underside. Their head shading remains dark farther back on the left side than the right. Like humpbacks and minke whales, fin whales have baleen and feed on krill, straining the tiny animals from the water. Fin whales are rarely seen breaching; usually you can see the spout, then a small black fin, and then an incredibly long back.

Just south of Anchorage, there's a place called **Beluga Point**. Believe it: it's a great place to watch for **beluga whales** passing by; there are a lot of them in Prince William Sound and Cook Inlet. We've seen pods of 30 or so in the past couple years, but that's nothing compared to the numbers there used to be.

Belugas are among the smallest of the true whales. An adult male is only about 13 feet long, and weighs about 3,000 pounds. When they're born, belugas are about five feet long and weigh only 100 pounds or so.

They start off a dark gray, but by the time they're five years old or so, they've faded to the familiar white color. A beluga can live up to 35 years.

Belugas like to live in groups; while recent newspaper reports in the Kenai suggest that the populations are way down, you'll still see belugas in bigger bunches than any other kind of whale. There have been sightings of more than 1,000 whales in a single pod in the arctic. There are about 70,000 belugas in the world, so they're not on the endangered list. Native hunting in Alaska takes 200 or 300 a year.

Belugas swim quite slowly, looking for fish, crabs, clams, and squid to chow down on. They've got sensational sonar, among the best of the whales, and that, combined with their size, means they're frequently in much shallower water than most whales. That makes it easier to watch them.

How to Kill a Whale

Killing whales isn't as difficult as it once was. If you're a Norwegian with no recriminations, or a Japanese hiding behind the façade of scientific research (but that doesn't explain the whale meat stores all over Japan, does it?), you chase them down in a large ship, aim a harpoon cannon at them, and when the harpoon hits the whale, the tip explodes, hopefully killing it before you have to waste another couple hundred bucks on a second harpoon.

But it wasn't always like this, and there's no real way to look at the history of the north without looking at the history of whaling. From the 17th century into the early 20th, whales provided lamp oil, corset stays, perfume bases, and a hundred other must-have items.

The best account of traditional whaling is, of course, *Moby Dick*. Author Melville had done his time on a whaling ship, and he knew what he was talking about. When a sailing ship spotted a whale or a group of whales, they lowered whaleboats – about 20 feet long – and chased after the whale. They drew close enough to lance it and harpoon it. This meant, really, getting right on top of the whale. Then the crew held on for the ride, trying to stick more lances in the whale and injure it enough to slow it down. It was incredibly dangerous, bloody work, and a whaling ship that didn't lose a few of the crew to accidents was a miracle ship. In Melville's words:

> *A short rushing sound leaped out of the boat; it was the darted iron of Queequeg. Then all in one wild commotion came an invisible push from astern, while forward the boat seemed striking on a ledge; the sail collapsed and exploded; a gush of scalding vapor shot up nearby; something rolled and tumbled*

like an earthquake beneath us. The whole crew were half suffocated as they were tossed helter-skelter into the white curdling cream of the squall. Squall, whale, and harpoon had all blended together, and the whale, merely grazed by the iron, escaped.

European and American hunters set out in ships a hundred feet or more long, getting near the whales in the small boats at the last moment. Eskimo and Inuit hunters paddled out after whales in their kayaks. The killing technique was essentially the same: lance it, wear it out. But the Native hunters were doing this in boats not much bigger than your couch at home.

By the way, if you're wondering, whale meat tastes kind of like greasy, rubbery tuna fish.

■ Orca & Porpoises

Orca

Orca, or killer whales – a term that has fallen out of favor with the politically (and taxonomically, as the scientific name, *Orcinus orca*, translates out to "one from the realms of the dead") correct, as they are neither killers per se nor whales – are one of the most exciting animals to spot in Alaska. They are not actually whales; rather, they're the largest member of the porpoise family.

Orca can be more than 30 feet long, and the dorsal fin on a male can be as much as six feet high. At birth, orca weigh roughly 400 pounds. A full-grown orca can weigh as much as nine tons, and can swim 34 miles per hour.

Orca live at least 50 years, barring anything unforeseen. They may live as long as 80 or 90 years. Females start calving at around 12 to 17 years old, about the same age as males become mature – noted by a change in their dorsal fins.

It's a good thing they live so long, as they tend to calve only once every five years or so, and half the calves die at birth. It makes for a population that is not ready to deal with stress.

Orca travel in pods, with anywhere from three to 25 animals moving together. There are no accurate estimates for how many orca travel in Alaskan waters, as the animals move very quickly and scientists are never sure if they've counted the same one twice.

There are also both resident and transient pods. In British Columbia, for example, the orca in Johnstone Strait are resident. There are also resident pods in Glacier Bay. But you can never be absolutely sure, when you spot an orca, if you're seeing a resident or simply some orca passing through. It's not unknown for transients to cover a range of over 1,500 miles.

In the past couple years, the orca population has been at the forefront of a problem all over Alaska: changing weather is changing feeding patterns due to changing weather conditions. The seal population of the Aleutians has diminished; the orca are switching to eating sea otters, but otters aren't nearly as nutritious as seals, so not only is the otter population taking a hit from being turned into snack food, the orca population is decreasing because of the simple fact of starvation.

The most distinctive feature of the orca is the black and white coloration. Dall's porpoise, which are similarly marked, are often mistaken for orca. However, the Dall's porpoise grows only to six or eight feet – an orca's dorsal fin can be that big. There are a couple of other differences in the coloring: an orca has a white patch behind each eye, which is not usually present on a Dall's, and their flukes are white on the underside, whereas a Dall's is usually white at the edges.

Dall's Porpoise

Dall's porpoise, which grow to a maximum size of 300-450 pounds and six to eight feet long – baby killer whale size – travel in fairly large groups, usually numbering 10-20 animals. They forage at all levels of the ocean, and are known to dive to depths of more than 1,600 feet. These are highly playful animals; if you see porpoise playing with the ship, they'll be Dall's. Extremely fast swimmers, able to top 35 miles per hour, Dall's porpoises will happily chase boats and play in the wake unless the boat drops below 12 miles an hour or so; then the porpoise seem to lose interest and drop away, looking for something more fun to do.

Harbor Porpoise

Harbor porpoise are also a fairly common sight, but you don't see them for long. They are darker, more sedate in their movements, and more shy in their approaches than Dall's porpoise. They are much smaller than a Dall's, growing to only 125-145 pounds, and perhaps four to six feet in length. They travel in small groups, no more than five animals, and they come up only briefly to breathe, making sightings fairly short-lived.

In Southeast, there's something of a cut-off line between Dall's and harbor porpoise, at Icy Strait. From there up, harbor porpoise dominate, and you rarely see a Dall's. To the south, the balance is opposite, in favor of the Dall's.

■ Seals, Sea Lions & Otters

Harbor Seals

Harbor seals, like harbor porpoise, are shy and difficult to spot. They come up quietly, take a quick look around with only their head and nose protruding above the water – and the black color can make them almost impossible to spot – then they disappear. And since they can dive to 600 feet and stay down for more than 20 minutes, you might be wasting your time hoping one pops back up.

Harbor seals grow to about 180 pounds. They're covered with short hair, and are usually colored either with a dark background and light rings, or light sides and a belly with dark splotches. They generally stay within about 150 miles of where they were born. They don't migrate, but they will wander about to find food – walleye, cod, herring, salmon, squid, and octopus, among other sea life. You'll sometimes see them surprisingly far upstream on bigger rivers, as they follow the salmon. We've seen them a hundred miles up the Stikine River. When a harbor seal dives, its heart rate slows to 15-20 beats per minute, about a quarter of its heart rate when it's at the surface.

DID YOU KNOW? *It is estimated that there are about 200,000-300,000 harbor seals in Alaska. It is hard to get more accurate that that.*

Sea Lions & Sea Otters

While harbor seals disappear when you spot them, sea lions and otters, on the other hand, are showmen. Sea lions jump, splash and play constantly, as do the otters. Steller's sea lions can grow to 1,200 pounds or more, and there's nothing quite like watching them at a haul-out. They are also known to be much less shy than seals – a diver told us of a few sea lions coming up behind them on a dive and swimming in circles around the divers while occasionally giving someone a playful nudge. Both seals and sea lions like to pull themselves out of the water and bask in the sun atop rocks. Look for them on channel markers and buoys.

Sea Lion or Seal?

How do you know if what you're looking at is a seal or a sea lion?

- Seals have short, clawed front legs; sea lions have long, broad front flippers.
- Seals don't have visible ears, but sea lions do.
- When they're out of water, seals lie down; sea lions sit up.

A CLOSE CALL WITH EXTINCTION

The Russians killed whatever seals and sea lions they came across – why not, they were out hunting anyway – but what they were really after were sea otters. Sea otters were once hunted almost to extinction as fur traders made fortunes on their rich, luxurious pelts – the first sealing expedition, in 1741, brought back 900 pelts. In 1800, Alexander Baranov estimated that, in the previous 10 years, more than 100,000 pelts had been taken. It was noticed quite early on that this couldn't continue – already by 1818, it was reported that "along the whole expanse of coast from Cape Ommaney to Kenai Bay, only two places remain where we can still hunt, namely, Lituya Bay and Yakutat; but even there, they are no longer native, but hide someplace farther along the coast to the southeast where they are more protected."

The Russians were letting the locals do all the killing, and contemporary reports show that they were really good at it, even without threats of violence from the Russians. "The Aleuts are the only people born with a passion for hunting sea otters. When they spot a sea otter, they surround it, and the person closest... gets to shoot him with a dart and has the right to claim the kill."

For more on Russian sea otter hunting, see K.T. Khelbnikov's *Notes on Russian America*, beautifully translated by Serge LeComte and Richard Pierce. It's one of the best accounts you can find of what the Russians were doing in Alaska.

Why were the Russians killing off the otters? So they could sell the pelts to China and trade for tea. The English had their opium trade for the exact same reason.

Now sea otters, quite well protected by law, are back, and there's a healthy population that can be spotted almost anywhere along the Alaskan coast.

Sea otters grow to six feet and live, somewhat communally, in kelp beds. Rather odd is that although they live in groups, they don't really interact with each other; there may be some play fights and mating behavior, but other than that, they pretty much pretend the other otters aren't there.

Their diet consists largely of fish, marine bivalves and sea urchins, and they're famous for using rocks to bash open tough shells. There's a flap of skin under their forelegs in which they can stash food or rocks.

FURRY FACTS

The fur of a sea otter is a miraculous thing: otters have up to 125,000 hairs per square inch, more than double of just about any other mammal. This high-density fur makes otters the prime target for coats, hats, boots, and anything else for which a dead animal might be useful.

The thickness of the hair is an evolutionary development in lieu of layers of subcutaneous fat. Most marine mammals have thick fat layers to keep them warm in the cold waters. Hair is all the otters have, and this is part of why they were so susceptible during the oil spill in Prince William Sound: the fur, matted with oil, lost its insulating capabilities and the oiled otters literally froze to death.

Even when it's working well, the thick fur has some drawbacks. A sea otter has a metabolic rate two times higher than average for an animal its size. The body is working overtime to maintain its core temperature. You'll see that sea otters generally keep their feet lifted out of the water – this helps keep the wet surface area to a minimum, and keeps the otter warmer. Should the otter get overheated, there is a solution: like polar bears, sea otters have extra blood veins in their feet. They can send blood through these veins, close to the surface of the skin, and cool off. It's estimated that 80% of the excess heat can be shed this way.

Although sea otters are very unpopular with local fishermen (who claim they ruin the fishing grounds and depopulate the fish), they're actually a very important species for the maintenance of a healthy environment along the coast. Sea otters eat urchins, abalone, and other animals that eat kelp. Without the otter predation, the kelp beds, which shelter numerous schools of young fish, would quickly be gone.

■ Fish

Considering that Alaska has something like 10 million lakes and the longest coastline in the U.S., it comes as no surprise that there are a few fish around. The species tally is about 300, really an astounding variety. That said, most people who come to Alaska are interested in only salmon and halibut.

But first, a fun fact: as of the last time anybody bothered to run the numbers – around 1997 – the average out-of-state fisherman spent $930 to catch a king salmon in Alaska. Halibut run a relatively cheap $230.

Salmon

There are five types of salmon in Alaska: **pink** (humpie), **chum** (dog), **coho** (silver), **sockeye** (red), and the prize of them all, the king, or **chinook**.

Now that we've said that, we're going to list a sixth type, the **steelhead**. Steelhead, long classified as a type of trout, were officially moved into the salmon category in 2000. For reasons that require explaining more about fish biology than you're probably interested in, there are a lot of fish experts who aren't real happy with this move. Yes, steelhead move from freshwater to saltwater and back. But that's about it on the similarities list, and the same attribute isn't enough to push the Dolly Varden (an ocean-going trout, which is what everybody thought steelhead were) into salmon land. All over the country, there are Ph.D. candidates getting dissertation material out of the debate. There aren't enough steelhead to make them important commercially – according to Fish and Game, of the 331 known steelhead streams in Southeast, only 12 support more than a thousand fish.

All salmon share the trait of returning to the waters in which they were born to spawn and die. During the summer months, this means rivers clogged with dying fish, and a lot of very happy bears.

The chinook, Alaska's state fish, is what all the fuss is about: they grow up to 100 pounds, and 30-pound fish are common. They also fight.

 DID YOU KNOW? *A few years ago, a man had a chinook on the line for over 24 hours. He lost it when his guide used the wrong size net and snapped the line.*

The chinook is considered abundant all along the Alaskan coast. The run is usually from May through July. The chinook is rather astounding in its run, traveling more than 2,000 miles in only two months – but there are some that, over their lifespan, travel more than 10,000 miles. Once returning to the site of its birth, the female lays up to 14,000 eggs. The fish in the run may be anywhere from three to seven years old; there is not a clear cycle for chinook. A full-grown fish has black spotting on its back and dorsal fin, and a line of black along the gum line.

 DID YOU KNOW? *Trolling is your best bet for catching chinook, using herring as bait. There are strict regulations on catching chinook, particularly in Southcentral; check with Fish and Game before heading out.*

While the chinook is the main trophy fish, a lot of people prefer the coho for eating. Coho, which grow from eight to 12 pounds, do not have the tail spots that kings do. Fins are usually tinted with orange, and the male has a hooked snout.

Coho spend a fair amount of their lives in freshwater; after hatching, the fish may hang out in estuaries through the summer and then move back into freshwater for the fall. They may spend as much as five years in freshwater before their saltwater period, which averages about 18 months.

AUTHOR TIP *Like fishing for chinook, your best bet is trolling with herring for bait. The run lasts from July into September, and coho fight enough to make chinook seem like logs.*

Sockeye, or red salmon, are probably the biggest part of the fishery, and they have been for thousands of years. They spend one to four years in the ocean, and then do the run home. Average weight is around four to eight pounds at maturity, but they can get bigger; some around 15 pounds have been caught.

There are a few places where there are landlocked species of sockeye, called *kokanee*. These stay pretty small, and you're not that likely to run into them. It's the ocean-going type that everybody's after, and they find them in abundance. In Bristol Bay alone, there are 10-20 million sockeyes caught every year. Most of them are caught with gill nets, which are a small step up from the drift nets you read about.

If you're fishing for them, troll like you would for any other salmon. There have been a number of closures on the Kenai for sockeye of late; the long-term effects of the Valdez oil spill are just now making themselves clear.

The other two species of salmon are caught more on a commercial than a sport basis. The pink, or humpback, grow to about four pounds. They're steel blue on top and silver on the side. They get their nickname, humpie or humpback, from the hump and hooked jaws that develop when they enter freshwater. Pink salmon mature in only two years. These are the primo fish for commercial fishermen; more than 45 million fish a year are taken, roughly half the total salmon catch.

Chum salmon, which are green-blue on top with small black dots, mature after roughly four years. They spend most of that time at sea, primarily in the Bering Sea or the Gulf of Alaska. A full-grown chum will weigh seven-15 pounds. There is a huge commercial fishery for chum in Alaska, primarily through gillnetting or seining; about 11 million fish a year are taken.

We've already mentioned the steelhead controversy – once a trout, now a salmon. There is another kind of very salmon-like trout, the Dolly Varden.

Dolly Varden are a mottled olive-brown, with dark marks. Mature males are bright red on their lower body, while the fins are red-black with white edges. They also develop a strongly hooked lower jaw.

The Dolly Varden run is from mid-August into November. They actually move in and out of freshwater for most of their lives, not migrating into the sea until they are three or four years old. They're still quite small at this time, only about five inches long. Spawning generally happens when the fish is five or six years old, and unlike other salmon, roughly 50% of Dolly Varden live to spawn a second time (steelhead also do this, which is one of the reasons for the controversy about whether they're salmon or anadromous trout). The fish can live as long as 16 years.

Dolly Varden never reach the size of coho or chinook – a full-grown fish is only about four pounds – but they are around all year.

Life Cycle

The life cycle of all the types of salmon are more or less similar – it's a matter of how long they do what that really changes.

At hatching, what you've got is called an **alevin**; this is a tiny little bit of a fish, with the yolk sack – that they're still living off of – remaining attached. They live in the gravel where they were born, six to 12 inches down in the streambed.

The next stage is the **fry** stage, where they start to look like real fish. They're about an inch or two long at this point, and they start to get vertical bar marks – like they'll get later when they're packaged and barcoded in the supermarket – to help them hide in the streambed. This stage lasts a couple of months.

Next, they turn into **fingerlings**, or parr. They've gotten bigger now – a couple of inches or so – and they may stay in this stage for anywhere from a couple of months (pink and chum) up to a couple years for sockeye and chinook. The bar lines have gotten darker, and they're really just building up strength for their final freshwater stage, the smolt.

As **smolts**, they're better than six inches long now, and they've lost the bar marks as they become silver for better camouflage in the open ocean. At this stage, they undergo a massive physical transformation, getting ready for the change from freshwater to saltwater: their gills essentially reverse, and their hemoglobin changes to cope with the loss of oxygen that comes with saltwater.

As soon as the fish hits saltwater, it changes from a smolt into an adult salmon. It's time to go out in the open water.

At their end of their lives, the salmon come back. The Walt Disney nature films you saw in school taught you they always come back to the stream where they were born. That's mostly true – salmon navigate by a sense of smell that can detect "one drop of vermouth in a 500,000-gallon martini." They know where they're going. However, there are always a few that don't want to go along with the crowd – about 8% decide that home ain't good enough, so they head out for other streams. This is good, as it can help populate new areas; it's bad, because, as we'll explain below, it gives alien fish a chance to move in where they don't belong.

AN UPHILL STRUGGLE

There is a bit of salmon behavior you're bound to see if you're traveling during the run months: salmon, gathered near a stream mouth, jumping. You'll hear various explanations for this behavior, ranging from "they're trying to catch bugs to eat" to "they're trying to shed scale parasites." The jumpers are actually female fish, loosening their eggs before heading up stream. Probably. Maybe.

Salmon populations, like those of so many other things, are declining rapidly. Some of this is due to over-fishing, some to climate changes. Each year, there are more fishing closures along the Kenai, and the commercial catch in Southeast declines as each year, the returns are getting a little smaller. Over the past hundred years, 232 genetically distinct strains of salmon (that's strains, not species) have gone extinct. Due to decreasing runs, the value of the salmon catch almost dropped in half between 1994 and 2000. Having an oil tanker worth of poison spilled into the ecosystem didn't do anybody any favors, either.

That said, there is some hope. The return of pinks was so large in 2001 that most canneries stopped taking them; there were too many to process. Fish returns run in cycles; there's hope that this huge return is a marker of the end of the bad years.

Why Hatcheries & Fish Farms are Bad

So, what to do about this overall decline in fish population? Screw with nature, of course.

The first idea was hatcheries – you can see them in work in a lot of towns along the coast. The idea here is that, if nature lets about one out of a thousand eggs actually grow into salmon and return to spawn, why not scoop some eggs up and increase the odds?

Hatcheries raise the fish in controlled environments. This makes sure that the salmon don't have any chance to develop the wild smarts they'll need to survive. It's a lovely way to dilute a gene pool, particularly when the hatchery-raised salmon breed with wild. Think how smart chickens are after centuries of domestication, how well they'd do in the wild. Same thing with hatchery fish.

Once a hatchery is up and running, it gets its own return of salmon. The fish are imprinted with marks, so they can be tracked. Once they make it up to the home hatchery, they're pulled out of the water, gutted, and the roe and smelt are mixed by hand. Oh, and all that valuable protein, the fish that once was, is discarded. It's the rule.

The life stages are then led in tanks, rather than the stream. Instead of having anything to do with Darwinism – which works for most species – survival becomes a matter of luck. A big part of the luck is surviving the diseases and filth that hatcheries tend to breed.

So the next bright idea is fish farms, which are illegal in Alaska, but common in Canada. The first problem here is that most fish farms are stocked with Atlantic salmon – nothing like bringing in alien species. Farms are built in streams, with holding pens for different stages. The concentration of fish in one batch of step ponds means there's a whole lot of fish waste churning out into the ocean – as much as from a town of 10,000 people. The fish are also packed in so tightly that they can hardly swim. The fish themselves are more susceptible to disease and pollution in this cradle-to-the-table captive cycle. Of course, that means they get antibiotics pumped into their food.

Canadian fish farms are allowed to shoot any marine mammals that might come by and see these pens as a free lunch – about 900 seals and sea lions are shot a year.

There's also the little detail that farm-raised fish are eating fish-meal pellets – ground up bits of other fish. The Worldwatch Institute looked into this and discovered that for every gram of farm-raised salmon that hits your dinner table, five grams of other fish were turned into salmon food. This really helps the part of the worldwide fishing industry that's out to strip the oceans bare. Estimates are that in British Columbia alone, this means a waste of 90,000 tons of edible protein.

Because the fish are eating unnatural food, they don't come out looking nice and healthy and pink like you want them to. But dyes fix that.

One more thing while we're on the subject – the increase of fish farms has devastated the traditional culture of the coasts. Towns that used to support 40 or 50 fishermen now support two or three.

Shall we talk about Frankenfish? Genetic engineering is turning out salmon that mature in a fraction of the time it takes nature. Like most genetically engineered products, there's no idea what the long-range effects of this might be. And if you think the fish are confined to pens, forget it: fish escape. Aliens enter the gene pool and the wild streams – Atlantic salmon have been found in quite a few Alaskan rivers. In 1997, a single fish farm in Washington State "lost" over 350,000 Atlantic salmon in one whack. Try and think of any way this is a good thing.

In 1980, 1% of the salmon market was comprised of farmed salmon; today that number is 56%.

Other Uses for Salmon Besides Your Dinner

Salmon aren't just out making salmon dinners. They're a vital part of the entire ecosystem, almost the base level, the cornerstone of the Pacific Northwest's economy, ecology, and culture. You can't understand anything about the Alaskan coast without taking salmon into account.

Besides yourself, there are 137 other animal species that depend on salmon at some stage of their life for animal protein – from bald eagles to bears, seals, and sea lions, and everything in between. The forest also depends on salmon. The rotting fish that die in streams after the spawn provide 17% of the nutrients found on the rainforest floor along a stream. About 60% of the nutrients that freshly hatched salmon depend on comes from their spawned-out parents.

When the fish disappear, the forest disappears, which makes everything else disappear.

Halibut

Halibut are a kind of flatfish, like enormous flounders. Like many fish, they're darker on the upper side than on the lower – the idea is that a predator fish getting under the halibut will look up and think the light color is just a patch of sky. Or so the theory goes.

FISHERMENS' TALES

This is one of those great Alaska stories, the kind of thing that could never happen anywhere else. A man was out fishing, and he caught a halibut. Not a little one, mind you. Estimates later put the fish at around 460 pounds. The man got the fish on deck, using a crane, but the fish wasn't quite dead, and it began to thrash around. The man slipped; the halibut's tail hit him in the head. Death was probably fairly fast for him, rather slower for the fish.

Halibut live on the bottom of the ocean, sometimes at great depth – up to 1,800 feet. Once hooked, a large halibut may get dragged to the surface and still find the strength to go back down six or seven times, diving several hundred feet. Most halibut fishermen carry guns to try and keep this game to a minimum. Gaffs just make the fish madder.

Halibut migrate in a clockwise manner, heading south and east through the Gulf of Alaska. Older fish are more likely to stay put. A halibut reaches maturity around the age of eight, and a female might lay as many as three million eggs a year. A halibut might live more than 25 years.

Halibut are extremely strong swimmers. This allows them to eat pretty much anything they want to. Its digestive tract is extremely small for an animal its size, so to maintain its metabolism, it eats all the time.

The vast majority of halibut fishing goes on around Homer, at the bottom of the Kenai Peninsula. If you're after flatfish, head there. However, there's also plenty of good halibut fishing in the outside waters of Southeast – try Sitka for the best the panhandle has to offer.

BARN DOOR HALIBUT

Four-hundred-pound halibut are rare, but one or two are caught every year, and probably thousands of hundred-pound halibut are caught each season. Fish this big – a hundred-pounder will be about six feet tall and three or four feet across, and maybe six inches thick – are called "barn door" halibut. They're the ultimate trophy, but the truth is, the little ones, 20 pounds and under, make for better eating. Removing them from the ecosystem also doesn't do nearly as much damage to the gene pool as killing the strong and big ones does, either.

Cooking Your Catch
Favorite Recipes

Once you've made your catch, it's time for dinner. We offer here two superb recipes, courtesy of Wrangell's Alaska Vistas outfitters (see the *Stikine River* section, page 196).

FOR SALMON:
Mix up a marinade of ½ cup of soy sauce, ½ cup of brown sugar, and ½ teaspoon of liquid smoke seasoning. Marinate fillets for at least six hours, turning them a couple of times. Cook in a pan over a low fire. Slide the fish back and forth in the pan, and use olive oil to prevent sticking. Turn over only once. Cook until the fish is no longer transparent – about five minutes per side, maximum. (This recipe also works well for steelhead trout.)

FOR HALIBUT:
Mix ½ cup of real butter, ½ cup of soy sauce, ¼ cup of lemon juice, and 2 tablespoons of Worcestershire sauce. Coat an aluminum tray with olive oil or nonstick cooking spray. Place halibut on the tray and cover with the sauce mix. Cook until the meat is no longer transparent (shouldn't take more than 10 minutes, tops). Use very low heat – halibut is easy to overcook.

You'll need some good sourdough bread to have with your fish. In the old days, of course, miners and homesteaders couldn't run out to the store for sourdough starter. Here's how to make your own, and then how to do something with it.

Sourdough Starter

This is a recipe for a "wild yeast" – the old 'sourdoughs' didn't have commercial yeast available and so had to made their own.

Take two medium potatoes, unpeeled, rinsed (organic are preferred). Boil them in enough water to cover them (about three cups). Cook until well done and fully soft. Mash potatoes in their cooking water and strain out the skins. Cool mixture to room temperature.

Select the container that your starter will live in: we use a clear gallon ice cream container, but Tupperware containers, wide-mouthed glass jars, or crocks work well. Avoid metal containers. Add about two cups flour (unbleached unleavened, good quality). Stir this mixture well (there will be lumps, but these aren't a problem). Add about a tablespoon of white sugar.

This is your starter. Keep it in a warm place (70-80°F is best), stir it daily, and add a little more flour and a pinch of sugar every 24 hours. You'll notice the mixture will start to bubble. When you have an inch or more of bubbles on the top, it's ready.

If you don't want to feed the starter daily, refrigerate it. The container should be mostly airtight, preferably – if you're using a mayo jar, punch a hole in the lid. Once the starter is chilled, it needs to be fed only once a week. If you've chilled your starter, set it out on the counter to warm for several hours before using. Save at least a cup of starter, add a half cup each of warm water and flour to bring the level up to about three cups. Remember your starter is alive – it can be kept and used for many years.

SOURDOUGH PANCAKES

Mix up night before:
1 C sourdough starter
2 C flour
2 C buttermilk
1 tsp salt

Add to mix:
2 tsp baking soda
2 eggs
3 T oil
2 T sugar
Fresh berries (be like the real sourdoughs, and go pick your own).

Cook on a griddle like a regular pancake.

Catch & Release

If you're not hungry, follow these basic steps to release the fish:

- Land the fish quickly and carefully.
- Don't lift the fish entirely out of the water.
- Use only a soft or knotless mesh net, and keep your hands wet while handling the fish.
- Use barbless hooks, and keep the fish underwater while you're pulling it. If you can't get the hook out, cut the line off the hook – sooner or later, the hook will rust out.
- Stick the fish into the current, or swish it back and forth in the water to revive it. Make sure the gills are working, and let the fish swim out of your hands.

A lot of catch-and-release fish still end up dying, due to improper release techniques. Some basic care keeps them out there and alive.

■ Playing with the Big Boys

 Okay, so let's say you've come to Alaska, fallen in love with the landscape and the fishing, and you've decided to do it for a living, to move up here and become a commercial fisherman. Here's what you'll have to do. And reading this should help give you an idea of what it takes to put fish on your plate back home.

First, you're going to need a boat. You don't need as big a one as you might think; for Southeast waters, a 38-foot boat is plenty. This can be crewed by two people, and anything bigger will have trouble getting to some of the best fishing grounds. Once you've got your boat, you'll need to rig it out: radar, GPS, all the electrical and mechanical systems a boat requires (and don't forget the Mustang survival suits); plus, you'll need shrimp pots, crab pots, halibut long lines, and a drift net and accompanying winch. In other words, all the stuff you'll need to actually drag the fish on board.

You've just spent roughly $250,000.

And you still can't fish, because you don't have a permit. You're going to have to find one of those that's for sale, and buy it, too. These aren't as expensive as they used to be, but to get yourself legal, you've just spent another $100,000. Because you actually want to make a living, you've rigged your boat for year-round fishing – everything from salmon to crab. If you're really ambitious, you can buy a dry suit and air tanks, and go after sea cucumbers for the Japanese market as well, but let's say that's a bit much.

Your big money item is going to be the salmon. With this kind of boat, on a pretty good year, you can figure you'll catch about 75,000 pounds of salmon. The number is going to vary with openings and government regulations, etc., but for now, let's call that good. Seventy-five thousand pounds of fish is a lot, right? Salmon goes for eight or 10 bucks a pound in the grocery store.

Doesn't work that way.

Let's say you've rigged your boat for a drift net. This method of fishing puts a net about a hundred feet long by twenty feet deep in the path of the fish. They swim into it and get stuck. The alternative is seining, where you surround the fish with a net and then drag them up like you've got them in a big sack, but that takes a bigger crew.

Half your catch will be pink salmon. At the cannery, you'll sell it for about 6¢ a pound. Yep, that's it. These are the bottom of the salmon ladder. Run the math: 37,000 pounds at 6¢ a pound. It adds up to beer money. Not much further up is a third more of your catch, the chum salmon. These sell at the cannery

Fishing gear, Chignik.

for all of 14¢ a pound. Boy howdy, now you're in business. You do better with the sockeye fishery: those are going to bring you as much as $1.10 a pound, and they'll make up a third or so of your total catch. They're your money fish. King salmon are, honestly, going to be negligible, as are coho. Less than 10% of your total.

Once salmon season is over, you can head out for halibut. These are caught on long lines. You put lines in the water, with hooks every 15 feet or so. Halibut live deep, so each line is going to be from 30-200 fathoms long (a fathom is six feet). Halibut season is long – from March through November – and it's not regulated with strict windows of fishing the way the salmon fisheries are, but there's another catch to it. Everybody who commercial fishes for halibut has an allowance, which is based on their historic luck at catching. If, over the period in question, you caught 30,000 pounds a year, your legal limit will be about 30,000 pounds. Because you're new to this game, you don't have an allotment. You'll have to buy someone else's. Get the checkbook out. It's going to cost you $50,000 to buy 5,000 pounds worth of permit. It's going to take you, according to those who run these numbers, seven years just to break even on halibut.

So let's move on. Shrimp. Lots of shrimp in the ocean. There are five good kinds in the waters of Southeast. You'll catch about 5,000 pounds of them in a good year, lowering baited pots into the water (one of the uses for all that pink salmon you caught), and then coming back and dragging them back up. Most shrimp fishers process the shrimp themselves on board now, selling them straight to the Japanese market in what's called a Japanese pack. For good-sized shrimp, you'll get $5 a pound, but you've spent a fair amount on processing; not to mention the cost of your time. Another problem: when your initial batch of pots get lost or damaged beyond repair, and it's time to buy new ones, consider this: a full outfit of 120 pots and line is going to run $15,000.

Crab season. Surely you can make money off crab. You'll need a hundred crab pots and line, so that will be a quick $13,000 you'll need to spend. In Southeast, the only real crab fishery is for Dungeness. Let's say you're not crazy enough to go after king crab in the Bering Sea (it's called the world's most dangerous job for a reason; you'd be better off being the guy in the freak show who has cannons shot at him). If you do decide to go for the Bering Sea, you'll need a bigger boat – at least 50 feet – and you'll have to shell out $300,000 for a permit. So let's skip that and stick with the Dungeness. You set your pots out, again baited with pink salmon, and come back to drag them out of the water later. On a good year, you'll catch 10,000 pounds of crab, but it comes mostly at the very beginning of the fishery. At the dock, you'll sell your catch for $1.25 a pound.

With all that fishing, have you been remembering to maintain your boat? The standard rule of thumb for a boat is that it costs 20% of its value in maintenance every year. These are not numbers we made up. We sat down and talked with commercial fishermen to get them for you. So that brings up the question of what the hell are these people thinking? They've got a half-million dollars worth of gear, and they're scraping by.

Well, it wasn't always like this. Twenty years ago, they made money fishing. Some people still do, although when you hear the stories of crew members who fished for a month and got a $20,000 cut, those are mostly lies. But with increasing competition, decreasing fish numbers, and all the vagaries of modern times, the fishing life just isn't what it used to be.

There are more regulations than you want to think about. There is constant strife with Canada over the coastal fisheries, and with the Japanese over the open seas fisheries. Openings can be ridiculously short – for example, near the Kuskokwim, in June and July 1997 and 1999, there were only two six-hour openings. Think you can make your living off 12 hours of work a year?

If you do get a decent opening, you come home extremely tired. We know people who slept on the boat at the dock because they didn't have the energy to last the 15 minutes it would take to drive home.

Processing the day's halibut catch.

Keep these hardworking people in mind the next time you're sitting down to a salmon dinner. Offer them up a toast.

Land Animals

There's nothing quite like seeing a grizzly or black bear walking along the shoreline, hunting for fish. Or, better yet, leaping into the water to catch its dinner and coming up, soaking wet, shaking itself. Spotting a moose feeding is an equally thrilling experience. Wolves are the hardest Alaskan wildlife to spot, and you should consider yourself very lucky if you see one.

■ Bears

Brown Bears

Brown bears, or grizzlies (now a politically incorrect – and somewhat taxonomically incorrect – term; stick with brown) are rarer and considerably larger than their black cousins. In Southeast, browns are most commonly seen on Admiralty Island, where they considerably outnumber the human population, near Wrangell, and on Baranof, Chichagof, and Kruzof Islands, around Sitka. In Southcentral, Kodiak Island is famous for its huge bears – some more than 10 feet tall. There are some nearly this size around Brooks Camp, on the Alaskan Peninsula.

More commonly, browns run seven to nine feet, with males ranging from 400 to 1,100 pounds. Females are about 20% smaller. Brown bears range in color from a dark brown to blonde. The easiest way to distinguish them is by the hump on their back, just behind the head. They have a life expectancy of about 20 years in the wild. These bears are bigger and faster and more dexterous than you can imagine. There is no thrill quite like watching a grizzly catching and eat a fish. You can find T-shirts in some of the roadside shops in Alaska that show a grizzly paw the size of a dinner plate; the caption says "Actual Size," and it's not a joke. The biggest grizzly track we've found was 17 inches long, heel to pug. And that was in a place where there weren't really big bears. And with those huge paws, the bears are astoundingly dexterous: watching a brown bear eat a salmon will reveal how easily the claws move, as delicate as a set of very sharp chopsticks.

Black Bears

More common than brown bears are black bears. They may be found on nearly every large island in Southeast and Southcentral (except the outer islands of Baranof, Chichagof, and Admiralty), as well as in coastal mainland areas. They average five feet in length and weigh from 150 to 400 pounds. A good-sized black bear is often mistaken for a brown bear because black bears are not necessarily black: they range from black to very light brown. In fact, there are two kinds of black bear that are white – the kermodie (also called the spirit bear), found around Princess Royal Island in British Columbia, and the gray-blue glacier bear, found near Yakutat. Black bears have a life expectancy in the wild of about 25 years.

Populations

Bear populations vary widely, depending on what the environment has to offer. Around Anan Bear Observatory, there are more than a hundred bears, living off the rich salmon stream; by contrast, at the North Slope, there may be only one bear (polar, this far north) per 300 miles. The average in the productive southern areas of the state – all the coastal regions except the Aleutians – is maybe one bear per 15-23 square miles. Obviously, territories overlap, and a lot of bears may be sharing the same food reserves. The official estimates for Southeast are 6,000-8,000 brown bears and about 17,000 black bears.

The life cycle of browns and blacks is fairly similar. Cubs (one or two, very occasionally three) are born during the mother's hibernation. Black bear cubs weigh only a few ounces at birth, and their birth may not even wake the mother. They attach themselves to a teat as the mother keeps on sleeping.

DID YOU KNOW? *In his 1555 book,* A Description of the Northern Peoples, *Olaus Magnus wrote that the "she-bear, a creature full of wiles, gives birth to shapeless cubs, which she licks with her tongue into a form like her own." Imagine a world that full of marvels.*

Rising from hibernation, the bears spend the first week or two not quite awake. Their metabolism, shut down during the winter, is still pretty slow. They come out of their dens, dig up a few skunk cabbage tubers

A black bear having a snack.

(which act as a laxative, helping to get things running again after the long sleep), and then go back to sleep for a while longer.

The bulk of the summer is spent eating, exploring, and teaching the young bears what they need to know. Bears are very playful and, while not particularly social, cubs can have a great time with each other.

Come fall and the first touch of colder weather, the bears seem to enter a kind of frantic mood, as they try to pack on enough fat to last them through the winter. They move down to salmon streams and start to gorge themselves on the return. A bear may eat parts of 50 fish a day – stomach, brains, some skin, the roe – the parts with the most fat, leaving the rest behind for birds to scavenge.

Come winter, the bears hole up in their dens. One of the last things they do before hibernating is eat some clay if it's available – sometimes you'll see scratch marks in clay banks, where a bear has tried to find some better-tasting clay. This is thought to help plug up the digestive tract for the winter.

Bear-Watching

If you want to see bears, the best places to go are the **Pack Creek** area on Admiralty Island; the **Anan Observatory** in Wrangell (one of the very few places in the world where you can see black and brown bears together – although the blacks tend to hide when the browns come around); **Fish Creek**, outside Hyder; or Kodiak, which has bears everywhere. The best time is during July and August, when the streams are full of fish and the bears are chowing down, getting ready for the coming winter.

Bear Safety

While virtually every story you've ever heard about bear attacks is likely to be untrue, you do not want to mess with bears in the wild. They are not like Yogi Bear waiting to steal a picnic basket. They're animals with jaws strong enough to take off your leg, and if you provoke one, it will react.

However, the bears really have no interest in you at all. In fact, they're usually appalled that you're even there, and most of the time they'll do anything they can to get away from you. This makes it fairly easy to stay safe. All you have to do is make sure the bear sees you first. To avoid untoward encounters with bears, there are a few simple precautions you should take. The easiest thing to do is avoid contact.

- ■ When hiking, **make some noise** to alert bears of your presence. Talk loudly, bang a stick against trees, or drop a few pebbles into an empty soft drink can and tie it around your waist so it clanks. Some people use small bells, which most Alaskans tend to call "bear dinner bells." We just call out "Hey, bear," at fairly regular intervals.

■ **Never smell interesting.** Bears have a keen sense of smell and poor eyesight. They are both curious and hungry. Bears are omnivores, like humans, and they'll eat pretty much anything – berries, fish, squirrels, whatever looks good. They are also known to eat camping gear if the right mood hits them. Cooking inside a tent is an invitation to disaster, as are strong perfumes or soaps. Keep all smells away from your campsite, and keep your food in a bearproof container or up in a tree, hanging from a rope (see the *Camping* section for more details, pages 81-82). If you're keeping food in the car, the trunk is safer than the interior – at least that way they won't tear up your upholstery if they want to get at your pretzels. Bears have only about six months to get fat enough to make it through hibernation, and so they get touchy about their food supply. When you consider a squirrel is only about 2,000 calories, you know it takes a lot of eating to fill a bear.

■ **If you see a bear cub, head back the way you came, away from the cub, as quickly as possible, without showing signs of distress.** Just go back the way you came, because where there's a cub, there's a protective mother nearby. There are more stupid people/bear altercations because of people wanting to pet the cute bear cub than all other causes combined. People see a cub out playing, and don't bother to remember that mom has claws big enough to whack your head off with a single blow. Stay away from cubs. Period.

■ **Bears always have the rights to berry bushes and fishing streams.** A single bear can eat 2,000 or more berries in a single day (and you have to wonder who counted seeds in bear scat, and for how long, to come up with that number), so a loaded bush is always tempting for a bear. Stay out of thick patches of bush, make noise. The bears don't want to see you – they just want to eat and get on with their business. Try not to walk into the wind; bears don't see well, but they do have excellent senses of smell and, face it, you don't smell as if you belong there. If the wind is behind you, your scent is carrying news of your approach, and that gives the bears time to leave.

■ **Never let a dog loose in the forest.** Leave your dog at home. Dogs and bears just do not get along. Even the calmest dog tends to freak out and think it's tougher than the bear as soon as it gets the first whiff of bruin. We've known people with weiner dogs that thought they could attack bears. Bears make dogs really, really stupid.

- **If you see a bear, don't run.** Food runs, so the bear's impulse is to chase. You will lose any race you have with a bear. On a dirt road, we once startled a bear. We were driving nearly 30 miles per hour; the bear passed us, and ran straight up a hill and out of sight faster than we could put on the brakes. This was not unusual; black bears have been clocked at well over 30 mph, and browns at 41 mph – that's a hundred meters in under six seconds. You don't stand a chance if you run and the bear decides to chase you.

- **Do not panic.** If you see the bear from a distance, detour around it. If you see an animal carcass, leave the area as quickly as you can without showing distress. Just go back the way you came, because the carcass has likely already been claimed by a defensive bear.

- **In closer quarters, the advice of bear experts is to stand your ground and speak to the bear in a firm tone of voice.** If the bear stands, it's not necessarily a threat sign: since bears have lousy eyesight, they stand to get a better look at things. Keep talking to the bear, let it know you're there and not interesting. Don't turn your back to the bear. Do not, under any circumstances, run. Again, that's what food would do. If the bear stands, try to look big – fan out your jacket, wave your arms, or if you are in a group, have everybody stand together. You can yell. If the bear doesn't leave, try to back away slowly – still facing the bear – but if the bear starts to follow, hold your ground. If you can, and if you have to, back up to a tree and start to climb. Climb high, though, because grizzlies can reach quite a ways. This won't work against black bears: they can climb better than you.

- If you're facing a bear and the bear woofs and runs, even in your direction, that's okay. **Hold your ground.** But if it holds its own ground and woofs, or pops its teeth together, it's time for you to back up. Keep facing the bear, don't run, don't panic, but give the bear some room.

- **If the bear turns sideways, that's not a good sign.** It's a threat posture. Just like you wave your arms to show the bear you're big, the bear is showing you its flanks to prove how big it is. Take this as a sign to start backing up, slowly.

- **If the bear follows you, drop your hat or jacket,** something that smells like you but doesn't smell like food. Most bears will investigate what you drop, and be satisfied.

- **Absolutely do not imitate the bear's sounds or postures.** This is the number two stupid thing people do, next to trying to pet cubs. If the bear is in a threat pose, you want to submit, not mirror it back.

- **Play dead only as an absolutely last resort.** Curl into a fetal position, keep your pack on for extra protection, and cross your arms behind your neck. Reports vary on which attacks are worse. Grizzlies tend to maul and get it over with. Black bears hang out and nibble, and are more likely to think you're food, or at least a really fun toy that they can swat around for a while. If you're attacked, hold still for as long as possible. Something that doesn't move loses its entertainment value, and the bear will probably get bored and leave pretty quickly. There's a new school of thought that believes instead of curling up, you're better off playing dead by laying flat on your stomach, hands laced behind your head. Nobody really wants to test this theory.

A bear track by the Stikine River.

- **Guns are pretty much useless against bears.** Unless you're either very lucky or a crack shot with an ice-cool head, calm enough to make Clint Eastwood look like he needs Ritalin, you'll just piss the bear off.

- **Pepper sprays can work from about 20 feet, but it's best not to get that close in the first place.** These sprays are the choice of locals. However, there are two warnings about it. First, it doesn't really work on wet bears. The capsaicin molecules don't bond with water, which is why you should head to the sink if you mace yourself with the stuff (which is what usually happens to people who carry sprays). It's not a good idea to go merrily tromping off into the bush figuring the pepper spray will protect you. The stuff is a last resort, at best. There have been a number of recent cases of people figuring that pepper spray, since it deters bears when sprayed in their faces, would also act as a kind of bear repellent. These people have sprayed pepper spray all over their backpacks and tents. The problem is, old pepper spray smells like dinner. Bears come running for it. If you're going to carry the spray, remember it works only when fresh – and not always then – and when the bear is standing right there looking at you.

- Here's a old settler story of what to do in the last resort, when you're being attacked by a bear: jam your fist down its throat and block its air hole. Maybe before the bear finishes chewing off your arm, it will suffocate. Maybe.

All of these precautions work in theory, but still depend upon the bear's mood. If the bear doesn't feel like being placated, it won't be. The bear doesn't know and doesn't care about the rules.

> 📖 Most forest service offices have a free brochure, *Bear Facts: The Essentials for Traveling in Bear Country*, that offers more details.

Finally, do not ever, for any reason, feed a bear. Bears are very, very smart. If they get food from a person once, they're likely to think it can happen again, and that's how you end up with bears foraging in garbage cans and rummaging around houses. When that happens, sooner or later, Fish and Game will have to kill the bear.

Why don't they just relocate them, you ask? Because bears are smart, and they know where home is. Relocated bears will do just about anything to get back home. They've been known to swim hundreds of miles, just to get back to that trash can. Even if they don't head right back, they're likely to start looking at human settlements as sources of food.

Here's the bottom line: A fed bear is a dead bear.

The best bear pictures ever were taken by Michio Hoshino; they're in his book **Grizzly**. The one true, cautionary bear tale we will tell is that Hoshino, who spent his life around bears and knew the rules as well as he knew his cameras, was killed by a grizzly, somewhere in Siberia. Hoshino was sleeping; the bear took offense at the color of his tent, or something. It's impossible to know. The point here is not that the bear killed him, but that he had spent thousands and thousands of hours in the wild photographing bears without any incident; the point is that, in the end, bears will do exactly what they want.

Nevertheless, bear attacks are extremely rare. Take proper care, and don't worry too much. We hiked in bear country for four years before we had even the most mild confrontation. Now, after so long doing this, we've had bears sneak up and smell our feet. We're still here to tell the story. Obey the rules, and remember the bear is boss.

■ Moose

Moose are the largest members of the deer family; they stand from five to seven feet at the shoulder, are covered in thick, coarse brown fur, and the antlers, which grow only on the male, can measure six feet from tip to tip. Most people think the moose is an ungainly looking animal, but they can move with surprising grace and amazing speed. Along the coast, they're most commonly found in Southcentral – Homer, Cordova, and along the Kenai – and near the larger rivers in mainland Southeast, like the Alsek, Chilkat, and Stikine. Although there are more than 150,000 moose in Alaska, it's quite unusual to see one along the Inside Passage.

For something to remember moose by, look for Michio Hoshino's book, **Moose**.

Moose are grazing animals, eating twigs and bark, grasses, moss, and water lilies. Willow is one of their favorite foods. In spring, you get the classic moose in a marsh as they feed on shallow water vegetation. Although moose live in small groups in the winter, during the summer months they tend to live alone; the males rarely sighted down from the mountains. Moose are very territorial and protective, especially of their young.

A full-grown male moose will stand about six feet tall at the shoulder. The rack of antlers can be six feet across, and the moose will weigh anywhere from 1,200 to 1,600 pounds. Female moose run about a foot or six inches shorter and 400 to 500 pounds lighter. Newborn calves weigh only about 30 pounds, but within five months – the onset of winter, as calves are born in late May or early June – they can weigh 300 pounds. Usually only one calf is born, but twins aren't uncommon. A calf stays with the mother for about a year; then it will be chased off to maximize the mother's chance to bred again. In the wild, moose live about 15 years.

Compared to many other animals in Alaska, moose are pretty sedentary. They do have distinct seasonal grounds, but it may only be a matter of traveling a few miles. A moose that has gone more than 75 miles has really traveled.

More people are injured by moose than by any other wild mammal in the Americas. The only other animal in world in the same damaging category are hippos in Africa. Moose are large, and their hooves are very sharp – and unlike horses, moose can kick forward or backward. They are not big, harmless Bambis. Sit and watch them all you want, but don't try to sneak up on one.

■ Wolves

You're not likely to see one, but keep your eyes peeled. A wolf sighting is more exciting than just about any other thing you'll see in the north.

The first wolf we ever saw chased us – we were on a motorcycle, and the wolf was crossing the highway. It heard us, its ears twitched, and it was off. The only sad thing was that we were going too fast to enjoy watching the wolf.

The first thing you have to be sure of when you see a wolf is to make sure it isn't a coyote. There are a lot more coyotes in the north than there are wolves. Coyotes are smaller in both body and head. Wolves have short, rounded ears, while coyote ears tend to be longer and pointed. If you're tracking, you'll see a wolf has front paws larger than its rear paws, whereas it's the other way around on a coyote.

It's estimated that there are 5,000-8,000 wolves in the state of Alaska. This works out to roughly one every 100 square miles. And yet, because of the massive negative publicity wolves have gotten ever since Little Red Riding Hood went home and lied her fool head off, there is legal hunting of 1,500 wolves a year in the state – and probably that many more are killed illegally. The population is barely holding its own, and is likely to slip fast if there's a bad year for the wolf food supply.

DID YOU KNOW? *It wasn't always like this. The wolf was considered a powerful animal to northern natives. The Kwakiutl believed that if a bow or gun was used to kill a wolf, the weapon became unlucky and had to be given away. Wolves were guiding spirits and companions. They were – and still are – simply beautiful animals to watch.*

The gray wolf, *canis lupus*, averages 40-80 inches long, nose to tail. They can be three feet high at the shoulder, and weigh 130 pounds. Their color tends to be a mixture of browns and tans and grays; usually the muzzle is a lighter color than the rest of the body.

Wolves are the quintessential pack animal, and the packs feed on caribou, deer, sheep, goats, moose... whatever they can catch. In hard times, they go after squirrels, marmots and other small game.

Wolves stick to their own territory. Wolves are so territorial that it is believed prey animals are often able to find the "no man's land" between two wolf packs and so travel through an area safely. For the wolves, being territorial may also be a terrible hazard: it makes them easier to hunt. There was the famed Headquarters pack in Denali Park, but the last of those wolves was killed in 1995 by big, tough, brave hunters whacking them with high-powered rifles from helicopters.

The gray wolf once ranged over nearly all the land north of what's now the Canadian border. They're reduced to pockets now, but some have been sighted around Juneau, and fairly good-sized packs exist near Ketchikan and Wrangell. And there's always hope of packs along the central coast.

Log in to **Friends of the Wolf** at www.alternatives.com/fowbc/fow.htm, or write to them at P.O. Box 21032, Glebe Postal Outlet, Ottawa, Ontario K1S 5N1, Canada.

For a great movie with some of the best wolf photography ever, try *Never Cry Wolf*, based on the book by Farley Mowat.

▪ Other Mammals

The coastal regions are host to a variety of smaller mammals: voles, beavers, weasels, mink, squirrels, mice, martens, porcupines, and so on. Most of these live quite deep in the forest and you're unlikely to spot them.

Sitka Black-Tailed Deer

In Southeast, you do stand a very good chance of seeing Sitka black-tailed deer, one of the smallest deer species in the world. They grow to only about 120 pounds. Adults are reddish-brown in summer and a dark brown-gray in winter. They have small antlers, usually with only three points to a side. With an expected lifespan of about 10 years, they flourish in the old-growth rainforest. The deer subsist on berry bushes and low forage and, although they are still common, their numbers are declining as the forest is clear-cut. While a new clear-cut is great fun for a deer in the summer months, with lots of new, low growth, there is nothing there in the winter months. Also, as the cut grows back, the change from the natural forest balance shades out the understory plants on which the deer depend.

When & Where

There are deer in or near most of the towns in Southeast, or you can watch for them from the ferry, as they often come down to the water's edge. But they are small and easy to miss.

■ Birds

Eagles

Most people go to Alaska hoping to see a bald eagle, but the truth is, it's harder not to see them. They're everywhere. These birds, which can easily weigh more than 20 pounds, were so common in Alaska that, from 1917 until 1952, there was a bounty on them. Hunters were paid as much as $2 per pair for talons. The bounty was put in place on the assumption that eagles ate too many fish. It was discontinued in 1952, when the birds joined the list of federally protected species.

There are more than 10,000 adult bald eagles in Southeast, and a few thousand more young eagles. Adults are distinguished by the trademark white head; adolescent eagles are a dull brown and are harder to spot. Most nests are close to the water's edge.

DID YOU KNOW? *Eagles build the largest bird nests in the world, some weighing up to 1,000 pounds. A pair of eagles will return to the same tree year after year, making the nest a little bigger each time. The nest is abandoned only when the tree threatens to give way.*

Eagles are easy to spot, once you get the hang of it: look at the tops of trees and keep looking for a white patch. Eagles are amazingly patient and can sit, almost unmoving, for hours on end. They do not generally hunt by circling around, looking for prey, the way you're probably used to seeing hawks. In Southeast and Southcentral, they're more likely to sit until something catches their eye – and they have great eyes, with vision roughly 20 times better than 20-20, and the ability to filter glare off water so they can see the fish moving beneath the surface.

Eagles dive for fish. An eagle's talons lock when they are under pressure and cannot be released until the pressure is alleviated. They can put as much as 6,000 pounds of pressure into each talon. All this means if the eagle grabs a fish that weighs more than it can lift, the eagle goes face first into the water. It doesn't happen often, but it's a memorable sight. After the face plant, if the eagle is unable to swim to shore with the prey, it is entirely possible that the weight of the would-be victim can actually exhaust and drag the eagle down, drowning it. Eagles are good swimmers, though, using their wings like arms to swim. Young eagles get a lot of swimming practice, because they have to learn to keep their wings up when they hit the water; wings down, they don't have the necessary strength or lift to get back up in the air, and they have to swim to dry land to take off. When you see an adult eagle hit, the wings are up and extended fully, ready for the powerful thrusts needed to get airborne again.

Eagle-Watching

Good eagle-watching spots include city dumps, outside fish processing plants, and around boat harbors. **Haines** is famous for the number of eagles that nest there – as many as 3,000 a year. **Homer** and **Cordova** also have large eagle populations. Here are some tips for spotting them.

- Look for white spots in the tops of trees. Eagles like to find the highest point they can, then sit there endlessly, doing a remarkable impression of life after taxidermy. Young eagles don't have the white heads that help you to pick them out against the dark backdrop, but they head for high points, too.

- If you come across an eagle on the ground, stay back. As with all wild animals, if you make the bird move, you're endangering it and making it burn calories it has better uses for.

- If you want good bird shots, you'll need a telephoto lens, fast film, and some luck.

- Find out when fishing boats are dumping leftover bait (usually in the late evening) and head down to the docks. There's nothing quite like watching a full-grown, 30-pound eagle hit the water at full speed.

Ravens

Ravens are smarter than your dog, meaner than your in-laws, and more articulate than the kid who mows the lawn. While all the tourists are watching eagles not move, ravens put on a nonstop show. There's a reason why, in coastal mythology, it was the raven, not the wolf, who was a trickster.

Ravens are corvids and, like all corvids, they're voracious, smart, and curious. According to Bernd Heinrich, whose book *Mind of the Raven* is one of the best nature books available, ravens are keyed to new things in the landscape. They've got phenomenal memories, and if they see something that wasn't there yesterday, they'll key in to it, fly down and check it out. Really, they're checking to see if this new stuff is food. But there are few kids who grew up around ravens who didn't set out gum wrappers just to watch the birds fight over tinfoil. We've also seen ravens quite happily flying around with butter tubs in their mouths, and the stories of ravens grabbing jewelry, silverware, and any other thing not nailed down are legion.

Ravens are incredibly articulate birds, capable of making more than a hundred distinct calls. They can also mimic – one near a friend's house has learned to scream "MOM!" just like her kids, and one near our place barks like a dog. A personal favorite raven sound is that of a huge, drippy faucet.

In his studies of ravens, Heinrich wanted to find out if the birds were as smart as he thought they were, so he gave them tests. They were able to figure out, for instance, how to carry more than one donut at a time (use one as a basket, or stick the beak through the holes). But in his real test, he hung meat from a string, to see if the ravens could figure out how to get at it. To eat, the raven would have to pull on the string, then step on it, reach down, grab it again, pull again, and so on, until the meat was finally in reach. There are no strings with meat in nature, so it's a pretty good test of abstract reasoning. It took wild ravens five minutes to figure this out. Crows never managed it.

Okay, they're not as decorative as eagles, and nobody has ever put them on money. But sit down and watch some ravens for a while. It's time very well spent.

Other Birds

There are more than 400 other bird species in Alaska, the majority of which are coastal animals. Many people go out to the Aleutians just to watch birds: mile-long rafts of shearwaters, murrelets, puffins flying everywhere like whirligigs. The trip is especially famed as a chance to see the whiskered auklet, but you don't need to get that far into the boonies.

In Southcentral, near Valdez, the Copper River Valley near Cordova provides an important migratory flyway for trumpeter swans and several species of ducks. The Copper River Delta is the only known breeding area for dusky Canadian geese.

The fun birds to watch along the coast are the alcids: the auks, murres, and particularly the puffins. Alcids are birds that can "fly" underwater. The Audubon Society describes them as "chunky, penguin-like seabirds, chiefly dark above and white below, with short wings and large webbed feet located far back on the body." This doesn't quite do them justice. Puffins, the ones you're most likely to spot (take a trip out in Resurrection Bay, near Seward), are kind of a symbol of the far north. Their colorful beaks and the way they fly – flailing their wings comically – makes them seem a kind of clown of the sea. And there are some oddities about them: for instance, their jaws are not hinged, but rather open and close something like a crescent wrench. This means they can stuff a lot of fish in their mouths at one time – one puffin biologist we know counted 42 fish in one bird's beak at a single time – but when they're done eating, they're so heavy they can't take off. If, say, the wake of a boat disturbs them, they try to get airborne, but just end up smacking face-first into the first wave they hit.

This does not mean that they're not amazing birds. A tufted puffin (the other common species in Alaska is the horned puffin) can dive a lot deeper than you can; and while it's down there, air squeezing out of the space between its feathers, it's as graceful as a seal. You can watch puffins underwater at the SeaLife Center in Seward (see page 361).

The Alaskan coast is noted for its huge tidal fluctuations. When the tide is out, shorebirds appear in full force, feeding off the exposed marine life. Sand pipers, plovers, several types of gulls and ducks, ravens, and more swoop down at low tide to feed on blue bay mussels, steamer clams, wrinkled whelk, file dogwinkle, sea urchins and even the occasional starfish left high and dry by the receding waters.

> Even if you're not a birder, it's useful to have a field guide for the trip. The definitive book is Herbert Brandt's *Alaska Bird Trails*, if you can find a copy, but that's going to run you at least $200. For something cheaper, see *Suggested Reading*, page 98.

■ Smaller Beasts of the Air

Guess what? Once you're in the North, you're quite a few steps farther down the food chain than you're used to being. Mosquitos and no-see-ums are a part of Alaska living.

Mosquitoes

A much bigger threat to your health and sanity than bears or moose are mosquitoes. They are bigger, meaner, and more abundant than you ever imagined. Shops in the North sell three-inch-long bear traps labeled mosquito traps, and they're not joking. There are 27 species of mosquito in Alaska, all of them waiting to bite into your soft hide. During the summer months, the biomass of mosquitoes in the North outweighs that of the caribou – there are actually swarms of mosquitoes in the far north of the state bigger than Rhode Island. The Alaskan mosquito's bite is enough to raise welts on a moose. There are many stories of animals going insane from mosquito bites; and there are reputable reports of caribou so drained of blood after a trip through bad mosquito country that they died. They're big, they're mean, and they're everywhere. And, as if the mosquitoes weren't enough, there are black flies, no-see-ums, snipe flies, and moose flies.

Anywhere you go in the North, something will want to eat you. So what chance do you have against them?

Simple measures are the best protection.

- Mosquito repellent is quite effective, especially those that include the chemical DEET. The more DEET the better, but if putting serious toxins on your skin doesn't thrill you, there are people – you can usually recognize them because they're busy scratching – who swear by Skin-So-Soft lotion.
- Wear long-sleeved clothing, and tuck the cuffs of your pants into your socks.
- Try to camp where there is a breeze – a wind of 5 mph will keep the mosquitoes down. In your RV, camper, or tent, make sure the screens are made of the smallest netting money can buy.
- In hotels, check the window screens before opening the window. Mosquito coils are popular, but they're not going to work outside of an enclosed area, and who knows what that smoke is doing to you?

No-See-Ums

Where the mosquitoes leave off, the no-see-ums start in. The same precautions work against these huge clouds of biting bugs. If you're camping, check all screens: they can get through the tiniest opening. Hydrocortisone cream is useful to alleviate the itch. There are also a variety of specialized products designed to do the same. Pick up a tube or two, and then prepare to accept the bugs. They're as much a part of life as the midnight sun itself.

If you're interested in knowing your enemy, get a copy of **The Mosquito Book**, by Scott Anderson and Tony Dierckins. The subtitle says it all: "More than you'll ever need to know about... the most annoying little bloodsuckers on the planet."

Finally, rest assured in the knowledge that there are no poisonous snakes or spiders indigenous to Alaska.

Tongass National Forest

Stretching the entire length of the Southeast Alaskan coastline and comprising 77% of Southeast's land, the Tongass National Forest is the largest national forest in the United States. A mid-latitudes rainforest or, as it tends to be called now, a temperate rainforest, it's often overlooked when the discussions about destruction of rainforest habitat begin. The Tongass includes roughly 14% of the world's rainforest area and, while the wholesale burning that has become the world's nightmare in South America isn't going on here, for decades the Tongass was losing acre after acre at an alarming pace.

■ History

The Tongass was named a national forest in 1908, following the Alexander Archipelago Forest Reserve, which had been established six years earlier. It stretches over 500 miles from north to south and incorporates more than 11,000 miles of coastline, or roughly half the total coastline of the continental United States.

■ Logging

The glory days of the Tongass were short-lived. By 1947, Congress had sold off thousands of acres for long-term logging. By the early 1970s, more than 600 million board feet of lumber were being taken out of the forest per year.

Official numbers claim that less than 5% of Southeast Alaska has been logged, but the numbers are deceptive: that's 5% of the total land area, which includes huge icefields (11% of the land), and of which more than 19% is above the tree line and another 16% muskeg or other non-forest regions.

While most cutting on national forest land in Southeast has currently stopped – there is still logging on private land and land controlled by the native corporations (more on that in a minute) – the overall plan has not changed. This plan is to chop 26% of the old-growth forest during the next 100 years. There is only 41% of the forest held aside as designated wilderness areas, national monuments, roadless areas, or stream buffers. In 1980, an act passed in Congress that allowed 4½ billion board feet of lumber per decade to be logged.

While the forest is currently protected from logging by a variety of laws, the efforts of those in Congress to get around those laws are amazing. There are proposals to exchange forest land for education dollars; to sell off state holdings to make them available for logging to private concerns (which would go against more laws than Bonnie & Clyde ever thought of breaking); and even as you're reading this, there is someone in a developer's office somewhere, hatching schemes. The idea is to get a toehold, just get the logging moving again, and from there the forces behind the cutting – who number the state's senators among their members – have a domino-theory attitude about it. Just get one tree cut, and the rest will follow.

One of Clinton's last acts in his presidency was to put in a full moratorium on logging in Southeast Alaska. The appeals have been many and various and, as of the time we're writing this, still ongoing.

While there is no doubt that trees have to be cut – houses need to be built, fireplaces stoked, furniture made, and the diminishing logging in Southeast has closed pulp mills and sawmills and nearly devastated the economies of some towns – the argument in Southeast (and with national forest logging everywhere) is exactly what's being done with the logs. The simple answer is that they have traditionally been sold to Asia (primarily Japan) for a loss. Yes, for a loss. Not a loss to the logging companies, but to the federal government – which affects you and me – who has been subsidizing the sales. The trees are getting sold for less money than the government spends putting in logging roads. Worse, the companies with the rights to take the logs out high-grade cut down everything in sight but take only out the very best, straightest, most knot-free wood; so for every tree taken out, a couple more are killed and left behind. The agreement with the government counts only the trees they take, not the ones they destroy.

The Multiple Use-Sustained Yield Act, passed in 1960, requires that all national forests be managed to provide a maximum benefit to all users, be they campers, miners, or loggers. The problem is, no one can agree on what maximum benefit is for others – only for themselves. With the decline of logging in Southeast and the change in natural balance of forests, now is a time of transition for the Tongass.

■ The Forest Service

Another big part of the problem is that, with no valid interpretation to work on, the National Forest Service makes the rules themselves. Their motto seems to be, "When in doubt, build a road and sell the timber for a loss." As Bill Bryson points out, there are over 378,000 miles of roads in national forests – that's eight times the length of the interstate highway system. In Bryson's book, *A Walk in the Woods*, he writes that you show the Forest Service "a stand of trees anywhere, and they will regard it thoughtfully for a long while, and say at last, 'You know, we could put a road here.'" As can be easily seen on Prince of Wales Island, our road-building tax dollars served only to open up our national forests to being stripped by private logging concerns.

It is necessary to separate the Forest Service and the people who work for it. On your trip, you will probably meet lots of Forest Service people ("Greenies," they're often called, not because of their jobs, but because of the color of the Forest Service vehicles, a sort of nauseating green). They are, with astonishingly few exceptions, good, helpful people who care very much about the wild. We've never yet met one who said he always wanted to grow up and become an official environmental terrorist. The employees of the Forest Service are not the problem, but their bosses are, the people back East who have never seen an inch of unpaved territory in their lives and who never get more wild than the area around G Street in D.C. The ultimate boss of the Forest Service is Congress; that means we're the boss, because the people in Congress work for us. Take a look at the forest and take the time to remind them of that fact.

There are also questions of interpretation. The Forest Service was never supposed to lock land away – that's the Park Service. The Forest Service is supposed to use the land for the maximum benefit of the nation. Multiple-use was always the byword. But that's exactly what they've been failing to do by selling off the logs for huge losses. Send up a yell.

■ Reforestation

Although any trip through the waters of the Tongass passes by mile after mile of untouched, old-growth forest, any trip through Southeast is going to be an education in clear-cutting. You cannot miss the bald patches of mountains, scarred by landslides of rock no longer held in by tree roots.

Reforestation efforts are largely left to nature. It's easy to spot old clear-cuts: they are a brighter green than the surrounding forest, since the balance of plants is reversed. In the old-growth areas, Sitka spruce is the dominant species, with Western hemlock second. However, in a clear-cut area, the hemlock quickly asserts dominance, leaving little room for the spruce to take root and grow. No surprise, then, that Western hemlock comprised 51% of logging activity – the companies are all for it coming back to dominate the land. Also in clear-cut areas, the usual lower-level plants, the berry bushes, devil's club, skunk cabbage and so on, are pretty much absent from the grow-back. So, while from a distance the new growth looks at least similar, from up close it seems practically sterile.

Logging on government land is, though appallingly ugly, strictly controlled. Cuts can cover only so many acres, and there have to be buffer zones between cuts and fragile areas such as streambeds. These restrictions do not hold for native-controlled land. The native corporations are free to strip entire mountains bare, to log right up to the water's edge, even in salmon spawning streams. And so they do. Logging in native areas makes the rest of logged areas in Southeast look like lovingly tended gardens.

It may take as long as 300-400 years for the natural balance of the land to reassert itself after a clear-cut, if it ever does. There are those – usually forestry officials – who say it takes only 40-100 years, but they're kidding themselves and lying to you.

Overall in the Tongass, hemlock comprises 60% of the forest; Sitka spruce 30%. They share the forest with more than 900 other species of plant. (Except for parts of Kodiak Island, the forest of Southcentral Alaska is largely similar.) This includes 200 species of vascular plants, 100 or so species of mosses and liverworts, around 350 species of lichens, and nearly 30 species of ferns. In the mature forest, there are roughly 150 species of birds and mammals, plus thousands of insect species calling the place home.

■ Economics

Now for the other side of the story. Logging has long been second only to fishing as the most important industry in Southeast Alaska; for many years, it kept the entire state's economy afloat. However, that's changing. The dive in Japan's economy (Japan imports more than $1.33 billion a year worth of Alaskan materials, three times more than Alaska's number two trading partner, South Korea) has dried up the timber market and the fishing market. (Now the Japanese will start bringing up all those logs they sank in a deep freeze in Tokyo Bay when the prices were good and the Forest Service was giving away huge swaths of forest.) Just between 1996 and 1997, Alaska's fishing exports declined more than 16%, and lumber exports were down more than 5%. That was before the serious slump hit Asia. Paper exports, once the staple of pulp mills around the state, declined 60.4% in just that one year.

There are other problems with the extraction industries. With growing environmental awareness, methods are changing – which usually means becoming more expensive – and with price drops (largely due to serious deforestation efforts in the Third World), logging has become less viable. The Sitka pulp mill closed its doors for good in 1993; Wrangell's sawmill closed in 1995; it's open again on a limited basis now, but the town lost one-third of its population when the mill stopped full production.

So all this is great for the forest, but lousy for the economy of the towns. There is nowhere for the people to turn; fishing has been decreasing throughout Southeast, and that really leaves only tourism. How many T-shirt shops can one small town support? Just take a look at Franklin Street in Juneau, and wonder if logging really isn't preferable to endless kitsch. Any rational human being, no matter how green at heart, knows logging must happen. People need jobs, people need wood. We simply argue that it should be done not on the basis of politics, but on the basis of best available science and maximum sustainable yield.

■ In the Forest

A walk into the rainforest is a must on any trip to Southeast. There are easy walks in most towns or, for the more ambitious, week-long treks. The Forest Service maintains more than 400 miles of paths in the Tongass. In many of the towns, you can go on a guided walk with a naturalist, who will show you a hundred things you'd never notice on your own, fill you in on the medicinal use of the plants, and maybe teach you how to make good fireweed honey (tastes just like the real thing).

Plants

In old-growth, the first thing that most people accustomed to continental U.S. forests notice is how thick the vegetation is: the trees seem to grow almost on top of each other. Whatever space there is between roots is filled with salmonberry, blackberry, blueberry, red huckleberry, and thimbleberry bushes, devil's club, and moss that glows a hundred shades of green. Bear bread covers the sides of both growing and fallen trees. Skunk cabbage shoots its yellow flowers toward the light. There are orchids and the carnivorous butterwort plant. It's an amazingly lush environment.

Plants Used by Natives

There is only one plant that is really dangerous to the hiker in the rainforest: **devil's club**, *Oplopanax horridum*. But even that had important uses for natives. Devil's club is a member of the ginseng family. One shop in Juneau actually used to sell devil's club branches as "Alaskan ginseng." Unsuspecting tourists would take it home, play with it, and find their hands beginning to swell. Devil's club can grow to seven feet tall, with leaves each more than six inches across. It grows in patches that can be impossible to cross, or grows solitarily in well-drained areas.

The problem with devil's club is the spines covering the plant's branches and undersides of the leaves. These yellowish-brown spines break off and dig into the skin of passing animals and hikers. If you don't get the spines out immediately, they can fester and infect; some people are allergic to the poison on the spines and can have quite a dramatic reaction. To most people, it may cause hives, itching, and blotches. Folk medicine says the only cure is to strip the bark from a stem, and rub the underside of it across the affected area, but just try doing this treatment without getting more spines in you.

The Tlingit boiled the stalk, spines and all, into a tea, which worked very well as a general analgesic for aches and pains. Prayers were offered to the plant when it was cut, apologizing and giving thanks. Boiled down to a thick sludge and mixed with seal oil (or Vaseline, if you don't have any seal oil available), it makes a great topical cream.

If you leave the trails, you will encounter devil's club. Be careful, move it out of the way by touching only the top sides of the leaves, and remember it's usually not as bad as poison ivy.

Another plant that was frequently used by natives is **skunk cabbage**. While this plant is not edible (although bears eat the tubers when they first come out of hibernation), the broad leaves were used the way Polynesians used banana leaves: fish were wrapped and cooked in the leaves. It added a certain savor to the fish. It was also medicinally useful as an anti-spasmodic and was made into teas for coughs and asthma.

Flowers

The rainforest is full of flowers. One day, on a walk in Wrangell, we counted more than 30 different flowers in less than a mile, right off the road.

What you'll see the most of is fireweed, characterized by its oval leaves and pinkish flowers. When fireweed starts to seed, it starts to produce a cottony substance that helps spread the seeds. You can make honey with the nectar, and the first shoots in spring are also edible.

You're also likely to run into a lot of columbine, paintbrush, and shooting stars, among the pink and purple flowers, and goldenrod and cinquefoil in the yellows.

The Forest Service has a nice brochure, ***Wildflowers of the National Forests in Alaska,*** that can get you started on identifying the different types.

Berries

There are almost 20 kinds of berries in the Tongass, from the abundant salmonberries to the harder-to-find blue huckleberries. Throughout summer, something will be fruiting, starting with the salmonberries and ending with the high bush cranberries. There are a couple of poisonous plants in Southeast that have berries, including **baneberry**, which can kill you with a couple bites.

 Here's the berry rule: if it sticks up above the leaves, don't eat it. If it hangs below, you should be safe. Or at least that's the rule we were taught, and we have not died yet, following it.

Trees

The soil in the forest is really quite thin – less than 15 feet deep or so in most places. This means that the trees, no matter how big they are (and some of the cedars can easily be 100 feet tall and 20 feet around at the base), have no tap roots, no deep anchoring system. Their roots go out horizontally instead of traveling downward. While this would seem to be a potential problem, it's actually how the forest regenerates itself.

The coastal area is frequently beaten by winds in the winter months. Hundred-mile-an-hour gusts are not at all uncommon. These winds rip through the forest and actually push trees over, uprooting them. Anywhere in the forest you'll see these great trees, sometimes with 20 or 30 feet of root sticking up in the air like a big fan.

The soil along the coast, in addition to being thin, is largely sterile. There are very few nutrients in it. The rain washes them away. As these wind-felled trees rot, they actually provide a rich base for new plant life. Lichens and mosses will start to grow on a fallen tree. Small vascular plants will begin to spring up. And, ultimately, the larger trees will take root on the decomposing fallen tree. You'll frequently see a fallen tree with what look like full-grown trees sprouting up from it. Sometimes you can spot arches of roots, seeming to hold a tree in the air; the empty space is where the fallen tree, now entirely rotted away, once was.

The fallen trees are called "nursery trees," and perhaps as much as 90% of the plant life in the coastal forests got its start on a nursery tree. The forests have provided a rich living to the natives living on the coast. Traditionally, about 50 different species of plants were used for food; dozens more were used for medicines.

How to Identify Trees

- **Sitka Spruce** (*Picea sitchensis*). Alaska's state tree, the Sitka spruce grows 150-225 feet high, up to eight feet in diameter.

Sitka Spruce lives 500-700 years. Its leaves are dark green needles, about an inch long, and they cover all the branches. At the top of the tree, light orange-brown cones develop, dropping to the forest floor and providing a favorite food for squirrels. Sitka spruce wood is commonly used now for making guitars. The Russians used it for the beams and decks of ships that they built in their Sitka boatworks, and for housebuilding. In World War II, it was used for airplanes – the British made two of their fighters from Sitka spruce, and of course that's what went into Howard Hughes's *Spruce Goose*. Walking in the forest, you'll find huge spruce stumps. Notice the niches cut in them a couple feet above the ground. Loggers, working a two-man saw, couldn't cut the tree at the base because their saws weren't long enough. So they'd cut these niches, insert a platform on which to stand, and then lop the tree from higher up, where the saw could go through. Spruce turned out to be a godsend to the early mariners. Not only was it good for repairing their battered ships, the tips of spruce buds can be made into quite a decent beer. As an extra benefit, it's loaded with vitamin C, and so serves as an anti-scorbutic. Captains Cook and Vancouver both served their men spruce beer, keeping them happy and relatively healthy at the same time.

- **Western hemlock** (*Tsuga heterophylla*). Western hemlocks are shorter than Sitka spruce – they grow to a maximum of about 150 feet – and they're thin, with a large tree reaching only about four feet in diameter. Maximum lifespan is about 500 years. The leaves are wider and lighter green than spruce leaves, and the cones are a darker brown. Bark is a gray-brown. Western hemlock loves to come back in clear-cut areas.

- **Mountain hemlock** (*Tsuga mertensiana*). It's not that easy to tell a mountain hemlock from a Western, but they are considerably smaller, growing to a maximum of 100 feet high and 30 inches in diameter. Their range is considerably more limited than the Western hemlock (Western can grow pretty much anywhere under the tree line, but mountain hemlock is restricted to the 3,000-3,500-foot elevation isotherm). The needles are more pointed than on Western hemlock, and the cones are considerably bigger.

- **Yellow cedar** (*Chamaecyparis nootkatensis*). The Forest Service is still trying to figure out why all the yellow cedar trees in Southeast are dying. The problem is, they've been dying off for a very long time, for at least the last hundred years or more.

It's a fairly delicate tree, temperature-wise, but scientists are not sure if the problem is a drop in temperature, too much snow during spring growing season, or a rise in temperature. Yellow cedars (which, like Western red cedars, are actually a kind of cypress), grow to about 80 feet, and perhaps two feet in diameter. They can live up to a thousand years, but they never get that big. The leaves are dark green and look almost like chains of beads; the cones are green and black, about a half-inch in diameter. Happiest at altitudes of 500-1,200 feet.

■ **Western red cedar** (*Thuja plicata*). Taller than the yellow cedar, the Western red cedar covers a wider range, from sea level to about 3,000 feet in elevation. The leaves are much like those of the yellow cedar, but more yellow-green in color. The cones are oval, as opposed to the round yellow cedar cones.

■ Alpine Meadows & Muskeg

The Tongass is not only forest. There are two other significant plant zones here: the muskeg and the high alpine meadows.

Muskeg is a mass of low, dead plants decomposing in a wet area. The dying plants make a rich soil that supports new plants ranging from the marsh violet and marigold to sedge, juniper, and swamp gentian. Few of the muskeg plants grow more than a foot tall.

Signs of spring.

The most important plant in muskeg is **sphagnum moss**, which holds as much as 30 times its own weight in water, and so preserves the marshy habitat necessary for muskeg.

Muskeg covers more than 10% of the Tongass, and shows up as a large, mossy patch in the middle of a forested area. Flightseeing over Misty Fjords opens huge vistas of muskeg for view. From the ground level, walking on muskeg is kind of like walking on a trampoline. The trick is missing the spots where the plantlife is not thick enough to support your weight: it's actually possible to drown in muskeg patches. Think of muskeg as a mat laid over a hole – just like an elephant trap in an old Tarzan movie. But here the hole is filled with water.

Some contend that muskeg is the natural climax of the mid-latitudes rainforest, the place where the forest is heading, forming when the trees have died of old age and no new growth has come in. The acidic level of the muskeg keeps new growth out. This is probably true for the rare pieces of flat land in Southeast; you can see patches where the muskeg is slowly taking over from the trees. But on the larger scale, the theory is debatable, as most of the forest is on slopes, while muskeg grows only on flat. Up on the hills, the climax forest is old growth spruce, cedar, and hemlock.

Alpine meadows (technically, sub-alpine meadows) exist between the frozen peaks of mountains and the tree line. The soil here is thin and acidic, and only low plants survive (on a sub-alpine meadow, there will be bushes or shrubs; true high alpine will be without them). The meadows are thick with lupine, lichens, heathers, low grass and sedge, and a walk across such a meadow will show a complex of inter-nested plants and roots that looks as complicated as an architectural diagram. Like muskeg, the meadow plants are very fragile and can show scars for many years after damage. Stay on the paths and walk with care.

■ Conservation Groups

Before you write to your congressman, get the facts from both sides. **Alaska Rainforest Campaign**, 320 4th St. NE, Washington, D.C. 20002, ☎ 202-544-0475, on the Web at www.akrain.org, works on both the Tongass and the Chugach National Forests. They're the central organization for forest conservation in Alaska, but the **National Forest Foundation** also concerns itself with the Southeast region, among others. Reach them at P.O. Box 1256, Norfolk, VA 23501. They also have an office in Sitka, next to Old Harbor Books, on Lincoln St.

The **Greater Ketchikan Chamber of Commerce**, 744 Water Street Upstairs, P.O. Box 5957, Ketchikan, AK 99901, has information from the logger's point of view.

For Canada, the **Forest Action Network**, Box 625, Bella Coola, B.C., V0T 1C0, ☎ 250-799-5800, maintains connections with a large network of conservation groups throughout B.C., specializing in the coastal rainforest.

We feel that both conservationists and loggers are correct; the trick is getting them to meet in the middle on the basis of best available science and best long-term results. The question is whether they'll ever get a chance to do so, given the political wrangling in Washington. But the one thing any sane person should realize right away is that clear-cutting just ain't the answer.

Glaciers

 Okay, after a while, the forest and ocean become overwhelming, and it's not certain you'll spot a grizzly bear or a whale. But one of the other great sights of Alaska is always on display, and you will see at least one, if not dozens. These are the glaciers.

There are, literally, hundreds of glaciers along the Alaskan coast, ranging from tiny cirque glaciers to the huge Juneau Icefields, which cover an area bigger than Rhode Island. The entire coastline of Alaska was once under ice, and, although the glaciers have been melting pretty quickly over the past decade, there's still a lot of ice out there.

■ Formation

Glaciers are, quite simply, old snow. Lots of old snow. They begin to form when newer snow falls on top of older snow, compressing it; more new snow comes in, and layer after layer forms. As the layers form, the crystals of snow undergo a slight change; where they touch, they squeeze out the air between them, and they near the melting point, allowing for an adjustment of the space between crystals. Individual snow crystals are packed in very, very tightly, keeping each other cool and forming thicker and thicker layers of ice.

The grand party time for glaciers was in the last ice age, which went from roughly two million years ago up to only 14,000 years ago. The glaciers you'll see were formed during this time, as the snows fell and the woolly mammoths cavorted.

Glaciers are not static entities; they can be considered frozen rivers and, like all rivers, they move. A glacier high on a mountain will obey the dictates of gravity and start to move downward. A few hot seasons will melt a glacier back. Most (but not all) of the glaciers in Alaska are retreating somewhat; this is partly due to global warming, and partly just the way things are. We are, after all, just in a warm spot between ice ages, and the freeze will return sooner or later. Glacier movement – forward or back – depends on a wide variety of factors, including weather, slope, and thickness of the ice. Sometimes one part of a glacier will move faster than another, causing a bulge of thick ice called a **kinematic wave**.

Glacial movement is not easy on the landscape around the glacier. While the ice itself isn't quite hard enough to do much damage, the stones and boulders that the ice picks up do a number on the ground. This is illustrated in the land around the Mendenhall Glacier in Juneau: as the glacier has retreated, it has left behind land that is stripped almost to the bedrock.

Because of the amount of rock and debris that a glacier carries with it, it leaves a clear record of its passing. When a glacier begins its retreat, it leaves a line of stones known as a **terminal moraine** to mark the peak of its advance. These are simply stones that were dropped or pushed by the leading edge of the glacier, and moraines can be huge and quite dramatic. There are also **lateral moraines**, where the glacier's sides once were.

Sometimes you can see where a glacier came through by what look like terraces on hillsides; this shows different movements of a glacier. Look to the hills outside Valdez for good examples of this. It looks like somebody has drawn huge lines on the mountainsides.

You can also look at the big picture of Southeast's landscape for a look at how glaciers shape the world: first, any mountain below about a mile high is rounded, smooth; those higher are rough and jagged. The glaciers in Southeast once covered the land at a thickness of about a mile. The sharp stuff now is what was sticking above the ice then. Also, consider the north-south alignment of most of Southeast: the glaciers pulled back to the north, after their southward travels. The bays, the inlets, the passages and channels are all the result of glacial action.

    📖   The best introduction to glaciers and glaciology is John Muir's ***Travels in Alaska***. The guy was a glacier nut, and the way he writes about them puts fun into the science.

■ Shapes & Colors

Although there are a considerable number of categories of glaciers. Mountain glaciers and tidewater glaciers are among the major types.

Mountain glaciers are found up on the peaks. A good example is Bear Glacier, near Stewart/Hyder, or the Juneau Icefields.

Introduction

Tidewater glaciers come right down to the sea: for example, Tracy Arm, the glaciers in Glacier Bay, and the 20 glaciers that empty into Prince William Sound. These are the glaciers that let you see the drama of calving, when huge chunks of glacial face break off and fall into the water. Watching a berg the size of your house come crashing into the sea is a sight you'll not soon forget. Not all chunks are that big, of course. There's a gradation of pieces, from the huge bergs all the way down to **bergy bits** – yes, that's really the term – the little pieces, backpack-sized or smaller, that can choke bays in front of active glaciers.

LeConte Glacier.

And when you're watching a tidewater glacier, don't forget that the glacier goes well below the waterline: some of them are five or six hundred feet deep. This means that chunks of ice can also break off below the surface and then suddenly shoot up – hence their name, **shooters**. If you think it's dramatic seeing a piece fall off, wait until you see a piece fall up.

The final point to make about glaciers is their stunning blue color. It's actually due to the pressure that the ice is under, how compact the ice crystals are – and how large, as some crystals can be more than a foot long. A walk on a glacier will reveal shades of blue that you never before knew existed.

DON'T MISS: *The best place to get close to a glacier is Mendenhall, in Juneau: book a trip that lets you walk around on top of this finger of the Juneau Icefields. For more dramatic glaciers, head into Glacier Bay, Tracy Arm, or check out Harriman and College Glaciers in Prince William Sound.*

The Aurora Borealis

 Besides wildlife and the glaciers, people go to the northcountry hoping to see the aurora borealis – the northern lights. The problem is, you're not too likely to see them from the coast. As most people travel in the summer, of course, it's too light to see the display; and year-round, it's too cloudy along Alaska's shoreline.

This is not to say sightings don't happen; just that you'll be lucky to catch one without going inland.

The aurora is produced by a high-vacuum electrical discharge, created by interactions between sun and earth. What you see – the glowing curtain of lights – is charged electrons and protons formed by the sun hitting gas molecules in the upper atmosphere. The aurora can be compared to a TV picture. Electrons strike the screen (or the air), getting excited and making a glow. The most common color for the aurora is a yellow-green, caused by oxygen atoms roughly 60 miles above the earth.

The lights get more intense the farther north you go. People in Montana occasionally see a display. In Fairbanks, they're practically as common as the moon, with 240 displays a year. There are those who say they can hear the aurora – sounds like a crackling – but so far scientists haven't been able to prove or record it.

Head outside on cool, clear nights, and look north. You never know.

Basics

Traveler's Information

i Alaska has one of the best-developed tourist programs in the U.S. Nearly every city has an information office of some kind. These addresses are listed in the *Basics* section of each city in this book. A few letters will bring you a ton of useful information. The address for the statewide **Alaska Division of Tourism** is P.O. Box 110801, Juneau, AK 99811-0809. ☎ 907-465-2012, fax 907-465-3767 or on the Web at www.dced.state.ak.us/tourism.

📖 Ask the Division of Tourism for a copy of the *Alaska Vacation Planner*.

There are also great links at www.state.ak.us – everything from how to make a cabin reservation to information on fishing and hunting regulations. For Southeast Alaska, drop a line to Southeast **Alaska Tourism Council**, P.O. Box 20710, Juneau, AK 99802-0710. You can phone for their Travel Planner at ☎ 800-423-0568, or visit them at www.alaskainfo.org.

The **Alaska Marine Highway** can be reached at P.O. Box 25535, Juneau, AK 99802-5535. ☎ 800-642-0066, fax 907-277-4829; www.dot.state.ak.us/amhs/. **Fish and Wildlife**, which has excellent links and a notebook series of information on animals, is at www.state.ak.us/local/akpages/FISH.GAME/.

For something cultural, try the **Alaska Native Tourism Council** at 1577 C St., Ste. 304, Anchorage, AK 99501.

Once you're in a town, you'll find helpful, knowledgeable staff at the local Tourist Information Office. These offices are a good place to check for new developments, addresses, and changes in local conditions or regulations. Each town can weigh you down with a ton of brochures and booklets. If you're planning ahead, drop them a line, and find your mailbox filled.

The towns have also all been working to improve their on-line presence. We list websites in the *Basics* section for each town.

When you're in a town and drop by the visitor's center, be sure to sign the guest book if there is one – the number of people going through affects the funding of these marvelously helpful places.

It used to be that, in the winter, everybody spent their time drinking and watching cable television. Now they spend it drinking and working on their websites. Almost every outfitter we mention in this book has a website. We give the addresses for the best and most useful of them, but don't stop there. If you're looking at listings and can't decide who to try, check them out on-line. Give these people hope for next winter.

■ Money & Communications

Money

Honestly, the most common question asked in Alaska is "Do you take U.S. money here?" Yes, and everybody has since 1867, and even more happily since Alaska became a state.

Mail Service

U.S. postal stamps are sold on the ferries. Most of the towns have either a main post office or a substation in the downtown area. Zip codes for towns are given in the *Basics* section for each town. And yes, just like using U.S. money, you can use U.S. stamps. Hang out at the post office on a busy cruise ship day and see if we're joking about people asking this. Over a half-hour, count how many people ask, "How much does it cost to send a letter to the U.S.?" Wonder if you're the only person in the world who ever went to school.

Telephone

The area code for Alaska is 907; for British Columbia it's 250.

When to Go, For How Long

 Most people head up to Alaska between late June and mid-August. At these times, the ships are booked, and ferries on the major runs are jammed with 600-plus people looking for space. There is no hope at all of getting a car onto a ferry without an advance – usually well in advance – reservation, and you can forget a stateroom unless you booked it back in January. The towns can be the same way – during peak season, five or six cruise ships can unload upwards of 5,000 people a day into a town with a population not much bigger.

If you're looking for a little more flexibility and a lot fewer people, travel in the shoulder seasons. May and September are gloriously beautiful months in Alaska and the crowds are not there. The ferries still have some empty seats, and you can probably get vehicle space with less than a week's notice – more on the runs to Bellingham, since locals take advantage of the lessening crowd to head south themselves. Seasonal businesses are usually open from May 15 through September 15. If you're traveling outside that time, call to make sure the providers you're interested in are open.

■ Winter Travel

Winter has its own charm along the coast. It's quiet, and Alaska is there only for itself and for the people who have made it home. Outsiders find the towns have buttoned down for the long haul to spring, the waters are often rough, and the dark is oppressive. It's not the cold that will get to you during an Alaskan winter, but the dark, with only three or four hours of daylight. People who move to the state from Down South aren't quite considered residents until they've made it through a dark season without running away. Travel in the winter can be very beautiful – the snow, the northern lights, the dark gray of the ocean. Yet this is more of a real Alaska experience than most people ever try to find.

■ How Much Time to Allow

You can do a round-trip from Bellingham to Skagway and back in a week. This allows no time to get off the ship, other than the couple of hours in each port that the ferry pauses. It's the same thing for most cruise ships: a week to cover over a thousand miles of territory. To really see begin to see Southeast, a minimum of two weeks is more reasonable, splitting the extra time among Juneau for the cosmopolitan air, Ketchikan for a great combination of city and wilderness, and Sitka for the history. Or drop one of the above and add Wrangell if you want something more wild. Most of the other towns are small enough to be seen quickly. Three weeks allows plenty of time for excursions, but it will still only give you a taste and will leave you longing for more.

Southcentral's main features are not the towns, but the excursions that can be made from them. For a Valdez-Kodiak loop, figure on a week to 10 days, plus extra time for your own amusements – fishing, hiking, wildlife-watching. Go to Valdez and Cordova for the wild, Homer for a blend of civilization and the wild.

The Aleutians run is a five-day round-trip on the Alaska Marine Highway. There's nothing in any of the towns that can't be seen during the stop-overs, and the real attraction of the trip is the ride itself, past the volcanoes and the huge rafts of birds, with the chance of spotting fin whales, killer whales, and Steller's sea lions. If you need to speed the trip up some (or want to stay a few days at the end), you can fly either to or from Dutch Harbor and cut two days off the trip.

■ Costs

Okay, time for some bad news. If you're going to have fun, you're going to be paying for it. Yes, there are a lot of free things you can do – endless hiking trails, wildlife watching, and more. And campsites are cheap, even if food isn't. But if you're going to do excursions and stay in even cheap hotels, guess what? A per-couple per-diem of $500 would not be out of line. It's simple math: hotel, $100; whale-watching trip for two, $200; meals, $100. Tack on a little for margin of error, and you're dropping a lot of cash.

Now, you're not going to go on an expedition every day; days spent on the ships traveling from port to port are cheap. And you can save by cooking some of your own meals, taking picnics – or, if you're on a cruise ship, eating one of the 14 or 15 meals a day that they offer. But be prepared, when you find something you want to do, to spend some money. Going to see the bears at Anan is minimum $120 per person; to do the same at Pack Creek will be double that and, at Katmai, quadruple. You can have a lot of fun in Alaska on the cheap. You can have even more if you figure out your priorities and prepare to shell out for them.

■ Land Connections

From either Southeast or Southcentral, you can connect to Alaska's automobile highway system. Now that the Alaska Marine Highway has a ship linking Southeast and Southcentral, you can get on the ferry in Bellingham, ride to Valdez or Seward, and then drive home. A quicker alternative is the old standby, taking a ferry to Haines or Skagway, then heading north or south on the Alaska Highway from there.

> 📖 For details on driving in Alaska, see our other book, **Adventure Guide to the Alaska Highway** (Hunter Publishing) for all you need to know.

HIGHWAY DISTANCES & TRAVEL TIMES		
	TRAVEL TIME	MILEAGE
Haines to Valdez	14 hours	702
Haines to Fairbanks	13 hours	662
Haines to Anchorage	16 hours	785
Skagway to Valdez	16 hours	761
Skagway to Fairbanks	14 hours	710
Skagway to Anchorage	17 hours	832

Climate Concerns

 No matter where you are along the coast of Alaska, you're going to get wet. Southeast is a rainforest: Ketchikan gets more than 150 inches of rain a year; Sitka gets over a hundred; some of the back sides of mountains get more than 200 inches of rain each and every year. Three hundred days a year of overcast weather is common throughout Southeast Alaska.

Southcentral isn't all that much better: Kodiak has the worst weather of any major city in Alaska. Fogs and socked-in clouds are common and, thanks to the Kenai Peninsula, which sits in the middle of the Gulf of Alaska, largely unpredictable.

Basics

LAUGHING AT THE WEATHER

The National Weather Service says that the Aleutians have "the worst weather in the world." During World War II, troops would joke that you could be standing in the Aleutians with your backside wet from pelting rain, your front baking from bright sunshine, and hail falling all around you.

▪ Weather Patterns

Now for the good news: it's almost never really cold. In the summer months, expect temperatures from the 50s to the low 70s. Nights drop into the high 40s. In winter, average temperatures along the coast rarely drop below zero, getting up into the 30s during the day. And, although it does rain frequently, there is little snow, even in the dead of winter (Stewart/Hyder is a notable exception). Even the rain itself is not such a problem: while there are cloudbursts, most days it's more of a constant, very thick and wet fog in summer, rather than what most people think of as rainfall.

AUTHOR TIP

If you plan to fly in and out of Alaska's coast, always be prepared for a delay. The clouds and fog can defeat even the world's best pilots. We cannot emphasize this enough – avoid tight connections. Because of the weather, flight delays are common. Be flexible and keep a sense of humor. Sooner or later, the plane will fly!

Summer usually has a single two- or three-week period of glorious weather, with deep blue skies, clear sunshine day after day, and temperatures in the 70s every afternoon. This tends to make local residents frantic: people close down shops and head out, fearful that every minute of sunshine is going to be the last one. Because there can be 20 hours of light per day in the summer, it's a little wearying on the locals, and the return of rain is almost greeted with a sign of relief. Two or three days of no rain and everybody is out watering their lawn; a week without, and the drought talk starts.

■ Clothing

How do you spot tourists in Alaska? They're the ones with umbrellas. Residents are firm believers in three things: **Gore-Tex**, a waterproof fabric, for all the outerwear, and **flannel** for layers of inner clothing, with a synthetic fiber like **Capilene** closest to the skin. Layers, rather than single thick garments, are a lot more comfortable when the temperature changes. The outer layer should be wind-resistant; it gets quite breezy on the bow of a ship. Any time you're going out on the water, bring an extra layer – a sweater, a sweatshirt – just in case.

Notice we're not saying a T-shirt for a base layer. The rule is "cotton kills." If you get wet, cotton does not wick the moisture away from your skin; it keeps it there, and it keeps you shivering. So don't forget the Capilene.

With Gore-Tex, there is one minor problem: it has a saturation point, after which it becomes really uncomfortable to wear. It's a high point, one you really have to work to hit, but once you do, you'll be sorry. The same miracle fabric that allows your body to breathe ultimately allows water to get in. The miracle fabric of Gore-Tex also tends to break down when it gets really dirty. If you're on a trip where you plan to get truly and completely soaked for a length of time – whitewater rafting, a fishing trip – or if you're going to get filthy dirty, you might be more comfortable with an old-fashioned rubberized raincoat. There's a reason why fishermen wear those thick rubber duds. You won't be comfortable, but you will be dry. The problem with the rubber clothes, besides making you feel like Gumby, is that if you work up a sweat in them, it feels like it's raining inside your clothes. The condensation can be fierce.

AUTHOR TIP

Often the difference between a miserable trip and a great trip is the gear you're wearing. If you're shivering to death or getting soaking wet, you're not going to enjoy the scenery all that much. If you need to watch the money, eat cheeseburgers for a night or two instead of the salmon dinner; but don't skimp on the rain gear.

Make sure your shoes are waterproof – either with Gore-Tex or some waterproofing spray – before heading out. If you plan to spend a lot of time on charter boats, invest in a pair of "Sitka sneakers," or gum boots. Waterproof hats with wide brims are good too, especially if you wear glasses.

When you're standing in the rain along the coast, unable to see more than a few dozen feet ahead of you, your flight out canceled for the day, think of this quote from Disraeli: "Nature, like man, sometimes weeps for gladness." Alaskan rain is just the sky crying with joy from being over the most beautiful territory in the world.

Health

 There are no special health worries or major health hazards involved in traveling along the coast of Alaska; nor are there any inoculations required by either the U.S. or Canada, should you venture inland. Still, there are a few things to keep in mind.

■ Aboard Ship

The shipping lanes run through developed communities, most of which have excellent hospitals more than capable of handling emergencies. From the smaller villages, air-evacs can be arranged. Cruise ships usually have a doctor for the basics, but not much more. The ferries have no trained medical personnel; some of the crew can perform first aid and there is a medical station for minor problems, but anything serious has to wait until the next port. In a dire emergency, Coast Guard air-evac can be arranged, but just speeding into port is usually as quick, as the choppers generally have to come from Juneau, Sitka, or Anchorage.

■ First Aid Kits

It's a very good idea to take along a first aid kit. You can buy a perfectly good one at any camping store. It should include several sizes of bandages, disinfectant, a small pair of scissors, moleskin, pain reliever, antiseptic cream, and tape. When choosing your first aid kit, keep in mind the number of people who will be using it. Here are a few other guidelines.

■ If you are currently taking any **prescription medication**, be sure to carry along an adequate supply for the length of your trip. If you have allergies, take along some antihistamines. The entire area is rainforest, and there can be pollen galore. On the good side, the constant rain generally keeps things from getting out of hand.

- Take along some **sunblock**. There can be more than 20 hours of daylight; also, the farther north you go, the greater the risk of sunburn. Choose a sunblock with an SPF of 15 or higher. No matter what the label says, it needs to be reapplied on exposed skin every couple of hours. Don't rub it in – rub it on for maximum effect. Yes, you can get burned even on cloudy days. Water is a fierce reflector.

- Perhaps most important, take along a massive supply of **mosquito repellent**. Those with the chemical DEET work best. If you don't want to be putting such a toxic chemical on your body, there are those who swear by Skin-So-Soft, a lotion available in most drug stores, and now jazzed up with a special repellent ingredient that doesn't smell like chemical waste. You'll find a lot of people who say it's the perfect mosquito repellent; you'll also find quite a few people who think mosquitoes like the way it tastes and smells, and flock to it.

DEET WARNING!

If you're using DEET, remember that it needs to be washed off with warm water and soap, and you need to be sure to clean your hands before touching food. DEET is nasty stuff, but mosquito experts (yes, there are such people, squinting through microscopes to identify the dozens of species that inhabit Alaska alone) swear it's the only thing that truly works.

There are a couple of other warnings about DEET. Children should not use a concentration higher than 10%. You should never use DEET on broken skin, nor should you apply it under your clothes (although a drop on the top of your hat brim will keep mosquitoes away without you having to put poison on your face – but don't touch your hat brim and then your face, and don't forget to throw the hat in the washer after the trip).

Don't mix DEET with any kind of skin lotion – the lotion drags the DEET down into your system through your skin, where you really don't want it. If you use DEET on your clothes, wash them as soon as you take them off. Remember that DEET is highly toxic, and treat it that way.

- Whether you go for DEET or some other concoction, take along some **hydrocortisone cream** to soothe the itch for the times when the mosquitoes and other biting insects have no respect for modern chemistry.

MOSQUITO ATTRACTORS

What actually attracts mosquitoes is the scent of the carbon dioxide you're exhaling. And yes, there really are people who attract more mosquitoes than their fair share. Put an attractor in a room with a regular person, and almost all the mosquitoes will go for him, leaving the other person alone. Attractors make excellent mosquito repellent – find one and always travel together!

■ Stomach Problems

Then there is the other bane of all travelers: the runs. If you're camping in the backcountry, you'll need a method of water purification. Due to the high concentration of animals in the forests, there is no pure and safe drinking water. Filters, such as First-Need, are expensive, but they don't have that nasty iodine taste. Iodine and chemical tablets are cheap, but you pay for them on the palate. Alternatively, just boil all water: bring it to a full boil for five minutes. Add one minute per 1,000 feet of altitude over 5,000 feet – an altitude it's pretty hard to reach on the coast. If you're filtering water out of glacial streams, your filter is going to get clogged pretty quickly, so remember to take spares.

The new filter bottles like Safe Water can be great for personal use. Fill it, squeeze it, and drink. We've used these all over the state without any trouble.

Drinking water in the towns and, of course, on the ferry is perfectly safe. On some of the cruise ships, you'll hear that the food and water aren't safe in Alaska, but that's only because the ship is trying to keep you under its thumb. Get serious. It's still the United States, subject to all the rules and regulations of back home. The truth is, Alaskan tap water in the bigger towns tastes better than bottled water and is just as pure. The only exception to this is some of the very small villages, such as Tenakee, which do not have potable water. In any of the small villages, check before drinking.

If you decide to trust nature and not treat the water in remote wilderness areas, pack some broad spectrum antibiotic, and remember most diarrhea goes away in three or four days. If it doesn't, or if there is blood or a fever, see a doctor.

■ Hypothermia

Out on your own, the biggest health risk is hypothermia, the number one killer of outdoorsmen. It can be easily avoided.

Basics

Hypothermia occurs when the body is unable to maintain its core temperature. To save the vital organs in the middle of the body, the system starts shutting down at the extremities: you lose feeling and function in your arms and legs, and breathing becomes difficult. A victim of hypothermia often shivers uncontrollably, showing a marked lack in coordination and sudden sleepiness.

Wet and wind in combination are the biggest factors in hypothermia. Should a member of your party display any of the signs above – victims often deny there is anything wrong beyond a slight chill – get them dry and sheltered. Hot drinks can help a mild case but, in an extreme case, they can cause choking. Also:

- Put the victim in a sleeping bag; if the symptoms are severe, strip the victim and yourself, then get in the sleeping bag together. Brisk rubbing in hopes of restoring circulation is not a good idea.
- Try to keep the victim awake. Do not let them drink any alcohol.
- Get them to a doctor as quickly as possible.

Remember, quick action saves lives. From personal experience, we can tell you that the person suffering from hypothermia has no idea what's happening. To the victim, things actually seem rather peaceful. So watch out for each other.

     For those who are heading out into the serious bush during cold weather (and remember, hypothermia can take hold at any time of year), take a look at the book ***Hypothermia, Frostbite, and Other Cold Injuries***, by James A. Wilderson.

To avoid hypothermia, go out prepared. Wear proper rain gear, proper warm clothes. Remember that cotton kills – keep that synthetic layer next to your skin. If the weather become extreme, take cover. It's that simple.

Boating

 There are 10 million lakes in Alaska alone, not to mention the rivers and, of course, the ocean. One of the first things early explorers to the North noticed was that the locals had better boats. While the Europeans sailed bulky ships that could barely turn, the locals, according to German naturalist and explorer George Stellar, were in boats "about two fathoms long, two feet high, and two feet wide on the deck, pointed toward the nose but truncated and smooth in the rear.... On the outside [the] frame is covered with skins, perhaps of seals, and colored a dark brown." Stellar had spotted a kayak, and it didn't take the Europeans long to figure out that these tiny boats could do just about anything. Meanwhile, in the interior, explorers and trappers were heading up the rivers in bark and skin canoes, some 30 feet long.

"STELLAR"

Many northern animal species are named after George Stellar, including the Steller's sea lion, the incredibly common Steller's jay and the now-extinct Steller's sea cow. (We choose to follow standard orthography – yes, we're spelling his name with an "a" whereas all the animal names have it with an "e." It's a transliteration thing.) The sad thing is that out of all the animals named after him, all the animals he first identified, the blue jay is the only one not extinct or endangered. The world used to be a place much more filled with marvels.

■ Precautions

The water in Alaska is still great – still perfect for paddling. But whether you canoe one of the wild rivers, kayak the fjords to watch glaciers calve, head out fishing or cruising, or just want to sit in a boat and watch the sky overhead, there are things you should keep in mind. Much of Alaska's water remains wild and remote, so excursions require a high degree of planning and self-sufficiency.

- Always **file a float plan** and itinerary with an agency, authority, relative, or friend. Should you end up stranded or in need of rescue, a search can be underway a lot more quickly if someone knows where and when to start. Details of the float plan should include the type, color, and length of your boat, the number of people, and even the color of clothes everybody's wearing when they head out (remember, it's a lot easier to spot a red jacket than a green one). It's also vital that you let those people know when you make it to your destination – don't get back to your hotel and sack out until people know you're safe.

- Get an accurate **weather forecast** before you set off and watch for any signs that conditions are deteriorating. Keep your eyes on the horizon and peaks for clouds coming in. Carry an emergency supply of food, clothing, and essentials separate from your other gear, in a waterproof container. This can save your life if you have to weather a storm.

Basics

- Have **PFDs** (personal flotation devices – life jackets) and wear them at all times.

- Be aware of the dangers, conditions, symptoms, and treatment of **hypothermia** – see above. Northern waters are always cold, and getting wet can kill you.

- Watch out for bears, marine mammals, and other wildlife. Salmon-spawning streams and berry bushes are prime bear spots. Marine mammals should be viewed only from a distance. It's illegal and dangerous to chase an animal (and an angry seal can easily capsize a boat). And remember, to most marine mammals, a guy in a kayak looks just like a killer whale. **Respect the animals.**

- If you're going out into the ocean, be aware of **tidal races and fluctuations**. Have – and use – charts and tables to ensure safe boating. The tides can move very fast in some spots, and the tidal variations are often extreme. Remember this when pitching your camp, and stay well above the high water mark.

- **Keep your camp bear-safe.** Keep all food in a bearproof container, or hang it from a tree branch at least 10 feet off the ground. Never cook in your tent.

- **Boil and purify all drinking water**, no matter where you land, and practice eco-sensitive rules of waste and sewage disposal. No-trace camping is the only way to go.

- Take some kind of **signaling device** with you for use in the event an emergency, such as a VHF radio, an EPIRM (emergency position indicating radio beacon), flares, or mirrors. More than one person on a trip should know how to use these. A flashing mirror can be spotted from forty miles away.

- Have a **contingency plan** in case a member of your party gets separated. Pick a spot to meet, and choose regular times to check in by walkie-talkie.

- If you capsize in the water, **stay with the boat**. Moving around only makes you lose body heat. The boat also is easier to spot for rescuers. A person bobbing in the water is a very, very small target.

- Finally, you need to plan a rational approach to **threatening situations**. Remaining calm is top priority. Then you can make a clear assessment of the emergency and take proper corrective measures. Find shelter, food, water, and keep a level head. That will just about ensure survival and rescue.

The odds of an emergency are remote – more likely, you will enjoy peace and safety on the water. But the more prepared you are for an emergency, the more relaxed your days on the water will be.

WHITEWATER CLASSIFICATION CHART
Class I . . . . Easy
Class II . . . . Intermediate
Class III. . . . . Difficult
Class IV . . . . Very Difficult
Class V. . . . . Exceptionally Difficult

Wilderness
Hiking & Camping

Along the coast, there aren't many roads. Sitka has 14 miles of main road, seven in each direction from downtown. Juneau has about 40, Ketchikan the same. Even where there are roads, like on the Kenai Peninsula, the roads open only a tiny fraction of the land. You could easily spend a hundred lifetimes hiking in the coastal backcountry and still have plenty to see.

■ Safety

The backcountry is wonderful if you're prepared, a terror if you're not. We emphasize the importance of preparation. Here are a few of the details you'll need to take care of before you lace on your (broken-in) boots.

- First, get maps. Topo maps are available in most towns. If you don't know how to read one, learn before you head out. All the modern global positioning systems (which are fine if it's not too cloudy) and tricky radios won't be as useful as topo maps and an old Boy Scout compass.

- For any lengthy hike or camping trip, tell somebody where you're going and when you expect to be back. Nobody will go out to search for you if no one knows you're lost.

- Practice no-trace camping. This means what goes in, goes out. Keep fires to a minimal size. Use only already-downed wood. Bury human waste at least six inches deep.

- Boil or otherwise purify all water before drinking it.

- Read the section on *Wildlife*, page 16, which tells you never to make your tent smell like a bear restaurant.

- Make sure to pitch your camp above the tide line. Tides along the coast can raise the water level dramatically, and it's not at all uncommon for novice campers to wake up right before their tent floats off. Even a mile or two up a river the tide can change the water level by several feet. Find good high ground to pitch your tent.

- Know your limitations. It's not at all uncommon for novice hikers to get in over their heads in the bush. Know the conditions of the hike before you set off. Local ranger stations are great sources of information.

- Whenever possible, when you're hiking, stick to the trail. The forest floor is extremely fragile, and just a few footprints can cause damage that will take years to recover.

📖 It's a good idea to pack a copy of *The Outward Bound Wilderness First-Aid Handbook*. It will get you through most emergencies, from having to splint a break to treating beaver fever. Another good book is *Leave No Trace,* by Annette McGivney.

■ State Campgrounds

If wilderness camping is a little too wild but you still want to spend some nights in a tent, the best campgrounds in the world are in Alaska. And they come with prices ranging from zero to about $12 per night. Most have firewood and water available; all come with incredible views and scenery.

■ Forest Service Cabins

One of the best ways to see the Alaskan bush is to rent one of the Forest Service cabins that are dotted about the Southeastern archipelago and the Southcentral islands and mainland.

Very, very few of these cabins are accessible by land; access to nearly all of them requires chartering a boat or plane. When chartering, be sure the pick up time and place are well understood. Go prepared for weather delays – bring a couple of extra days worth of supplies in case you get fogged in and the pilot can't reach you. You do need to figure in the cost of the charter into your overall cost of the stay. Rates run about $150/hour for chartering boat transport up to $400/hour for larger planes.

Reservations

For the past couple years, there has been a central reservation system in operation. You no longer go to the local Forest Service office; instead, you can book sites in the whole state on-line or by phone.

AUTHOR TIP

Reservations for cabins can be made 190 days in advance. If you know when you'll be in an area, it's a good idea to call in right on the 190-day deadline and ask what's available and which forms you'll need. The best cabins are booked up without a break. The local ranger stations keep notebooks with the vital statistics of each cabin. These include attractions in the area, fish most often caught, and visitor comments, which can be useful for determining a cabin's condition. The visitor comments also tell of any recent bear activity.

Your reservation will be confirmed no sooner than 179 days in advance. All applications must be accompanied with payment – the cabins run $25 or $35 a night – the more popular cabins are the more expensive ones. You can get a cabin for seven days between April 1 and October 31, or for 10 days the rest of the year. Checkout time is noon. It is usually possible at any time of the year to get an immediate booking for the less-popular cabins. Even those are lovely and offer a real taste of life in the Alaskan bush.

To book a cabin, you'll need a credit card; payment is due when the reservation is made. You can make a tentative reservation on the phone (not on the Web), but they have to get your payment within 10 days (cashier's checks or money orders only) or the reservation is canceled. Cabins are reserved on a first-come, first-served basis, and, again, the most popular cabins, such as the one at Anan Bear Observatory, book up almost immediately. Phone ☎ 877-444-6777 (toll-free) from 4 AM to 8 PM Alaska time between April 1 and Labor Day; the line is open 6 AM to 3 PM the rest of the year. You can visit the website at www.reserveusa.com. For more information, phone the Forest Service Information Center at ☎ 907-586-8751, or on the Web at www.fs.fed.us.

The only real drawback to the system is that by getting your reservation this way, you'll miss the chance to pick up local info on which cabins are the best. However, there's also no need to panic; there are a lot of cabins, they're all lovely, and you will find something, even if you start looking around only a day or two in advance.

There is one final caveat: plain and simple, the reservation website is lame. If you want, say, any three days out of a given week, you have to think up all the permutations and enter them, one by one, until you hit

Basics

cabin availability. There are no hints given – you're just throwing blind. If you have to be at a specific cabin on a specific day, the on-line system works. Otherwise, you're better off calling.

Cabin Types

There are four types of cabin used by the Forest Service: A-frame, Hunter, Pan-abode, and Alpine. The A-frames have a second floor, which opens up a bit more sleeping space. The others have similar interiors, but only a single floor. All of the cabins can hold at least four people, and usually six, and sometimes more.

Many of the cabins have oil-burning stoves, but stove oil is not provided (although there's frequently some left behind; still, it's not the kind of thing you want to count on). Check the type of stove in the cabin; if you need oil, five or 10 gallons is plenty for a week's stay. Wood is provided for those cabins with wood stoves, but you'll have to split it yourself.

The cabins do not have any bedding, electricity, or cooking utensils. There is no running water, and stream water should be boiled for a full five minutes or otherwise purified before using. There's no such thing as a safe stream. Cabins are run on an honor system: take care of them, and pack all your garbage out.

Charters

 To get to the Forest Service cabins, or simply to get out and enjoy the beauty of Alaska away from the towns, you'll need to charter. Charter operators are listed in each town section in this book, but they represent only a fraction of what's out there. You can charter a tiny boat, a huge yacht, or a plane that holds anywhere from two to six people, or more. Need a helicopter? It can be chartered.

Flight companies all work on a similar basis. They have a flat per-hour charge, which varies with the size of the plane. With a six-passenger plane fully loaded, chartering can be surprisingly cheap – less than $100 per person. For a plane that holds three passengers and a limited amount of gear, the going rate is anywhere from $180-500 per hour of flight time, depending on the town and the operator, so shop around. The planes can fly you into forgotten lakes where the fish are just waiting to bite, or a customized sightseeing package can be arranged.

AUTHOR TIP *If you're being dropped off, always allow for delays due to inclement weather on the pick-up. Pack enough supplies in case this happens.*

■ Boats

Boat charters lean toward fishing or sightseeing, or a combination of the two. When chartering a boat, be up front about what you want to do and what you hope to accomplish. Even the most experienced captain can't guarantee you'll catch a fish, but different species need different tricks and lures, and a good captain knows where and when your chances are the best.

If one charter company is considerably more expensive – or cheaper – than any of the others, find out why. At a basic level, charters should include all fishing gear, some kind of refreshments, and at least some help on processing the fish.

MONEY SAVER: *Some charters run cheaper trips, not because they skimp on the service, but because they run in a different area. For example, in Homer, the lower-cost charters stay out of the deep, rougher water where the really big fish are; however, they can take you into hidden, quiet bays, and they often offer more excitement, since they use lighter tackle.*

Before booking the trip, ask how long a half-day or whole-day charter lasts, find out exactly how much time you'll be on the water, how long the captain has been working the area, and ask about their license. You should also find out what they do for you on board. With some charters, you hardly even touch the lines, which isn't too exciting for the avid fisherman.

Finally, find out what kind of boat you'll be on. Charters range from Boston Whalers with Alaska cabins – basic, serviceable, and far from comfortable, but great for serious fishing – to luxury cabin cruisers.

AUTHOR TIP *The only way to ensure you get what you want is to let the captain know what you're after. Make your expectations known, match the ship to your needs, and you'll have a great time.*

Expeditions & Outfitters

We list expedition providers who are going to give you a good time, the most bang for your buck. If we list something that seems really expensive, there's probably a reason for it – you'll have an amazing time despite the cost. It's our belief that the wise traveler knows when to blow a few bucks and when to save.

Along the coast, you'll have chances to kayak, hike on glaciers, trek through the rainforest, fly into remote lakes, take jetboats up rivers, and do just about any other thing your outdoors dreams ever included. Whatever you want, Alaska's got it, and there's somebody out there ready to help you get there.

■ Prices

For all goods and services listed in this book, every effort has been made to keep the prices listed accurate. That doesn't mean that the prices won't change before you get there. Oddly, prices on a lot of expedition trips have been going down over the past few years, as more and more competition has moved into the state.

■ Selecting an Outfitter

Before you get to a town, it's good to have some idea of the expeditions you want to go on. Give a call around, and book as early as you can. While, say, day-kayaking trips can usually be booked a couple of hours in advance, you can never be sure when a cruise ship is going to come in and fill up all the spaces.

As with charters, it's wise to ask and find out exactly what the trip entails. It's also a good idea to ask who else will be on the trip. If you're an experienced kayaker, you don't want to spend hours floating while novices weave back and forth in dead flat water. Conversely, if it's your first time in a boat, you don't want to be out there feeling you have to keep up with a bunch of hot dogs.

The key to a good trip is talking with the people you're going to travel with. They want you to have a good time; you've just got to find the people whose idea of a good time is the same as yours.

For Cruise Ship Passengers

If you are coming off a cruise ship, these things happen a little differently. The ship gives you a list of expeditions it books. These are usually rated for difficulty (which don't always make sense – a gentle walk in the woods near Ketchikan is given the same rating as the rather difficult Dyea hike, so take these ratings with a grain of salt) and are very strictly scheduled, so people will have plenty of time to get back to the ship.

On the ship, they'll tell you that if you don't book in advance, you may find the operators fully booked. That is sometimes true, particularly on flightseeing trips, where there's a limited number of planes. However, just as frequently, you can go ashore, find a small operator who doesn't meet the ship's criteria for getting listed on board (an ability to handle a very large number of clients at once, and a million dollars worth of liability insurance) and head out on a trip that's more intimate and interesting than something booked via the ship's crew.

The other thing about booking on the ship is that it will cost you more. The ship, of course, takes its own cut, usually tacking on an extra 20-30% to the cost of the expedition. If you've got your cell phone with you, you can save a lot of money by calling and booking trips a few days ahead on your own.

When you get off the ship in most of the larger towns, you will be all but assaulted by people wanting to take you somewhere. If you haven't booked off the ship, or booked ahead, and you're interested in taking an excursion, talk to these people.

▪ Reservations

A busy cruise ship day – and there can be days when 5,000 people or more are in these small Alaskan towns – can overwhelm the services. Everything may be booked up. For cruisers, this is the balancing act – pay too much and end up on a herd expedition, or try to find the smaller providers who have a little more to offer. For ferry passengers, there's the frustration of finding nothing but full flights and expeditions.

For anybody, cruise ship passenger or ferry traveler, if you're booking on your own, calling a day or two in advance can help avoid disappointment.

Fishing & Hunting

▪ Rules & Regulations

 You must have a fishing license to take advantage of the rich fishing grounds along the ferry route. One-day licenses are available for $10. A three-day license runs $15; $30 for a month; and $50 for a year to non-Alaskan residents. Many charter operators sell licenses, and almost any store near the harbor will have them.

Catch allowances vary from place to place and species to species. For full information, write to **Alaska Department of Fish and Game**, Box 25526, Juneau, AK 99802-5526. They have a fantastic website at www.state.ak.us/local/akpages/FISH.GAME/. You can order licenses by mail from Fish and Game, 1111 W. 8th St., Room 108, Juneau, AK 99801, ☎ 907-465-2376, or order on-line. The same people also provide information on hunting rules and regulations.

In general, a nonresident hunting license is starts around $135; species-specific tags run from the low hundreds to the low thousands of dollars, depending on the animal. Bear tags start at $200, and most big game trips must be planned well in advance to qualify for the tag drawing (a lottery system is employed to select the lucky applicants).

We don't go into great detail on hunting in this book. If you're a hunter, we suggest you call Mark Galla at **Alaska Peak and Seas**, in Wrangell. He's been guiding for a very, very long time, and he'll go all out to get you the hunt you're after. We've traveled with this guy, and he's everything you'd want in a guide. ☎ 907-874-2454.

Photography

 While you're out there, you might as well get some pictures. Film and videotape are readily available in all but the smallest villages – and there, it's usually obtainable but expensive.

■ Tips

Every person you talk to along the way will have different advice for taking good photographs. Here are just a few general guidelines.

- The weather patterns of the Alaskan coast provide a few special challenges for the photographer. First, many cameras are not water-resistant, much less waterproof. Check all seals and read your warranty. Take along plenty of lens cleaner and check for saltwater spray when taking pictures.

- Ever-present rain means that it's often dark, so faster film is needed. You lose something in the grain of the picture, but you gain latitude in what you can shoot. Kodak makes some excellent fine-grain 200 speed films. Fuji has good 400 speed film. The darker it is and the bigger your lens, the faster the film you'll need.

- It's best to have at least two lenses for your camera: a wide-angle that takes in the range from wide angle (24-35mm) through standard focal distances (50-70mm), and a telephoto zoom (a 60-300mm works very well). This first lens is for shooting the landscape. The horizons are big, the mountain ranges go on forever. If you're hoping to get any good mountain shots, the wide-angle lens is required. Remember when framing your shot to include something to offer depth: a nearby tree, your friend, a stream. Just aiming at distant mountains gives a flat, uninteresting picture. Because of the range of these lenses, they're also useful for all-purpose shots: around town, at the campsite, personal photos, etc. This is the lens most cameras come with when you buy them. A 50mm focal length offers a view close to that of the human eye.

■ The most important lens is the telephoto zoom. It is easier to use and faster to adjust, which is a definite bonus when you're trying to shoot fast-moving animals. A telephoto lens with an adjustable 60-300mm focal length offers maximum flexibility with minimum weight. With a 300mm lens, you can really pull things in. If you want really good, dramatic animal pictures, you'll need an even bigger lens to cut the distance. Six hundred millimeters is workable; a thousand is better, if it's in your price range. But keep in mind that at those focal lengths, camera stability and light become an issue. You'll need a tripod and faster film as the lens gets longer.

AUTHOR TIP *At the photo store, they'll tell you to add a skylight filter to all your lenses as cheap protection against scratches on the lens itself; however, a lot of professional photographers wonder why anybody would put a $20 piece of glass on the end of a $200 lens.*

■ Alaska is a land of contrast, and your photographs should take that into account. With the varying sky, the white mountain peaks, and the dark forests, automatic light meters can get confused. A polarizing filter and a medium grade graduated neutral density filter can do wonders for still photographers.

■ Above all, be sure you know how to use all your gear before you take it out. Shoot a couple of rolls of film around home, to make sure everything works and that you know how to operate it.

■ Have the camera loaded and ready at all times. Wildlife rarely appears when you're ready for it. To keep off the dust, put the camera in a holster, but leave the top of the holster loose so you can get to your camera in a hurry.

■ The best time for photographing animals is in the dawn and dusk hours. In summer, these hours, for all practical purposes, extend from about 5-8 AM and 7-10 PM. In the winter, it may be noon for sunrise and three o'clock for sunset. Remember that animals don't always do what they're supposed to. Personally, we have yet to see an animal when and where we expect to, so keep a sharp look-out at all times of day, especially around sources of water, where the animals go to drink.

Do not, under any circumstances, chase after moose or bears to photograph them, unless you want to become part of ranger folklore about the many ways people find to kill themselves.

■ Digital Cameras

You'll face a couple problems with digital cameras: first, downloading your pictures. Bigger towns have Internet cafés where you can take care of business, but you're going to want to bring quite a bit of extra memory with you. And second, the trip is really not the time to learn how to use your new camera. With a film camera, there's a margin of error. Not so with digitals.

> **HOW TO TAKE PICTURES OF DOTS**
>
> You're on a boat, looking at a whale. You see 10 people rush to the rail, tiny little cameras glued to their eyes, snapping away. When they get home, anxious to see the whale pictures, what do they find? Little dots on the water.
>
> Here's the truth: Little disposable cameras take little disposable pictures. Worse, the resolution is poor, so there is virtually no hope of pulling out detail later if you want to enlarge an image.
>
> Even good pocket cameras won't take decent pictures for you unless the animal is practically standing on your head. Their lenses aren't any good, their zooms are even worse.
>
> If you're shooting around the campfire, a pocket camera will do. If you want shots that really show how dazzling Alaska is, you're going to need a real camera.

■ Video Cameras

For the video photographer, get the biggest zoom available in the lightest camera and carry at least one extra battery. Recharging is no problem on the ships, but some of the smaller towns are run on generator electricity, which can fluctuate dramatically. Watch for unusual heating in the equipment when charging.

You make a tradeoff with video. While watching your tape back home will give you that feeling of "being there" again, you're never going to get the single stunning image that sums up the whole trip for you. And you'll never get the detail that a still camera can offer. On the other hand, a still camera image will not let you hear the cry of an eagle.

Shopping

Thanks to the diverse cultural influence along the Alaskan coast, there's a shopper's paradise out there. And due to the influx of tourists over the past 10 or 15 years, there's no shortage of places to spend your money. In the *Shopping* sections in this book, we do not give details about standard-fare tourist shops. There are plenty of those and we figure you can find them yourself, if you're looking for T-shirts and *ulu* knives for the people back home. What we describe here are shops where you can find unusual, beautiful, and quality pieces that you're going to treasure for the rest of your life.

■ Russian Delights

All along the coast there are stores specializing in items of Russian origin. These range from Pepsi T-shirts written in Cyrillic letters to beautifully painted icons ornately framed in gilt, like those you might see in a Russian Orthodox church. Juneau and Sitka are good places to look for these. Some of the most popular Russian items are trade beads, originally brought to Alaska to trade with the natives for fur, food, and other necessities. Some of the beads are gloriously beautiful, their deep blues shining with the patina of age. Look in Kodiak and Haines for earrings, bracelets, and necklaces made of trade beads. The Russians brought a huge variety and there's something to suit every taste. A strand of reds can be had for under $20; a nice strand of blues starts around $100. The beads were once used as currency, but that backfired on the Russians after a while – everybody had too many of them, and the island people did not travel much, so the beads became worthless for trade.

■ Artists

Alaska's natural riches brought settlers to the area and those same riches keep the artisans going today. There is a very large contingent of artists in Alaska, ranging from the high-culture groups in Homer, to the more tourist-oriented hordes of bear bread painters. Bear bread is a fungus that grows in the rainforest; artisans gather it and paint designs on it. Some of the best artists incorporate the shape of the bear bread with a scene of, say, seals on a haul-out. Virtually every town runs exhibits of its local artists in the summer months.

Basics

■ Indian Crafts

On the more traditional side, Tlingit and Haida artworks are among the most popular. These highly geometric carvings and lithographs feature natural objects – whales, beavers, bears, etc. – but with a touch that makes the centuries-old design look like the cutting edge of art. A wide variety of shamanistic objects, such as drums and rattles, are available as well. Traditional canoe paddles, which start around $500, make a fine souvenir of a trip on the water.

Aleut, Indian, and Eskimo artisans all make stunning masks. Higher quality pieces are made from cedar wood or animal skin. Designs range from the simplicity of an Eskimo face mask, usually made to resemble a real person, to the complex Kwakwaka'wakw designs from the southern edge of the Panhandle, which represent Raven, a key figure in Southeast mythology.

Whalebone, ivory, and baleen carvings are all readily found. When choosing a piece, look for fine detail. A truly good piece will simply feel right; lately, there have been a lot of okay copies flooding the market, which have started to crowd out the marvelous. Spend some time, get something worth having.

BRINGING YOUR PURCHASES HOME

Keep in mind that it is illegal to purchase items made from endangered species. Certain animal products may be bought if the animal was killed by a native and the item was "substantially altered" by a native artisan. Unpainted or uncarved walrus tusks, for example, are illegal and may be seized. If they're painted or carved by a native, though, they're perfectly legal. Canada bans the import of virtually any animal product into their territory. Ivory, baleen, many types of fur, whalebone, bear, or seal products all must be shipped home through the U.S. if you are planning to enter Canada on any part of the trip. You can obtain a special importation permit, but the mail is a lot easier.

The exception to these import/export strictures is fossilized whalebone and ivory. They can be legally moved through either country. Fossilized ivory carves easily, and there are some beautiful artworks made from it.

For more information on restrictions, write to the Department of the Treasury, U.S. Customs Service, Washington, D.C. 20041, or Customs Office, 1001 W. Pender St., Vancouver, B.C. V6E 2M8.

■ Ethical Issues

Although many of the products for sale in Alaska and Canada are made from endangered species, strict controls are enforced in both countries. The bone, ivory, and baleen (a kind of strainer that replaces teeth in some kinds of whales; pieces of it can be 10 feet long) come from animals that were hunted under subsistence regulations and used for food by native villagers. Although this is sometimes abused – reports of headless walrus carcasses are not uncommon – when you buy these products, you are supporting a traditional way of life, one that predates European civilization by thousands of years.

■ For Cruise Ship Passengers

On the big ships, before you hit a town, there's a talk offered, and there's a list of retailers the ship suggests you do business with. Of course they suggest these places: they're getting kickbacks. In some towns, the ships own the stores.

The economic power of the cruise ships puts some interesting dynamics into the Southeast Alaska mix. When Juneau put a head tax on cruise ships – five bucks per passenger – suddenly several of the cruise lines started telling their passengers that Juneau was a bad place to shop.

The lesson here is the same lesson all travelers should pay attention to: look around, get advice, and then do what feels right to you.

Independent vs. Cruise Ship Travel

■ Cruise Ship Travel

For years, Alaska's towns have courted the cruise ship market, and they have been highly successful at it. Over the past decade, the number of ship passengers has nearly tripled. In 1990, for example, Ketchikan got 236,000 cruise ship passengers in town during the summer season; in 1998, that number was 520,000. In 2001, it was over 620,000 – and that in a year when tourism was down around the state. Consider that Ketchikan has a population of around 17,000, and you can imagine the economic impact that the cruise ships have. The official number (or one of them, at least) is that cruise ship passengers spend an average $60 per day on their trips. As most towns on an Alaskan cruise are about a day apart, each city stop can depend on a fair chunk of cash being dropped on them, and this keeps a lot of businesses going through the winter months.

On the down side, that many day-trippers in a town has got to have a negative effect on the town itself. A look at the shopping center on the dock in Ketchikan, the bottom of Franklin Street in Juneau, and the monstrous proposal for a deep-water dock in Sitka, show the effects that rampant development for the cruise market can cause. Developing for the cruise market can also be something of a dead end: over the past couple of years, ships have been bypassing Sitka, going to Skagway instead. This has almost killed Sitka's downtown, which depended heavily on cruise passengers.

There's also a serious pollution issue to address. Cruise ships are the most polluting industry in the state, and that's not just because of the smokestacks – it's also because too many of the big ships are still going with the idea that if they hide something in the water, nobody will notice. The number of dumping violations handed out to the big cruise lines are astounding. In the summer of 2001, Coast Guard personnel were on board one cruise ship in Juneau when the ship decided to illegally dump wastewater into the channel. Everything goes overboard, the minute nobody's looking. According to state tests done in 2000, only one in 80 samples of cruise ship wastewater met federal standards. Seventy percent of gray water – water headed down the drain from showers and kitchens – contained fecal bacteria counts as high as 50,000 times the standard for treated sewage.

Keep an eye on your ship. Check with the Center for Marine Conservation, 1725 DeSales St. N.W., Washington, D.C. 20036, ☎ 202-429-5609, www.cmc-ocean.org for more information.

There are two trends in cruise ship travel: bigger and smaller. The past couple years have seen the first megaships in Alaskan waters – vessels nearly a thousand feet long and holding more than 2,000 passengers. Toss in the crew, and you've got over 3,000 people on these boats – which makes each one of them one of the dozen or so biggest cities in Alaska. If you want to have fun, see shows, do a little shopping, eat more food than many Third World countries get in a year, these are great deals. They're cheap, they're comfortable, and they are self-contained traveling worlds, destinations in and of themselves.

DID YOU KNOW? *On any given day in the peak of tourist season, 45,000 people are riding cruise ships in Alaskan waters. If the ship population were a city, it would be the fourth largest in the state.*

If you're out to see Alaska, remember that big cruise ships travel at night, so they can put you by the shopping the next morning. You might be a lot happier on a smaller ship. It's almost frightening to see a large ship go by you in a channel, and there's nobody outside (see the end of the next chapter, *Transportation*, for more details).

The other direction the Alaskan cruise industry is moving is toward small ships, carrying fewer than a hundred passengers. These give you a close-up, intimate experience of the state – as a general rule, the smaller the boat you're on, the better your view. The smaller ships can go places the larger ones simply can't, and they tend to offer more adventures, like kayaking trips in secluded areas. They're a lot closer to independent travel, but the scut work – hauling bags around, finding a place to sleep, and all the other little details that tend to eat up vacations – are handled for you. Again, take a look at the end of the next chapter for more on this.

The two types cater to entirely different markets. Small ships are more expensive and more intense. Large ships are more like being in a really fun college dorm. Pick what you like, and go for it.

■ Independent Travel

Recently, Alaskan officials have determined that independent travelers spend an average of (and again, this is only one of the official numbers) $161 per day during their trip – renting cars, booking hotels, going to the grocery store and the sporting goods store.

Independent travelers are easier on the town: they don't come in groups of 5,000, and locals can still go about their business without running into tourist jams. The independent traveler fits in more easily, and, truthfully or not, is thought to be more interested in the local scene.

Because of all this, there has been a marked increase of late in the state's attempt to market to the independent traveler. Some towns are better at this than others (Wrangell is a good example). Some towns, naturally, have more to offer. But it is interesting watching the changes, and expeditions and excursions for the independent are becoming easier and easier to find. There seems to be a shift in the state's tourism mentality, from "get as many through as quickly as possible" to "get people up here and get them to stay a while."

This book is largely geared toward the independent traveler, but the cruise ship passenger will find plenty of useful information here. We don't believe you can see Alaska properly on a six-hour stopover, but cruise ships are great for coming up and getting a taste of the state, finding out where you want to come back to and spend some time.

The Good Traveler

RESPECT Okay, we're going to preach for a minute. But this stuff is important. Because Alaska is a nice, comfy part of the United States, some of the questions that the average traveler would ask on a trip to a less-developed part of the world get overlooked. However, Alaska is, quite honestly, more remote, more fragile, and more pristine than your standard eco-tourist destination in the rainforests of Belize. The questions of the impact of tourism are just as important here as they are in a Thai village where the locals are giving up farming for the easier fleecing of tourists instead.

■ What Makes a Good Traveler?

What keeps the traveler welcome, beyond the open wallet? In any area where tourists frequently outnumber locals, there are some interesting paradoxes involved. First, the local economy depends on people coming in from Outside and parting with money. This explains the T-shirt shops, the ceramic polar bears, the genuine Alaskan ulu knives. For your six days and five nights, or however long the trip may be, the locals' main idea is to get your money.

But the tourist is widely disparaged, looked upon as a lower life form, prone to insult and abuse at the hands of locals who aren't directly making their money off the tourism industry (and anyone who has lived in a tourist town knows this). This holds true anywhere in the world. The people who live near the Pont Neuf in Paris aren't that thrilled to see the high school tour buses roll up. "Tourons" and "zombies" are some of the nicer descriptive terms you can hear in any tourist town.

The combination of point one and two, above, take us to point three, that attracting tourists for tourism sake, the development of a particular locale into a tourist spot, tends to ruin what brings people there to begin with.

Development invariably leads to homogenization – the arrival of chains and out-of-character buildings and shops – and the debasement of local traditions and flavor. The shopping mall in Ketchikan, right next to the cruise ship dock, illustrates this. No matter how great the town is – and it is great – too many people are going to go away with the memory of it as a junky yard sale.

In Alaska, because of the size and remoteness of most towns, these dynamics, while holding true, take on a slightly different form.

Nobody is considered Alaskan until they've made it through a winter; that's the first test, although there are those who will tell you that it takes years to lose *cheechako* (newcomer) status. Make it through the dark without going crazy, and everybody figures you're here to stay.

However, even without surviving the dark, the non-group traveler is going to find a new world of hospitality, at levels never before expected. A traveler stopping to stay for a few days is a source of entertainment. In most Alaskan towns, everybody knows everybody else as well as they want to – they just spent that long winter together with nothing for distraction but ESPN2; people from Outside can be a tremendous, welcome distraction. You end up with offers that astound you: boat trips, plane trips, free fish – in short, made to feel a part of the community. In return, you should show that you are interested in the town, the people, the culture. There are some simple ways to ensure this, ways that will actually make your trip even better.

- Keep your money in the towns you visit. Go to the local café, not the McDonald's. Try a B&B instead of a motel chain that is headquartered in the Bahamas for tax reasons.

- Related to this is the question of what you buy. Elsewhere we talk about the question of purchasing items made from endangered species. We're not ashamed to have pieces of baleen in the house; we met the guy who killed the whale, met a bunch of the people who ate it. Local economies and customs are supported. However, this may not be the case when you buy something as harmless as a bag or a T-shirt. Was it made locally? Was it at least decorated locally? Buy local products, local arts and crafts that reflect traditions.

- Practice low-impact traveling. The visitor to a town consumes considerably more resources than a local. However, particularly in the smallest places, supply cannot keep up with demand. There are coastal villages where all power is run off generators and where water comes in through a cistern system. Even parts of larger towns – the outskirts of Homer or Ketchikan – can have limited water supplies in summer. The smallest settlements have no organized sewage system, with waste simply being dumped into the ocean. Be aware of local conditions and situations and do what you can to limit your use of precious local resources.

- Even when you're traveling alone, try to form a group when you head out into the wilderness. This is important for safety reasons alone, but it also means less strain on the environment. A bonus to this is you'll get better rates for a group booking – sharing a charter is a lot cheaper than paying for the whole thing yourself.

The idea is to practice a kind of sustainable travel, travel that gives you the best bang for your buck and leaves the place in a way that the locals can live with – both economically and emotionally.

THE ESSENCE OF TRAVEL

Travel is the ultimate force for good in the world. It brings people closer together, it promotes understanding, and it can get you out of a rut. It's good to get out and see just how big and full of wonders the world is. There is no reason in the world for a tourist destination to turn into an overdeveloped nightmare; no reason in the world for Mexican beach resorts to have Hooters restaurants, no reason in the world for the largest KFC restaurant ever built to be across the street from Mao's tomb in Beijing. You travel for local flavor, the feeling of the different, not to find everything is exactly the same as it is at home. The communities of coastal Alaska have everything you're looking for. The better you treat them, the better they'll treat you.

Suggested Reading

We scatter suggested reading materials throughout this book, offering up titles that relate to a particular topic or town. Here, to get you started, are some good general books to look for.

With over 45,000 miles of coastline in Alaska, you're lost without a program. Navigational charts are widely available in bookstores along the ferry route.

MONEY SAVER: *If the charts are too expensive, specific, or bulky, try the* Alaska Atlas & Gazetteer, *published by DeLorme Mapping.*

Finally back in print is the masterful ***Exploring Alaska and British Columbia***, by Stephen Hilson. It's a collection of charts and fascinating facts. If you get only one book on the state, make it this one.

For a scientific skew on the landscape, ***Roadside Geology of Alaska*** by Cathy Connor and Daniel O'Haire, can't be beat. The ferry routes are covered in full.

Jonathan Raban's ***Passage to Juneau*** hit the best seller lists. It's got some great insights on the cultures and topography of the archipelago, and if it drags a bit in the middle, he does bring it all around in the end.

Those interested in Southeast's flora and fauna should pick up a copy of ***The Nature of Southeast Alaska***, by Rita M. O'Clair, Robert H.

Armstrong, and Richard Carstensen. It is occasionally a little skimpy on weights and measures, but marvelously informative.

One of the most popular birding books used by the U.S. Fish and Wildlife people is *Seabirds: An Identification Guide*, by Peter Harrison.

Fishermen need *Alaska Sport Fishing Guide*, by the Alaska Department of Fish and Game, and *Fly Fishing Alaska*, by Anthony J. Route.

Discover Southeast Alaska with Pack & Paddle, by Margaret Piggott, lists excellent hikes and kayaking routes in Southeast. Andrew Embick's *Fast and Cold* is a comprehensive guide to whitewater paddling in Alaska. *The Stikine River: A Guide to Paddling the Great River*, focuses on the best and most accessible river in Southeast.

If you're looking at the mountains, try *Alaska Ascents: World-Class Mountaineers Tell Their Stories*, by Bill Sherwonit. To get even farther out, state-wide, buy *The Alaska Wilderness Milepost*, from Pacific Northwest books.

The first person to bring the Alaskan coastline to the English reading public was John Muir. His *Travels in Alaska* shows a deep understanding and appreciation of the land. Muir would hit a village and immediately start looking for a trail into the mountains and icefields. (When you're reading it, don't worry – the dog Stikine comes out okay.)

The Wolf and the Raven: Totem Poles of Southeast Alaska, by Viola Garfield and Linn Forrest, is an excellent introduction to the most famous artwork in Southeast. For the legends behind the totems and the native culture, *Heroes and Heroines: Tlingit and Haida Legends*, by Mary L. Beck, is a good choice.

Where the Mountains Meet the Sea, from Alaska Geographic, provides a detailed examination of Southcentral's coastline. *The Aleutians*, another Alaska Geographic book, has excellent photos of the islands, plus informative text on the Aleuts, the Russians, and the war years. They also publish a similar book specifically on Dutch Harbor. *Extreme Conditions*, by John Strohmeyer, is the most complete look at Alaska's oil industry and the effects of the spill.

For those using the AMH as a connection to the Alaska Highway, *Adventure Guide to the Alaska Highway*, by the same authors as the book you're now holding, will get you where you need to go. See the last chapter of this book for more details.

Not a single title, but an entire series for history buffs, "**Materials for the Study of Alaska History**," published by Limestone Press, has wonderful Russian source material, beautifully translated. Some of the recommended titles include *Two Voyages to Russian America, 1802-1807*, by G.I. Davydov, and the two-volume *Notes on Russian America*, by K.T. Khlebnikov.

■ Bookstores

In the towns, the best bookstores are **Parnassus**, in Ketchikan, and **Old Harbor**, in Sitka, which has one of the finest assortments of Alaskana books you'll ever see.

> ### THE BEAUTY OF THE WILD
>
> Remember that much of the North is wilderness, meant to stay that way. There are huge areas where no roads are allowed – or could even be built. There are huge tracts of land that haven't changed since the last ice age. Once you set off into these places, you're on your own. In Juneau, you used to be able to buy postcards with a quote from the *Idaho Law Review*. Nothing we've seen better sums up the beauty of wilderness areas than the following:
>
> *A venturesome minority will always be eager to get off on their own... let them take risks, for God's sake, let them get lost, sunburnt, stranded, drowned, eaten by bears, buried alive under avalanches – that is the right and privilege of any free American.*

The Best of Alaska

 It's a huge area, the coast. How to narrow things down? Here are some of our suggestions for the best Alaska has to offer. We know you'll enjoy them as much as we do.

■ Top Picks

Best Long Trip

Raft the Stikine River with Alaska Vistas, in Wrangell. You've got 150 miles of river in the middle of nowhere, incredible scenery, beaches full of wolf tracks, all in the company of one of the best outfitters in the state.

Best Day-Trip

Hike the Mendenhall Glacier in Juneau with Northstar Trekking. Instead of the usual fly-up-and-stand-twiddling-your-thumbs-on-the-glacier trip, these people lace you into crampons, hand you an ice axe, and take you out for a hike on the top of the glacier.

Best Salmon Fishing

Head for the Russian River, on the Kenai Peninsula. It's an easy drive from either Homer or Seward. Lots of room to be off by yourself, only a medium-sized bear population, and salmon that are big enough that you won't have to lie about the size of your catch.

Best Halibut Fishing

Homer. Flat out. Go, get a charter, catch a fish the size of your front door. There's not even a close second.

Best Wildlife Viewing

Anan Bear Observatory. Yes, Pack Creek outside Juneau is more famous, but it's a hassle to get a permit. You can show up in Wrangell most mornings and be watching bears by afternoon. Also, it's the only stream where you've got a chance to see both brown and black bears. If you're after only brown bears, get your wallet out, and book a flight from Homer or Kodiak to McNeil River. It's where *National Geographic* goes to get its grizzly bear pictures.

Best Whale-Watching

Orca Expeditions, Juneau. Ever had a whale come up right next to your boat, its mouth wide open? It happens to these people all the time.

Best Bird-Watching

The Copper River Delta, outside Cordova, is one of the most important migratory flyways on the continent. Stop by and watch nesting trumpeter swans. Oh, and maybe a half-billion or so other birds flying around.

Best Hike

The Chilkoot Trail, starting in Dyea, outside Skagway. It was good enough for thousands of miners; it should work for you, too.

Best Russian History

Sitka. The church itself is a loving replica, but the Bishop's House is original, and there's no other spot in the state to give you an idea of what Russian Alaska was like. There's even the ghost of a Russian princess.

Best Native History

Ketchikan. Go see the astounding totem pole collection at Saxman. Yet more poles at Totem Bight. The town is also the center for the new wave of totem carving, which incorporates modern elements into classic forms.

Best Kayak Day-Trip

If you're in Southeast, head to the north end of the road in Juneau. Put in around the Shrine of St. Therese, and paddle the small islands in the channel. If you're in Southcentral, Homer's Kachemak Bay is what you're looking for. Yukon Island has wildlife, good views, and a cool natural arch you can try to shoot the boat through.

Best Long Kayak Trip

Glacier Bay. Get dropped off, paddle up the East Arm, where cruise ships are forbidden. Plan to start looking for a job in Alaska after the trip, because nothing else will ever satisfy again.

Best Ferry Ride

For a long day-trip, take the monthly run from Juneau to Pelican. Incredible scenery, and since the route goes through Icy Strait, a near certainty of seeing whales. For a long trip, book the Aleutians run. It's like nothing you can begin to imagine: both bleak and lush, stark and opulent. Bring your binoculars: you'll see rafts of birds miles long.

Best Trip That Doesn't Involve Boats or You Working Yourself

Not feeling too active? Ride the White Pass & Yukon Route train (Skagway), and be glad you were never a gold miner.

Best Romantic Escape

Alaska's full of remote lodges and beautiful inns. But how about something different? Get the *Rain Haven*, a vintage houseboat (Wrangell), and have it anchored in a quiet bay, where nothing moves but you and the wildlife.

Best Museum

Sheldon Jackson, Sitka. Jackson was an inspired collector, anxious to document the Native lifestyles he was trying to ruin. The collection he left behind makes every other museum in the state look like a garage sale.

Best Russian Church

Dutch Harbor, Aleutians. The Russians built their onion-domed churches all over the Alaskan coast. None match this one for splendor, both of construction and setting. Worth the trip to Dutch all by itself.

Best Place to Sit and Hang Out

In Southeast, Gustavus. All directions are given from the crossroads. Don't worry about getting lost, there's only one way. In Southcentral, Seward. More relaxed than Homer, and better restaurants to boot.

Best Place to See What Alaska's Like When the Tourists Go Home

Wrangell. The restaurants close at 3 PM. No movie theater, no bookstore, but there are three hardware stores. There's also easy access to the best wilderness in Alaska and people who have stuck through hard times because there's no place in the world they'd rather be.

Best Place to Sit and Watch the Tourists Go By

Skagway. A town with only 400 permanent residents, there can be 6,000 cruise ship passengers a day in town. And yet it's still a fun, beautiful place to be.

Best Way to be a Tourist in Alaska

Okay, if you're not interested in the hassle of doing it all yourself, let somebody else do it for you. Book a trip on Glacier Bay Cruiselines. Week-long cruises, tiny ships, and they go places nobody else does.

THE SECOND LAW OF THERMODYNAMICS

We go to great lengths to make everything in this book as accurate as possible. However, as physics teaches us, things inevitably change. Hotels get more expensive, restaurants go out of business with alarming frequency, operators buy new boats and run different trips. Good places go bad, bad places turn into the best places you've ever been. If you find any inaccuracies, drop us a line at comments@hunterpublishing.com.

If nothing changed, we wouldn't need to rewrite this book so often. So keep your eyes open, and remember: it's a guide, not a bible. There's a big state out there, just waiting for you to have fun in it.

Basics

Transportation

There are a few thousand islands along Alaska's coast. That means you're going to need boats. Lots and lots of boats.

The Alaska Marine Highway

Almost 10 years ago, this book began as a guide to the Alaska Marine Highway. If you're an Alaskan living on the coast, the ferries are your equivalent of a bus system. They're the lifeline that holds the towns together. If you want the real Alaskan experience, the ferries are for you.

The Alaska Marine Highway runs nine ships to 34 ports, covering over 3,500 miles in two essentially separate routes, **Southcentral** and **Southeast**. For convenience, we have broken the Southcentral route into two sections: Southcentral, which includes Prince William Sound; and Southwest, the run from Kodiak to Dutch Harbor. The 1,600-mile Southeast route is the longest single ferry route in the world. The Southwest run, which connects Kodiak and Prince William Sound with the far-flung islands of the Aleutians, touches the most remote places of the U.S. accessible via public transportation. And now there's a cross-Gulf trip that goes from Juneau to Valdez and Seward, letting you take in the entire coast without having to hop in a plane or a car.

The Alaska Marine Highway transports more than 400,000 passengers annually (most of them in the peak summer months) and more than 111,000 vehicles. The system directly employs almost 1,000 people and contributes more than $150 million to Alaska's economy.

■ History

The ferry started in 1960, only a year after Alaska gained statehood, when a ballot issue passed to create the Alaska Marine Highway as a division of the Department of Transportation.

Prior to the state taking over the ferry business, several private companies had sent ships into Alaska's waters, often using Seattle as a base port.

During the fine, heady days before World War II, a one-way fare on one of these private lines from Seattle to Ketchikan was $31.50; you could get from Seattle to Unalaska (Dutch Harbor), a nine-day ride, for only 80 bucks.

The first government-run ferry to ply Alaskan waters was a converted Navy LCT (Landing Craft Tank), named the M/V *Chilkoot*, which ran from Juneau to Haines and Skagway. Operations started in 1949, and the ship ran without any competition until 1957, when the Alaska Steamship Company sent seven ships north from Seattle into Alaskan waters. The ASC's ships were primarily interested in commerce, stopping in Cordova and Seward to meet the railheads, Valdez to get the road link, and Ketchikan and Juneau almost as afterthoughts. The Alaska Steamship Company was, until the summer of 1998, the only company to ever regularly route ferries across the Gulf of Alaska – something the Alaska Marine Highway began doing only with the launch of their newest ship, the *Kennicott*.

M/V *Chilkoot* was taken over by the Territorial Board of Commissioners in 1957; two years later, the ship was replaced by the M/V *Chilkat*. The *Chilkat* was a great improvement, but strictly limited: it had a carrying capacity of only 15 vehicles and 60 passengers. Still, the running of these ships proved the feasibility of a ferry system in Alaska. The demise of passenger service on the Alaska Steamship Company made it imperative that some ships started heading north hauling people as well as freight.

■ Politics

Before the Alaska Marine Highway could start sailing, there were politics to take care of. It was decided that the first ships would operate in Southeast, and immediately towns began fighting to have the ferry come to their dock. Annette Island, home only to the insular community of Metlakatla, sent letter after letter to the governor, stating (correctly) that Annette had the best airfield in Alaska, and so was a natural stop for the ferry. Sadly for Annette, the ferry system decided that with the airstrip, they didn't need the ferry, and so the island was bypassed for years.

Valdez and Sitka had different problems: the proposed ferry terminals were outside of town. How, Valdez asked, were tourists supposed to get into town to shop? What benefit was the ferry going to be to the community if it docked three miles away? Well, the earthquake solved that problem, and the ferry dock is now in the heart of downtown.

For Sitka, the problem was even worse. The ferry system couldn't run full-sized ferries through the narrow passages all the way into Sitka. Instead, the Alaska Marine Highway docked at Rodman Bay, 60 miles south of town. From there you had to transfer onto a feeder ship to reach town. That, too, took years to straighten out, although now that Sitkans have a convenient dock near town, they're talking about building a road to Rodman Bay, just so they'll be able to drive somewhere.

The initial cost projections for linking the communities of Southeast together by ferry stated that $15 million would be needed. Bond issues were floated and bought. Ships were ordered and the first Alaska Marine Highway vessel pulled out of Seattle on September 3, 1962. Within a year, two more ships were operating in Southeast, and the M/V *Tustemena*, the *"Tusty,"* was working in Southcentral. In its first full year of operation, the AMH transported 83,000 passengers and 16,000 vehicles.

The system steadily added new ships, reaching a glitch only in 1967. Alaskan voters had already approved the construction of two new ships for the Marine Highway. When the B.C. Ferry system's ship *Queen of Prince Rupert* ran aground, it was decided that a new ship should be purchased immediately, since there was only one vessel still traveling between Seattle and Prince Rupert. No suitable ship was found in the U.S., but a new 354-foot, 1,300-passenger ship, M/V *Wickersham,* was found for sale in Sweden. Quick studies determined buying this ship would save Alaska $4 million over the cost of building one from scratch, so the ship was quickly purchased. The problem was a U.S. maritime shipping law known as the Jones Act. This law stated that no foreign-built ship could be registered to a U.S. port, nor carry vehicles, passengers, or cargo from one U.S. port to another. The State of Alaska looked to get a waiver, but none appeared, and the state had to sell the ship and go back to building from scratch.

■ Growth

The Alaska Marine Highway is in its fifth decade now, looking to the future. Express trips between major cities have been started and regular service across the Gulf of Alaska has been initiated. There are plans for building some smaller ships for commuter runs as well – Juneau to Haines and Skagway, an echo of the first days of ferry transport in Alaska. By 1996, all the ships of the Marine Highway had undergone full refurbishment, and on shore, new terminals are being built – $200 million worth of expansion and shore facilities are in the works.

The AMH is one of the most civilized means of public transportation in the world. The ships are fast, friendly, cheap, and comfortable. The scenery absolutely cannot be beat. The AMH is a travel bargain, and there's more than one cruise ship passenger out there, looking at the ferries, wishing they'd used them instead. The AMH is the real Alaska.

Transportation

Ferry Technicalities

First, directions on the ferry are given in nautical terms: bow (front of the boat), stern (back), port (left side), and starboard (right side). Whales don't wait for you to translate ship-speak, so memorize these.

Distances & Travel Times Between Southcentral/ Southwest AMH Ports		
	TRAVEL TIME (hours)	NAUTICAL MILEAGE*
Whittier to Valdez	6¾	78
Valdez to Cordova	5½	74
Cordova to Whittier	7	97
Cordova to Seward	11	144
Valdez to Seward	11	144
Homer to Seldovia	1	17
Homer to Kodiak	12	136
Homer to Port Lions	10	134
Seward to Kodiak	13¼	185
Kodiak to Port Lions	2½	48
Kodiak to Chignik	19	138
Chignik to Sand Point	9¼	138
Sand Point to King Cove	6¾	98
King Cove to Cold Bay	2½	25
Cold Bay to Dutch Harbor	18¼	237

* 1 nautical mile = 6,080 feet

■ Reservations & Planning

It is rarely difficult to get on a ferry as a walk-on passenger. If you're bringing a vehicle or want a stateroom, you will need do some advance planning. Staterooms for the peak summer months are usually sold by January, or about a month after they go on sale. Vehicle space is available a little later but, if you are planning on bringing an RV or large truck, the sooner you book, the better.

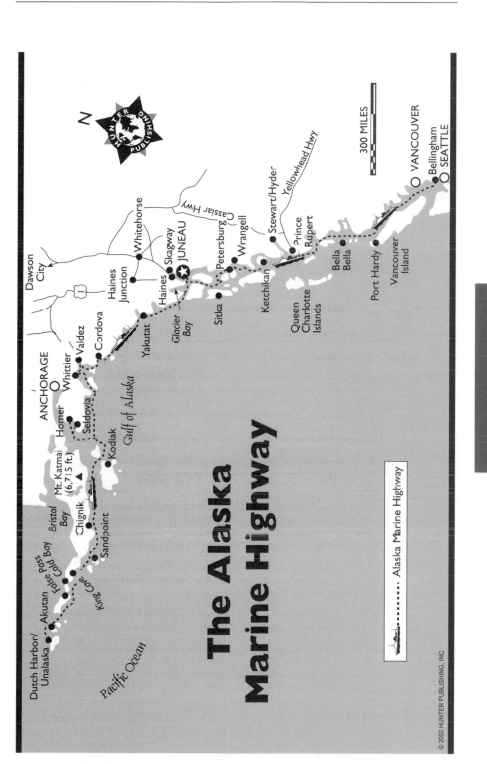

The Alaska Marine Highway

Transportation

Distances & Travel Times Between Southeast AMH Ports		
	TRAVEL TIME (hours)	MILEAGE (nautical)
Bellingham to Skagway	67	949
Bellingham to Skagway, via Sitka	82	1,116
Bellingham to Ketchikan	37½	595
Prince Rupert to Skagway	33¼	430
Prince Rupert to Skagway, via Sitka	47¼	584
Prince Rupert to Ketchikan	6	91
Hyder to Ketchikan	9¾	143
Ketchikan to Wrangell	6	89
Wrangell to Petersburg	3	41
Petersburg to Juneau/Auke Bay	7¾	123
Haines to Skagway	1	13
Juneau/Auke Bay to Haines	6¾	91
Sitka to Juneau/Auke Bay	8¾	132
Petersburg to Sitka	10	156

In summer, there can be a two- to three-week wait for vehicle space on the more popular runs. Advance planning is essential from May through September. In winter, though, the ferry is nearly empty.

Walk-on passengers can't book a through-ticket, get off at stops en route for a day or two, and get back on any ship headed to the destination port. You'll need to book each stop. However, this doesn't run more than $20 or so over the single-destination ticket with no stops.

Get a schedule from the Alaska Marine Highway, ☎ 800-642-0066. They're on the Web at www.dot.state.ak.us/amhs. Printed in a slightly confusing color-coded format, the schedule lists sailing times from each of the ports. Note that sailings from Bellingham leave only once or twice a week. If you have questions about the schedule, call and ask the reservations personnel.

AUTHOR TIP *The ferry system does maintain a standby list, which works on a first-come, first-served basis. If your chosen sailing is full, you can ask to be put on the list.*

■ Check-In

Departure and check-in times are printed on the tickets. In larger ports, take the check-in times very seriously. If you're not in line, you can miss your spot. In some of the smaller ports, things are a lot more relaxed, but it's always a good idea to check with the local terminal. In all but terminus ports, call the terminal an hour or so before check in to see if the ship is running on time. The AMH does a remarkable job of sticking to the schedule, but delays do happen in the changeable weather of Alaska.

Walk-on passengers don't really need to check in – that's more for the vehicles. Still, you want to show up a bit early, particularly if you're going to be looking for a spot on the deck or in the lounge to sleep. Figure 30 minutes before departure as the absolute latest to board. Always check locally for changing rules and conditions.

■ Prices, Deals & Passes

There are a couple of special price deals.

Senior Discounts

Those 65 and over can board the *LeConte, Aurora, Bartlett,* and *Tustemena* for 50% of the regular adult fare (on a space-available basis). There are restrictions on this in the high season, and the rate applies only to your body: cabins, vehicles, and meals are all extra. The offer is also only good for Alaskan ports.

Passengers with Disabilities

Passengers with disabilities can obtain a $25 pass that allows them space-available travel on the AMH. The pass entitles the bearer to sail at discount rates on selected sailings. The rules and regulations are long and complicated, so check with the ferry office. This deal is limited to those with 70% or more disability. There are elevators on all ships except the *Bartlett,* which has a stair climber – the AMH wants to know when you book if you'll be using this. The *Columbia, Malaspina, Matanuska, Taku, Kennicott,* and *Tustemena* have wheelchair-accessible cabins available. The AMH is willing to try to make special arrangements. Call the office for more details.

Vehicle Charges

Charges vary according to the size of the vehicle, and prices do not include the driver's transportation. There's also a fare category for kayaks, canoes, and bikes. It's quite cheap to put your kayak on the ferry – about

$40 for a Bellingham to Juneau trip, or the equivalent of a single day's kayak rental in town. Those with large RVs should be prepared to back the vehicle down the ramp into an assigned spot in very tight location.

AUTHOR TIP

Ferry personnel will help direct you, but get comfortable with maneuvering your vehicle before leaving home. If you're bringing a bike, motorcycle, kayak, or anything else that can roll, bring your own tiedowns. You can secure your vehicle to stanchions on the ferry floor. Car deck personnel will help you and, if they can find some, you might get some rope out of them, but it's better to come prepared.

■ Ferry Regulations

Baggage Allowances

You are permitted to carry as much baggage as you want in your car. Foot passengers are allowed only 100 pounds, although it's never checked. We walked on once carrying upwards of 150 pounds of camping gear, and called out jokingly to the purser, "We're seriously breaking the hundred-pound rule." She called back, "As long as you're lugging it, I don't care."

A baggage cart comes off the ship at each port in Southeast; load your stuff on that, and retrieve it on board. There are storage lockers on all ships, which run 50¢ or a dollar (quarters only).

Restrictions

The ferry does not keep a refrigerator for your fish catch, nor does it allow explosives, flammable materials, or corrosives on board. Handguns are not permitted in Canada, even in Canadian waters as you pass through. Handguns will be confiscated, and failure to declare one can result in seizure of the weapon, your vehicle, and possibly you (for more on Canadian Customs, see the Alaska Highway section at the end of this book). RVs must turn off propane tanks before loading. Small gas containers are allowed, but must be sealed and checked by ferry personnel before loading.

Pets

Pets are allowed on the ship, but they must be in a container or in your car and kept on the car deck. The ship does not make any facilities available for pets. You can go down to the car deck to tend to your animal only on car deck calls, which are limited to times in port and, on the longer runs, to three very specific times per day that last only 15 minutes. It's a cold, miserable, lonely trip for an animal. You'll need a current health certificate (issued within the past 30 days) to get your pet on board.

AMH Vessel Information Table

	Columbia	Matanuska	Malaspina	Taku	Aurora	LeConte	Tustemena	Bartlett	Kennicott
Date Completed	1974	1963	1963	1963	1977	1974	1964	1969	1998
Length (ft.)	418	408	408	352	235	235	296	193	382
Beam (ft.)	85	74	74	74	57	57	61	53	85
Loaded Draft (ft.)	17	17	17	16	14	14	14	13	17.5
Gross Tonnage	3,946	3,029	2,928	2,624	1,328	1,328	2,174	933	5,110
Horsepower	12,350	7,400	8,122	8,122	4,300	4,300	3,200	3,468	13,380
Service Speed (kts.)	17	16	16	16	14	14	13	12	17
Crew	66	50	50	42	24	24	37	24	56
Passenger Capacity	625	500	500	475	250	250	210	190	748
Staterooms	91	108	84	44	0	0	26	0	99
Berth Capacity	312	256	274	106	0	0	68	0	320
Vehicle Capacity	158	108	107	83	44	44	42	41	120

Transportation

Smoking

Smoking is allowed only outside and in the bars.

■ Sleeping On Board

Staterooms

Staterooms are booked for the entire length of your trip – that is, for example, if your run is Bellingham to Juneau, you buy the cabin as a unit for three nights. The ships have two- and four-berth cabins (*Aurora, Bartlett* and *LeConte* do not have any staterooms). Not all rooms have private bathroom facilities. Those with full facilities are slightly more expensive, as are rooms with outside windows.

AUTHOR TIP *Avoid inside cabins if you get claustrophobic. They're comfortable, but dark and confining. It may be worth the extra money for an outside cabin.*

It is occasionally possible to get a stateroom by going on the standby list. You generally stand a much better chance of getting a four-berth cabin on standby. Check with the terminal and again with the purser on board. A lot of people book cabins in advance, and then decide not to use them. So, even during the busy season, if you're one of the first 10 or so people to get on the list, your chances are pretty good.

Roomettes

The *Kennicott,* in addition to the usual cabin facilities, also has roomettes. These are purely basic: chairs and a table that converts into a bed, and a second bed that folds down. Nothing else, not even linen (you can rent pillows, sheets, and blankets from the purser). They're not exactly the height of luxury, but they are very cheap, about a quarter the price of a regular stateroom. You're not going to be doing anything besides sleeping and stashing your gear there, so how much luxury do you need, anyway? These are one of the real bargains of the fleet.

"Camping"

If you don't want a room, you can camp outside in the solarium on any of the ships, or in the open area on the back end of the cabin deck (preferable, quieter) of the *Columbia*. Tents are allowed, but in these areas only, and in high season spaces fill up fast. Every chair in the solarium will get occupied right away, too. There is nowhere to stake a tent, although a roll of duct tape serves nicely – and if you have a big roll you'll make friends quickly with all the people not wise enough to read this book. Bring a rope

"Camping" spots fill up quickly on board ferries.
Many passengers stake a claim to deck chairs in the solarium.

or two for good measure, since it's not uncommon for tents that have been inadequately tied down to blow right off the ship in rough weather.

The *Columbia* has room for maybe 20 tents, the *Malaspina* and *Matanuska* maybe half that number. This is a lovely way to travel, providing time outdoors with a private sheltered area. You will want a rainfly, though, just to be sure, although the aerodynamics of the ships keep things from getting too bad.

If you want to sleep outside in a tent, forget about it on the *Kennicott*. The solarium also is not suitable for sleeping out. It's more exposed than on other ships, and considerably smaller and harder to find a patch of deck or a lounge chair to call your own. Once you do have a spot, the windows are too high to see out of.

Sleeping in the forward lounges and observation lounge is permitted on all ships. No baggage is allowed in the observation lounge and no food or drink is permitted in the forward lounge. Both places can get noisy, but they are darkened at night, a blessing for those who find the white nights of summer a little much to take. Technically, you cannot stake out a space by leaving gear in it. In practice, though, such claims are usually respected.

There are public showers available on all ships except the *Bartlett*.

■ Dining

Every ship has a dining area. These range from those found on the *Tusty*, which opens for only three hours a day, to the snack bar on the *Columbia*, which never closes. There are also vending machines.

The Food

Snack bar and restaurant meals on the smaller ships are fairly limited, but reasonably priced and quite good. At the other extreme of choice, the dining room of the *Columbia* will surprise you with its gourmet meals. Just-caught shrimp are picked up in port and cooked only an hour or two later. Non-seafood dishes are created with delicious sauces and no detail has been spared to make the dining outstanding. You absolutely can't beat the view out the restaurant windows. Figure on $6-8 for a meal in the snack bars, double that for something in the restaurant.

AUTHOR TIP *If you're bringing your own food (not a bad idea for variety), keep in mind that there is nowhere to cook on the ship – campstoves are strictly forbidden – but there is always hot water available, which is good for instant oatmeal, soups, and teas.*

■ Special Programs

The Alaska Marine Highway not only wants to take you from place to place, they want you to have a good, educational time getting there. In the summer high season, the AMH has a couple of on-board programs.

Naturalists – from the Forest Service or Fish and Wildlife – are placed on the larger ships. They present programs on the landscape, the people, and the wildlife along the ferry route. Before arriving in port, lectures are given on the town's history and attractions. Programs are announced on the ship's PA just before they start.

If, for some warped reason, you're tired of scenery, on the longer runs there are cheesy Hollywood films shown at regular intervals in the TV lounges. Sometimes you get a good documentary, but usually the films are just something to keep kids from running around.

■ The Cross-Gulf Trip

There is one ferry run we don't cover in quite the same detail as the others in this book: the cross-Gulf trip from Juneau to Seward. It goes once a month, on the *Kennicott*. It's two days, either way, and along the route, if the weather holds for you, you can get some beautiful views of the

Fairweather mountain range and Prince William Sound. However, unlike the other ferries that hug the shoreline, the cross-Gulf trip goes quite far out into open water, so the mountains are a long way off. It's not usually a rough trip, so those prone to seasickness don't need to worry much.

The Kennicott

We hate to say this, but we have to: nobody likes the *Kennicott* and, if you've got a choice, we suggest you stay away from it. The ship was not really built with human beings in mind. It was built as a multi-purpose ship and, as we all know, the more things you do, the fewer you do well. The *Kennicott* is rigged for emergency oil spill clean-up, and to come to the aid of vessels in distress. It's ultimately slated to take over the *Tusty's* run in the Aleutians, so it's built solidly. It's a clean, shiny ship, and after the *Columbia* caught fire late in 2000 (it's back running, fully renovated now), we heard quite a few ferry people say they wish it had been the *Kennicott* that had burned, preferably to the waterline.

It's not a bad ship. It's just uncomfortable and very sterile-feeling. It's fine for short runs and, of course, if you're going cross-Gulf you have no other choice. But if you're going to be taking a long run, and there's a choice, you're probably going to be happier on a different ship.

■ What the Ferry is Not

Saturated with TV images of cruise ships, a lot of passengers get on board expecting to find the *Love Boat*. No such luck. These are working ships. There is no doctor on board (in a medical emergency, air-evac can be arranged); the purser is swamped under a complicated work load and schedule (the purser on the *LeConte* never gets more than five hours straight sleep). There's no pool, no shuffleboard, and you don't have to wear a tux for dinner. But you'll find the AMH's people friendly and interesting. Often, they are just as excited as you are when a breaching whale or a passing pod of porpoise is spotted. This is the real Alaska.

Cruise Ships

The Alaska Marine Highway gets about 400,000 passengers each year. Cruise ships bring more than 600,000 passengers to Alaska. The ships run the gamut of size, shape, and luxury. In 2002, the first megaship, carrying more than 3,000 passengers, started traveling in Southeast. There are also lovely small ships, carrying as few as a couple dozen passengers.

The advantage to a cruise is the elimination of hassle. These companies make it a point to take very, very good care of you, and once you've gotten your luggage to the line, you never have to move it again. You know when you'll dock where (and it won't ever be in the middle of the night, the way the ferry tends to be) and, in short, the complication level is cut way, way down. Plain and simple, it's why people go on cruises.

The disadvantage is the loss of time – which can, in and of itself, be a good thing, if you've got a tight schedule. If you've got only a week to see Alaska, get on a cruise ship. They cover a lot of ground, and do it for a low price. Just be prepared for the fact that it will leave you wanting, and by the time you're off the ship, you'll be planning a long, slow vacation for next year.

If you're going to opt for a cruise, the most important thing is to know what you want out of a trip. There's a world of difference between a 1,000-foot-long ship with a casino and nightly Vegas-style shows, and a small line where the ship is simply a pleasant way to get to the real attraction: Alaska. The only way you're going to get on the ship that's right for you is to know what you want. With the variety, there's something out there for everyone.

■ Cruising Alaska

For years, we passed cruise ships by when we were writing this book. The only lines making serious inroads in Alaska were the big lines (see below), and we didn't honestly think we could recommend one of those cruises. This book is written specifically for travelers who are looking to get outside. Sure, people on the ships have a very good time. We've never heard a single person say otherwise. But they don't see Alaska, and anyone who has gone on one will be the first to admit that fact. We see our job as showing you Alaska, not the cruise ship casino, and so we've passed the ships by for the first three editions of this book.

However, as the big ships have gotten bigger – in 2002, when Princess takes up its 3,000-passenger ship, it will be the size of the fourth-largest town in Southeast Alaska – there has been a backlash.

■ Small Ships

The largest ship that the Alaska Marine Highway runs is just over 400 feet long. At that size, it's the largest ship that goes through the Wrangell Narrows; it's the only large ship that stops at towns off the main line of the Inside Passage, which, in summer, can be a pretty well-beaten path.

The definition of a small ship, and the small ship cruise experience, then, is one that can get you where even the ferry can't. We're talking ships under 200 feet long – sometimes much under – which still offer the full luxury experience of a cruise but get you outside, where you can smell the rain in the trees and put your feet on paths where there might be bears.

On a small ship, you get all the advantages of the big ships – pampering, more food than a sane person feels comfortable seeing, getting to cover a lot of territory in a short time – and you also get some of the advantages of independent travel: more adventure. With the rise of the small ships, you can finally take a cruise and really see Alaska. And not only see it, experience it.

Glacier Bay Cruiseline (☎ 800-451-5952; www.glacierbaycruiseline. com) runs small ships – the biggest is just over 100 feet long. Here's how good they are: when we tried it, they took us places we'd never been before. We grew up in Southeast Alaska and have been writing guides to Alaska for more than a decade, and the glorious surprise of waking up off an island we'd never seen before was more wonderful than can easily be described. Finally, a cruise we can honestly call a good deal.

This company is a branch of the same company that runs the lodge at Glacier Bay, and targets itself toward the active traveler. Each day, there are kayak trips and hikes ashore. They runs four ships, ranging from ultra-luxury to relatively bare bones, but decked out for the very active traveler. The ships are big enough to be comfortable, small enough to go into remote bays and nooks and crannies that you'll never find on your own. The service is as outstanding – if not better – than you're going to find on a big ship. But instead of crowding the rail with a thousand other people for a glimpse of wildlife, you're on a boat with maybe 50 or 60 other travelers, each with lots of space.

There are several routes to choose from: Ketchikan to Glacier Bay run, which takes in Wrangell, Sitka, Juneau, and Skagway along the way; prices start around $2,700 for the eight days. There's also a weekly Juneau to Sitka run, stopping in Skagway and Glacier Bay, for a couple hundred cheaper, as well as a few other shorter runs. It's a bargain. You're going to spend this much money anyway, unless you're planning to spend every night in a tent. If you're looking for a cruise, don't bother to look any further.

There are also add-ons available, with extra days in Glacier Bay, or trips to the interior. After looking at all the small ships, and all the big ships, this is the one that we think gives you the best bang for the buck.

If you can't get on one of their ships, there are a few other small lines well worth trying. Remember, with a small ship, you're paying more than you would on a megaliner, but you're seeing more, too.

Cruise West has four-day trips in Southeast, for just under a grand (☎ 800-888-9378; www.cruisewest.com). At the other end of the price spectrum, **American Safari Cruises** runs yachts through Southeast.

Transportation

An 11-day run will hit you up for about $3,750 (☎ 888-862-8881; www. amsafari.com). And finally, still on the high end, **Lindblad**, known for basic ships and very good educational programs, does eight days in Alaska for about $3,750 (☎ 800-397-3348; www.expeditions.com).

■ 800-Pound Gorillas

Big ships are destinations in and of themselves. You'll see more of the ship than you will of Alaska, no matter what the brochures promise. It's always an eerie thing to see one of the big ships passing by and yet not a single person is outside looking at the scenery. There's simply too much to do on board, from shows to casinos to movies to more food over the course of a week than the average person in the world sees in a year. Think of the big ships as resorts that move. That's what they try to be, and that's what they do very well, and if that's what you're looking for, you'll have a great time on one. However, you're not going to see much in the way of wildlife off one of the ships – the water is a long way off when you're 13 decks up – and the ships travel mostly at night, so they can drop you off in towns first thing in the morning.

That's your chance to get out and be in Alaska. Skip the shopping street, and head out. All big cruise lines book excursions – see the previous chapter (pages 86-87) for how to best survive the booking desk.

What the big ships do, they do well. You get a quality resort experience at a low price. It's a temperament matter. If you're looking to enjoy solitude in the great outdoors, skip it. If you're looking to have a lot of fun with friends, this could be for you.

Over the years we've been doing these books, we've talked with hundreds of passengers off the big cruise ships. Most of them are having a tremendous amount of fun on the ship; very few of them think they're really experiencing Alaska. That said, if a big ship is for you, don't plunge in and book on the first one you come across. Read up on the line in the cruise ship magazines. Check them out on line – most of the ships have virtual tours now, so you can get a good idea what you're getting into. Ask around. Odds are, somebody you know has been on one of the ships somewhere. The more information you go in with, the happier you'll be.

Remember, once you're on board that the ship's goal is to make money off you. Cruise ships are astonishingly profitable – due in large part to most of them being flagged in tax havens and staffed with Third-Worlders. But another way they make their bucks is to tack on surcharges on everything you do. Any expedition you book on the ship will cost you more than if you do it on your own. Part of making money off you is to keep careful track of you. One cruise line sends out letters to its passengers that say it's not safe to eat or drink in Alaska towns. Yeah. Right. Last time we checked, Alaska was still a state, subject to all the same health regulations as everywhere else. And it's the only state we'll drink the tap water.

To sum it up: think of your week on the big cruise ship as a week at a really, really good Las Vegas casino. When you get around to looking out the window, you're going to have amazing scenery, and you'll be content with short runs into the towns along the way. But if what's outside the window is your main goal, this might not be the way to go.

What you need to look for is your level of comfort, above your price point. Any of the lines listed below can put you on a ship for a week, for under a grand. Maybe you won't get much of a room, but you'll be moving. From there, prices can go up to the suites on Princess ships that come with three televisions (why?) and a hot tub.

Look for hidden costs – drinks are almost always extra, for example – and keep in mind that your shore excursions are going to cost, big time. And don't forget the end-of-the-cruise tip.

Finally, remember that although the resort/cruise ship is the permanent bastion of the middle class, they try to maintain upper class distinction: check for dress codes.

So, if this sounds like what you're after, head to the websites or call for brochures. The main lines running big ships in Alaska are **Royal Caribbean** (☎ 800-398-9819; www.royalcaribbean.com), **Celebrity** (☎ 800-722-5941; www.celebritycruises.com), **Holland America** (☎ 877-932-4259; www.hollandamerica.com), **Princess** (☎ 800-PRINCESS; www.princesscruises.com), and **Norwegian** (☎ 800-474-5678; www.norwegiancruises.com). Princess in particular has a lot of add-ons – they own lodges all over the state – that will give you a good look at Alaska.

Transportation

Southeast
Seattle to Prince Rupert

Dixon Entrance

Prince Rupert

Skeena River

Kitmat

Skidgate

Queen Charlotte Sound

QUEEN CHARLOTTE ISLANDS

Bella Coola

Bella Bella

Pacific Ocean

Port Hardy

Powell River

Courtenay

VANCOUVER ISLAND

Nanaimo

VANCOUVER

Victoria

Bellingham

Port Angeles

Seattle

N

100 MILES

© 2002 HUNTER PUBLISHING, INC

AMH Route

Southeast Alaska & the Inside Passage

On April 1, 1867, the *New York World* reported that "Russia has sold us a sucked orange. Whatever may be the value of that territory and its outlying islands to us, it has ceased to be of any to Russia." The article went on to say that, "The purchase of the Russian territory renders it morally certain that we shall some day acquire [British Columbia]."

The few who made positive comments about Seward's Folly, as the purchase of Alaska was called, echoed these sentiments. The only good thing about owning Alaska, they said, was that it would cut British Columbia off, making it easier for the United States to annex the land. People knew Alaska was worthless. If it wasn't, the Russians wouldn't be selling it.

On October 18, 1867, at 2:30 PM on a partially cloudy day – incredibly rare for Southeast Alaska in October when it usually pours without a break – Prince Maksoutoff signaled Captain Pestchouroff to lower the Russian flag atop Castle Hill in Sitka. There was a salute of guns, then the captain turned to General Rousseau, the U.S. representative, and ceded the territory of Alaska to the United States. The U.S. flag was raised by General Rousseau's son.

General Rousseau reported: "Three cheers were then spontaneously given for the United States flag by the American citizens present, though this was no part of the programming, and on some accounts I regretted that it occurred." Rousseau hadn't much wanted to be in Alaska at that moment of what could have been national disgrace. And perhaps he was the last person to regret a visit to Southeast Alaska. The Inside Passage is the state's most popular tourist attraction, drawing close to a million people a year. But in the vast spaces of Southeast, it is never crowded. There are countless untouched, unnamed islands, glaciers flowing from the high mountains, and a thick, impenetrable forest.

The *New York World* was a little premature calling Alaska a "sucked orange." The Interior is full of minerals and oil. Southeast has rich timber industries and fisheries, both of which are rapidly being supplanted by tourism as the region's main support, trading on the natural beauty and the rich culture of the Tlingit and the Haida. The switch to a tourism-based economy is giving sections of the land and sea time to recover from more than a century of natural resource exploitation (but take a look at the discussion of the effects of mass tourism on pages 96-98).

Southeast and the Inside Passage today are a strange, tantalizing mixture of sophistication – the state capital of Juneau, the music festival in Sitka – and wildness, with thousands of acres of untouched land, and bears wandering village streets. More than any other part of Alaska, there's something for every taste in the Southeast and along the Inside Passage.

Bellingham

The Alaska Marine Highway's southern terminus and home port, Bellingham, gets little of the attention it deserves. Most people hurry through the town, anxious to get farther north, but Bellingham is interesting and pleasant enough to be a destination in itself. And now that Seattle and Portland have been overrun with people looking for Paradise, Bellingham is also one of the Pacific Northwest's most liveable cities (it's been getting a lot of magazine press for this recently, and long-standing residents aren't that pleased about their newfound fame), a lovely spot between the towering peak of Mt. Baker and the glistening sea.

■ History

People have been living around what's now Bellingham for over 10,000 years, but it wasn't until 1774 that the place started getting noticed. The Spanish laid first claim to the Bellingham region, but did nothing with it. Twenty years later, Captain George Vancouver sailed in, charted the entire region, and changed the Spanish name Bashia de Gaston to the more Anglo-Saxon Bellingham Bay.

Even with a name easier to spell, nothing happened here until the mid-1800s, when coal was discovered nearby. That brought a base of workers, and the first sawmill was opened in 1852. The Fraser River gold rush turned Bellingham into a boomtown, as the last gasp of civilization before hitting the Cariboo gold fields.

Bellingham has long existed in the shadow of Seattle. The fight for the terminus of the transcontinental railway was decided in favor of the more southerly town and, when the Alaska Marine Highway looked for a Washington State port, Seattle was it. It wasn't until 1989 that the ferry terminal moved north to Bellingham.

Bellingham is a city of Victorian houses, with a nicely restored semi-Bohemian downtown and 60,000 residents (about 150,000 total, with the outlying areas included). These folks have escaped Seattle for the quiet forests and bays of the north. Bellingham is a place to linger and enjoy.

■ Basics

i The Alaska Marine Highway serves Bellingham four times a week, twice northbound and twice southbound – although this can change, so be sure to check the schedule early. Check-in time for a northbound trip is usually three hours before sailing, and the AMH is serious about that. Be there early, especially if you're loading a vehicle or planning to get in line for deck space. Loading here is like watching a gigantic jigsaw puzzle go together. The **ferry terminal** (local ☎ 676-8445; or 800-642-0066) is in Fairhaven (off I-5 at exit 250). From north on the Interstate from Seattle, get off at the first exit; there's finally a sign there – lacking for years – that points the way to the ferry terminal and the "Fairhaven Transportation District." It's a straight shot down to the water from the exit.

The **train station** (☎ 800-USA-RAIL for the national line; 734-8851 locally, if you can get somebody to answer the phone) and the bus depot are next to the ferry terminal. The terminal is within walking distance of a good shopping area for books and restaurants, but if you want supplies for the trip, there isn't much selection. Stock up before you head to the terminal.

There's no way to get from Seattle to Bellingham by ferry; if you can't drive yourself, try **Greyhound Bus**, ☎ 733-5252 or 800-231-2222. An alternative is the **Airporter**, ☎ 360-380-8800, which goes from the Seattle airport to the Bellingham airport (stopping at a few of the larger hotels). It costs $32 from airport to airport. From the Bellingham airport, it's easy to get a taxi down to the AMH terminal; it'll run you about $20. Figure on three to four hours total for the trip up from Seattle.

The **Visitor's Center** is at 904 Potter St., ☎ 671-3990. Take exit 253 off I-5. They've got info and guides for the entire area around Bellingham, and can easily fill however long you've got until the ferry leaves. If you pick up a map here, be prepared for major confusion: Bellingham changes its street names about every other block, and a two-mile drive on a single street could mean three or four street names.

Rent a car from **Budget**, ☎ 671-3800; **U-Save**, ☎ 671-3687; **Avis**, ☎ 676-8840 or 800-831-2847; or **Hertz**, ☎ 733-8336 or 800-654-3131.

Taxis are run by **Yellow Cab**, ☎ 734-8294; **City Cab**, ☎ 734-8294; and **Checker Cab**, ☎ 398-8294. There's a central dispatch line at 734-TAXI.

Visitor information on-line at **www.kulshan.com**. There are a variety of Internet cafés in the Fairhaven district, near the ferry terminal.

Bellingham's zip code is **99226**. Phone numbers have area code **360**, unless otherwise noted.

Southeast

■ Museums & Attractions

WHATCOM MUSEUM OF HISTORY AND ART: This museum at 121 Prospect St., ☎ 676-6981, is open Tuesday-Sunday, 12-5. The museum is housed in a gorgeous old red brick building, which is highly distinctive. Free admission. Don't make a special trip, but if you've got time, it's worth the stop.

KID-FRIENDLY

WHATCOM CHILDREN'S MUSEUM: A little more lively is the Whatcom Children's Museum, 227 Prospect, ☎ 733-8769. Hands-on displays, a science center, puppet theater, and more, including a toddler area for the very small ones. Admission is $2.

FAIRHAVEN DISTRICT: Bellingham's main attraction is the Fairhaven District, right near the ferry terminal. This is a historic area, with most of the buildings dating from the turn of the century, now refurbished and full of tourist shops. There are also remains from a 3,000-year-old Indian campsite. Fairhaven was built up on the hopes that Bellingham would be chosen as the terminus for the Great Northern Railroad; when those hopes went bust, so did Fairhaven. The influx of visitors waiting for the ferry has brought it back, though. The district only covers four blocks: park anywhere and walk. **Village Books**, on 11th St. off Harris, has a good selection of new books; **Eclipse**, a block down Harris, is the place for used books. The entire area is studded with color from the past. At what was once the **Royal Bodega Saloon**, on 12th between Harris and Mill, a committee of 25 men once formed a vigilante group to handle crooked card dealers. Much of the original road building was done by chain gangs (if you refused to work, you got chained to a jail scow at Padden Creek and left for people to stare at). The downtown was fairly wild around the turn of the century, with **McKenzie Av-**

enue serving as the red light district and **11th Street** hosting the bars – as well as an opera house that seated 500 people.

Historic buildings in Fairhaven include the **Marketplace**, corner of 12th and Harris, which was built in 1890, and the **Fairhaven Hotel**, opposite the Marketplace, which looks alarmingly like the Addams' Family house. If you're architecturally inclined, pick up a Fairhaven Walking Tour brochure from the visitor's center for a guide to a dozen buildings in the area. It's a nice walk, even if you're not really into architecture.

For a look at what the grand life was like in the old days, when it was great fun to be filthy rich and have lots of servants to push around, drive out to the **Roeder Home**, 2600 Sunset Drive, ☎ 733-6897. The house was built in 1903, and offers a great look at a slower, more luxurious time – don't miss the built-in vacuum cleaning system.

There's a **post office** next to the Colophon Café, inside Paper Dreams.

SQUALICUM HARBOR: This area was built up fairly recently, hoping to be a less historic alternative to Fairhaven, but it hasn't taken off as planned. Built around the small boat harbor, it has some good restaurants, a small display of aquariums that can help you get a handle on local marine life at the **Marine Life Center**, open 8 AM to 9 PM daily, as well as shops to supply you with any kind of boating supplies/services you might want. If you're interested in getting nautical charts for the ferry route, you'll find them at **Redden Marine Supply**, 1411 Roeder Avenue, ☎ 733-0250, just up the street from the main Squalicum building. Figure on about $16 per sheet for navigational charts for U.S. waters, $17 for Canadian – this means that a complete set for the ferry route will run you several hundred dollars, but you can pick up select sheets for places you're particularly interested in. If you need some last-minute camping or paddling gear, there's an **REI** branch at 400 36th St., ☎ 647-8955.

There are more fish at the **Bellingham Maritime Heritage Center Salmon Life Cycle Facility**. Okay, so they need a better name. Still, it's a good place to go see how your dinner starts off. There's a hatchery, fish ladder, holding ponds, and more. It's on Whatcom Creek, where Dupont Street turns into Prospect Street. ☎ 715-0283.

SCULPTURE/FLORAL GARDENS: Bellingham claims fame for its sculpture gardens. There are two good ones: **Western Washington University Outdoor Sculpture Museum** – no small potatoes, they've got Noguchi here – and the **Downtown Outdoor Sculpture Walk**, which makes a loop starting at the Whatcom Museum. The advantage of the latter is that it passes some of Bellingham's many art galleries.

Big Rock Garden and Gardens of Art, 3000 Sylvan St., ☎ 734-4167, has a huge flower garden and a Japanese-style garden, among others. Open from March 1 through November 1.

Southeast

SEHOME HILL ARBORETUM: Just above Western Washington University is the Sehome Hill Arboretum, offering 3½ miles of trails that lead through a gardener's paradise.

MUSIC FESTIVALS: The annual music festival held at Western Washington University has classical and jazz musicians. ☎ 360-676-5997 for dates.

If you want to try something different, get **gold panning** equipment from the old gas station at 12th and Harris, and head out to the local rivers. You're not likely to pay for your vacation, but if you got lucky, you wouldn't be the first to find gold around here, either.

On Saturday nights during the summer, there are **open-air movies** shown in Fairhaven, in the park in front of Fairhaven Village. Bring your popcorn, or a little of the produce you've stashed aside from the farmer's market in the same spot on Wednesdays.

■ Adventures

Steam Train Rides

The **Lake Whatcom Railway** runs steam train excursions on Saturdays and Tuesdays, from mid-June through August. Leaving from Wickersham Junction, the ride goes at 11 AM, 1 PM, and 3 PM, and costs $10 for adults, $5 for under 18. ☎ 595-2218 for more information. Of late they have been having to use a diesel engine from time to time, so if the motor is more important than the ride, call first to check.

Boat Charters

If you want to get a quick foretaste of life on ships, take the **Lumni Island Ferry**, ☎ 676-6692, just a couple of minutes from Bellingham. The island is home of the Lumni tribe of coastal Indians and is full of art galleries selling traditional crafts. It also has a large eagle population, and Legoe Bay is one of the few places in the U.S. where you can watch reef-net fishing for salmon. It's illegal most places, but on Lumni tradition holds sway. The ferry leaves regularly from Lumni Shore Drive.

There's a **foot passenger ferry** that goes from Bellingham to Victoria, one of Canada's most beautiful cities. ☎ 738-8099. That's a vacation in and of itself, though. The cruise does go through the San Juans, so you've got a good chance of seeing killer whales and more. It's $79-89 for a return fare. Used as a day-trip, you get five hours in Victoria, plenty of time for high tea at the Empress Hotel.

The cruise to Victoria goes through the San Juans because they're right out there in the channel in front of Bellingham. They're the town's playground, but they're a playground with nearly a hundred orcas in residence.

You've got a lot of choices for getting into the islands. **Sail the San Juans**, ☎ 800-729-3207 or 671-5852, runs six-day trips in a 50-foot sailboat. If that's more than you have in mind, there are plenty of day-trip options. The **San Juan Island Commuter**, 888-734-8180 or 734-8180, runs day-trips from Bellingham to Friday Harbor. It's only $35 for the round-trip, or there's a run with more time to watch whales and less time in town for $30.

Much the same is the **San Juan Island Shuttle Express**, which runs through the San Juans with a stop off in Friday Harbor. ☎ 888-373-8522 or 671-1137. Check them out on line at www.orcawhales.com.

San Juan Boat Tours, 800-232-ORCA, or 378-3499, does the orca thing for $39 for a three-hour trip. **Whale Spirit Adventures**, ☎ 376-5052, runs a small boat – remember, when you're on the water watching animals, smaller boats are always best. You pay more, but the trips are longer, and you'll see a bit more. Finally, there's **Whales 'n' Tales**, ☎ 877-734-8866 or 734-8866. Full-day trips are $55 for adults. They also run sunset cruises on Thursday nights, with storytellers from the Whatcom Museum. A fun way to get local history, for only $15.

Fishing

If you can't wait to get to Alaska, you could kill a few days fishing Bellingham. Try **Trophy Charters**, ☎ 378-2110, or **Eagle Point Charters**, ☎ 966-3334. Rates start around $125. Check at the visitor's center for more operators if these guys are booked up.

Kayaking

To get closer to the water, **Moondance Sea Kayak Adventures**, 2448 Yew Street Road, ☎ 738-7664, has three-hour trips for $40, full days for $70. They also have some paddling classes – a one-day class, on a lake, teaches you to paddle, brace, get out of the boat in an emergency, and gives you an idea of how to roll (although you probably won't succeed for a while); the two-day class teaches you all the above, plus how to handle the boat in extreme conditions. If you're a novice paddler hoping to do some real trips up north, this is good use of a couple of days. One day costs $70, two days, $185. The company also runs multiple-day excursions in the Bellingham area. Check them out on-line at www.moondance-kayak.com. **Leisure Kayak Adventures**, in Friday Harbor in the San Juans, has two-hour trips for $35. ☎ 378-5992.

Driving Tours

If you're not interested in getting into the water, Bellingham is an ideal city for walking or driving in the country. Head north out of town to **Lynden**; the drive takes about half an hour. The **Lyndale Pioneer Museum**, 221 Front St., ☎ 354-3675, is one of the great little museums of the Northwest. A huge buggy and antique car collection and an entire village reconstruction are inside. Open Monday through Saturday, 10-5 in summer; Wednesday through Saturday, 10-4 in winter. Admission is $3.

Take the Mt. Baker Highway out of town. Your first stop can be the **Mt. Baker Vineyards**, 4298 Mt. Baker Highway, ☎ 206-592-2300, which are open for tastings Wednesday through Sunday, 11-5. Once you get beyond the town of Deming, the views of Mt. Baker just get better and better. The mountain is the dominant feature of Whatcom County's landscape at 10,778 feet. It's the second most active volcano in the Cascade Range (Mt. St. Helens is the first). The Lumni Indians call the mountain *kulshan*, which roughly translates to "broken off," a perfect name for a volcano. There was a gold rush in the area – a year after a rich strike in 1897 there were more than a thousand claims staked around the mountain as everybody looked for what started it all: bits of gold "as large as peas." The gold pretty much petered out around the end of World War II.

There are some good features along the drive out to the mountain: stop at **U-Pick Berry Farm**, Mile 11, for strawberries, raspberries, and blueberries. The **Kendall Creek Hatchery** is at Mile 21, open for tours.

It's 58 miles from Bellingham to the end of the road at the foot of Mt. Baker. From there, you have views not only of Mt. Baker, but also of **Mt. Shuksan** (9,038 feet) and **Table Mountain** (5,628 feet). Trails lace the terrain here, including one to the summit of Table Mountain. Another good choice is the **Heliotrope Trail**, which leads to views of the Coleman Glacier.

Skiing

Finally, if you're here in the winter, you might as well head out to the **Mt. Baker Ski Area**, at Mile 52. Lots of new trails have been constructed in the past couple years.

Hiking

If you're looking for hikes closer to town, take a drive along **Chuckanut Drive**, south of town. The road hugs the coastline and you can stop at one of several beaches enjoying the lee protection of Lumni Island in Larabee State Park. You'll have views of the San Juan Islands and Puget Sound. The **Interurban Trail**, with its trailhead right off the road, is a popular six-mile hike though Arroyo Park Canyon. The best swimming beach is just past the trailhead. Directly across the street from the Larabee State Park campground is the **Viewpoint/Fragrance Lake Trail**. It's .9 miles up to the viewpoint – a steep trail that makes good use of switchbacks through forest where it seems every inch of the forest floor is covered with ferns – and another mile past that to the lake. The visitor's bureau has a sheet listing more hikes in the area.

■ Food

Whatever you want, you can find it down in Fairhaven. This used to be a black hole, where no good food ever was found, but over the past couple years, it has become the place to go to fill up. No reason at all to look around the rest of the town. Best of all, you can walk here from the ferry terminal.

The **Colophon Café**, inside Village Books (11th and Harris), has incredible African peanut soup, good veggie sandwiches, and gourmet coffees. Prices from $5. ☎ 647-0092.

Stanello's, 1514 12th St., ☎ 676-1304, has a white pizza (made with alfredo sauce) that's a Bellingham favorite. $7-$15.

Dos Padres, 1111 Harris St., ☎ 733-9900, serves Mexican specialties. Try the carne asada for $9.75. Other dishes range $8-$13.

For fish and chips, go to the double-decker bus – **Jacci's Fish and Chips**, at 11th and Harris. Six bucks buys you lunch.

Kind of hidden behind the bus is **Skylarks**, a local favorite. Soups, sandwiches, and Thursday nights, all-you-can-eat BBQ.

For a fancy dinner, try **Le Chat Noir**, inside the Marketplace at 12th and Harris. Poached salmon for $15. Another option is **Dirt Dan Harris'**, across from Village Books, which is open only for dinner. Steaks from $20, one of the best wine lists in town.

Got a furry friend with you? The **Doggie Diner**, run by the same people as the Colophon, is at 1007 Harris, and while you chow down, so can Fido.

If you're determined to look at the rest of the town for food, try **Eleni's Family Restaurant**, 3720 Meridian, which has good souvlaki and shish kabob, plus less exotic fare for a cheap $5-$8. ☎ 676-5555.

Il Fiasco, 1309 Commercial St., ☎ 676-9136, has Bellingham's best Italian food. Prices $10 and up.

Two luxury meal suggestions: **Chuckanut Manor**, 302 Chuckanut Dr., ☎ 766-6191. Steak and seafood from $13-20; they also have a kid's menu. Alternatively, **Top of the Tower**, atop the highest building in town, at 119 N. Commercial, 15th Floor, ☎ 733-6332, has okay food in a good atmosphere with great views.

Bellingham has what the *Beer Travelers' Guide* calls one of the best pubs in the States: the **Boundary Bay Brewery & Bistro**, 1107 Railroad Ave., ☎ 647-5593. It's open daily and tours of the brewery are available.

Finally, to stock up for the trip ahead, go to **Mercato Italiano**, 1006 Harris. A serious Italian deli. Good hard cheeses and meats that can keep for days without refrigeration – just what you need for a few days on the ferry. They also serve focaccias for lunch, which are exquisite.

There's a health food store, the **Community Food Co-Op**, at the corner of Forest and Holly. Good restaurant inside.

■ Accommodations

 The **Fairhaven Inn**, downtown, has beautiful rooms overlooking the water and the ferry terminal. A choice location, it's a great place to stay. Doubles from $139-159. Worth stopping in just to see the bird cage in the lobby.

I-5 exit 252 is "Motel Row" in Bellingham. Sell-outs of the whole street are rare, and any of them are going to give you a double for $100-120. Bellingham has two **Best Westerns**: 714 Lakeway Drive, ☎ 671-1011, and the **Best Western Heritage** at Meridian Plaza, ☎ 647-1912. The Heritage has great service and a location that's central to everything. Other motel chains represented are **Hampton Inn**, 3985 Bennett Dr., ☎ 676-7700 or 800-426-7866; **Quality Inn**, 100 E. Kellogg, ☎ 647-8000; a **Day's Inn** in the same price range at 125 E. Kellogg, ☎ 671-6200 or 800-831-0187; and a **Ramada**, 215 N. Samish, ☎ 734-8830 or 800-228-2828.

Cheaper, but really no less comfortable are the **Shangri-la Motel**, 611 Holly St., ☎ 733-7050 (rooms from $40); **Travelers Inn**, 3570 Meridian, ☎ 671-4600 (from $60); and the **Travel Lodge**, 101 N. Samish Way, ☎ 733-8280 (rooms starting at $50).

Bellingham has some fine and very reasonably priced B&Bs. The Bed & Breakfast Guild of Whatcom County, ☎ 676-4560, can help book you into a place. Some good choices include **A Secret Garden**, 1807 Lakeway, ☎ 671-5327 or 800-671-5327, which has two rooms (ask for the Rose Room, with its claw-foot tub) and big breakfasts. The height of luxury for $65-80. **Big Trees**, 4840 Freemont St., ☎ 800-647-2850, is in a restored Victorian home, surrounded by the trees that gave it its name. It offers a good chance to see inside one of the lovely homes in Bellingham's historic area. **The Castle**, 1103 15th St., is near the ferry and convenient to Fairhaven shopping. Rates range $45-95. ☎ 676-0974.

The **North Garden Inn**, 1014 N. Garden, ☎ 671-6414 or 800-922-6414, has rooms in a huge, gorgeous Victorian house. Prices run $45 with a shared bath, $79 with a private bath.

For a water view, try the **DeCann House**, 2610 Eldridge Ave. ☎ 734-9172.

The visitor center keeps a book of photos and stats on local B&Bs. Stop in and take a look to see what suits you best.

Finally, if you're on your way home from a hard trip through Alaska, spend a night at the **Chrysalis**, 804 10th St., which is a full-service spa. Rates start at $139. ☎ 756-1005.

■ Camping

The best place to camp is back in **Larabee State Park** (see page 131). Beautiful walk-in sites are the choice locations, which run $14 per night. Sites with hookups are $20. ☎ 676-2093. It's popular, so you'd better call well ahead for reservations. Just head out Chuckanut Drive and you'll find it. It's about 20 minutes from the ferry terminal.

For RV travelers, there's the **Bellingham RV Park**, 3939 Bennett Dr., ☎ 752-1224 or 888-372-1224. Full hookups for $20.

There's also an RV park out at Mt. Baker – the **Mount Baker RV Park & Campground**, ☎ 599-1908 or 888-250-7077, 10443 Mt. Baker Highway. Full hookups for $22.

Bellingham to Ketchikan

- The Southern Inside Passage -

■ The Route & Its History

With passengers on board and cars loaded, it's time for the ferry to pull out. Travelers without staterooms are frantically searching for a place to bunk down – tent spots on the fantail and seats in the forward lounge fill quickly, so be prepared. Those with rooms are exploring the ship, finding the dining halls, purser's office, and the best spot to sit and watch the scenery. It's nearly two days from Bellingham to the first stop in Ketchikan, so there's plenty of time to get used to shipboard life.

If you're on a cruise ship heading out from Seattle, you're likely to be passing much of this at night. Keep an eye out for **Mt. Baker** – can't miss it, unless it's been swallowed by clouds – and pick the trail up from there. For cruise ship passengers who are starting in Vancouver, you'll wake up tomorrow morning about the same place AMH passengers do.

Southeast

Almost all cruise ships and all the ferries of the AMH keep navigational charts in prominent positions – check near the purser's counter or in the stairwells. As mentioned above in the Bellingham section, if you want to buy your own charts (and have the space to carry them), they are readily available in most towns for about $15 and up a sheet. The *Columbia* also has a GPS (Global Positioning System) in operation, with screens by the purser's office and in the TV lounge showing the ship's exact position.

 DID YOU KNOW? *In the old days all navigation was done by dead reckoning: the pilot looked out the window and steered according to what he saw. In a fog, blasts of the whistle would be sounded; a good pilot could tell the ship's location by the echoes of the whistle, just like a dolphin navigating at night.*

Today the ship's navigation systems include radar, GPS, and a dozen or so other glowing machines on the bridge. The radar system is so sensitive that it shows floating logs; the ships are maneuverable enough that they can get around the logs, if the pilot deems it wise, without the passengers ever noticing a change of course.

The ferry leaves Bellingham in the evening; you don't get much chance to see the scenery as the ship heads north. As you're leaving Bellingham, the large mountain behind the town is Mt. Baker. You're in Canada only 20 miles north of Mount Baker – long before most passengers have settled down for the night. An hour or so past the border, the bright lights to the starboard (to the right) are Vancouver. Soon after passing into Canadian waters at Point Roberts, the ship enters the **Strait of Georgia** and parallels the coast of **Vancouver Island**. The island has been largely clear-cut: patches of trees seem almost an oddity by the north end of the island where the heaviest logging has taken place.

While the forest in Alaska is the Tongass, down here it's the **Great Bear**. It's all an extension of the same thing. The main difference you'll see as you head farther north is in the profiles of the islands: through the Canadian stretch, the up-close islands are mostly pretty flat, nothing at all like the 4,000-5,000-foot peaks rising straight out of the water that you'll encounter farther north. There's also the little detail of clear-cuts. Canadians have made no effort to keep the cuts off the main routes. You'll pass hillsides stripped to the dirt through here, much worse than anything you'll see farther north in Alaska.

After traveling through some fairly wide stretches of water, the ship enters **Johnstone Strait**. This will be the first morning of your trip (or the last evening of the trip, right before you go to bed, if you're southbound). In this narrow passage of water there is a resident pod of orcas, and sightings from the ships are common.

At the northern tip of Vancouver Island is **Port Hardy**; the AMH does not stop here, but the B.C. Ferry system does. If you've driven Vancouver Island, here you can load your car on a B.C. Ferry ship to Prince Rupert, and catch the AMH northbound there. From Vancouver Island's northern tip of Cape Scott to the southern tip of Calvert Island, the route travels through Queen Charlotte Sound, one of only two large patches of open water on the Inside Passage.

The sea here doesn't hit land again until northern Japan. Queen Charlotte is the first test of one's sailing ability, because all that open water means you'll feel waves from a gusty day outside Tokyo. On a clear day, your ship will go through the sound in about 60-90 minutes. At the other extreme, one winter a ship belonging to the AMH fleet battled waters here for 42 hours without getting through. They finally had to turn back because they were running out of food on board. But travel through Queen Charlotte Sound is rarely worth worrying about. The ship is likely to pitch and roll some during the crossing, but in summer months storms are rare, and it's unusual for the ship to take, at worst, more than a few hours to get through.

TIPS FOR SEA TRAVELERS

If you're prone to seasickness, try taking Dramamine before symptoms start. Ferry personnel say they don't see much difference in comfort levels among those who take Dramamine, or use patches or acupressure bracelets – except the Dramamine people fall asleep and miss the scenery. However, some travelers swear these methods work.

There's an interesting story to the place names along this stretch of coast. George Vancouver was the guy who got to decide what everything was called, and you can watch his mood change with the names: on a good day, things are named after his crew: Johnstone, Dixon, Whidbey; on bad days, when – as so frequently happened – his crew pissed him off, or when he saw something too grand for a mere crew member, he got out his copy of *Debret's* and started naming things after people he wanted to suck up to: Queen Charlotte, for example. Watch for the **Coast Mountains**: Silverthorne is 9,700 feet tall and always ice-capped. The land is punctuated by tiny inlets, regularly broken by fine rivers pouring into the ocean. These rivers are almost hidden by dense tree growth, which comes right to the water's edge.

There are three lighthouses in Queen Charlotte Sound. **Egg Island Lighthouse**, built in 1898, still shines to warn mariners in a 16-mile radius. The middle of the three lighthouses, Egg Island is set at the entrance to Smith Sound, guarding the navigation path into Fitz Hugh Sound. It was nearly washed away during a storm in 1948.

DID YOU KNOW? *Queen Charlotte Sound ends as the ship passes by the point of Cape Calvert, which has a little bay. The bay was used as shelter by natives for centuries as they hunted the waters of Queen Charlotte Sound. If the wind shifted direction, the bay became a nightmare of high waves, hence its name – Grief Bay.*

Fitz Hugh Sound was the home of the Nootka Indians. Not as well known to the outside world as the neighboring Tlingit, Haida, and Tsimshian, the Nootka fared badly in their confrontations with Europeans. Their habit of smearing themselves with grease (excellent mosquito protection) kept them free of the affections of European sailors and some of Europe's nastier contact diseases, but a contemporary report noted that the "Purification Ceremony" – a good, long bath – that European sailors required of Nootka women was "performed... with much piety and devotion." This, from Europeans who still thought bleeding was the height of medical science.

VANCOUVER'S BEER RECIPE

Vancouver and his men were all up and down this area, searching for riches and a route to the Northwest Passage, around Hunter Island, Denny Island, and continuing north toward Alaskan territory. It was while in this region that they learned to brew beer from spruce needles. Here's how: Boil 10 gallons of water, six pounds of molasses, and three ounces of ginger for three hours; add two pounds of the outer sprigs of spruce fir – spruce tips – for five minutes in the boil. Strain, add milk yeast, then wait two days for fermentation. It not only gets you blitzed, it works well as an anti-scorbutic, as the spruce tips are quite high in vitamin C.

Vancouver and his men coerced natives into bathing, and explored this rich wonderland which Vancouver noted in his journal as a land that was "as desolate and inhospitable a country as the most melancholy creature could be desirous of inhabiting." The famous captain wrote those words near King Island, now suffering from patches of clear-cut, but no doubt once as beautiful as most of the Inside Passage, if a little wilder with its cliff-scarred northern end.

Traveling through **Lama Passage**, the ferry skirts King Island, then passes between Hunter, Campbell, and Denny Islands. Bella Bella is on Campbell Island, and it's a stop on the B.C. Ferry route, but the AMH and the cruise ships keep moving by.

LAMA PASSAGE

Lama Passage was named for the Hudson's Bay Company ship the *Llama*, a 144-ton vessel that was part of HBC's half-hearted investigations of this area. HBC tried, but never quite came to terms with Canada's far west. The *Llama* first sailed this passage in 1833, heading north to found Bella Bella as a company town. The original town site is south of the current community, almost where Hunter Channel meets Lama Passage.

The ship next travels up the **Finlayson Channel**, between Swindle Island and Roderick Island. Finlayson is actually made up of three reaches. The ferry goes up the **Fraser Reach**, where trees meet the water (up to 1,000 feet deep through here). The ferry crews say if they hit the side of the ship in the reach, they might scrape some paint off the boat, but that would be about the limit of the damage, the drop-off is so steep.

The reach meets the **Tolmie Channel** (reports from the steamship days of travel said that in Tolmie bear and deer were commonly spotted swimming across the channel) and the two become the Graham Reach between Princess Royal Island and Sarah Island. Princess Royal is one of the largest islands in the Southeast archipelago, and is the home of the kermodie bears, *Ursus americanus kermodia* or *Eurarctos kermodia*.

KERMODIE BEARS

Kermodie are white bears, even though they're a subgroup of the black bear family. They live only on Princess Royal and Gribell Islands, with a smaller population in the Kitmat Arm of Douglas Channel. Smaller than the usual black bear, kermodie are a creamy white, with a yellowish undertone. They're also known as spirit bears, since their white fur gives them a spirit-like appearance.

There are almost no settlements out here. Occasionally the ship passes the ruin of a cannery or a tiny operating works, but mostly it is mile after mile of quiet bays and inlets, mountains, water, and sky. With the weather system that dominates this region, seeing the mountain tops is rare, but it does happen. Most of them peak out in the 3,000-4,000-foot range, and have subalpine meadows above the tree line. Higher peaks are snow-covered; in the Grenville Channel, which leads to Prince Rupert, the mountains are as high as 3,500 feet above sea level, with bases as much as 1,600 feet under water.

Southeast

GRENVILLE CHANNEL

The name of the Grenville Channel well illustrates one of the common facts of early exploration: you had to name things after the people who gave you the money to go out. In this case, Lord Grenville, the secretary of state, who gave Vancouver the commission for exploration of the Northwest Passage.

In the Grenville Channel area you'll start to see signs of clear-cut logging. There are also a lot of scars from landslides; the topsoil here is terribly thin, and the mountains very steep. It doesn't take much to get a slide rolling that can clear off half a mountain.

Prince Rupert is the last major town that the ferry passes; B.C. Ferries makes this town its northern terminus. It's about a 12-hour run from Port Hardy. The cruise ships never stop here, and the AMH does not stop at Rupert on its northbound run from Bellingham – you cannot get from Prince Rupert to Bellingham on the AMH. The AMH continues north, past the old village of Metlakatla and Dundas Island. Now it's back on the AMH Route, going from Prince Rupert to Ketchikan.

If you're heading south, though, this is a stop for you. In fact, if you're not on a Bellingham-bound ship, it's where your trip on the AMH ends.

Prince Rupert

If you're on a cruise ship, or if you're on the AMH heading northbound, you're not going to stop here. Prince Rupert is a stop only for southbound ferries on the AMH. The Alaska Marine Highway's only Canadian port, Prince Rupert is a lovely little Victorian-style town, easy to get in and out of, and with lots of stuff to do in the surrounding area. Southbound ferries make this a terminus, and the ships unload people ready to drive the last few hundred very scenic miles back down to the U.S.

■ History

Prince Rupert, a town founded in 1906, is now home to about 18,000 people. The town was originally planned as the terminus of the Grand Trunk Pacific Railway, run by Charles Hays.

The planning for this railway was immense – more than 12,000 miles of territory surveyed, nearly 900 miles of right of way blasted through solid rock, and costs rose to more than $100,000 per mile before the railway line was completed. Plans for Prince Rupert were equally grandiose, and publicity started early.

DID YOU KNOW? *There was a contest for naming the town. The rules were that the name had to have 12 letters or fewer, and represent the Northwest Coast. Prince Rupert, second cousin to Charles II and son of Frederick of Prussia, was the first governor of the Hudson's Bay Company. His name just happened to fit.*

Plans for the town were for it to have over 50,000 people almost as soon as it was incorporated. While the rail line did go through, and while Rupert did serve as the terminus, the enthusiasm about making the town a northern showplace died an icy death. When Hays went down on the *Titanic*, all his grandiose plans for the port – situated in the third largest and deepest ice-free harbor in Canada, among its other attractions – went down with him. When he died, there were about 200 people in town.

That didn't necessarily hurt the town. While Hays envisioned something to compete with Vancouver, what happened instead was slow, controlled growth, leaving behind a pleasant little city that still maintains a very busy port, especially for pulp and coal.

■ Basics

If you're on a cruise ship, you can skip this section. The Alaska Marine Highway uses Prince Rupert as its secondary southern terminus. Southbound ferries that terminate here – ships that go on to Bellingham do not stop in Rupert – leave you with a very enjoyable drive farther south, through the Yellowhead Highway and southern B.C., or you can hop a B.C. Ferry and go a bit farther south, to the northern tip of Vancouver Island, before you start driving. Either option is more than scenic.

The area code for Prince Rupert is **250**.

The local **AMH** number is ☎ 627-1744. There's a **B.C. Ferry** run every other day from Rupert to Port Hardy on the tip of Vancouver Island. The trip takes 12 hours and it is always run in daylight to provide maximum scenic enjoyment. Ferries also go from Rupert to Skidgate in the lovely Queen Charlotte Islands. Local phone number in Prince Rupert for B.C. Ferries is ☎ 624-9627; toll-free in B.C., ☎ 800-663-7600.

Rupert's road connection is via the **Yellowhead Highway**, a smooth road in excellent condition. The road intersects with the Cassiar Highway and the main approach route to the Alaska Highway.

Air B.C., ☎ 624-4554 or 800-663-3721 in Canada, or 800-766-3000 in the U.S., links Rupert to Terrace and Vancouver, among other destinations. **Taquan Air** flies into Prince Rupert, connecting the town to Ketchikan, only 45 minutes away. ☎ 800-770-8800. For local charter flights, call **Harbor Air**, ☎ 627-1341.

Greyhound Bus connects Rupert to Edmonton and Prince George with daily departures. ☎ 800-661-1145.

Rent a car at **Budget**, ☎ 627-7400, or **Tilden Rental**, ☎ 624-5318.

Skeena Taxi, ☎ 624-2185, serves the Prince Rupert area.

There's an excellent **Visitor Information Center** next to the small boat harbor at Stiles and Market. It's open from 9 AM in summer. ☎ 624-5637, 800-667-1994, or write Box 669, Prince Rupert, B.C., V8J 3S1.

Internet access is available at **Java Dot Cup**, 516 3rd Ave. West, ☎ 627-4112.

PRINCE RUPERT AT A GLANCE

QUICK TOUR: Rupert has great displays in the Museum of Northern British Columbia. Stop in and see how the HBC used to live, then head over to the Kwinitsa Railway Museum to see how trains changed Canada.

DON'T MISS: The archaeological tours offered by the museum are a great value and a good way to get onto the water; the North Pacific Cannery Village Museum shows you how lucky you are to have never been a fish canner.

BEST FREEBIE: Rupert is a walking town. Just take a stroll from the archaeological museum down to the train museum, around the point toward the ferry terminal. Look one way, there's a beautiful town; look the other, and you'll see nothing but ocean and islands and fishing boats coming and going.

AUTHOR TIP *Prices in this section are in Canadian dollars – the continuing fall of which makes pretty much everything in Rupert a great bargain. However, the volatility of exchange rates means you should take all prices listed here with a grain of salt – things are going to change fast as the currency market moves.*

■ Museums & Attractions

There isn't a whole lot to do in Rupert – the town is most useful as a way to get somewhere else, as it's a port for both the Alaska Marine Highway and the B.C. Ferry system – but you're not going to regret a couple of days wandering, either.

MUSEUM OF NORTHERN BRITISH COLUMBIA: Start touring the town here. Check for guided heritage walking tours of the downtown area. The museum has a good assortment of Native artifacts, including a reproduction of a petroglyph known as the "Man Who Fell from the Sky." It's a full-sized outline of a human body. There are also regular guided programs to the carving shed behind the museum, which offers a look at a totem pole in the making, and in which films are shown on the history of totem poles. Admission is $5.

In the summer, the museum runs **archaeological tours**, selling tickets in the Tourist Infocentre. The tour, which is really more historical than archaeological, takes you out on a boat to the old village of Metlakatla, stopping along the way at other points of interest. A knowledgeable guide fills you in on how to spot old Native villages (watch for green swaths of land or parallel rows of rocks leading into the water), and offers a history of settlement in the area. It's a good introduction to local Native culture, and the price can't be beat: $24 for a 3½-hour trip. For more information, contact the museum at P.O. Box 669, 100 1st Ave. East, Prince Rupert, B.C. V8J 3S1. ☎ 624-3207.

FIREHALL MUSEUM: This site details Rupert's historical fire stations, with the highlight of the exhibition being a 1925 Reo Speedwagon fire engine. It's just up the street from the Tourist Infocentre. Admission is by donation. ☎ 627-4475.

KWINITSA RAILWAY MUSEUM: Walk west along the waterfront to reach the museum. Along with an interpretive exhibit – a detailed history of how the railway has influenced Prince Rupert – the museum also features videos and has a good gift shop. It looks small on the outside, but this is a must-see. Admission is by donation, suggested at $1.

NORTH PACIFIC CANNERY VILLAGE MUSEUM: The other standard attraction of Prince Rupert is actually a few miles out of town. Head out on the Yellowhead Highway and take Route 599 – there's only one way to go and you can't get lost. Follow 599 for six miles, and you'll reach the North Pacific Cannery Village Museum. Like coal mining communities in the Eastern U.S., cannery communities in the West were towns unto themselves, with housing, stores, entertainment, and more. The North Pacific Cannery opened in 1899, and ran continuously until 1981. It's been reopened as a museum, showing the details of the canning process and how the canneries stayed alive. The museum offers excellent displays (ever wonder how they made cans before the machinery took over?) and good interpretive signs. Tours are run every hour, or you can walk the grounds yourself. Admission is $8 for adults, and well worth it.

INDUSTRIAL ATTRACTIONS: One other industrial operation runs tours in Rupert: the grain elevators. Touted as the most modern grain elevators in the world, they are located on Ridley Island. From the Yellowhead, take the Ridley Island Access Road; the elevators are just across the bridge. These free tours are at 9:30 and 11 AM.

Just beyond the grain elevators is the Ridley Island Terminal coal depot. Entire mountains in the Peace River area are disappearing and being sent to Japan. Here's your chance to watch the process. No tours are offered, but you can see the ships and conveyers.

■ Adventures

 Prince Rupert is salmon country. Mid-May to mid-July, the place is a fisherman's dream come true. Even if you're here as late as September, you can pick up on the coho run.

There are a ton of local operators. Check with **Seashore Charter Services**, ☎ 624-5645 or 800-667-4393 first. They book with a wide variety of ships, and can get you out with the people who will best match your needs. Remember, always before booking a charter, see what you're getting yourself in for, what's provided and what isn't, and what kind of boat you're going to be on. There are plenty of choices out there, and something that's just right for you.

Once you've caught the fish, **Prince Rupert Seafood**, #7 Cow Bay Road, ☎ 627-4806, can freeze or vacuum pack your catch.

If you're looking to kayak, contact **Eco-Treks**, ☎ 624-8311. They've got quick paddles for novices, from $40. They also rent kayaks.

Harbour Air, ☎ 627-1341, runs flightseeing trips, including flyovers of the Khutzeymateen wilderness – Canada's only grizzly sanctuary. A look at it will run you about $200.

■ Food

The place of choice is **Smiles**, at 113 George Hills Way, in Cow Bay. The menu includes seafood, wonderful carrot cake, and other desserts. In business since 1922, it has the best food in town, and the most popular – you may have to wait for a table. Prices start around $6. Nearby is the reservations-required **Cow Bay Café** (☎ 627-1212), at 205 Cow Bay Rd. The meals change according to what's fresh, but the food is always outstanding. Prices from $12.

For a nice night out, try **Boulet's Seafood** (☎ 624-9309), in the Fairview Terminal near the Alaska Marine Highway (AMH) dock. They serve crab, salmon, and more in a deluxe atmosphere (with deluxe prices). Reservations are required.

At the other end of the scale is the **Green Apple**, at 301 McBride. Stop in for a fill-up of fish and chips. This is Prince Rupert's place of choice for a quick meal.

▪ Accommodations

Most of Prince Rupert's hotels are located along 1st, 2nd, and 3rd Avenues, between the ferry terminal and downtown. **Crest Motor Hotel** (☎ 624-6771 or 800-663-8150), 222 1st. Ave. West, is the nicest place to stay in town. Doubles start at $140. The **Moby Dick Inn** (☎ 624-6961 or 800-663-0822), 935 2nd Ave. West., is conveniently located, features room/car packages, and has a pretty good restaurant on the premises. Doubles start at $80. The **Inn on the Harbor** (☎ 624-9107; 800-663-8155) at 720 1st Ave. has good views and rooms starting from $80.

The **Aleeda Motel**, ☎ 627-1367, at 900 3rd Ave West, is out near the ferry terminals. Doubles from $70. In the same neighborhood is the **Totem Lodge**, 1335 Park Ave., ☎ 624-6761, with doubles from $75.

As with most towns, turnover in B&Bs is huge. If you can't get into the **Cow Bay B&B**, 20 Cowbay Rd., ☎ 627-1804 – which offers luxury touches for only $100 – it's easiest just to ask at the Info Centre, where there will be plenty of brochures on local spots.

▪ Camping

There are two places to camp in Prince Rupert. The **Park Avenue Campground** is just a mile from the ferry terminal. Not much atmosphere here, but it's very convenient. Tents can get in anytime; RVs need reservations. The place is a big grassy patch by the roadside. ☎ 624-5861.

Just 14 miles outside of town on the Yellowhead Highway is **Prudhomme Lake Provincial Park Campground**, which features 18 nice spots, no facilities, but lots of trees and scenery.

▪ Leaving Prince Rupert

Rupert is a primo jumping-off point, with easy access to Alaska and Canada's interior. If you're not on the AMH, you still have options. First, you can drive out. For extensive details, pick up a copy of our *Adventure Guide to the Alaska Highway*, also from Hunter Publishing.

To get farther south by sea, take the B.C. Ferries. There's an every-other-day run from Prince Rupert to Port Hardy, on the tip of Vancouver Island. The trip takes 12 hours, and it is always run in daylight to provide maximum scenic enjoyment. Ferries also go from Prince Rupert to Skidgate in the lovely Queen Charlotte Islands. ☎ 624-9627; or toll-free in B.C., ☎ 800-663-7600.

Prince Rupert to Ketchikan

Soon after passing Rupert the ship moves into the **Dixon Entrance**, the other large patch of open sea the ferry goes through in Southeast. As with Queen Charlotte Sound, Dixon Entrance is a fairly fast crossing – about 45 minutes on a good day – but it can get rough and slow things down. Those prone to seasickness should be ready. None of the cures work after you've already started to show the symptoms.

The warm water from the Japan Current comes here, hits the mountain air, and sends off tremendous banks of fog from time to time. The plant life around the Entrance reflects the warming influence of the current; there are a lot more ferns than you'll find elsewhere.

You cross into U.S. territory at 54 degrees, 40 minutes north latitude, as the ship passes Wales Island to the mainland side, and approaches Duke Island on the sea side. Wales Island has a tiny speck of land, hardly more than a rock, known as Tongass Island due west of it. This was once the site of Fort Tongass, built by the U.S. soon after the purchase of Alaska from Russia. Sixty men were stationed here before the fort was finally abandoned as pointless. The U.S. had no interest at all in its Alaskan holdings and didn't feel like sending anybody up here.

Before the post was established, the island was famous for some of the finest totem poles in Southeast. As an example of how totems changed with the times, it's said there was a pole on Tongass Island that had a representation of a ship under full sail. It sat in front of the house of the first woman to see such a ship. There were also poles with likenesses of Secretary of State Seward and Abraham Lincoln. There was even supposed to be a pole with a telescope attached and the legend "Captain James Cook, 1778." After the village was abandoned, the poles were, seemingly, open game.

 DID YOU KNOW? *In 1899, the Seattle Chamber of Commerce and the* Seattle Post Intelligencer *took a pole from Tongass Island. It didn't quite fit on their ship, so they sawed it in half. Descendants of the villagers sued and won a settlement, but the pole stayed in Seattle.*

It takes just over three hours to get from the U.S. border to Ketchikan. The ferry skirts Annette Island, once home of Southeast's finest airport and, in the days before the ferry, thought to be the spot for Alaska's next great boom. Now there's nothing on the island but **Metlakatla**, a village that traditionally discouraged tourism but that's now starting to open itself up (see page 179). The ship sails between Race Point and Mountain Point. As houses become visible on the mainland, engine speed is cut for arrival in Ketchikan.

 DID YOU KNOW? *Passing Duke Island and entering Revillagigedo Channel, there's an area of strong magnetic disturbance. In the days before radar, this caused mariners many troubles in the narrow passage; it's still marked on all navigational charts.*

Ketchikan

Although its name is no stranger than many others in the state, Ketchikan has something of an obsession with the history and etymology of the town's name. You won't find a piece of promotional literature without some discussion of the mystery of its name.

KETCHIKAN

The official story is that the name comes from the Tlingit word *Kitcxan*, meaning "Where the eagles' wings are." This is supposed to refer to the shape of the sandspit on Ketchikan Creek. Close to this is another story, that the name comes from *Kach Khanna*, which means "spread wings of a prostrate eagle." Not quite as flattering, but close to the same story. However, if you talk to a few of the old timers, they'll tell you the name really comes from a Tsimshian term that means "place of the big stink." They're talking about Ketchikan Creek again, but this time what happens when the huge masses of spawning salmon die after their run.

If it wasn't bad enough that the city has a name nobody can agree on, just try to get people to pronounce the island's name – Revillagigedo. Blame Vancouver. He was sucking up to minor royalty, as he wrote, "On this occasion I cannot avoid a repetition of my acknowledgments for the generous support we received from Senor Quadro, acting under the orders of the Conde de Revilla Gigedo.... In commemoration therefore... I have not only adopted the name of the channel after that nobleman, but have further distinguished the land north of it by the name of the Island of Revilla Gigedo."

■ History

Thanks to the massive salmon run, the area was a Tlingit summer hunting and fishing camp for centuries before the arrival of European settlers, who opened a salmon saltery in 1883, and a cannery in 1887. The town of Ketchikan itself is now the fourth largest in Alaska, with a population around 9,000 and about the same number again in the surrounding areas. It was incorporated in 1900.

Ketchikan was known for its Wild West air in the old days. The houses of ill repute on Creek Street were still running in the 1950s, and long-time residents may entertain you with firsthand accounts of people bleeding from bar fights and alcohol being smuggled into the bars during Prohibition.

■ Ketchikan Today

The Ketchikan of today is a lot calmer. It's probably one of the friendliest towns in Alaska and one of the most liveable towns in Southeast, except for the insane problem of parking (if you see a space, grab it – most likely you'll never see another, as the town has roughly twice as many cars as people) and the even more dire problem of the weather. Ketchikan gets more than 150 inches of rain a year. The city's mascot is the rainbird. Even other Southeast residents recoil in horror at Ketchikan's weather. On the other hand, it doesn't snow much, and it never gets really cold.

Like most Southeast communities, Ketchikan hugs the mountains, making the town long and narrow. Because people have had to head up the mountains for land to build, the town has a kind of teetery air, with wooden stairs leading to the next level, and the next, and roads that seem to head almost vertically up the mountains. This is a beautiful town and you'll see more eagles and floatplanes here than elsewhere in the state.

There is the air of a boom-town building around Ketchikan. **Misty Fjords National Monument** is one of the hottest scenic spots in Alaska, and the base for all trips into it is Ketchikan. Nearby **Prince of Wales Island** is considered to be Alaska's next boom town (or, in this case, boom island), but so far it has no facilities to handle an influx of business, so Ketchikan has become the hub for trips to the logging camps, fishing resorts, and backcountry of the island, the third largest in the U.S. We've been saying this for 10 years now in these books. Really. Everybody promises. It's right around the corner.

The nearness to the wild and the relatively large population of the town make it a great place for a stop that combines outdoor adventure with history and culture.

■ Basics

i Ketchikan is served almost daily by the **Alaska Marine Highway**. Connecting ports are Bellingham, Metlakatla, Hollis, Prince Rupert, Stewart/Hyder, and Wrangell. The ferry terminal, ☎ 225-6182, is two miles north of downtown, next to the post office.

Cruise ships dock right downtown, next to the tourist information center.

Alaska Airlines, ☎ 225-2141 or 800-426-0333, connects Ketchikan to Seattle, other Southeast communities, and Anchorage. All fixed-wing wheeled planes take off from Gravina Island, which is directly across the channel from Ketchikan proper. You have to take a ferry to the airport, which costs $2.50 ($5 if you put your car on it) and takes about 10 minutes. It runs regularly from just past the ferry terminal. Don't forget to allow yourself extra time for the trip. ☎ 225-6800 for more information. You can call the **Ketchikan Airport Shuttle**, ☎ 225-5429, for pickup at your hotel or at the airport. The cost is about $8-$12, depending on distance.

Charter floatplanes mostly leave from the city side of the Tongass Narrows. **Taquan Air**, 1007 Water St., ☎ 225-8800 or 800-770-8800, schedules flights to Metlakatla and other villages.

Pacific Airways, ☎ 225-3500, does much the same. Charter rates start around $400 an hour – for this you book the entire plane, so you can split the cost with someone else going your way. **Pro-Mech Air** flies to Metlakatla and Prince of Wales Island and also offers flightseeing trips. ☎ 225-3845. **Island Wings**, ☎ 225-2444 or 888-854-2444, runs great trips into Misty; chartering starts at about $250 an hour. **Air One**, ☎ 888-388-1189, runs scheduled flights around the smaller towns.

Alaska Car Rental, ☎ 225-5000 or 800-662-0007, offers some of the best car deals in Ketchikan. There's also **Avis** on Gravina Island, ☎ 225-4515 or 800-831-2847, and **Practical**, ☎ 225-8778.

Alaska Cab Co., ☎ 225-2133; Sourdough Cab, ☎ 225-5544; and **Yellow Taxi**, ☎ 225-5555, all operate in Ketchikan.

 MONEY SAVER: *If you're planning on doing a lot of sightseeing, renting a car is probably cheaper. Ketchikan is long, narrow, and very spread out.*

The **Ketchikan Visitor's Bureau** is at 341 Front St., right next to the cruise ship dock. They're open daily 8-5 (summer), and 8-5, Monday to Friday, for the rest of the year. The very helpful staff will answer any questions or help you plan an itinerary.

Southeast

📖 Ask for a copy of the ***Ketchikan Guide*** and the ***Ketchikan Walking Tour Map***. ☎ 800-770-2200 or 225-6166 for a free information packet.

Inside the Visitor's Bureau are a variety of tour operators looking to take you out flying, fishing, rowing, boating, or hiking. Even more station themselves outside the center whenever a cruise ship comes in. This is action central for trips around town. See the *Adventures* section, below, for more details.

The **Forest Service Visitor Center**, on the corner of Mill and Stedman, is one of the best Forest Service offices in Southeast. Load up here on maps to Misty Fjords and information about the Tongass National Forest. If you haven't made reservations in advance for a Forest Service cabin, you can book one here. Shoot for one of the 14 cabins in Misty Fjords. ☎ 225-3101.

For short ferry stopovers, several different companies offer quickie tours of Ketchikan. Representatives often wait at the dock when the ferry comes in. Alternatively, call the Visitor's Bureau to make advance arrangements for pickup. Prices start at $15.

Internet access at **Soapy's Station**, two locations: one right next to the tunnel at the north end of the cruise ship dock, the other upstairs in the mall at the south end. Keep your time card and use it again in Juneau.

Ketchikan's zip code is **99901**.

KETCHIKAN AT A GLANCE

QUICK TOUR: Visit the Totem Heritage Center; Check out the Southeast Alaska Visitor Center; get a ride out to Saxman, for the best collection of totems in Southeast.

DON'T MISS: Saxman. You'll hate yourself if you miss this; fly out to Misty Fjords – a landscape that makes Norwegians cry in envy.

BEST FREEBIE: Gotta send you out to Saxman on this one too. Best totem poles in the state, no admission. Bring a hat.

■ Museums & Attractions

 SOUTHEAST ALASKA VISITOR CENTER: Located behind the Spruce Mill/Salmon Landing complex, on Mill, the center has exhibit rooms featuring displays on a wide variety of Alaskan topics, including the rainforest, native traditions, and the Southeast ecosystem. It is a good place to get a handle on the different ecosystems of Southeast and how they all interact.

Ketchikan

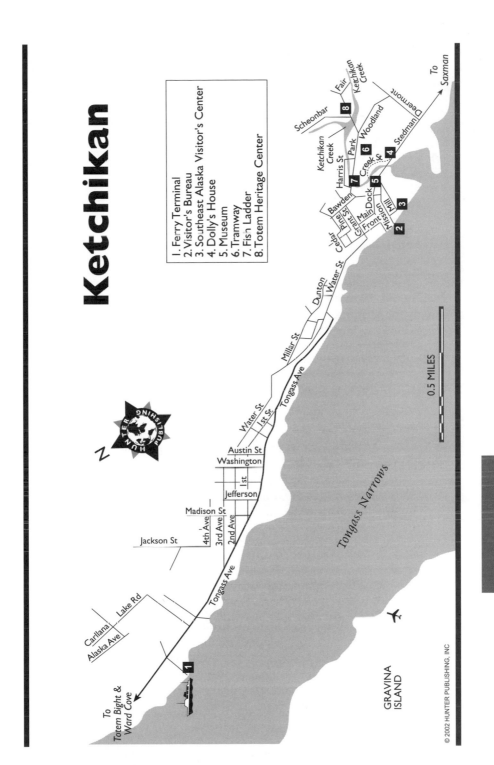

1. Ferry Terminal
2. Visitor's Bureau
3. Southeast Alaska Visitor's Center
4. Dolly's House
5. Museum
6. Tramway
7. Fish Ladder
8. Totem Heritage Center

0.5 MILES

Tongass Narrows

GRAVINA ISLAND

To Saxman

To Totem Bight & Ward Cove

Southeast

There are also good displays about what people do in the region – mining, fishing, and so on. Every half-hour there's a film shown on Native traditions. It's open May through September, 8:30-4:30 daily, and October through April, 8:30-4:30, Tuesday through Saturday. A good first stop on any trip. Admission is $5. For more information, ☎ 228-6214.

In the basement of the center is Trip Planning. This is a room with videos and references for pretty much every attraction in Alaska. You could spend half your trip here trying to decide where to go. They can help you book Forest Service cabins and pretty much steer you in any direction you're interested in.

AUTHOR TIP *If you're going only to Trip Planning and don't want to see the exhibits in the Visitor Center, tell the cashier upstairs; you won't be charged to go down.*

Next door is the **Great Alaskan Lumberjack Show**. Once upon a time, there was a real mill here; now there are bleachers and guys training for the strenuous world of lumbersports. Yeah, there really is such a thing. The show pits two teams on events such as speed chopping, log rolling, pole climbing, and anything else you can logically think of to do with logs and sharp implements. The guys are not just going through the motions – their summer job working here lets them train for the big money events elsewhere, so they put on quite a show. It ain't cheap, though. For the 30-buck admission price, you'd better be really sure you want to be a lumberjack. Three shows a day, ☎ 225-9050.

TONGASS HISTORICAL MUSEUM: 629 Dock St., ☎ 225-5600. Open Monday through Saturday, 8:30-5, and Sunday, 1-5. Admission is $3. The museum has an outstanding collection of Tlingit objects: bentwood boxes, baskets, button blankets, and items of daily use. They also have a good display of fishing equipment with an explanation of all the different types of fishing boats moving in and out of the harbor.

MONEY SAVER: *You can get a pass that takes in the museum, the hatchery, and the Totem Heritage Center for $9.95, which saves you three bucks over single admissions. Ask at the desk.*

CREEK STREET: The museum is right around the corner from Creek Street, which was once Ketchikan's red light district. One of the stories about Creek Street says that when Ketchikan was dry, the sheriff, who was part of the smuggling action, kept things pretty liquored up despite the laws. Almost every house on the street was once engaged in illicit business, and some even had specialties among the customers: one house took only halibut fishermen, because they paid the best. During World War II, up to 30 houses were operating; prostitution was not outlawed until 1954.

Today Creek Street is a combination of private houses, shops, and a museum, **Dolly's House**. It's usually open only if there is a cruise ship in town. The house is at #24 Creek St. and has been refurbished to glorify its seedy past. A good look at the wild past of the Far North. Admission is $4.

WATCHABLE

WILDLIFE

While visiting Creek Street, stop to look in the creek itself. Salmon run up through here and, when they do, it's not uncommon to see harbor seals almost as far up as the museum.

DON'T MISS: Ketchikan is probably the best place in Alaska to watch or photograph floatplanes. Dozens of them take off and land in the water by the visitor's center. During peak season, Tongass Narrows looks like LAX.

BLUEBERRY FESTIVAL: If you're here in August, don't miss the Blueberry Festival, a last gasp for the summer season. General fun and games, plus what may be the only slug races in the world.

CAPE FOX WESTMARK: Between Dolly's House and the museum is the free tramway up to the Cape Fox Westmark, which offers some good views of Ketchikan. The hotel has some of the most interesting and lovely totem poles in Ketchikan. They're all new and, although they follow traditional designs, they incorporate modern elements, such as a mirror or new colors. The poles are also smaller than the huge monument poles you'll see elsewhere. This style was more commonly seen incorporated into house structures. Compare these with some of the older totems.

■ Totem Poles

There is no better place in Alaska for seeing totem poles than Ketchikan. There are two outdoor parks: Saxman and Totem Bight, plus the incomparable Totem Heritage Center, which offers historic totems in varying states of decay and disrepair, as well as historical displays about totems in Southeast.

TOTEM BIGHT: Located 12 miles north of downtown in an open-air setting stand 15 poles showing the various styles of pole carving. None of them is original: most were carved in the 40s. There is also a reproduction of a Native lodge house, complete with a colorful design painted on the front. Traditional villages had dwellings much like this, with poles standing in front of houses that stretched along the beach – often the only flat land in Southeast. Totem Bight is a lovely spot, good for a picnic or for a walk through the forest that surrounds the poles.

SAXMAN: Saxman is 2½ miles south of downtown. It has more and even better poles than Totem Bight – in fact, it has the largest outside collection of poles in the world.

The village of Saxman, which occupies one square mile of territory, has a population of 410. Although it seems to be in the middle of Ketchikan, it actually has a strong sense of self-identity as a Native village. It is an incorporated village, with a full-time staff of eight running the town.

SAVING THE POLES

The totem collection got its start in the late 1930s, when efforts were made to "rescue" poles from abandoned villages. This project was actually run by the Forest Service and the Civilian Conservation Corps, and it caused a fair amount of debate in Native circles. Natives reasoned that the poles were never made to last. No effort had ever been made to preserve a pole before. When a pole got old and rotted, it was allowed to fall. Village elders put a lot of thought into the issue before they finally came down on the side of preservation as a means of showing their history.

The poles in Saxman line the street and are set in a small field in front of a clanhouse. There are 24 poles in all, including two that are located on a small branch trail near the clanhouse: these have been allowed to lie on the forest floor to show what decaying poles look like, to show the natural lifespan of a pole.

Highlights of the collection include the **Lincoln Pole**, which has the head of Abraham Lincoln carved at the top. The pole was erected not to commemorate the president, but the U.S. revenue cutter *Lincoln*, which had helped cement a peace treaty between two Tlingit tribes.

There is also a rare **ridicule pole** in the park, a pole erected just to make someone feel stupid. In this case, they're making fun of William H. Seward, the guy who bought Alaska from the Russians. The locals feasted in his honor and treated him like royalty, but he failed to offer gifts in return, which was not only incredibly rude, it labeled him as an extraordinary miser. The pole, two over from the Lincoln pole, shows Seward with his nose and ears stained red, a mark of stinginess.

Chief Ebbits, the man behind the ridicule pole, also has a **memorial pole** in the park. It's the one at the far left of the field, with two bears shown at the top. Lower down is a wolf figure holding a shield; the shield represents that the person owning it also has at least 3,000 blankets or 20 slaves – a rich, rich man. A bit lower, Chief Ebbits showed he was not a man to forget any slight – there's a figure that's upside down, which represents a man who owed the Chief and never paid. Next to the pole display there is a **carving shed**, where in summer you can usually find one or two carvers hard at work. The cedar smell in the shed is heavenly. If it isn't too busy, you might get a quick lecture on totems.

Traditional Tlingit design on a lodge house, Ketchikan.

Several of the operators downtown will take you out to Saxman, where locals "read" the poles – as much as is possible – and take you through the **Tribal House** (note the lovely beaver design on the front), and into a theater for a film on the Native history of the region. If no one is around (check at the store across from the poles), you're free to wander around yourself.

For only a buck, you can get a pamphlet with the stories of most of the poles down at the **Native Co-Op**, in the old school building at the foot of the hill.

TOTEM HERITAGE CENTER: There's one more stop for the seeker of Native history. The Totem Heritage Center, 601 Deermount, ☎ 225-5900, is open daily 8-5 in summer, and Tuesday through Friday, 1-5, in winter. Admission is $4. You can also buy an entrance ticket that includes the hatchery (just across the river) for $7.95, or one that includes the hatchery and the museum downtown for $9.95.

The center is dedicated to the preservation of totems. Natives decorated their poles with only a few colors, primarily red and black, the colors generally preferred throughout the Pacific Northwest. Pigments used in dye were mixed from common substances: black from coal, reds from iron ore. The rarer blue was made from copper.

Southeast

The Totem Heritage Center has 33 poles, though most are not displayed due to their fragile condition. The poles in the main exhibit are well recorded and flyers tell the "story" of each one. It's worth a visit here just for the historic photographs of the villages, when the poles were still an integral part of daily life.

There is also a room of older poles, heavily deteriorated, too fragile to stand. These old cedar giants will – more than any newly painted pole – give you a sense of the history of Southeast. There's a good gift shop, with some unusual stuff, just inside.

The center is keeping traditions alive through a wide variety of classes. You can, with enough study, actually gain a certificate of merit in basketry, carving, or regalia. The classes, mostly given in winter, include making traditional paddles, history classes, making moccasins, warp spinning, cedar bark weaving, and much more. Many of the courses last only a couple days, and the price is very reasonable. If you're around in the winter months, check it out.

In summer, graduates from the program, or sometimes the local elders, give frequent demonstrations of their craft at the center. Check at the ticket counter for what's going on when you get there. It could be a pole carver, a basket weaver, or a halibut hook carver, among other possibilities.

POLE PRESERVATION

In addition to the basic question as to whether the poles should be preserved, one of the main problems for keeping totem poles intact is that cedar, the wood used for carving, rots from the inside out. Painting the wood is one of the quickest ways to start the rot, as it cuts off the cedar's "breath." When the first totem preservation efforts were made, it was usually decided to paint the poles, both to imitate their original coloring and to save them from the elements. Unfortunately, this had the opposite effect. Traditionally a form of storytelling, or a memorial, poles really weren't expected to last all that long.

■ Hatcheries & Eagle Centers

 DEER MOUNTAIN TRIBAL HATCHERY & EAGLE CENTER: Cross the bridge to the left of the center, and you'll reach the center, which was built back in 1954. Over 300,000 fish are released here each year; a 2% return of adult fish is considered pretty good, and they hope for a 3%-5% return. There are the fry tanks, where the young fish are raised, and the return tanks, where adult fish come back, actually having to work their way up a fish ladder to get into the quiet pools. The adult fish are removed from the pools, the roe or smelt taken out. The female fish, by law, have to be discarded at this point; the male fish are donated to charities.

There's an underwater camera set up that allows you to see inside the tanks. A lot of fun to stop for a look from a fish-eye view.

WATCHABLE WILDLIFE

The salmon run is exciting. The streams and creeks become filled with writhing masses of salmon. Because the different varieties of salmon run at different times, there's something going on here pretty much all summer. However, if there's no cruise ship in town, particularly late in the season, call to make sure the place is open before you come out.

The other attraction at the hatchery is the Eagle Center, an aviary with two injured bald eagles. One is missing its right wing – a losing argument with a gun – and the other has a permanently damaged wing (didn't see the power line). The eagles have it pretty good; there's a small stream with fish in it, should they decide to get their own food, or they can just wait for the keepers to throw in mice. They are, oddly, a mated pair. Eagles mate for life; these two just happened to hit it off at the center.

An eagle was born here in 2000. The parents killed it. Steps are being taken to see to it this issue doesn't arise again. As the adults cannot fly, they obviously can't teach the young proper eagle behavior; really, they can't teach much beyond how to sit on a log and wait for food.

They're also doing raptor rehab here now; they're not as kitted out as the Raptor Center in Sitka, but they're a vital part of a statewide bird rehabilitation effort.

You can tour the hatchery and center for $5.95 per person – the multiple-entrance deal noted above for the Totem Heritage center is a much better bargain, so don't buy admission for the hatchery alone. ☎ 252-5158. It's open daily from May 15 through September 30, 8:30-4:30.

DID YOU KNOW? *Ketchikan has made the Guinness Book of World Records. No, not for rainfall, but for the town's one and only tunnel, which is next to the cruise ship dock. It's said to be the only tunnel in the world that you can go through, around, or over. Above the tunnel is Ketchikan's ritziest residential area.*

■ Adventures

Organized Excursions

As mentioned above, the Visitor's Center is tour central. There's an operator there ready to take you just about anywhere. If you just want to see the town, in addition to the usual quick tour offered straight off the ferry, you have a number of possibilities.

Gray Line runs a 4½-hour tour that includes a visit to Totem Bight, flightseeing Misty Fjords, and a look at the salmon falls. It runs daily and costs $179. Gray Line offices are at 3436 Tongass, ☎ 225-5930. Some shorter city tours are also offered.

Southeast Alaska Native Culture Tours runs a two-hour program that introduces local Tlingit, Haida, and Tsimshian cultures. ☎ 225-5158. **Specialty Tours**, ☎ 247-8625, offers downtown tours, as do **Ketchikan City Tours**, **Totem Tours**, **Trolley Tours**, and **Little Riding Tours**, all of which can be booked in the Visitor's Center, ☎ 228-6214. Two hours should run you about $20. Longer tours that include Saxman and Totem Bight go around $45. If all you're interested in are the poles, you're a lot better off getting a taxi or renting a car. For something a little different with a car, try **Classic Tours**, where you get taken around in a '55 Chevy. ☎ 225-3091.

Seahorse Ventures runs horse-drawn carriage rides through downtown during the summer season. ☎ 225-3672.

AUTHOR TIP *Cruise ship passengers need not worry about getting back in time to board their ship before it leaves the dock. Local operators know the schedules and will get you back long before the ship leaves.*

For ferry passengers, the availability of a tour largely depends on the presence of cruise ships. If there are a lot of cruises in town, the buses probably won't come out to give the quick tour for those on the ferry. If you're only in town on a stopover, there isn't much of anything you can get to in Ketchikan if the buses don't show. The interesting things are too far from the ferry terminal to reach on foot.

Hiking

There are a few worthwhile hikes around Ketchikan, though many paths go through muskeg, so water-resistant boots are a good idea. For the unambitious looking for an introduction to the rainforest, just drive out to the campground at the north end of the road. Easy walking paths lead to a waterfall deep in the old-growth forest. A gorgeous spot.

Deer Mountain offers a more taxing hike, climbing a steep 3.3 miles to a wonderful view of the Tongass Narrows, Saxman, and Prince of Wales Island. The trail leaves from near Deer Mount, marked on the walking tour map and just a short walk from the city park. At the end of the trail is one of the few easily accessed Forest Service cabins in Southeast – make reservations well in advance (☎ 877-444-6777 or go on-line at www. reserve-usa.com).

If you want a longer walk in, you can actually get to this trail from the other side, by getting on the **Silvis Lake Trail**. Drive south from town until you run out of road; you'll see the trail signs. It's a difficult hike, but worth it. It's two miles to Lower Silvis Lake, three miles to Upper Silvis Lake. The second part of the walk is the harder. If you continue past Upper Silvis, after about another 1½ miles you'll hit a left turn in the trail; this is the end of the Deer Mountain Trail.

Several trails lace the area around **Ward Lake**, out toward the pulp mill. There's a 1.6-mile loop through the forest, with a healthy growth of devil's club. It's a very gentle, easy walk, accessible to just about anyone; there are a couple of bridges that prevent full wheelchair access, though.

Another 1½-mile boardwalk (plus about a half-mile of gravel trail), known as the **Perseverance Lake Trail**, crosses Ward Creek and heads through muskeg to a lovely lake. The trick to this trail is navigating the several hundred steps in the boardwalk, which can be very slippery. The trailhead is out off Ward Lake Road, at the Three C's Campground entrance.

WATCHABLE *In addition to having a number of trails lacing around it, Ward Lake is prime wildlife-watching territory, particularly for birders. Keep an eye peeled for trumpeter swans, goldeneye, bufflehead, and more.* **WILDLIFE** *There is a beaver lodge on the lake (start watching around twilight for the best chance of spotting one).*

Lower Second Waterfall Lake has an unwieldy name, but the three-mile hike is a nice one. The path is not usually tended. The trailhead is at Mile 17.5, North Tongass Highway. The lake is good for trout fishing and is kept stocked by the Fish and Game people.

Diving

Not many people expect it, but the Ketchikan area has some of the finest scuba diving in the world. Bring your own gear or rent some at **Alaska Diving Service**, 4845 N. Tongass, ☎ 225-4667. They have wet and dry suits available to certified divers and offer lessons to those who are not certified. If you can't dive and don't have the time to learn, Alaska Diving can set you up with snorkeling gear and wetsuits.

Winter is an especially fine time to dive, because the water is crystal clear then. You owe it to yourself to find out what's really going on underwater, since so much of Southeast is ocean.

WATCHABLE *In the water you can expect to see wolf eels, bright gardens of anemones, starfish, sea urchins, abundant seals, sea lions, otters, and maybe the occasional king salmon.*

WILDLIFE

Kayaking

If you've never paddled a kayak before, prepare yourself for a treat. If you have, you already know that it's the world's most peaceful form of transportation. The waters around Ketchikan are calm and the scenery fantastic. After a few days of seeing everything from the height of a ferry or cruise ship deck, looking out from a kayak seems to open a new world.

Southeast Exposure, 574 Water St., ☎ 225-8829, the town's oldest kayak operator, rents kayaks and runs guided kayak trips into Misty Fjords, the Barrier Islands, or shorter trips around town. Half-day trips start around $50. They also run four- , six- , and eight-day excursions. Contact them for a current schedule. They also rent bikes, $6/hour, $12 for four hours.

An alternative is **Southeast Sea Kayaks**, ☎ 225-1258, on the Web at www.ktn.net/sekayaks, or go talk to them at their booth in the Visitor's Center. Two-and-a-half hour guided paddles are $68. They also do longer trips that combine the best of luxury and paddling: mothership-supported kayak tours. Paddle all day, sleep comfy on the big boat at night. Prices start at $900 for four days. They also rent kayaks if you're going to head out on your own. Prices are $55 per day for a double, $40 for a single, with rates dropping for longer rentals.

Boat Charters

Many people come to fish or watch wildlife, and the easiest way to do this is to book a charter. While there is no shortage of operators in Ketchikan, it is also one of the most expensive cities. The prime destination for trips is Prince of Wales Island. (See pages 170-179 for more details.)

All the places in Ketchikan are going to charge you about the same: prices should be $125-135 per person for a half-day, $175 for six hours (not everybody will do these mid-length trips), and $200-225 for a full day on the boat.

Major Scales Charters, 1204 Black Bear Rd., ☎ 225-9115, is one of the more popular places; they've been in business a long time.

Knudson Cove Marina, 407 Knudson Cove, ☎ 247-8500. They also rent skiffs.

Ketchikan Charter Boats, Inc. runs several boats in all sizes. Trips are customizable. Contact them at 422 Water St., ☎ 225-7291 or 800-272-7291.

Deer Mountain Charters, ☎ 225-9800, and **Ketchikan Sport Fishing**, ☎ 255-7526 or 800-488-8254, are also good choices.

Experience One Charters runs the usual fishing trips, but they also rent skiffs and camping gear. Talk to them in the Visitors Center, or ☎ 228-6214.

If you get tired of fishing and whale-watching, the charters can take you exploring some of the caves that wind through the Ketchikan area. This is for the experienced only. Many of the caves are on Prince of Wales Island, but there are a significant number west of Ketchikan on Revillagigedo Island, in the George Inlet and Carroll Inlet. The Forest Service estimates that there are several thousand caves in the Ketchikan area, many only 30 feet long or so, others stretching to more than 500 feet. So far, only 57 have been completely explored.

Don't investigate these caves without taking all the proper precautions, including registering your destination with the Forest Service. There are some long-term plans to open some of the caves to make them easily accessible. For now, you'll need all the proper gear.

Rock Climbing

For something above ground, call **Kave Sports** at ☎ 225-5283. They are the local rock climbing connection and can outfit you as well as give valuable advice.

■ Misty Fjords

No visit to Ketchikan is complete without a trip to Misty Fjords National Monument, just 22 miles east of town. Charter boats and planes are a common sight here, and on a heavy cruise ship day it might seem as though every one of Ketchikan's 80 or so floatplanes are in the fjords at once.

The fjords offer a dramatic landscape of steep granite cliffs towering nearly 3,000 feet above the ocean and laced with waterfalls that give the rock a sheen like something alive. There are meltwater lakes, muskeg fields that seem to go on forever, Alaska's southernmost glaciers, and smooth, smooth waters.

Wildlife is abundant in the more than 3,500 square miles of park land in Misty Fjords: bears, mountain goats, harbor seals, porpoises, and humpback whales all pass through here. You might even spot wolves, beavers, wolverines and otters.

The area has a long, although scattered, history of human habitation. Archeologists have dated Tlingit, Haida, and Tsimshian remains back as far as 10,000 years. Sea kayakers are likely to see some of the many pictographs that dot the rocks of the shoreline. Later settlers tried running canneries, fox farms, and logging operations within what are now the boundaries of the park.

For the fisherman, Misty Fjords is a paradise of enormous lake trout, grayling, Dolly Varden, and cutthroat. Nearly half of the salmon that spawn in Southeast do it in one of the many rivers that flow out of Misty Fjords.

Although Misty Fjords is more or less pristine, like many places in Alaska, there have been compromises with development. More than 150,000 acres were exempted from the strict regulations covering the rest of the park to allow mining of a molybdenum deposit, one of the richest in the U.S. However, you won't see any traces of the mines. In fact, due to a worldwide slump in molybdenum prices soon after development began on the mine, the company controlling the exemption never got far in their plans to dig. There's a road and a shack, but that's about it. And it's well off the route of the sightseeing tours. The one thing you will see is a navigation station – huge white poles sticking up in the air, still functioning leftovers from the days before satellites scanned the world.

    📖   A good map of Misty Fjords is available at any Forest Service office. They also offer a separate map specially designed for kayakers.

Most trips into Misty Fjords head up the **Behm Canal**, threading through a pass bounded by mountains over 2,500 feet tall, toward **Rudyerd Bay**, a narrow passageway that includes the steep cliffs of Punchbowl Cove. Eight major rivers flow into Rudyerd Bay; countless more tiny streams and creeks trickle into the bay's calm waters.

The **New Eddystone Islands** and **New Eddystone Rock** are highlights along the way. The rock is a monolith that seems to come straight up from the water, while the islands are comprised of cliffs that suddenly thrust above the water's surface. Vancouver named them both in a little fit of homesickness, as they reminded him of "the lighthouse rock off Plymouth." He met some locals here, who were unusual for having nothing with them to trade or sell – although they tried to get him to the village where they could trade fish skins for cloth, "blue cloth seemed to be the most esteemed."

Make sure to watch for roosting eagles at the top of New Eddystone Rock. Maybe you'll get lucky and spot some.

The best way to enjoy the fjords is by boat, staying at least one night in the monument. If you're really ambitious, you can take a boat the length of Behm Canal, along the backside of Revillagigedo Island, and return to Ketchikan from the other direction. With that much time, you can get off the boat and enjoy some of the hiking trails maintained by the Forest Service. Trailheads are visible from the water – they're marked with large orange and white diamond-shaped signs.

You can camp anywhere in the fjords, but follow a few simple guidelines:

- Keep to the trails.

- Practice low-impact camping.

- Carry out whatever you carry in.

- Build as small a fire as possible.

- Bury all human waste away from water sources.

- Keep your tent area as odor-free as possible and never eat inside it; interesting smells – food, or even soap – can attract bears.

The Forest Service maintains 14 cabins in Misty Fjords. They're usually pretty well booked up six months in advance. If you know that far ahead of time exactly when you'll be in Ketchikan, it's worth checking with them to see if any are available. There isn't a bad cabin in the bunch. You'll have to charter a plane to reach the cabins, most of which require one to two hours of flight time.

CAUTION

While it's quite easy to catch fresh fish for your dinner, remember that the clams may be poisonous. Avoid eating local bivalves.

Almost every charter operation in Ketchikan can take you into the fjords. If you're looking to camp or kayak, negotiate a drop-off rate, but be sure the pickup time and place are well understood by everyone.

Misty Fjords Kayaking

For the kayaker in the fjords, the possibilities are almost limitless. If you look at the area on a map, it appears something like a hand, with the Behm Canal as the hand and the fjords as the fingers. Rudyerd Bay offers about 20 miles of shoreline to paddle; much of it is too steep to land on, but the farther you go in, the more opportunities there are. The bay has enough twists and turns and fingers of its own that you can happily paddle in here for days.

To the south of Rudyerd is Smeaton Bay, which actually travels into the area that is, while part of Misty, not a designated wilderness area. But you're not likely to notice all that much. Smeaton splits into two arms; taking the north, the Wilson Arm, dead-ends after about six miles at the juncture of the Wilson and Blossom Rivers. Fishing licenses, available in town, are required for the Fjords.

 Remember that the water is cold, the weather sometimes very unpredictable. While the fjords are fairly sheltered, they can also act as great big wind funnels. Go prepared and let someone know where you're going to be and when you'll be back.

For a guided trip, contact **Southeast Sea Kayaks**, ☎ 225-1258 or 800-287-1607. These are great people, and they run a four-day guided trip for $708, six days for $950.

📖 Southeast Sea Kayaks sell the *Misty Fjords National Monument Trip Planning Guide*, which includes topo maps designed for kayakers, showing the best destinations and camping areas. It's also got cabin locations, hiking routes, and info about the dozens of lakes in the park. A bargain for $14.

Misty Fjords Flightseeing

If you can't get into the fjords by boat, then try flying over. A 90-minute flightseeing trip will introduce you to a landscape like nothing else in Southeast. Looking down, you lose some of the power of the towering cliffs, while gaining an appreciation of just how vast the fjords are. The best bargain in flightseeing is at **Island Wings Air Service**, ☎ 225-2444 or 888-854-2444, on the Web at www.islandwings.com. This is a one-plane operation, and it's a small plane – it takes only three passengers – so you get the most intimate, uncrowded view of the fjords; you're also taken around on a longer flight than most other operators offer. And while the others give you a "lake landing" that lets you get out of the plane only long enough to stand on the float, Michelle puts you on shore for an hour or so to let you look around. The basic run is $179, but there's a better bargain for $250 that includes a two-hour hike on one of the Forest Service trails.

AUTHOR TIP *Book your trip early. With only one plane, space fills up fast and this is one you don't want to miss. If you can't get on this one, try another outfitter.*

You'll never forget a flightseeing tour over Misty Fjords.

Alpine Helicopters, ☎ 247-6601, has landings in the backcountry for $159. A two-hour trip that includes a quick fly-by of the Fjords is $228.

Taquan Air Tours, 1007 Water St., ☎ 225-8800, handles most of the other flying business in the fjords. Landing in the fjords costs $179 – but remember all you get to do is stand on the plane's float for a minute or two. They also have a couple of shorter tours. Call ahead to see what will fit into your schedule and price range.

FLOATPLANES

One of the amazing things about floatplanes is just how smooth they are. Takeoffs and landings are more comfortable than on the average wheeled plane; sometimes, unless you're looking out the window and see that there isn't a wake from the floats anymore, it's hard to know you're even in the air.

If it's a major cruise ship day and you can't get on with either of above two operators, any of the other air operators listed back in the *Basics* section will take you out to Misty.

Southeast

Misty by Ship

Goldbelt has a day-trip to Misty by ship. It's quite a different view than you're going to get by air. Price is $145 per person. ☎ 800-820-2628.

However you go into Misty, you're not going to be disappointed. The scenery is entirely unlike anything else you're going to see along the Alaskan coast.

■ Shopping

Ketchikan is the first or last stop of most cruise ships, so there's no shortage of stuff to buy. The trick is, among the gigantic tourist traps of T-shirt shops, jewelry stores, and things to mail home to relatives back east, finding something worthwhile. But there are some shining lights.

Carver at the Creek, on Creek Street, is a closet-sized shop that sells the work of Norman G. Jackson, who is one of Southeast's best Native carvers. It ain't cheap, but it's worth every penny. ☎ 225-3018.

Downtown, **Eagle Spirit Gallery**, 310 Mission, has great masks. Very high-quality items. ☎ 225-6626.

Back on Creek Street is the **Hide-A-Way** giftshop, Native-run, which has real halibut hooks, plus smaller prints and lithographs of Native designs. High-quality stuff, reasonable prices.

For more standard tourist fare, **Sockeye Sam's**, north of the cruise ship dock near the tunnel, tries a little harder to find unusual items. Not so many T-shirts, but some really interesting local food products, including wild berry and salmon foodstuffs. Well worth a look inside.

Tongass Trading Co., 201 Dock St., has only a few tourist items, but they're a good place to get outfitted for excursions. Wet and cold weather gear is sold on the first floor.

Ketchikan has one of the finest bookstore in Southeast Alaska, possibly in the state. **Parnassus Books**, upstairs from **Alaska Eagle Arts**, has an eclectic selection of reading material to get you through the night, or even through all of Alaska. Also in the same building is **Soho Coho**, which has some really fun Alaska stuff, and good art.

At Saxman, the **Saxman Arts Co-op**, right on the main road at the foot of the totem poles display, has a wide selection of arts and crafts from local artists. Each piece comes with a card, letting you know exactly who made it. Very reasonable prices.

■ Food

The **Good Fortune Restaurant**, #4 Creek St., ☎ 225-1818, has a nice menu of Chinese specialties. Their dinner combos are worth the prices, which start around $12.

Cape Fox Westmark's dining room, the **Heen Kahidi**, is a good place for lunch, serving steak and seafood, with a good view of Tongass Narrows. Prices start from $8. Located at 800 Venetia Way, ☎ 225-8001.

For an excellent Sunday brunch, try **Annabelle's**, 326 Front St., ☎ 225-6009. Go early or late: at peak, it's jammed as people fill themselves on the sourdough pancakes. For breakfast takeout, the **Creek St. Café & Bakery**, on Steadman near the Creek Street bridge, is the place.

Harbor Lights, 2131 Tongass, ☎ 225-7111, has pizza from $12 for a small one. Another place to try for pizza or sandwiches is the **Pizza Mill**, 808 Water St., ☎ 225-6646. It looks a little down and out, but it serves good food, starting around $10. Mexican food is offered at **Chico's**, 435 Dock St., ☎ 225-2833. Cheap and tasty.

The **George Inlet Lodge** is nearly at the end of the road, heading south from town. A favorite "night-out" spot with locals, it offers reasonable prices and a great atmosphere. If you're going out on a weekend night, call ahead for reservations, ☎ 225-6077. If you don't have transportation, they will pick you up from town.

If you're coming off the AMH and need something other than ferry food but don't want to go into town, stop by **The Landing**, directly across the street from the ferry terminal in the Best Western hotel. It serves steak and seafood, with most entrees costing around $20.

New to town is the **Ketchikan Brewing Company**, at 607 Mission St. Microbrews, smoke-free atmosphere. Stop in for some spruce tip beer, and be sure to ask them the distance to the church doorknob. It matters to them. Finally, for fast food downtown, inside the Landing, at the south end of the cruise ship dock, there's some very basic pizza, hot dogs, and nacho places.

■ Accommodations

Ketchikan's most convenient lodging is downtown. The **Ingersoll**, the granddaddy of Ketchikan's hotels, is directly across from the Visitor's Center, at 303 Mission St., ☎ 225-2124. They offer spacious, comfortable rooms, some with excellent water views, from $110. Nearby is the **Gilmore Hotel**, 326 Front St., ☎ 225-9423, which has been redecorated to look like something from the gold rush era. Rooms above the bar can get a little noisy, but it's still a good choice.

Doubles in high season run upward from $80. Closer to Creek Street but away from downtown is the **New York Hotel**, 207 Stedman St., ☎ 225-0246. Nicely decorated rooms run from $89 in season. Out toward the ferry terminal is the **Best Western Landing Inn**, 3434 Tongass Ave., ☎ 225-5166. Rates start around $120.

The swank address is at the **Cape Fox**, on the hill above town, 800 Venetia Way, ☎ 225-8001. Accessible by cable car from Creek Street, it has rooms from $160 in summer. The restaurant on the property is a bargain, and don't miss the totem poles in front of the hotel and the art collection inside.

The **Narrows Inn**, a couple of miles past the ferry terminal, has doubles for $85. The water-view rooms with little balconies are great on clear days. The **Super 8** has doubles with water views from $120.

If you want to stay in a B&B, Ketchikan has plenty. The easy way to find one is to call the **Ketchikan Reservation Service**, ☎ 247-5337 or 800-987-5337. They book for about 20 different properties, and make sure everybody is up to a good standard. You can check out the various options on the Web at www.ktn.net/krs/. Most selections run around $80 for a double. Another option is **Alaska Traveler's Accommodations**, ☎ 800-928-3308, or 247-7117, on the Web at www.alaskatravelers.com. They can book you a room in a variety of B&Bs.

The cheapest lodging in town (without bringing your own bed) is at the **Alaska Rain Forest Inn**, 2311 Hemlock St., ☎ 225-9500. Beds in the bunkhouse start at $21; there are some private rooms for $45. There's also a **Youth Hostel** inside the United Methodist Church. Bring your own bedding. Rates for non-members run $10 per night. ☎ 225-3319.

There are some world-class fishing resorts located on Prince of Wales Island that use Ketchikan as their base. (See the *Prince of Wales* section for details on these dream escapes, pages 177-178.)

■ Camping

There are four very nice public campgrounds outside Ketchikan proper. Three are in the Ward Lake Recreation Area: take the Tongass Hwy. seven miles north of the ferry terminal and turn at the Ward Lake cutoff. All sites have water and run $8 per night. **Signal Creek** is one mile beyond the turnoff on the south end of the lake; **Three C's** is just a half-mile north of Signal Creek; **Last Chance**, the nicest of the three, is located on Ward Creek, two miles beyond the parking entrance to Ward Lake. **Settler's Cove** is at the end of the Tongass Hwy., at Mile 18.5 by the beach. Camping fee here is $6.

Additionally, **Clover Pass Resort**, 14 miles north of town, ☎ 247-2234, has RV hookups.

Stewart-Hyder

Once a week, the Alaska Marine Highway makes a run from Ketchikan to Stewart-Hyder with the **M/V Aurora**. It's not used much by tourists, but if you're looking to get onto the road system from Southeast Alaska, this is your last chance until Skagway and Haines. Conversely, for drivers, it's the last chance to get off the highway for a thousand miles or so.

Stewart and Hyder together form a single small community, stuck on a spur road off the Cassiar Highway.

The town of Stewart (population 1,200), which is in Canada, is primarily interesting for its juxtaposition to Hyder (population 100), which is in Alaska. Hyder residents tend to use Canadian money, attend Canadian schools, and use the Canadian time zone. Both towns have all services, a definite preference for Canadian currency (despite the U.S. dollar's higher value), and are on a different time zone than the rest of Alaska.

 DID YOU KNOW? *Stewart is the northernmost ice-free port in Canada, but it still gets more snow than you can believe: in one 12-month period, Stewart-Hyder received 1,104 inches. That's the third largest snowfall ever recorded for a year in one spot.*

■ History

The towns lie at the head of the **Portland Canal**, a 90-mile-long saltwater fjord. George Vancouver came to this canal on July 29, 1793, looking for the Northwest Passage. Obviously this dead end wasn't it, but he wrote about this place, "salmon in great plenty were leaping in all directions. Seals and sea otters were also seen in great numbers." Actually, had communications been better at the time, Vancouver might have skipped the canal entirely (his diary entry when he left said he was "Mortified with having devoted so much time to so little purpose"). In August 1791, the *Columbia-Rediviva*, a U.S. ship, was in the canal when "one canoe came alongside in which was six men extraordinarily well armed with spears daggers bows and arrows covered with mats in the bottom of their canoe." There was a bit of talk, a bit of trade, and a landing party was put ashore. The landing party didn't come back, so the ship tacked in and there, "I saw my worthy friend Mr. Caswell laying dead in the bottom of the boat... stabbed upwards of twenty places." The ambush was apparently in retaliation for the actions of an earlier ship, the *Hancock*, which had opened fire on the locals.

Southeast

The U.S. Army Corps of Engineers came here in 1896; and with the big gold rush in the Klondike two years later, the area was swamped with would-be prospectors. A few got lucky here, and both towns boomed for a brief period. Just before World War I, there were 10,000 people in town. When the boom went bust, about a dozen remained.

This area was originally going to be the terminus of the transcontinental railway – every town along the Canadian coast was hoping to be the end of the line – but the terrain leading in was simply too rough to cut a train line. The terminus got moved south to Vancouver, and Stewart-Hyder languished until the 1960s, when mining concerns moved in. The biggest of them, a copper mine, shut down in 1984. Today both towns are quiet, but pleasant. There's not a lot to do here, but that's part of the attraction.

■ Basics

 The **Stewart Infocentre** is in the Chamber of Commerce Building on 5th Ave.; the **Hyder Visitors Center** is on the right as you drive into town. Hyder's museum is also there.

Although there is an international border here, nobody pays much attention to it (although this could be changing with increased security concerns). The only marker is a storehouse from 1896. If you take this run on the ferry, U.S. Customs is in Ketchikan.

Hyder is worth a visit for a look at the bars. The walls inside many bars are covered in money, a tradition from the mining days. A miner would tack a bill to the wall, scribbling his name on it, as insurance against coming back broke from prospecting. Getting stuck in Hyder was known as being "Hyderized," and after a good look around town, you'll see why a small savings deposit was a good idea.

The towns get a little wild at the beginning of July for a combination Canada Day/Independence Day celebration, with parades, fireworks, pig races, and more.

STEWART-HYDER AT A GLANCE

QUICK TOUR: Are you kidding? The whole town is a quick tour.

DON'T MISS/BEST FREEBIE: Drive out to Bear Glacier. Okay, there are better glaciers farther north. But here's your first taste of ice; Fish Creek Bear Observatory – it's only three miles from town, and you don't need a permit to show up and watch the bears. From July into September, here's the best action in town: the toaster museum. Yeah, really. Where else do you get a chance like this?

■ Weather conditions have made Stewart the town of choice for filming Hollywood movies. *The Thing* (the John Carpenter version), *The Iceman*, and *Bear Island* were all filmed here. The Stewart Tourist Info-centre can show you some of the leftover movie props. If you're really desperate for entertainment, they'll put you in touch with a tour company that specializes in taking people around to local movie locations.

■ Scenic Drives

The link to the Cassiar Highway makes for an interesting side trip if you've got a car. It's a 40-mile access road, smooth and delightful, traveling between tight mountain ranges. You'll see several glaciers along the way; Bear Glacier, at Mile 15, is the best. Come here in early morning light for top-notch photos. There's a pullout where you can look across the river to the glacier. Look up at the old highway, several hundred feet up. The glacier used to reach all the way across the valley. A few miles farther is a huge accumulation of snow, which looks like a glacier, but is in reality the remnants of avalanches. You meet up with the Cassiar at Meziadin Junction, near the foot of the Skeena Mountains. Turn left to get to the Alaska Highway (two days north); a right turn leads south toward Kitwanga and Prince George. Either direction is scenic, but if you're looking for a way onto the Alcan, it's a lot easier to make the road connection at Prince Rupert, Skagway, or Haines.

■ Adventures

Hiking, Boating & Flightseeing

If you're looking for a place to hike or boat, head to **Clements Lake**, seven miles northeast of Stewart. Other options are the **Sluice Box Trail** (the trailhead is near the dump), a nice short overview trail; or the **Titan Trail**, with the trailhead off Salmon River Road. The hike is 4.7 miles up to the Titan Mine. **Vancouver Island Helicopters** has short flightseeing tours of the area. ☎ 636-2442.

Bear-Viewing

The Fish Creek Wildlife Observatory is three miles outside Hyder; it's the easiest access of any of the bear observatories in Southeast. From July into September – as long as the fish run holds out – both black and brown bears show up to gorge on the salmon return here. There's a platform for viewing, and Forest Service personnel are on duty from 6 AM to

10 PM. Bring lots and lots of film, and read the bear section on pages 42-47 for how to behave at the platform. And remember: bears don't like flash bulbs. Never surprise anything with a mouth bigger than your head.

■ Food

Check out the **Bitter Creek Café**. The menu here includes pizza and Mexican dishes. **Fang's Garden** offers Chinese food. And for the trip ahead, whether it's going to be by car or boat, stop in at **Brother's Bakery** for rolls, fresh sandwiches, and a good selection of meats and cheeses.

■ Accommodations

There are some nice places to stay in town. All hotels – whether in Alaska or Canada – use the 250 area code, and prices are quoted here in Canadian dollars. Canadian hotels tack on a 15% bed tax to their rates.

The **Grandview Inn** (☎ 636-9174) has rooms from $67. The **Sea Laska Inn** (☎ 636-2486) has rooms with shared baths starting around $50. Some rooms with private baths are available. It also has RV hookups. The **King Edward Hotel** (☎ 636-2244) starts at $80 for a double.

■ Camping

You've got couple of choices. The **Rainey Creek** municipal campground is on 8th Ave., ☎ 636-2537. Spots start around $13. The **Bear River Trailer Court** is a better bet for RVs. They're just off the Bear River Bridge, in Stewart. ☎ 636-9205.

Prince of Wales Island

The third largest island in the United States, Prince of Wales must have once seemed like the Garden of Eden. Unspoiled areas retain that flavor: rich forest, abundant wildlife, and a somewhat milder climate than many other regions in Southeast.

However, over the years, Prince of Wales has seen one of the highest concentrations of logging in all of Alaska. The land is piebald with clear-cuts and, because much of the island is Native holdings, more or less exempt from the moratorium on Tongass logging, there is no end to the cutting in sight.

Of course, all the logging accounts for part of the island's appeal. There are more than 2,000 miles of logging roads on Prince of Wales – some stretches in much better shape than others – and that means just about every nook and cranny of the island can be explored.

Of course, as we discuss elsewhere, the logging does create other problems. Besides the fact that it's astoundingly ugly and ruins habitat, there are more subtle issues at hand. At Stanley Creek on Prince of Wales there was a huge pink salmon die-off in 1993; the final attribution of blame was to higher stream temperatures caused by logging – a forest stream in Alaska is unlikely to ever get a bit of sunshine until all the trees around it are stripped out. Federal laws require stream buffers, which are not really enough, but Native corporations are not held even to these minimal laws; nor are they held to maximum-size requirements, so you'll know when you're in a Native clear-cut – it looks a little like pictures of Hiroshima after the bomb dropped.

Growth continues on Prince of Wales. Mines are re-opening: there are healthy deposits of molybdenum, beryllium, thorium, and chromite. The entire southern end of the island is, supposedly, rich in minerals, just waiting for an ambitious miner to extract them.

 DID YOU KNOW? *Marble from Prince of Wales Island was used in the construction of the State Capitol in Juneau.*

Plans for everything from new logging development to scuba diving resorts are underway for Prince of Wales. So far, this hasn't fed a lot of cash into the local economies (except Ketchikan's, where most of the entrepreneurs are based), but the towns have been growing rapidly, and you should watch for big changes over the next decade. Prince of Wales is Alaska's next hot tourist development spot, focusing on the areas that still have trees – and make no mistake, there are a lot of them. Hotels and tourism companies are scrambling for a toehold on the island, with luxury fishing lodges claiming the most remote areas.

See it now.

■ History

The island was probably first sighted by a Spanish expedition that left San Blas, Mexico on January 25, 1774. They kept heading north, and they're credited with being the first non-Russian Europeans to explore this part of Alaska. They came up through the Queen Charlottes, and on August 18 claimed the area around Nootka Sound, which led to further Spanish claims in Southeast – something that survives in names like Cordova and Valdez. It's assumed that this expedition sighted the southern tip of Prince of Wales.

Southeast

Over the next few years, things are going to change on Prince of Wales, as the Alaska Marine Highway starts its fast ferries. The first, a ship to be called *Prince of Wales*, is going to make twice daily Ketchikan-Hollis runs, probably starting in early 2002. The second ferry, as yet unnamed, will link Coffman Cove, at the north end of the island, with Wrangell and Petersburg. Once that's running – maybe by spring 2003 – this will be ground zero for the best time you can possibly have in Alaska.

Despite the heavy logging, the huge chunks of clear-cut and the flurry of hopeful development – still much of it just talk – Prince of Wales Island remains much as it was when the Spanish saw it. A stunning island in a stunning spot. One of the true glories of Southeast.

■ Basics

There are six fair-sized communities and a number of small villages on Prince of Wales, comprising a total population of around 10,000-12,000 permanent residents. In the summer, that number swells with seasonal loggers and fishermen. The island covers an area of 2,231 square miles, and it's only 15 miles west of Ketchikan; it's also not too far from Wrangell.

The Alaska Marine Highway regularly serves Hollis. The only other way to reach the island is by charter plane. Check the Ketchikan section (page 147) for operators. **Taquan Air** (☎ 225-8800) has scheduled flights – mail runs, mostly – to many of the villages, as does **Pacific Air**, ☎ 225-3500. **Scott Air**, ☎ 846-5464, is in Craig, and they're a good company to charter a plane from.

There are no tourist information offices on the island, but the Chamber of Commerce in Craig can send you the very nice booklet *Explore Prince of Wales Island*. ☎ 826-3870, on line at www.princeofwalescoc.org.

A cab company operates in Craig: **Chief Wiah Cab**, ☎ 826-3375, and in Klawock you can try the **Screaming Eagle Taxi**, ☎ 755-2699. You can rent a car from **Wilderness Rent a Car** in Craig, ☎ 826-2205.

An alternative is to rent a car in Ketchikan and take it to Prince of Wales by ferry. Check with Ketchikan's rental offices for restrictions. Rent an RV in Craig from **POW Island Getaway**. ☎ 826-4150.

DON'T MISS: *Thanks to all the logging roads, the best way to get around the island is on your mountain bike. Strap your tent on the back and head out. You're unlikely to find a better wilderness experience.*

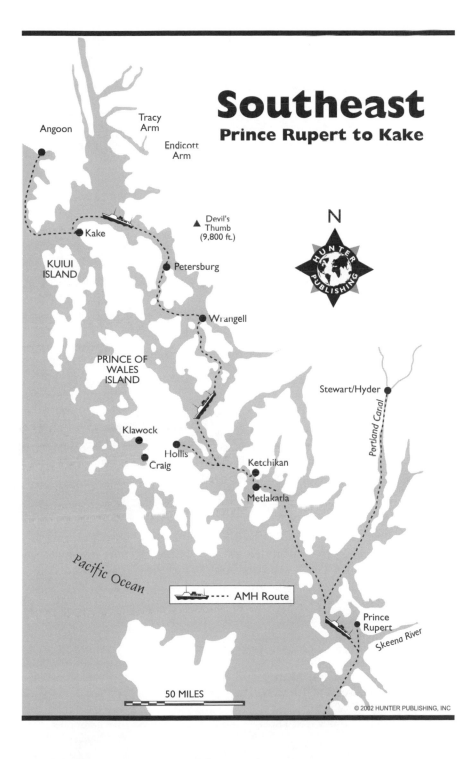

Southeast
Prince Rupert to Kake

N

Angoon

Tracy Arm

Endicott Arm

Kake

KUIUI ISLAND

Devil's Thumb (9,800 ft.)

Petersburg

Wrangell

PRINCE OF WALES ISLAND

Stewart/Hyder

Klawock

Hollis

Craig

Ketchikan

Metlakatla

Pacific Ocean

AMH Route

Prince Rupert

Skeena River

Portland Canal

50 MILES

© 2002 HUNTER PUBLISHING, INC

Southeast

📖 The Forest Service office in Ketchikan, ☎ 225-2148, sells a good road map/topo map of Prince of Wales. The map is an absolute necessity if you're going to explore the maze of logging roads on Prince of Wales. They can also help arrange a stay in one of the Forest Service cabins on the island.

Basic services – gas, food, and limited lodging – are available in all six towns. There are a number of small cafés and each town has a grocery store.

■ Adventures

 The joy of an independent trip to Prince of Wales is to get out in the serious Alaskan bush. The clear-cutters haven't completely stripped the island bare, and there remain plenty of places where you can hide from civilization. Keeping that in mind, don't expect much from the towns.

Most of the towns offer nothing but a gas station, a post office and a school (Craig had a Burger King, but it closed when the high school moved). Grocery stores will have basic necessities, but it's pretty common to head to Ketchikan for major shopping. You're not coming here to be amused by the towns; you're here for the wilderness. However, if you want a couple hints about where to get started, try **Alaska Native Personal Tours**, run out of Craig. Three hours takes you through Craig and Klawock. It's a good chance to get the local take on the island. ☎ 755-4848 to see what tours are running when you're in town.

Hiking

There aren't many trails on the island for hikers – a grand total of 16, adding up to less than a dozen miles. Remember it's a working island, not a vacation island, and if you want to hike you're probably better off on a more remote section of road than looking for a trail. If you insist, you can hike the **Soda Lake Trail**, located about 14 miles south of the junction of the Hydaburg Road. It's a 2½-mile trail that heads up to a natural soda springs. Southwest of Hollis, try the **One Duck Trail**, a 1½-mile walk that goes pretty much straight uphill.

Caves

In addition to the usual hiking and fishing, Prince of Wales also has a huge variety of caves. More than 700 square miles of the island are laced with caves, some of which are only a few feet deep, others several hundred feet deep. Only two of these have been developed for tourists.

Cavern Lake Cave was formed by an underground flow of water through limestone. There's a trail that leads back to the cave, with a viewing deck, or you can walk down to the entrance. Since the cave is full of water, any attempts to enter are an invitation to hypothermia, the biggest killer of outdoorsmen. To reach the cave take Highway 929 from Klawock 18 miles to Road 20. Turn left. After 40 miles you hit the intersection with Road 27; turn left again. Two miles later you'll see a large gravel pit on the left, which serves as the parking area for the cave.

El Capitan Cave has a lead-in trail, a boardwalk, and an interpretive area, complete with toilets. The cave itself floods and has quite a few vertical shoots. Only experienced spelunkers should pass the entrance. You can, however, join a tour offered by the Forest Service daily at 8, 10, 1, and 3. Reservations are required and can be made at the Thorne Bay Ranger District, ☎ 828-3304. Bring a flashlight and hardhat, and be sure to dress warmly and for wet conditions.

 Unless you take a tour, you're on your own in these caves. Leave your itinerary at the Thorne Bay Ranger Station, but don't expect much help if you get lost. Searches are run by the Alaska State Troopers (☎ 755-2918), who are not trained spelunkers. Alaska law allows them to charge you for the rescue.

Canoeing

If you've got a boat to bring to the island you can use the **Honiker Divide Canoe Route**, which covers 34 miles. Put in near Coffman Cove. The longest portage is about two miles; the trail leads from Coffman up Hatchery Creek to the Thorne River. You can get more information on the trail from the Thorne Bay Ranger Station.

■ Totem Poles

 When you look at totem poles in Ketchikan, you'll see that most of them originally came from a place called Old Kasaan on the island. This is a village on Skowl Arm, about 30 miles from Ketchikan, near Hollis. Old Kasaan was a Haida village, and it thrived for quite a while in a small clearing on a gravel shore here. The first row of houses was situated just above the tide line, and in the old photos, you can see how many totem poles lined the beach.

The village is abandoned now – most of the descendants of the residents moved off to Kasaan, about 12 miles away and next to a salmon cannery – and whether or not your presence is welcome at the ruins is highly debatable. There's not a whole lot to see anyway. Between the raiders and the weather, the forest has had plenty of chance to take the territory back.

■ Food

 Unless you're at one of the resorts, don't expect gourmet dining. In fact, you're best off bringing in your own food. In Klawock, try the restaurant at the **Fireweed Lodge** or **Dave's Diner**. In Craig, **Ruth Ann's Restaurant** is probably your best choice.

■ Accommodations

There are only a few hotels on Prince of Wales Island (not including resorts), but more are appearing fast. **Fireweed Lodge**, ☎ 755-2930, is in Klawock. It offers double rooms starting at $95.

The **Log Cabin Resort & Campground**, also in Klawock, has large log cabins from $100, smaller ones from $35; RV spaces with full hookups for $23; and 10 tent spaces are also available. They also rent boats (canoes are only $20 a day) and fishing equipment, and run charters. If you've arrived by private boat, you can moor here. Box 54, Klawock, ☎ 800-544-2205 or 755-2205.

Haida Way Lodge, ☎ 826-3268, is in Craig, seven miles south of Klawock. Rooms start at $90 and some include a kitchenette. The lodge is within easy walking distance of Craig's downtown, where there are a couple of restaurants.

Ruth Ann's Motel, ☎ 826-3378, starts at $90, and is conveniently located. They can also book you charters, and their restaurant is your best choice for food in town. There's also the **Inn of the Little Blue Heron**, ☎ 826-3606, with doubles starting at $80. A nice spot.

For the cheapest bed, head to the **TLC Laundry & Rooms**, ☎ 826-2966. A spot in the bunkhouse goes for $39.95.

McFarland's Floatel, ☎ 828-3335, is on the other end of the island, near Thorne Bay. They rent fully furnished cabins and can set you up with hunting and fishing guides and charters. Cabin rates start at $220 per day. They've also got charters and car rentals. They've been around a long time and know what they're doing.

AUTHOR TIP

Most of the limited visitor services on Prince of Wales are seasonal; many more are filled by loggers. Check before you go. You might take a tent along with you, just in case rooms are short, or try booking into one of the Forest Service cabins.

Resorts

The waters off Prince of Wales Island offer some of the finest fishing in Alaska. The remote location makes it a prime spot for the wealthy fisherman to run off and hide. They can spend a week or so being pampered by night, and fishing non-stop by day. The resorts have a reputation of being accessible only to the very rich, but if one breaks down the services, the prices are more than reasonable. Three days of charters in Ketchikan, a hotel at night, and two reasonable meals a day, is going to run $1,200 or more per person. Get into that range and you might as well enjoy the added benefits of a lodge.

The prime spot on Prince of Wales, and one of the nicest lodges in Alaska, is **Whales Resort**, near Whales Pass on the northeast side of the island. It offers a five-star chef, luxurious surroundings, and immaculate 28-foot boats with knowledgeable captains. The lodge holds only 24 people, so the staff/guest ratio is nearly one to one. The guest rooms are large and comfortable, with VCRs and all amenities. There's also a huge game room. All-day private use of boats, all meals, and processing and packing of the catch are included in the price, which starts at $2,100 per person for three days, including airfare from Ketchikan. Contact Whales Resort at ☎ 800-877-2661; www.gageoutdoor.com. An amazing place.

Waterfall Resort, closer to Ketchikan, is an old cannery converted into a resort. Accommodations are in small but well-appointed worker's houses. Waterfall holds about 80 guests at a time. They run a fleet of 21-foot fishing boats, put four guests on each boat, and package your catch. All meals are included, as is the flight from Ketchikan. Rates start around $2,800 for four days/three nights. Contact Waterfall at ☎ 800-544-5125; www.waterfallresort.com. The best description we've heard of this place is that it's a fishing "ashram."

There are some slightly cheaper alternatives, although you're still going to be looking at very close to $500 per night/person – but remember that price includes lodging, food, and the boat you're going to fish from. **Clover Bay Lodge** is only a 15-minute flight from Ketchikan. It's got 12 rooms. Instead of the big cruisers that you go fishing on in Waterfall or Whales Pass, here you go out in more basic skiffs. ☎ 800-354-0137. Four nights, with three days of fishing, runs $1,525.

Shelter Cove Lodge, ☎ 826-2941 or 888-826-FISH, www.sheltercovelodge.com, fishes off pretty nice boats. Their lodge is also a bit more swank than Clover Bay. Rates start at $2,060 for a four night/three day package. Comparable is the **Sunnahae Lodge**, ☎ 826-4000: nice boats, nice location, more fish than you'll believe. Packages start at $1,795 for three days. ☎ 888-826-8500.

Southeast

Alaska Best Fishing has three day/two night saltwater packages from $1,150; freshwater is only $900. If you haven't got so much time, **Lemire Charters**, ☎ 826-3007, runs two-night packages out of Klawock starting at $1,045.

If you can afford it, these resorts offer a great way to spend a few days; you'll probably never again have a chance to be so pampered while so far out in the boonies.

WATCHABLE

Any one of these resorts can also point you to great whale-watching waters. Humpbacks and orcas are common in the area.

WILDLIFE

■ Camping

If you want to try Prince of Wales on your own, choose a road and head out. It's that simple. The island is a patchwork of clear-cut and thick forested areas, with 2,000 to 3,000-foot mountains punctuating the land. You can set up camp nearly anywhere, but keep away from the villages as they are privately run by the Native corporation as part of the Alaska Native Claims Settlement Act. Also keep an eye out for "Private Property" signs. But the majority of the island is national forest, and that means you own it and you can camp there.

CAUTION

Remember to boil all water before drinking it and be sure to take all proper bear precautions. This is wild territory.

Trout (found in most of the streams and lakes) make a good dinner, or you can try casting for salmon from the shore. Red snapper and halibut also abound.

There are quite a few organized RV campgrounds, but don't feel restricted to them. There are only two public campgrounds. Again, there's no reason to stick to the beaten path. The **Eagle's Nest Campground** has 11 sites off State Highway 30, about 18 miles west of Thorne Bay. Fee for camping is $25 per night, and there is potable water available. Pack out all garbage. A boardwalk trail leaves the campground and parallels Ball's Lake, which has good fishing for cutthroat trout. Watch for bears.

Lake Number Three Campground has only two spaces, on FD Road 2030-790, about 20 minutes from Thorne Bay. This area was clear-cut in the 1980s and is not as scenic as the other campground, but it does offer a good close-up view of how the forest grows back. Another 300 years or so and it will all be good as new.

The **Staney Bridge Campground** also has only two sites and it, too, is situated in a clear-cut area. There's no water here. Staney Bridge is six miles south of the intersection of FDR 20 and FDR 2054, or about 90 minutes from Thorne Bay. Two more sites are at Horseshoe Hole, a quarter-mile away. In Craig you can camp in the **city park** on Graveyard Island.

Metlakatla

In the first three editions of this book, we described Metlakatla as a village that actively discourages tourism. But things change. Faced with few economic prospects – the lumber mill and fish cannery are dying – the town decided to open itself up. Then it kind of changed its mind. They decided to open up only to cruise ships, that they could get rid of in a couple hours.

While not all the locals are entirely happy about any this, enough agree with it to ensure that things are going to be changing rapidly over the next few years. What you find if you go now is a sleepy little village with eight churches and no bars, and a local culture that is trying to either find or redefine itself after a hundred-year brush with history and a missionary known as Father Duncan. It's an interesting town to see right now, but be prepared before you go: depending on who you meet, you could get anything from a warm welcome to the bum's rush.

■ History

Metlakatla is properly known as New Metlakatla. Old Metlakatla is in Canada, near Prince Rupert. Old Metlakatla was held together by the **Reverend William Duncan**, who was such a successful missionary that a bishop was sent in to help him with his ever-growing congregation. Duncan had converted more than a thousand people, and his church in Metlakatla was the largest in the West. However, he didn't take well to supervision – actually, the man was more than a little bit of a control freak – and so he and a band of followers split off and founded New Metlakatla on Annette Island.

It wasn't really quite this easy, of course. First Father Duncan sent out people to find an island that matched his requirements. Then, once Annette Island had been settled upon, he had to get permission, not only from the Canadian government to pack up and move so many people, but from the U.S. government to get hold of the island. He was not a man to be dissuaded. In 1887, 883 people packed up and headed north with Father Duncan; most of them traveled by canoe, but they also had a small ship with them, the *Glad Tidings*.

The village was designed in its entirety by Father Duncan. Everybody got a corner lot, all the original lots had water views, and the church and school were the center of everything. As an example of the level of control

Father Duncan maintained over the town, the school was a boarding school. Never mind that the kids lived, at most, a few blocks away. They were allowed home only on weekends.

Although his parishioners were Tsimshian, Father Duncan, like missionaries everywhere, wasn't that interested in the Native culture. It was quickly banned in any manifestation, and this led to several attempts on his life by those who had not yet seen his particular light.

Father Duncan's spirit remains. It's impossible to have a conversation with someone in town without his name coming up – maybe you'll hear about the troubles he had with Sheldon Jackson, his contemporary who was founding schools in Sitka, or maybe you'll simply hear his name mentioned when you notice that the town is still growing according to his original blueprints. He's been dead a long time, but you'd never guess it after spending a day in Metlakatla. The town is still attempting to shake off his presence, to reassert the Tsimshian identity. The longhouse, the revival of totem carving, the language being taught in the schools, all go against what Father Duncan was about.

There was a brief time in Metlakatla's history when more was going on. At the time of the first ferry run, back in the early '60s, Annette Island was supposed to be the new happening place in Alaska. It had one of the best airports in the state, capable of landing jets, and it had Tamgas Harbor, a huge natural harbor that could accommodate the largest ships. What it didn't have was a work force, and the villagers weren't as thrilled with plans for expansion as the entrepreneurs were. The airport is still there, doing nothing but growing weeds. The Coast Guard base has pulled out, and what's left is a very conservative village looking to preserve the best of its Tsimshian heritage and religious past.

Tourist facilities are very limited here (although beginning to grow) and the villagers have nightmares of being overrun and losing what they love about the town. However, at the same time, they're also building a road that will stretch to the far side of the island. Upon its completion, a ferry service will be inaugurated that will run to Saxman, giving easy access to town. The road will be a scenic abomination, completely ruining the lovely views of the waterfall that was one of the main reasons Father Duncan chose the spot for his village, but it will mean locals can go to the movies for less than $100 – roughly the cost of a round-trip plane fare to Ketchikan, plus a meal.

The locals refused the terms of the Alaska Native Claims Settlement Act, and so continue to live in what is the only Indian reservation in Alaska. Their special status allows them continued use of fish traps, illegal everywhere else in the U.S. Their logging activities – following the usual Native disregard of even the appalling standards of clear-cut the Forest Service allows – can be seen on the mountain opposite the town. The reservation factor also means that Metlakatla is the only spot in Alaska that's eligible to have a casino. So far, the religious base of the town has voted one down at every opportunity.

It's a weird place. By law, you're not really allowed to be there for more than 24 hours, but you can stay at a hotel. It's a heavily isolationist community, but they're bringing cruise ships in as often as they can – flash the cultural program, feed them some salmon, and get them back out of town. It's hard to say what's going to happen next here.

■ Basics

 You can get to Metlakatla by **AMH**, but watch the connections. The ideal day to go is Saturday (check the schedule), when there are two ships, so you can arrive in the morning and catch the evening ship back to Ketchikan. You can also fly into Metlakatla from Ketchikan with **Taquan Air**. The daily flight takes about 15 minutes. ☎ 225-9668.

You can get in touch with the **Metlakatla Tourism Office** – very nice people – at ☎ 877-886-8687, or www.tours.metlakatla.net.

METLAKATLA AT A GLANCE

QUICK TOUR: It's all you're allowed. Look around and get your can off their island.

DON'T MISS: Father Duncan's cottage. They don't make preachers like this anymore.

BEST FREEBIE: Observe the many effects of xenophobia, religion, and the desperate need for a local economy. Metlakatla is a sociology experiment that's still going on.

■ Museums & Attractions

 There are only a few sites of interest. It's the town itself that's most interesting for the glimpse it gives of the lifestyle in these parts.

FATHER DUNCAN'S COTTAGE: For something to do, tour Father Duncan's Cottage, which has been nicely restored as a museum, showing things the way they were when the good Father was still alive. It displays photos of Old and New Metlakatla, and the second phonograph Edison ever made is inside, despite frequent bids from the Smithsonian to get hold of it. It's fun to see how wide the Father's interests were – he started a local band, studied the science of opthamology, acted as the local doctor

Southeast

and schoolteacher, and was constantly investigating territorial and federal laws, searching for means of keeping his village safe. Father Duncan is buried behind the **Father Duncan Memorial Church**, at 4th Ave. and Church St. The church is a copy of the original, which burned. Only the original pulpit was saved and is ensconced in the new structure. It's quite a lovely piece of work, with inlays of light and dark wood. ☎ 886-4441 for more information.

BOAT HARBOR & LONGHOUSE: At the boat harbor is a tribal house. There is a similar one in Old Metlakatla, as both villages are trying to stimulate a resurgence of traditional arts. It'll probably be open Monday-Friday, 1-4:30 PM. Even if it's closed, it's worth stopping by to take a look at the **mural** on the water side. The mural depicts the four clans – eagle, raven, killer whale, and wolf – coming together in harmony in Metlakatla. This is very unusual, as most artists depict only their own clans. In front of the tribal house are a couple of newly erected **totem poles**, locally carved.

For cruise ship passengers – excursions are being sold from Ketchikan – there is a **salmon bake** held in the tribal house. If you roll up, and if they have room, you can tag along for $27. And if the cruise ship is in and the tribal house is open, check next door at the **Artist Village**. Good local art.

■ Adventures

Hiking

You can get a nice overview of the town by hiking up **Yellow Hill**, visible directly to the east. The hill is about a mile and a half from the town center, and it's a 30-minute hike to the top. For a longer hike, head out the airport road to Purple Mountain Road (about 2.7 miles), where you can hit the **Purple Lake Trail**, a steep 1.8-mile hike up to the lake.

Metlakatla is small enough that you can walk anywhere, and addresses are pretty much useless. Wherever you are, you're not more than five minutes from where you want to be.

■ Food

For food, try the **Leask's grocery store**. There's also a small café in the **Metlakatla Hotel**, along with **Cindy's Seafood & Coffee** on the west end of Western Ave. If they're open, head to the **Chester Bay Café** for pizza or **Uncle Fred's Café**, for specials.

■ Accommodations

Stay in the very small **Metlakatla Hotel**, ☎ 886-3458, where doubles start at $95. There's also the **Tuck 'em Inn**, ☎ 886-6611, with rooms from $65 a night; an extra 10 bucks also gets you dinner.

Camping on the island is discouraged. You can check at the mayor's office in the municipal building (☎ 886-4868) to see if any B&Bs have opened.

Wrangell

I f you want the real Alaska, the best of Alaska, this is the place to come. While the larger towns in Southeast have been developed and try hard to turn a pretty face to the outside world, Wrangell is a working town that just happens to be an incredibly fun place to visit. It's got all the comfort of the bigger towns, none of the tourist traps, and it's close to amazing wilderness. It's friendly, it's relaxed, and it's beautiful, offering long walks in the forest, some of the best bear-viewing in the state, and easy access to the last great undammed river on the continent. Unless you show up for the town's fourth of July bash, you won't see anything that even resembles a crowd.

This is what Alaska is like after the tourists go home; places like Wrangell are why people move to the state to begin with. If this is your idea of a good time, there's no way you'll ever want to leave Wrangell. The town calls itself "Alaska's Hidden Jewel," and they're not kidding.

■ History

You won't be the first to think this is a great spot. Wrangell has among the oldest records of habitation in Southeast. Petroglyphs, only a mile or so from the ferry terminal, have been dated to be more than 8,000 years old.

Despite the long factual history, legend gives Wrangell only about a thousand years of settlement, when Tlingit Indians migrated down the Stikine River to Wrangell Island. European settlement dates to around 1834, when there was a town known as Redoubt St. Dionysius on the site of what's now the city of Wrangell.

Vancouver was the first of the English captains to come this way. Somehow, he missed the Stikine River. It's huge, it pours tons of silt into the ocean, and a blind man could see the effects of the river. But he was not in the best of moods by this point in his trip, and he just sailed right by.

Southeast

Vancouver did make a note of an encounter with the locals, though, surprised by the sudden appearance of 20 canoes from behind a small low projecting point of land that seemed to contain not less than 250 Indians.

> *Our party immediately put themselves on the defensive, and made signs to the Indians to keep off; to this they paid no attention, and Mr. Johnstone... ordered a musket to be fired over them; but this having no effect, a swivel gun loaded with grape shot, was fired, sufficiently ahead of them to avoid doing harm, but near enough to shew its effect.*

Still the Tlingit did not retreat, so Vancouver's men got out of there: "A light breeze springing up, favorable to the boats, they kept sail all night."

Wrangell Island is rather unusual in the history of Alaska: it's one of the very few places that was ever under British control. In 1834, the same year as the founding of the original town, the British and the Russians fought a battle over rights to the Stikine River, which was not only rich in natural resources and was a trading mecca, but also cut into the heartland of British territory in Canada. The British ended up leasing Wrangell from the Russians – who thought it was pretty much played out when it came to furry things to kill anyway – for the steep price of 2,000 land otter skins per year.

By 1840, the British had firm possession of Wrangell Island, leaving the Russians with their vast territories to the north. At this time of dual control, Redoubt St. Dionysius was given the rather more wieldy name of Fort Stikine. Even more unusual, there are records of the natives making an impassioned case for their traditional rights to the land. Usually such episodes are lost to history, but Chief Shakes actually won the battle for the rights to the Stikine. There is still a Chief Shakes in Wrangell – Shakes is a hereditary title/name.

The balance of power among the Natives, the British, and the Russians held until the 1867 sale of Alaska, surviving even the influx of miners when gold was found on the Stikine River in 1861. The gold petered out quickly, though, and under the new United States government – or lack thereof, since the U.S. showed virtually no interest in its new toy for many years – Wrangell flourished until 1884.

A cannery was built in the 1880s and it was quickly followed by a lumber mill. The 1890s brought the gold miners back when they attempted to use the Stikine as a quick way up to the Yukon. One of the men who passed through on the way to the Klondike was Wyatt Earp, fresh from the shootout at the OK Corral. Wyatt had just gotten married, and he was looking for a quick way to make money. He landed in Wrangell, and the town offered him the job of sheriff. He looked around, and said that the town was "hell on wheels, filled with con men, gun men, prostitutes, ne'er do wells, and gamblers, all of whom had come to make their fortunes by taking advantage of prospectors straight from the gold fields." He turned the job down and fled north.

WITCHES OF WRANGELL

There was a year or so of ugliness around 1878, when the Wrangell Indians went on a witch-hunting spree. A suspected witch was stripped, then her hands, feet, and head were all tied back into a single knot behind her back. Until she confessed, she was fed only saltwater, beaten with devil's club, dragged over the rocky beaches, had spruce needles jammed into her skin and was set afire. The witch hysteria died out as quickly as it had started and the residents went back to being prosperous.

John Muir was also a frequent visitor to Wrangell and used the town as his base for exploring Southeast by canoe in 1879 and 1880. Muir visited the Stikine River and Telegraph Creek, and wrote about the local Indians. His journeys are chronicled in his book, Travels in Alaska.

The hill right in the center of town, now called Mt. Dewey, was once called Muir Mountain. The story, as Muir tells it, is that a storm was brewing, and he wanted to get somewhere where he could see the full force of it, to hear the language of nature." He climbed the hill, and proceeded to build a campfire in the pouring rain. Yeah, okay. Sure. But he goes on, saying that he had flames leaping from his fire, 30 to 40 feet high:

> Soon I had light enough to enable me to select the best dead branches and large sections of bark, which were set on end, gradually increasing the height and corresponding light of the hut fire. A considerable area was thus well lighted, from which I gathered abundance of wood, and kept adding to the fire until it had a strong, hot heart and sent up a pillar of flame thirty or forty feet high, illuminating a wide circle in spite of the rain, and casting a red glare into the flying clouds.

This glare caused a little problem: the light in the clouds made a great show, a portentous sign in the stormy heavens unlike anything ever before seen or heard of in Wrangell. Some wakeful Indians, happening to see it about midnight, in great alarm aroused the Collector of Customs and begged him to go to the missionaries and get them to pray away the "frightful omen."

Southeast

John Muir: founder of the Sierra Club, closet pyromaniac.

■ Wrangell Today

Wrangell now supports about 2,000 people, most of whom work in the fishing or logging industry. This balance is rapidly changing toward tourism, with the 1995 closing of the sawmill (it's open now on a limited basis) and the decline of fishing activity. Only a few years ago Wrangell was a quiet place in a very scenic setting and, unlike most large towns in Southeast, the townsfolk didn't really care if you came or not. Now, with the collapse of its economic base, Wrangell is trying to draw visitors, with many of those who once worked at the mill turning to charter operations. The town gets only two cruise ships a week, both of them very small. Wrangell recognizes that it's a lot better off trying to draw the independent traveler as opposed to working the cruise ship market. So, while there are a few more tourist shops appearing, the town still feels real.

It's a little slice of heaven. How can you not love a town off in the middle of the rainforest where there's still enough loopy optimism that most of the houses have sun porches?

■ Basics

i Wrangell is served five times a week by the Alaska Marine Highway. The ferry terminal is conveniently located near downtown, and a two-hour stopover is enough to see most of the town's major attractions, but not nearly enough time to have any fun. The local telephone number for the **AMH** is ☎ 874-3901. Check your back-on-board time carefully; more people get left at Wrangell than any other stop. It's really just a sign that they should have planned to stay, though.

Alaska Airlines makes daily stops in town, connecting it to Southeast, Seattle, and Anchorage. ☎ 800-426-0333. For charter plane service, contact **Sunrise Aviation**, ☎ 874-2319.

There is a **tourist information office** by the cruise ship dock, south of the ferry terminal, in the Stikine Inn. They've got the helpful staff and array of brochures that one comes to expect in Alaska. There are also a few pamphlets and a copy of Wrangell's tourist newspaper available at the ferry terminal. ☎ 367-9745, or 800-FOR-WRGL. It's open 9-4 daily. Wrangell also has a great website: www.wrangell.com. An e-mail sent here will connect you with most of the outfitters on the island.

The **Forest Service** office is at 525 Bennett St., ☎ 874-2323. They sell a Wrangell Island Road Guide that's well worth buying if you're going to check out any of the back roads away from town. Get information here on

Anan Bear Observatory, too (see below). You can also make local Forest Service cabin reservations here, if you didn't do it through the on-line service (www.reservcusa.com). They've got an expanding program of informative walks and hikes; check in to see what's on the schedule.

Star Cab, ☎ 874-3622, and **Porky's Cab**, ☎ 874-3603, run the town's taxi services.

You can rent a car from **Practical**, at the Wrangell Airport. ☎ 874-3975.

Rent a bike from **Rain Walker Expeditions**, in the booth on City Dock.

Internet access is available at the **public library**, behind the post office.

Zip code: **99929**.

WRANGELL AT A GLANCE

QUICK TOUR: Head out to Chief Shakes' Island, one of the most authentic feeling tribal houses left. You'll take in the entire downtown on your way; if you've still got a few minutes, head to the museum, which has the oldest house posts left in Alaska.

DON'T MISS: Take a ride on the Stikine. Best is to spend a week or so rafting it; if you can't do that, a day-trip shows you the lower river; golf. Really. Just because you can; from July through early September, go to Anan. Brown and black bears, stream stuffed full of salmon. What more could you want?

BEST FREEBIE: You've got two choices in Wrangell: go through town to Chief Shakes' Island, check out the totem poles, and watch the boats come and go; turn the other direction, you've got Petroglyph Beach, and hints of something older. Wrangell is also the best place to see how Alaska's dogs are in charge: hang out downtown and watch the dogs driving their trucks.

■ Museums & Attractions

PETROGLYPHS: At low tide, visit Wrangell's petroglyphs. Check the tide tables; at high tide a lot of the glyphs are underwater. From the ferry terminal, turn left and follow the road for about a half-mile. Signs mark the turn for the beach. From the overlook (which has replica petroglyphs), most of the petroglyphs are to the right. Among the 47 known glyphs – there's always a chance a few more will get found – there's a spawning salmon, a killer whale, and a few glyphs that look more like doodles than anything else. This is the largest concentration of petroglyphs in Southeast Alaska.

There are two cultures represented in the petroglyphs, the Tlingit, and something older and not clearly identified – the Tlingit culture was entirely oral in its record keeping, and there are no stories of who might have been here before them. If you look at the position of the beach, you can see how it was probably a watch station, as there are views a long way down both directions of Zimovia Strait from here. Indeed, the petroglyphs may be nothing more than the scratchings of a bored sentry.

In the past, visitors were allowed to make rubbings of the petroglyphs, but that is now technically forbidden. Too many people were careless in their methods and the petroglyphs started to degrade (5,000 years of tide and wave didn't do as much damage as 10 years of tourism). So when the state took the beach over, and put up the new overlook, they also put in some replica stones. You're quite free to make rubbings of these, or you can save the time and buy a rubbing in town.

Do not try to walk back to the ferry terminal along the beach. You will not make it. Also keep in mind that on the average ferry stop, you really don't have time to get out here and back. To be safe, you've got to figure on an hour for the round-trip – 15 minutes each way, there and back, and a half-hour of looking.

WATCHABLE *In August, petroglyph beach and also the area around the ferry terminal are good places to see great blue herons. The birds, which can grow to a couple of feet tall, are pretty common in the area,* **WILDLIFE** *hanging out on the beach and fishing. Petroglyph beach also frequently has harbor porpoise nearby.*

WRANGELL MUSEUM: The museum is in the Community Center on Church St., about a five-minute walk from downtown (a bit more than half a mile from the ferry terminal). ☎ 874-3770. It's open daily and admission is $2. The museum houses a pretty good collection of Tlingit artifacts and items of local history as well as a few petroglyphs for those who didn't make it out to the beach. It's worth coming into the museum to see the house posts from Chief Shakes' house, the oldest extant house posts in Alaska.

WRANGELL TOTEM PARK: Properly known as Kik-Setti, the park is a collection of a half-dozen replica poles on Front Street, about a 10-minute walk from the museum or the ferry terminal. Note how these poles, with considerably more elaborate carving, differ from those in Ketchikan.

CHIEF SHAKES ISLAND: There are more poles on Chief Shakes Island. Follow Front St. until it forks, then take the right fork toward the boat harbor. It's about five minutes from Totem Park.

AUTHOR TIP

Don't bother coming out here on anything less than a one-hour ferry stopover, just to make sure you have enough time to get here, enjoy it, and get back.

Chief Shakes was one of the few natives to win an argument against colonial powers in Alaska. However, he wasn't the only Chief Shakes: the title has been passed on and exists even today (depending on who you talk to).

On the island, there is a replica Clan House, which contains some interesting historical photographs and tribal artifacts. The house is open when the cruise ships are in, or by appointment (ask at the museum). There's a $2 admission fee if you can find anybody to let you in.

There are also some very nice poles on the island. Take a look at the Bear Up the Tree Pole, only carved with paw prints along its long sides and topped by a crouching bear.

A small boat harbor in Wrangell.

Right by the entrance to the tribal house is the grave of the son of one of the Chief Shakes. He was killed, and as the chief himself had just converted to Christianity, the whole town watched to see what would happen. Traditionally, the chief should have gone out for blood. But instead, he let the law take its course and didn't enter into the fray himself.

Of all the tribal houses you'll find in Southeast, this one has one of the most authentic feels to it; sitting alone on the small island, the poles surrounding it, the modern trappings of town seem to drop away. If you've got time, it's a good place to just sit and watch the world go by for a while. This spot has been the center of the Tlingit's cultural life for a long time; look across the island to the Marine Bar, which is where the Russians and British had their trading posts, and you can imagine the uneasy relationship that must have existed.

Southeast

The most famous of the Chief Shakes is buried just across the channel from the island. Go back to Front St. and take the left fork, which becomes Case Ave. The grave is behind a white fence, two minutes along the walkway. There's not much to see, but the fence itself is interesting historically: traditional Russian graves were surrounded by white fences, and the funeral style was widely copied by Native groups in Southeast.

The **Our Collections Museum**, a quarter-mile from the ferry terminal along the road to Petroglyph Beach (look for the old truck with plants growing out of it) is a little difficult to describe. It's a private museum, open by appointment (☎ 874-3646), and usually when the ferry is in. Think of someone who has lived in Alaska for 70 years and never threw anything away. Instead, it all goes on display. There is a century's worth of irons, PVC pipe chewed by animals, and pretty much anything else you can imagine. It's probably the most honest look at what it takes to live up here you're going to find. Reactions to the museum are really love/hate; nobody's indifferent to it, though.

■ Town/Naturalist Tours

For something to do around town, contact **Rain Walker Expeditions**, ☎ 874-2549. They have guided town tours, which include Shakes Island and the Tribal House, for $22. They also run guided hikes on some of the trails around town. Marie is a trained naturalist, and she'll show you details of the forest that you'd never notice on your own. Definitely worth a morning of your time.

■ Garnets

Wrangell has one thing that you won't find anywhere else in Southeast: a major garnet deposit. Located right near the mouth of the Stikine, the garnets were first collected by the Alaska Garnet and Manufacturing Company, which, according to *Roadside Geology of Alaska*, was the first corporation in the world composed entirely of women. The garnet mine was deeded to the children of Wrangell in 1962, and the local kids meet every ferry they can, selling the semi-precious stones.

Some are polished, some are still in the rough stone matrix (because it's really a hassle to get them out). These are deep purple garnets, not those wishy-washy green stones that you usually see. You can get a small stone for a couple of dollars, quite a big one for under 10 bucks. It is possible to go to the mine yourself, but the garnet ledge has been hit heavily over the past few years, and until somebody goes in with some fairly heavy equipment, you're not going to find a lot.

Southeast
Wrangell to Skagway

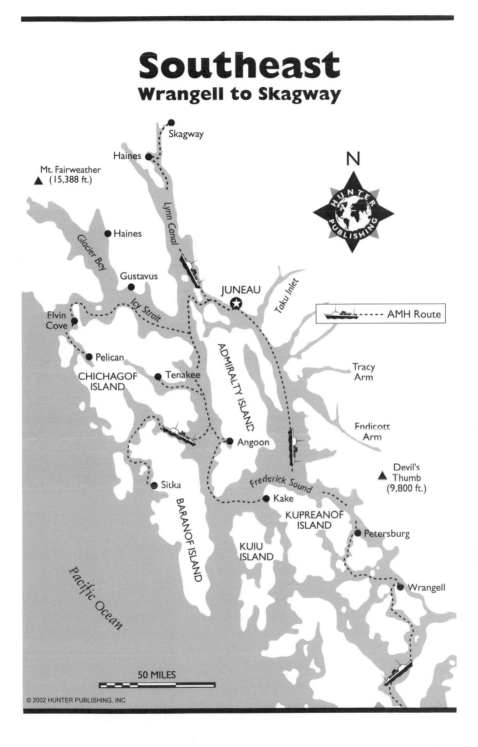

Skagway

Haines

Mt. Fairweather
▲ (15,388 ft.)

N

HUNTER PUBLISHING

Haines

Glacier Bay

Gustavus

JUNEAU ☆

Lynn Canal

Taku Inlet

Icy Strait

Elvin Cove

Pelican

CHICHAGOF ISLAND

Tenakee

ADMIRALTY ISLAND

Tracy Arm

━ ━ ━ ━ AMH Route

Endicott Arm

Angoon

Devil's Thumb
(9,800 ft.) ▲

Sitka

BARANOF ISLAND

Frederick Sound

Kake

KUPREANOF ISLAND

KUIU ISLAND

Petersburg

Pacific Ocean

Wrangell

50 MILES

© 2002 HUNTER PUBLISHING, INC

Southeast

You've also got to charter a boat to get to it, which will run you at least $100 (although a lot of Stikine day-trips stop at the ledge). Finally, you'll need a permit – check for that with the visitor's bureau, or ask your boat captain.

AUTHOR TIP

If you decide you want a stone after you've left town, call the visitor center; they maintain a list of children who'll sell via mail.

■ Adventures

Although there may not be a whole lot to do in town, Wrangell is still one of the nicest, most enjoyable towns to just hang out in anywhere in Southeast Alaska. It's where we lived while we wrote this book, and think about it – we've been everywhere, and this is where we chose to stay.

That said, one of the best things about Wrangell is that you can get out of it so easily. While being a very comfortable town to stay in, it's really in the middle of the deep wild. It's near the Anan Bear Observatory, and it's the closest community to the Stikine, the fastest free-flowing river and part of the largest undammed river cachement left on the continent. Although you'll also find operators for the river working out of Petersburg, they're coming in from a ways off. For people in Wrangell, the river is their backyard, and everybody with a boat goes there every chance they get.

Why do people live in Wrangell? Because everything around the town is one big playground for adults. The town makes it easy in summer to stop and talk to the outfitters: there are three offices next to City Dock that pretty much give you the run of the town. **Alaska Waters** has their office inside the Stikine Inn; **Alaska Adventure Reservations**, a co-op of four outfitters, has a small shack across the street; **Alaska Vistas** has a larger shack next door – and a java machine inside.

One caveat: most outfitters have minimums on trips. If you're traveling by yourself or with only one companion, you're better off looking for a trip to ride along on than trying to create one yourself. Taking out only two people doesn't even pay for the outfitter's gas.

Golf

From the sublime to the slightly ridiculous: Wrangell has a golf course, Muskeg Meadows. The town was given an enormous grant to build this – for reasons that must make sense only to some drunken government flunky. The community really came together to build the course – on "work party" days, there would be 30 or 40 people out working on it.

And it paid off. Now the course is up and operational, and it's a lot more impressive than you might think. It's even USGA approved, with a blue rating, if this means anything to you, of 70.2/119. The grass still hasn't all set in, and you putt on astroturf, but it's only $15 to play a round (club rental another $10). During summer, there are tournaments nearly every weekend, and it's not at all unusual to see boats coming in from Petersburg, full of golfers. The town has so taken to golf that Angerman's, the sporting goods store, has given over an entire aisle to golf toys.

If you don't golf, the course is also a great spot just to go for a walk. There are nice views, and always a chance of seeing moose or bear. The course is a half-mile out past the Forest Service office.

Kayaking

Most people planning to kayak near Wrangell are headed for the Stikine (see page 196). The area right around town is okay for day paddles, but if you head out north, going into the channel beyond the airport, you can easily get stuck in very, very nasty tide rips. It can get hairy out there. Rent kayaks from Alaska Vistas or Rain Walker Expeditions. Both have offices at City Dock.

Kayakers at LeConte Glacier.

Alaska Vistas (☎ 874-3006) also runs guided trips in the Wrangell area. A day-trip to Aaron Creek, on the back side of the island, is $190 per person, as is a day in Knig Slough, off the Stikine River. Their longer six-day trips are bargains. For $1,300, you can get a guided trip, paddling from Shakes Glacier to LeConte Glacier; a trip from Shakes Glacier back down to town, enjoying the lower reaches of the Stikine; or a paddle from Wrangell to Anan, where you can watch bears. They've also got trips to the nearby South Etolin Wilderness. Any of these outings would make your whole trip. Check them out on-line at www.alaskavistas.com.

Hiking

Although the town itself is tiny, Wrangell Island has a fair network of roads and a lot of trails. Walk in the footsteps of John Muir's pyromania days by climbing Mt. Dewey to see the campfire site. The trail is just above downtown – signs everywhere point to it – and it takes only 10 minutes or so to get to the top, where there are good views of the town and the strait. The sign at the trailhead says it's a strenuous hike, but that's only because the Forest Service "improvements" have fallen into disrepair and become harder to deal with than the trail.

There's a loop trail that starts behind the Elementary School, near the intersection of Church St. and the Zimovia Highway. The loop is 1½ miles, and leads through the woods and past patches of muskeg. At Halloween, this trail gets decorated like a haunted house.

> 📖 Head to the Forest Service office for a map – most of these roads were put in to take trees out, and the Forest Service is the one who put them there. Get a copy of *Wrangell Island Road Guide*. The map includes helpful topo features and it shows the location of Forest Service cabins on the island and across the Eastern Passage. The Forest Service also has a good brochure, *Hiking Trails and Recreation Facilities*.

Head south of town to **Pat's Lake**, a lovely little spot with excellent berry picking in season. Four miles past Pat's Lake is **Thom's Lake**. The area around the lake has quite a few hiking trails and is a popular spot for picnicking locals.

Another good hike is the **Rainbow Falls Trail**, starting at Mile 4.6 on the Zimovia Highway, across from the harbor. It's a .8-miles, one-way hike through the rainforest, on a largely boardwalked path. If you're just getting warmed up at the top of the trail, you can branch off onto the **Institute Creek Trail**, which follows the ridge line to **Shoemaker Overlook**, in a high alpine meadow. The views up here on a clear day are wonderful. If you're looking for a hike that allows you to explore a little of the rainforest, this is a nice one. If you've rented a bike in town (check at

Rain Walker Expeditions, in the booth on City Dock), this is a nice ride out, with a bike trail most of the way. Park the bike at the harbor, and go for a hike. A very good way to see some of the town and a really beautiful trail.

If you're really ambitious, once you get to the top of the Institute Creek Trail, you can link up with another trail that brings you back down the mountain the long way – it's about eight miles, and you need to allow two days to do it. At the **Nemo Campsites**, there are some really nice trails. Try the **Three Sisters Viewpoint Trail**, a quick and easy loop, and the **Anita Bay Overlook**.

Salamander Ridge Trail is south of town 27 miles, via Forest Roads 6265 and 50050. It's a mile-long trail up to a subalpine meadow with great views. Across the Strait from Wrangell, on Etolin Island, there's the **Kunk Lake Trail**, 1.3 miles, which leads to the lake shelter that offers a skiff and paddles you can use. The trail is partially boardwalked, and it makes a nice getaway from town.

LeConte Glacier

In addition to the Stikine River and the Anan Bear Observatory (see below), Wrangell is close to the LeConte Glacier. It's more common to go to the glacier from Petersburg, but it's not all that far from Wrangell, either. **Sunrise Aviation**, ☎ 874-2319, runs flightseeing trips to LeConte Glacier and the Stikine River Delta. Their shortest trip costs $100. For that you get an hour flyby of the Stikine Icefield, including great views of LeConte, Shakes, Great, and Flood Glaciers. They'll also take you up to Endicott Arm or to Anan; prices vary depending on the plane type and number of people.

To get closer to the glaciers, call **Breakaway Adventures** (☎ 888-385-2488 or 874-2488, www.breakawayadventures.com; you can also ask at the Alaska Adventure Reservations shack, or in the River's Edge gallery). For $135 (another 20 bucks if you want to stop in Petersburg), they'll take you up to LeConte Glacier. The channel in to the glacier is usually choked with icebergs and bergy bits, but the boat Breakaway uses – the nicest jetboat in Wrangell – can handle it, and get you right up to the face. Watch for harbor seals on the ice floes, and killer whales in the mouth of the inlet. LeConte, part of the huge Stikine Icefield, is the southernmost tidewater glacier in North America, and it's melting fast, so you're almost guaranteed to see calving, huge chunks of ice falling off the glacial face, when you're there. It's one of the better glacial shows in Southeast.

■ The Stikine River

 If you want to be alone in the most beautiful countryside you can imagine, the Stikine (stik-EEN) River is for you. John Muir called it "a Yosemite 100 miles long," and we're convinced the only reason he didn't rave more was that he didn't have time to go any farther upriver. The farther you go, the better it gets.

The Stikine River – the name comes from the Tlingit for "Great River" – is about 400 miles long, starting deep in British Columbia. Fed by literally dozens of glaciers, the water in the river is a murky silver, laden with silt. Enormous runs of salmon return to the river each year.

The watershed of the Stikine is one of the largest on the continent, and it is the largest (over 20,000 square miles) that is un-dammed. It's also the fastest navigable river on the continent, flowing upwards of five knots. At its widest, the river's a bit less than a mile across, but most places are considerably more narrow, perhaps averaging a hundred yards or so from bank to bank.

The Stikine was supposed to be the original route to the gold fields of the Yukon – it took would-be miners from the coast to the interior faster than any other means, and it didn't have any of the nasty mountains or glacier crossings that other routes did. The big problem was getting from Telegraph Creek up to Teslin Lake, where you could load gear onto a boat and head north. The *Klondike News*, on April 1, 1898, wrote, "The portage of 150 miles from Telegraph Creek to Teslin Lake is one that the traveler will never forget, even though made over a wagon road, and we would advise our friends to wait until the long-talked-of railroad is completed and go over this route by Pullman Car." Of course, if you had waited, you'd still be waiting. Although hundreds of miners tried this route in the first years of the rush, not many made it. The miners traveled in winter, and the first thing that got them was the fairly constant 60mph headwind that howls down off the glaciers all winter long. Gold is worth only so much.

Telegraph Creek, the only real community on the river (three streets, one shop, one church – although there is a little more town up the hill), is connected to the interior of British Columbia by road (see our *Adventure Guide to the Alaska Highway* for information on getting to or away from Telegraph by road). Not much that was ever supposed to happen at Telegraph ever did. The town was founded to support the telegraph line – it was easily accessible by river, a nightmare to reach by land – and it was, at one time, going to be the next big boomtown. Never happened.

If all you want to do is see Telegraph Creek, **Breakaway Adventures**, ☎ 874-2488, **Alaska Vistas**, ☎ 874-3006, and **Alaska Waters**, ☎ 874-2378, all run charter trips, and can help put together a package with lodging, etc. Figure you'll need three days: one up, one down, one there. Prices start around $700 per person, depending on the boat and what you need, as well as how long and how many people are going. Alaska Waters also has late-season trips that include lodging, starting at $725 for three days/two nights.

Traveling on the Stikine

 DON'T MISS: You have quite a few options for getting onto the river from Wrangell. Our choice, and our choice for the single best thing you can do along the entire coast of Alaska, is to raft the Stikine, from Telegraph down, with **Alaska Vistas**. They are the only outfitters to regularly run raft trips down the Stikine. For a paltry $2,500 – only a bit more than hiring a jetboat just to get you to Telegraph – you get first and last nights at a hotel in Wrangell, another night near Telegraph Creek, and six days traveling and camping on the river. Each evening is capped off with the best food you have ever eaten in your life. You travel in a self-bailing river raft, with plenty of time to get out and hike around, enjoy the scenery, and sit back and relax in camp. This is one of the best deals in the state, and the trip's river time will be some of the best days of your life. Contact them at ☎ 874-3006, or check out their website at www.alaskavistas.com. We have been lucky enough to experience a lot over the 10 years we've been writing these books. This is, quite simply, the best thing we've done in the North, and there's no way to recommend it highly enough.

You'll be happiest in life if you just plan on spending several days on the river. However, should that be impossible, you can still get a taste of it by taking a day-trip up from Wrangell. Alaska Vistas, Alaska Waters, ☎ 800-347-4462, and Breakaway Adventures, ☎ 874-2488, all offer six- to eight-hour jetboat trips up the Stikine from mid-April through mid-October, for around $150. All these trips take in the main channel, Shakes Glacier, and maybe or maybe not a stop at the hot springs. All three operators are good people who'll show you just how beautiful the river is. Breakaway Adventures also has twice-weekly four-hour trips on the river for only $65. This takes in the same scenery, but in a lot less detail. If it's all you have time for, or all you can afford, go for it; it's a great deal. But it will leave you wanting more. Phone or stop in at the Alaska Adventure Reservations shack or in the River's Edge gift shop for the schedule.

Kayaking the Stikine

Few travelers go up the river past Telegraph Creek. Right past the town is the Grand Canyon of the Stikine, an area with Class IV and V white-water (*Paddler* magazine calls it one of the great river runs in the world; *National Geographic* did the Canyon with the best paddlers in the world, helicopter support, and a huge budget, and they still almost didn't make it). Below the town, there's nothing more than Class II, and the very fast current (about five knots) that makes running the river a blast – all 150 miles down to the river's mouth by the Wrangell airport.

That's not to say the river is easy. There are snags, sweepers, logjams, and changing currents, meaning that you have to pay constant attention to what you're doing. The river braids and twists, and you could end up detoured way out on a slough. The water is cold, and hypothermia is a constant hazard. We've met a lot of people who went out here unprepared and ended up swimming; and most Wrangell jetboat captains who run the river regularly have more than a few rescue stories to tell. Go prepared, or don't go at all.

You can rent kayaks from **Alaska Vistas** (☎ 874-3006) or **Rain Walker Expeditions** (☎ 874-2549). Both also have offices on City Dock.

EXPERIENCING A JETBOAT RIDE

These small, ugly metal boats (a lot of them are actually made in Wrangell) have massive engines and no propellers. They move on the same principle as an octopus: suck water in, spit it back out very hard. This means that they can move very quickly in very shallow water – perhaps as little as eight inches. In the hands of someone who knows what they're doing, a jetboat is incredibly maneuverable. They turn on a dime and are remarkably smooth. A jetboat river trip is not something you'll forget quickly.

Traveling Safely on the Stikine

The main complication of traveling the river is that the channel is never the same twice. Huge amounts of silt are coming down the river, and the soft banks are cut away as the river digs new courses for itself. The lower reaches of the river, in particular, are heavily braided, with as many as 10 or 15 small channels reaching out. No chart can keep up with the river. In winter, storms howl through the Stikine valley, combining with deep freezes; you can pass acres of trees where the tops have been simply sheared off through a combination of freeze and breeze.

The lower reaches of the river are tidal, which can cause other problems. Plus, the water is really, really cold. Should you fall in, not only are you going to be dealing with the possibility of hypothermia, you've also got to worry about so much silt getting between the fibers of your clothes that it can drag you down before you have time to get hypothermia. The river requires attention and respect; it's not a simple float. There is no really fast water on the lower river. There are some riffles, rated as Class II, but nothing at all to worry about. You're not going to find yourself ripping down uncontrollable whitewater on the lower part of the river (up in the canyon above Telegraph is another matter entirely).

Because of the remoteness of the river and the very few people traveling on it above Shakes, you have to assume you're on your own when you head out. Be prepared for emergencies. There is enough jetboat traffic running between Wrangell and Telegraph that you can't go for more than a day or two without seeing a boat go by – unless you're in one braid and they're in another. However, even if a passing boat sees you, manners dictate that they just wave and keep on going. They're not going to stop unless you're signaling – they don't want to interrupt your wilderness experience. To the usual first aid kit and emergency equipment, add a good signalling device.

Know what you're doing. People go into the river, end up swimming (one woman was saved only when her bra strap caught on a tree branch and kept the current from dragging her under), and when they finally flag down a jetboat, their first words are "Never again." It's the most beautiful river you'll ever see, though, as long as you respect it and know what you're doing.

Camping

Camping on the Stikine is one of the great pleasures of life. There are plenty of wide beaches, sheltered by alder, pine, and spruce. Camp well above the water level – floods are generally seasonal, but anything is possible – and practice all bear safety precautions. Most beaches we've been on have bear signs. You can get your water out of the river, but either boil it and wait for the sediment to settle, or filter it. If you're going to filter, keep in mind what all the sediment is doing to your equipment.

 This is a wilderness area. Be responsible and make sure to practice no-trace camping at all times.

Preparing for the Stikine

Anybody can go on the river at any time, although there are a lot of times you wouldn't want to be out there. No permit is required. The prime season for running the Stikine is May-August. There are heavy spring floods before that, and in late summer the wind begins to howl up the river, making paddling downriver a bit of a nightmare. In winter, the entire thing freezes up.

If you are going to run the river on your own, the put-in point is Telegraph Creek. As mentioned above, you can get there by driving in from the Cassiar Highway, or you can hire a jetboat in Wrangell to take you up. You can also fly, but regulations make it impossible for you to fly your

Southeast

boat into Telegraph, unless you can collapse it and fit it inside the plane. Canada no longer allows boats strapped to the outsides of airplanes.

Alone, the trip will cost you between $1,000-1,500 to get a jetboat ride from Wrangell to Telegraph. The ride takes about eight hours. Any of the operators who run the river will book a boat for a Telegraph run.

 MONEY SAVER: *You are renting the entire boat, so if you can find someone to share the ride with, it'll be cheaper.*

It's about three to four days (six hours a day) in a canoe or a kayak to get downriver from Telegraph to the mouth of the Stikine. Obviously, the more you want to get out and explore, the longer it's going to take. For however long you plan to stay on the river, remember that you are on your own. You need to be entirely self-sufficient.

 AUTHOR TIP *Telegraph is your last chance to stock up on anything. There are only two stores and in both pickings are thin and expensive. Get what you need before you get to the river.*

NATIVE GLACIAL MYTHS

Native mythology has quite a story about the Great Glacier. It seems that, when they were first moving into the area, they found the river entirely blocked off by the glacier. There was, though, an opening in the glacial face through which water moved. They sent a couple of people up over the ice to see if the water came out anywhere, then sent a log through to see if it made the trip okay. Then they sent the most expendable member of the society, someone's grandmother. When she got through alive, everyone else decided it was okay for them to follow, and the journey continued.

Accommodations

There are two B&Bs on the river, one just below the Great Glacier, one on Farm Island. There's no real way to contact them in advance; if you're interested, just show up, and the odds are there will be a room available. There are also six Forest Service cabins on the river, plus another six on the delta, which are not quite as nice in the scenic department but still great places to stay.

Most people plan their pick-up around the Great Glacier. There is a developed picnic site here, and it's an easy place to tell your ride home where you'll be. There's an easy half-hour hike back to the glacier's pond, with great views of the glacial face and floating icebergs. If you fly over the area, you can see that the glacier once reached much farther ahead;

there are two concentric rings, moraines, that show how far up the glacier once moved.

Side Trips from the Stikine

A popular side trip on the river – where most of the jetboat traffic from Wrangell is headed – is to **Chief Shakes Hot Springs**, which is on a slough by the Ketili River. It's about two miles off the main channel, and at high water levels, paddling up to the spring is quite doable; if the water is running fast, particularly at the mouth of the slough, you can pretty easily line your boat up past the rapids. Once you hit the springs, you'll find the water is a toasty 122°. There's an indoor pool (reasonably safe from mosquitoes, but with no view) and an outdoor pool that overlooks a meadow. On summer weekends, most of the view is likely to be kids from Petersburg and Wrangell and their coolers full of beer.

There is another hot springs on the river, **Warm Springs**, across from the Great Glacier and just above the Choquette River, marked on many maps, but it has leeches.

> Before hitting the river on your own, pick up a copy of *Stikine River: A Guide to Paddling the Great River*, by Jennifer Voss. It has better coverage of the river above the Grand Canyon than it does below, but it's great for outlining preparations.

Stikine Conservation

The mere fact that the Stikine River is huge, remote, and fairly pristine means that there are a lot of people who want to *do* something to it. The additional fact that many of its tributary rivers are rich in coal, gold, and other goodies, means that the Stikine is facing serious threats. It's the last great undammed river on the continent, but that may not be true much longer.

The **Iskut**, perhaps the Stikine's main tributary, was the site of mining activities for years – the mine actually just closed between editions of this book. When it was still in operation, you'd see a large plane flying low overhead; it was taking ore out of the mines on the Iskut, two or three loads a day. Before the plane was used, a hydroplane was used, a behemoth that literally killed the river. The turbulence it kicked up in the Iskut entirely changed the river's habitat, rendering the area largely sterile. Additional silt flowing into the Stikine, where the boat also went, made the river shallower and wider, greatly increasing bank erosion.

The ever-present possibility of the mines on the Iskut reopening are one problem; the huge coal deposit on the Spatsizi is another. There is simply no way to extract it without damaging the Stikine's downriver flow.

Finally, there have been plans for years to dam the Stikine at the Grand Canyon (above Telegraph Creek). The river depends on regular flood cycles to maintain its equilibrium; without them, the river will die, the fish in the river will die, and the world will have lost another beautiful natural feature just so people can run their hairdryers.

FRIENDS OF THE STIKINE

The Friends of the Stikine Society has been around for a long time, trying to keep the river alive. They lobby actively for preservation of the river and its headwaters and, while a few of their positions may verge on over-conservation – in Wrangell and Telegraph Creek, there are fears that the FOS is trying to outlaw jetboats, which would cut off Telegraph and send Wrangell's economy into a tailspin – they are the only ones fighting for the river. Friends of the Stikine Society, 1405 Doran Rd., North Vancouver, B.C., Canada, V7N 1K1. ☎ 604-985-4659; www.panorama-map.com/z-pointsite/STIKINE/stikine.html.

Bringing Back the Dream

Long before the days of jetboats, the kind of ship used on the Stikine were huge riverboats. In the earliest days, sternwheelers that had a small enough draft to make it up past the flats; later, huge ships with tunnel drives and still tiny, tiny drafts. The last of these ships, the *Judith Ann*, was running as late as 1969. And she's still around. Sort of.

In her prime, the *Judith Ann* carried 12 passengers and four crew members between Wrangell and Glenora – just below Telegraph. She did the run in three days uphill, 12 hours coming back down, and she made weekly runs between May and October. A ticket for the ride in 1954 would have cost you $55, and even in 1961 she was a bargain for $70. You'd travel in reasonable comfort in two-berth staterooms, and the views off the railings couldn't have been better. The last owner of the *Judith Ann* decided to bring the boat back to the river. She'd been drydocked for years, but he set up house in it and went to work. When he passed away, his son took on the dream.

Now, the son and the **Stikine River Historical Society**, are undertaking a nearly half-million-dollar project to fully restore the *Judith Ann* and have her making trips on the river again. Yes, they could build a new boat easier and cheaper, but it wouldn't be nearly as much fun. It's a good dream to have. You can see the boat, still drydocked, about 12 miles out the Zimovia Highway. They've got a great website at www.stikineriverhistorical.org, with lots of good history on river travel. In town, you can phone them at ☎ 874-2664. It's the kind of thing that's worth having back in the world.

■ Anan Bear Observatory

First, an admission. Like the Stikine, this is one of our favorite places in the state. Everything we write about Anan is biased by the fact that we think coming here is a jaw-dropping wildlife experience in one of the prettiest places you can imagine.

Anan is about 40 miles southeast of Wrangell Island, on the mainland. It is, quite simply, Southeast's prime bear-viewing spot. It doesn't have the fame or the traffic of Pack Creek on Admiralty Island or Kodiak, but what it does have is a local population of about 80 black and 20 brown bears – this is really the only place you'll ever see black and brown sharing a fishing stream (although the black bears tend to hide the minute a grizzly shows up). It's also a wonderful place to see eagles, salmon, and harbor seals. The end of July is the peak of the salmon run, and prime visitor season, but you'll see bears any day during the salmon runs – most of the summer.

Anan was a traditional gathering place for area Tlingit during the salmon season. The name meant "place to sit down," because there was a truce in effect at Anan. Instead of worrying about rivalries, everybody just came and took advantage of the salmon run, which has been estimated at around three million fish a year returning. But that was before commercial fishing decimated the run. Commercial fishers went down the middle of the river channel, practically dredging the fish. The return now is about 300,000 per year, and there have been some attempts at strengthening this number. A bypass was put around the waterfall, which did result in more fry leaving the river, but actually fewer fish returned. The theory was that the bypass would allow weaker genes into the gene pool, fish who couldn't hack it out in the open ocean.

Today, the only fishing that's going on is by the bears, the birds, and the seals. There are thousands of birds on the gravel banks most days; by the end of the season they're so gorged on leftovers from the bears that they mostly just sit and screech at each other. Boats are met by watchful Forest Service personnel – this is one of the prize postings in Southeast.

The advantage of going to a place like Anan is that the bears tend to ignore you and go about their business. Instead of fleeing for the woods as soon as they see you, they bounce around in the stream – watching a yearling pounce and throw fish is an experience you'll never forget – and work on getting fat enough to make it through the winter.

There is a half-mile trail from the beach to the observatory building. Bears can be anywhere along here, which gives walking the trail kind of a jungle-movie feeling, as you walk past munched-on skunk cabbage (loosens the digestive tract after hibernation), dug-up sand banks (helps plug up the digestive tract before hibernation), and see tracks that remind you a grizzly has claws bigger than your head.

Remember that no food should be taken ashore. There are some bearproof containers right at the trailhead if you need them. You are in bear country. Behave accordingly. The bears here are used to people, but that doesn't mean they're big pets. Rangers and outfitters carry guns and bear spray for a reason. The odds of a bear being shot are almost zero (it's only happened once, when a photographer chased a grizzly, and we all know the wrong one died that day), but each year a few bears get maced for being too aggressive. The bears are wild... and they're much bigger than you.

The multi-level observatory platform overlooks the falls. This means that you can see bears fishing both upstream and downstream. There's a photo blind that puts you right down across from a couple of tiny caves where the black bears go to hide when the browns show up. You have to sign up for stints in the photo blind, and you can have only an hour a day down there, so what you see is something of a matter of chance, but sign up as soon as you arrive at the platform.

The platform does have a small covered area, but mostly it's like a big porch; dress like you're going to be outside all day, 'cause that's what's going to happen. While you're at the observatory:

- Speak softly.
- Don't use flashes. If you have a pocket camera with an automatic flash, put black tape over it – one day someone flashed a few bears and it was three days before any bears returned to the area. Of course, the other thing that the bears could do is be startled and charge you. Not a good thing.
- Don't rush from one side of the viewing platform to another. The more slowly you move and the calmer you are, the less likely it is that you'll spook the bears.
- The observatory really isn't the place for young kids. Every year there are kids who try to pet bears (yeah, the bears come up that close), and it's hard to keep small kids quiet, so all they're doing is messing up everybody else's experience. Also, what we've seen with kids on the platform is that they get bored a lot sooner then the parents, and so the parents end up having to leave a lot sooner than they want to.

■ There really isn't much to keep the bears from going onto the platform if they want to – only a little wooden fence that's not even waist-high – but they really aren't that interested in you. The river is so choked with fish that by the end of the summer the bears are eating onlys the bellies, the brains, and maybe some of the skin – the fattiest parts. That gives them plenty to do without even paying attention to you.

AUTHOR TIP   *The one downside to the observing area is that the outhouse is off the platform, at an area where several bear trails converge. Open the door slowly on your way out, and look before you step.*

The bears are known to the Forest Service rangers and to most of the outfitters. The same bears come back time and again, so the rangers look at behavior patterns, growth, the appearance of injuries, and so on. Most – but not all – of the bears have been named (not that the bears care), and observations have been going on long enough that the second and third generations of some families are hanging out near the observatory.

On a good day, you may see a dozen bears in only a few hours. The best afternoon we had was just the two of us and the ranger on the platform, and more than 20 bears. A bad day is only two or three. But there is nowhere else that you will get so close to bears doing what bears do in the wild.

If you're looking to stay at Anan for a while, be aware that the lone cabin is booked well in advance. Contact the **Forest Service** for booking information, and do it right at 190 days before you want to go (☎ 874-2323; www.reserveusa.com). Practice all bear precautions or be prepared to be bear lunch. Absolutely no food should ever be left – or probably even eaten – outside the cabin. Anything that is left outside is liable to be munched on, as some have found much to their sorrow when they've gone out in the morning and found their expensive collapsible kayaks turned into rags of canvas. The cabin has two bunks, plus a sleeping platform. As with all Forest Service cabins, bring your own bedding and fuel oil.

Anybody with a boat can show up at Anan any time they want to. If you're booking a ride from town, there are two categories of trips you can take: guided and unguided. This is kind of a warped thing the Forest Service started to do a couple years ago to keep the numbers down. Anybody with a boat can take you on an unguided trip; it'll run you about $120, and you'll get dropped off at the beach and left to walk the trail by yourself. Technically, the transporters, as these boat captains are called, can't advertise the fact that they can take you to Anan. At least that's what the Forest Service says. The First Amendment kind of sees things differently. For transport, call **Alaska Peak and Seas**, ☎ 874-2454.

Southeast

The other category of trip is to go with a guide. These people will walk up the trail with you, rather than just leaving you at the beach. However, back in the Forest Service's fairy tale book of rules, these people are allotted only a specific number of visitors/days. Some of the smaller outfitters, who visit Anan only as a sideline, don't get enough days to last very far into the season. Others are lucky enough to book all their days well in advance, so in a busy year, it might take a few phone calls to get a guide. Yeah, it's all politics, but you might as well know how things run.

To get the guide to walk up the trail with you, figure on the trip costing $150-175. To a lot of people who aren't comfortable with the idea of walking up a trail in bear country, the extra money is more than worth it. We've heard people scream, "I'm not walking up that trail unless there's somebody in front of me with a gun." Of course, we've also heard the rangers say, "I'd walk up the trail smeared in bacon grease." Find your own comfort level somewhere between the two extremes.

Stikeen Wilderness Adventures, ☎ 874-2085, or 866-874-3006, has the most Anan days in town. Minimum of four people, $175 each. Stop in and talk to them in their office at City Dock.

Alaska Waters, ☎ 800-347-4462, has six-hour trips to Anan for $165 in the months of July and August. **Breakaway Adventures**, ☎ 874-2488, does the trip for the same.

■ Fishing

The bears come to fish, so you might as well do it yourself. Any of the guides listed above can arrange fishing trips. There are also a couple of fishing specialists.

Alaska Peak and Seas is the place to call for fly-fishing, fresh or saltwater. Prices range depending on what you want to fish for and how many people are going, but figure in the $150-200 ballpark for a full day. ☎ 874-2590.

Alaska Charters and Adventures, ☎ 874-4157 or 888-993-2750, on the web at www.alaskaupclose.com, is your other specialty choice. Full-day rates are $195/person.

■ Shopping

Angerman's, 2 Front St., ☎ 874-3640, is a well-stocked sporting goods store. If you're going fishing, stop here first and pick up your supplies.

The **River's Edge** has the town's best supply of local arts. It's located in the Stikine Inn, and it's the home studio of Brenda Schwartz – you'll see her paintings all over the state, watercolors of boats and landscapes painted on nautical charts. Unless she's out in a boat herself, she's in the shop painting.

The **Alaska Waters Gift Shop** is run by the same people who do the Alaska Waters trips (see below). They're also in the Stikine Inn, right by the front desk.

If you're coming off the ferry and need toothpaste or other necessities, the B&B directly across from the terminal, **Fennimore's**, opens its store for all ferry arrivals. It also has a good gift selection.

■ Food

There's not much in the way of luxury dining in Wrangell and, after 3 PM, even your less luxurious choices start to diminish. For a splurge night out, head to the **Waterfront Grill**, inside the Stikine Inn. Excellent seafood, from about $15. They've also got steak, pasta, and chicken dishes.

For casual dining, most people go to the **Diamond C Café**, 215 Front St., ☎ 874-3677. There are burgers and sandwiches, good breakfasts, with prices in the $6-8 range. It closes at 3 PM, though. While it's open, it's where the town's movers and shakers hang out. Maybe the only restaurant you'll ever go into where the people are talking about the declining quality of available seal livers.

For quick pizza, try the **Hungry Beaver**, inside the Marine Bar, 640 Shakes – next to Shakes Island – ☎ 874-3005. $10 and up. Excellent pizza, open for dinner at 6:30 PM, although you can get bar food all day.

J&W's, on Front St., is Wrangell's fast-food answer. Surprisingly good fish baskets and the best ice cream in town. You can fill up for five bucks or so. A half-block farther up the street is the **JR Fish Co.**, which not only serves seafood, it sells the raw product as well. Great place to pick up supplies before heading out to the beach for a clambake. If you want to eat in, the soups are wonderful and the fish dishes are the best in town. Prices from $8, lunch only. Across the street is **Jitterbugs**, one of Wrangell's two espresso stops; the other is down on City Dock, inside the Alaska Vistas building. Follow the signs that say **Java Junkie**.

If you're looking for fresh prawns, take a walk on the docks when the boats come in for the day. Just ask around – somebody will be selling them – and you can cook yourself up a feast. There are two **grocery stores** in town, both right in the downtown area.

Southeast

■ Accommodations

 Wrangell's limited accommodations fill quickly in summer, especially if one of the town's fishing derbies is in progress. Book ahead. The town's chamber of commerce website, www.wrangell.com, links you to most of these places.

Our first choice to stay in town is to stay out of town: **Rain Haven**, a beautifully restored and refurbished vintage houseboat – all mahogany and cedar. For certain weeks of the season, the boat is taken out to a quiet spot in the surrounding islands and anchored. While you're out there, you get not only gorgeous solitude and a great place to stay, you get the use of kayaks and a chance to find out how big and quiet Alaska really is. We get it anchored near Anan, and then paddle in each day to watch bears. In the evening, we sit on the sun porch and watch the water. There aren't many better lodging experiences in Alaska. The galley (kitchen) is already stocked with staples, so all you need to bring are perishables. It's fully plumbed, and the boat can sleep up to five, although that would get a bit tight. Prices for remote stays are $150 per person per night, plus transportation out to the anchorage. Even if it's in town, it's a lovely place to stay, anchored at the dock. Taxi rides to and from town are included in the $100 per night (additional people $15 each) rate. ☎ 874-2549, or check it out on the web at www.rainwalkerexpeditions.com.

Harding's Sourdough Lodge, 1104 Peninsula, ☎ 874-3613, offers clean, basic rooms, in a nice quiet setting. There's also quite a fancy honeymoon suite. There has been a lot of renovation done here, and it shows. Homestyle, all-you-can-eat breakfasts and dinners are served at the lodge. Let them know if you need a ride in from the ferry terminal. Prices around $100. It's your best hotel bet in town.

The **Stikine Inn**, Box 990, ☎ 873-3388, just one block from the ferry terminal, offers doubles from around $100. It's within easy walking distance of practically everything. You also can't beat the views if you get a waterside room. There are suites with a refrigerator and microwave. But the hotel is up for sale, and has been allowed to run down a little over the past few years.

Roadhouse Lodge, Mile 4 on the Zimovia Highway, ☎ 874-2335, is the farthest from town, but has a nice view of the water. Rooms run from $75. This place has character to spare, and there's a good restaurant on the premises, which has the only salad bar in town.

Wrangell has its share of B&Bs, some of them outstanding values. **Rooney's Roost B&B**, 206 McKinnon, ☎ 874-2026, behind the post office, has been fully renovated over the past year or so and is now quite a lovely spot. Rooms with shared baths from $75, private from $100.

Above: Russian Cathedral, Dutch Harbor.

Below: Black Bear, Anan Bear Observatory.

Above: Lumberjacks, Ketchikan.
Opposite: Salmon drying, Akutan.
Below: Alaska Marine Highway ferry.

Above: Beached kayak, Juneau.
Opposite: Creek Street, Ketchikan.
Below: LeConte Glacier.

Above: Wrecked ships, Sand Point, Shumagin Islands.
Opposite: Waterfall, Stikine River.
Below: Salmon headed upstream.

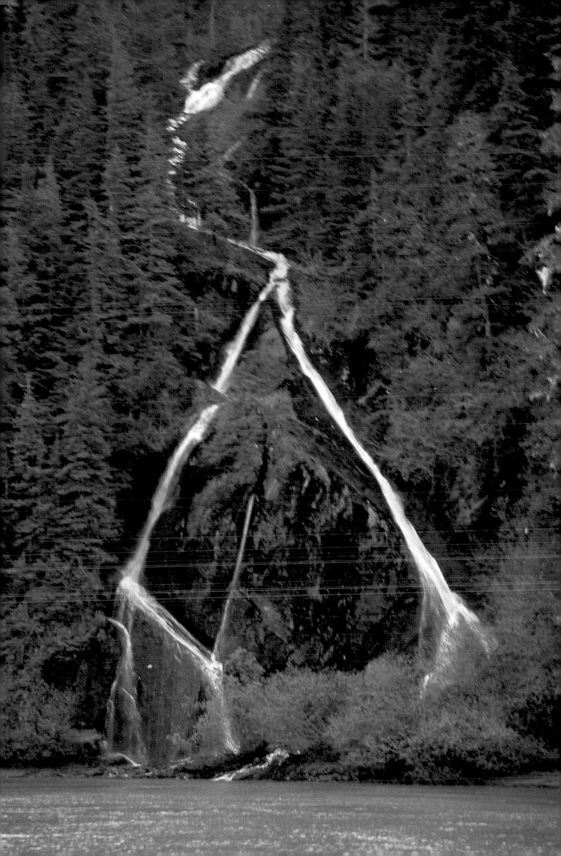

Above Totem Bigh poles Ketchikan.

Below: Ice climbing on Mendenhall Glacier.

The Anchor, 325 Church St., ☎ 874-2078, is a B&B with rates starting at $67. They're one of the oldest B&Bs in town. The **Grand View**, two miles out on the Zimovia Highway, has doubles from $90. They have four rooms, including one that's apartment-style. They've also got a hot tub and bikes guests can use. ☎ 874-3225.

Fennimore's Trading Post and B&B, ☎ 874-3012, is right across from the ferry terminal. Private entrances and baths, nice big rooms with microwaves and fridges, and there are bikes for guest use. $70 for a double. The **Zimovia B&B**, right near downtown, is new, well considered, and you get a sauna in the room. Also some of the cheapest rates in town. ☎ 874-2626.

The **First Presbyterian Church**, 220 Church St., ☎ 874-3534, has a dorm open from mid-June through Labor Day. $15 per spot, bring your own bedding. It's within walking distance of the ferry terminal.

■ Camping

The primo spot to camp in Wrangell is at **Nemo Point**. This is a free Forest Service campground. There are no hookups for RVs, but there is an outhouse. For tenters, there is a walk-in-only campground with truly stunning views. The only problem with the place is that it's 16 miles out of town – just keep heading south.

You can pitch your tent at **Pat's Lake**. Nice sites are $8. There are also four other campgrounds farther south from Pat's Lake, including **Upper** and **Lower Salamander Creek**, both with free tent sites and firewood.

If you need a place to stay for just one night close to town, it's okay to pitch a tent in the **city park**. Free, and much nicer than it sounds. Great water views, good trees, large fireplaces and free firewood. For $2, you get use of the town's pool, showers, and weight room.

Shoemaker Bay RV Park, Mile 5 of the Zimovia Hwy., has above-average views. Rates run $8-15. Partial hookups are available and there are showering facilities, as well as a pool and a weight room.

Alaska Waters has the only full hookups in town. Just a few minutes from downtown, sites are $17.50 a day. ☎ 800-347-4462. There's a telephone and showers at the site. These are the only two campgrounds in town with facilities of any kind.

Southeast

The Wrangell Narrows

If you're planning to travel on a cruise ship, don't read this section – it will just frustrate you, because odds are your ship is too big to go anywhere near here.

Between Petersburg and Wrangell is the single most difficult navigational stretch in all of Southeast: the Wrangell Narrows. The Alaska Marine Highway's M/V *Columbia*, at 418 feet long and 85 feet wide, is the largest vessel that runs the Narrows; cruise ships must go around.

The Wrangell Narrows is 21 miles long and averages a half-mile wide, closing in to a bare 100 yards in places. The shoreline looks close enough to touch. Equally hazardous to ships is the water depth – vessels must time their passage carefully according to the tide. The *Columbia* needs 21 feet of water – 16 for the draft, five for steerage. The Narrows is 19 feet deep in places. Back in the 40s, it was dredged to 26 feet at low tide, but so much silt has accumulated in the years since that some stretches have become completely unnavigable. This in itself wouldn't be so bad, but the sands shift, creating sandbars that the navigational charts can't keep up with. In 1998, the *Taku* briefly ran aground in the Narrows. She had to wait for the water to rise in order to float off the unmarked sandbar.

In addition, icebergs can frequently be a navigation hazard, coming in from the LeConte Glacier. Sometimes these bergs are big enough that the ferries either have to wait for them to float off elsewhere, or simply follow along behind them. As a final difficulty, the tide flows into the Narrows from both directions. This means, in essence, that a ship moves upstream half the time in the channel, downstream the other half. There's no great confluence where the tide forces meet, but the guys steering the boat can certainly feel the difference.

The Narrows looks like a slalom course, with buoys and markers defining the path through which vessels must weave. There are more than 70 of these markers, maintained by the Coast Guard. The ship keeps red buoys on the right as it heads north.

At the wider areas it is possible for ships to pass each other. Before the days of radar, ships sounded their horns at the entrance of the Narrows, at Port Alexander. If two ships were there at the same time, the one closer to the exit of the Narrows – whichever end – had to back out. A captain's nightmare.

 DID YOU KNOW? *It takes 46 course changes for a large ship to maneuver through the slalom course at the Narrows.*

When in open waters, the ships of the Marine Highway travel as fast as 20 knots, but they rarely exceed 10 knots in the Narrows. As an extra precaution, lookouts are placed on the bow of the ship. The lookout listens for approaching vessels and is responsible for dropping emergency anchors in the very remote chance of an accident or loss of power. The ships of the Marine Highway are equipped with radar so sensitive they can show raindrops, but their information on closing speed and distances is limited.

And all precautions aside, if it's foggy everything comes to a dead halt. The Narrows are one of the main factors in scheduling on the Alaska Marine Highway; they are only passable at high tide, so ships tend to leave Petersburg and Wrangell at odd hours.

There are quite a number of houses along the Narrows. As you get closer to Petersburg, these are connected by the town's road system, but farther back they're boat-only access. Most of these were actually homesteads, given away in Alaska's last free land grab.

Most guidebooks suggest trying to get passage through the Narrows at night: the buoys and channel markers are lit up and it looks something like floating through a Christmas tree. It is dramatic at night. However, the only way to really appreciate the Narrows is to travel in broad daylight. Watching the split-hair precision of the ship as it weaves a course as fine as a seamstress' needle is a lot more interesting than a bunch of colored lights.

WATCHABLE

WILDLIFE

Because the Narrows are so narrow, there's a good chance of seeing wildlife on land – Sitka black-tailed deer are fairly common, and around creek mouths there's always a chance of spotting bear.

Petersburg

Alaska's Little Norway, Petersburg sits on a corner of **Mitkof Island**, under the shadow of the towering, spiky Devil's Thumb, a 9,000-foot peak of the Coast Mountain Range on the mainland. Thanks to the difficult water route into Petersburg, nearly all cruise ships pass the town by and the only regular influx comes from passengers on the Alaska Marine Highway. Petersburg remains largely a town for the locals who are, incidentally, some of the friendliest people in Alaska.

Southeast

■ History

The town's name has nothing to do with Russia – Petersburg was founded in 1896 by Peter Buschmann, a Norwegian immigrant. From the beginning, Petersburg was a paradise for commercial fishermen. By 1900, the Strait Packing Co., the local cannery, already employed more than 150 people. Five years later, there were two more canneries operating at full capacity.

■ Petersburg Today

Nothing much has changed in the past 90 years. Petersburg remains Southeast's busiest processing port and home to Southeast's largest fishing fleet, with lumbering falling to a very distant second in economic importance. Tourism may not even make the top 10, especially now that the express ferries are bypassing the town. Petersburg is a lovely, liveable town, perfect as a base to get out and around the island, but if you're looking for a lot of standard attractions, look elsewhere. It's not much different from the way it was described in the 1937 WPA Guide to Alaska: "The lawns are close-cropped and gay with flowers, and autos speed along the plank streets. On rafts in the harbor are floating houses painted with red lead, complete with window curtains. Lanky blond Northerners lean against the wall." In 1938, Petersburg had the only traffic light in Alaska.

A large percentage of the population claim to be descendants of the original Norwegian settlers. The town retains an air of Norway: some residents speak Norwegian, houses are decorated with rosemaling, and Norwegian Independence Day is celebrated every May 17th in the town's biggest yearly bash.

ROSEMALING

Rosemaling is a kind of decorative painting, featuring floral motifs. The flowers and leaves are painted on panels, which are then put up on the sides of the houses as trim.

■ Basics

The ferry terminal is one mile south of town. In summer, Petersburg is connected daily with Wrangell and Juneau. Sailing times can be a little peculiar, depending on the hours of the tide. The local phone number for the **AMH** is ☎ 772-3855.

Most cruise ships pass Petersburg by, partially because of the hazards of navigating the Wrangell Narrows, but more because the town put a head tax on cruise ship passengers. A few small lines do make it to town, docking next to the small boat harbor, closer to downtown than the ferry.

Alaska Airlines flies into Petersburg daily. ☎ 800-426-0333 or 772-4255. Charter air services to Mitkof Island include: **Kupreanof Flying**, ☎ 772-3396; **Pacific Wing**, ☎ 772-4258; and **Temsco Airlines and Helicopters**, ☎ 772-4780.

For renting a car, try **Avis**, ☎ 772-4716. For a taxi, call **City Cab**, ☎ 772-3003. Rent a bike from Northern Bikes, ☎ 772-3978. You can't park in the harbor lots to wander the downtown; go to the staging area at Ira and Second, where parking is a buck an hour, but you won't get a ticket.

The **Petersburg Chamber of Commerce** runs a very good information office at the corner of First and Fram. It is open Monday-Friday, 7:30-5. Write Box 649, ☎ 772-3646.

    📖   Don't miss picking up a copy of the ***Viking Visitors Guide***, Petersburg's annual guide to the town.

The **Forest Service office** is upstairs in the Post Office & Federal building, downtown at Nordic and Haugen. They sell a map of Mitkof Island, well worth picking up, and have extensive handouts on area hiking. ☎ 772-3871. The Forest Service is open 8-5.

    📖   The best booklet to get is ***Hiking Trails***, which covers Kupreanof, Mitkof, Woewodsk, and Kuiu Island trails. The free guide includes specific difficulty rankings of the trails, plus a full description and history of each trail.

Internet access is available at **mitkof.net**, a computer store that rents out Internet access, 110 Harbor Way, across from the main harbor office.

Petersburg's zip code is **99833**.

Petersburg's big show is the **Little Norway Festival**, on the weekend closest to Norway's Independence Day, Syttendemai, May 17th. The festival runs for four days, with dancing, music, skits and more. Reservations are a must for lodging.

The **Fourth of July** brings bed races, logging events, and fireworks.

At Christmas, the town of Petersburg gives itself a present, **Julebukking**, during which merchants open early on Christmas Eve, setting up tables of goodies and spirits in appreciation for the business they've done that year. The townsfolk wander from store to store, eating, visiting, and enjoying the Christmas spirit.

Southeast

■ Museums & Attractions

THE CLAUSEN MUSEUM: Located at the corner of 2nd and Fram Sts., ☎ 772-3598, the museum is open 10-4 in summer, with a $2 admission charge. The museum has a good assortment of fishing equipment – probably the best displays in Southeast for explaining all the different kinds of boats – and some interesting exhibits on fox farming. Petersburg, like many of the islands of Southeast, was a hot spot for fox fur farming until the 1920s.

HISTORIC DISTRICT: In town, Hammer Slough is Petersburg's historic district. Located about half a mile north of the ferry terminal, Hammer Slough is especially pretty at high tide, when the warehouses and old houses with rosemaling are reflected in the water.

Quite a few Steller's sea lions pass through Frederick Sound – the water in front of Petersburg. In 1993, there was a pod of orca (killer whales) moving through at the same time as the sea lions. The sea lions, a favorite snack food for orca, all headed for shore, coming right up into the harbor fingers, but not all of them made it in time.

VIKING BOAT: Near downtown, next to the Sons of Norway Hall, is the *Valhalla*, a replica of an original Viking boat. It was built in 1976 for the nation's bicentennial, and has actually sailed, although if you look at it you'll wonder what kind of nuts the Vikings were, going out to sea in boats like that.

EAGLE'S ROOST PARK: Petersburg has a massive concentration of bald eagles. Heading out the road to the north end of town you'll pass Eagle's Roost Park, just beyond the seafood plant. Eagles are everywhere in Petersburg, but the park is a nice spot to have a picnic or just to sit and watch the water (if you can find a spot around the eagle poop everywhere). On a clear day you'll see the Coast Mountains, which are dominated by Church Peak (6,552 feet), Rodgers Peak (4,000 feet), and the dramatic Saw Peaks, which look like an array of teeth around the 5,000-foot line. The most famous of these mountains is Devil's Thumb, which towers more than 9,000 feet above the icefield and is considered one of America's most challenging climbs.

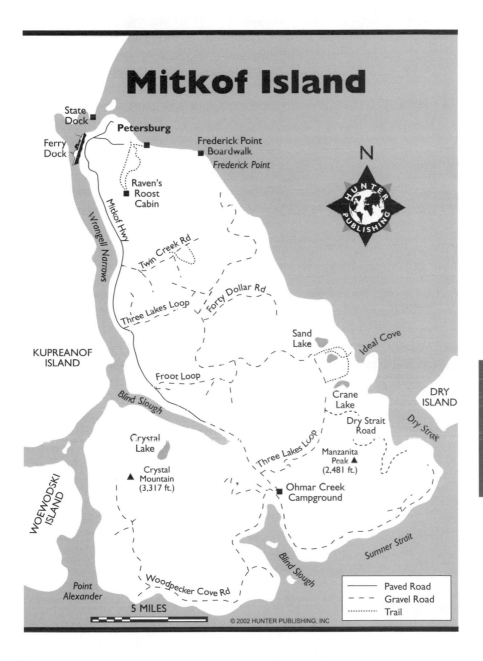

Mitkof Island

State Dock
Ferry Dock
Petersburg
Frederick Point
Boardwalk
Frederick Point
Raven's Roost Cabin
Mitkof Hwy
Wrangell Narrows
Twin Creek Rd
Forty Dollar Rd
Three Lakes Loop
Sand Lake
Ideal Cove
N
KUPREANOF ISLAND
Froot Loop
Blind Slough
Crane Lake
DRY ISLAND
Dry Strait Road
Dry Strait
Crystal Lake
Crystal Mountain (3,317 ft.)
Three Lakes Loop
Manzanita Peak ▲ (2,481 ft.)
Ohmar Creek Campground
WOEWODSKI ISLAND
Sumner Strait
Point Alexander
Woodpecker Cove Rd
Blind Slough
5 MILES

——— Paved Road
– – – Gravel Road
·········· Trail

© 2002 HUNTER PUBLISHING, INC

Southeast

SAVED BY DEVIL'S THUMB

According to legend, the local Indians survived the Great Flood by climbing Devil's Thumb. On the way up they found many bears and mountain goats, and this is one explanation for the use of animal tracks on totems in the Wrangell/Mitkof Island area, to tell their story of climbing the Thumb.

📖 For a good account of climbing the Thumb, pick up a copy of Jon Krakauer's *Eiger Dreams*.

SANDY BEACH PARK: Located almost at the end of the paved road heading north, has some picnic shelters and good water views. Down on the beach there are a few petroglyphs, visible at low tide.

The best attraction in Petersburg is the wilderness south of town, much of it readily accessible thanks to Forest Service roads. Heading this way, you have 18 miles of paved road, and then another lengthy stretch of dirt road that runs not quite alongside the Wrangell Narrows; if you've got time and a tough enough car, you can drive all the way around the island. Mitkof Island is laced with logging roads, all in pretty good shape and passable for most vehicles (although RVs or vehicles with low ground clearance might have some trouble).

FALLS CREEK: At Falls Creek, about eight miles out on the main road, there is a good picnic area and an old fish ladder. Depending on the time of year, you can see pink and coho salmon or steelhead trout using it.

BLIND SLOUGH: About 18 miles south of town, this is a popular picnic spot with locals. There is also good salmon fishing in the area in season. Blind Slough is also a migratory stopover for trumpeter swans, who stop here from mid-October to early December; about 75 swans winter here. You've got a chance of seeing the swans in the shoulder seasons. In summer, watch for great blue herons, kingfishers, and other shore birds. Also keep an eye out for blue grouse along the roads and lesser yellow-legs in the muskeg.

Right by the slough is the **Crystal Lake Fish Hatchery**, just before the pavement ends. They raise chum, king, and coho here. Although there are no organized tours, you're welcome to have a look around to see what's happening. ☎ 772-4772.

■ Scenic Drives

 Three Lakes Loop, a 45-minute drive to the end of the road, is a favorite. Another option is to drive south on the **Mitkof Highway**, along the Wrangell Narrows (the road is just far enough inland that there aren't any good views). The road heads down along Blind

Slough and Ohmer Creek, around the corner of Mitkof and along Sumner Strait and Dry Strait, where the tidal fluctuation leaves huge mud flats. It's 32 miles to the end, where you have great views and the satisfaction of coming to a place that only bored local teenagers ever see.

WATCHABLE *Deer are everywhere along this road, especially after you leave the pavement. The Petersburg area has a rapidly growing Sitka black-tailed deer population, and every year the number of animals on the* **WILDLIFE** *roads increases. There's also a good chance of seeing black bears.*

■ Adventures

Hiking

There are a lot of good walks around Petersburg. Be sure to pick up a copy of the island's hiking guide at the Visitor Center. Some of the trailheads can be a little tricky to find.

The **Frederick Point Boardwalk** at the north end of town, past the Sandy Beach Recreation Area, is a mile-long walk through rainforest and meadows. Because the old dump is just over the hill, it's a good place to spot bears, but a bad place to walk your dog. The path ends in the deep forest, with some lovely views of the mountains across Frederick Sound.

The **Three Lakes Loop Road**, which heads up the hills on the west side of Mitkof Island, not only serves as one of the town's favorite picnic spots, it's also the trailhead for the **Hill Lake Trail**, a really easy berry-picking route, and the similar **Crane Lake Trail**, where moose sightings are becoming increasingly common. There's also a picnic table and a rowboat at each of the lakes for public use, but you may need to hunt around a bit to find the oars. People tend to hide them in the bushes and pretend the boats are private. Come up here on a clear day for unbeatable views.

The **Raven's Roost Trail** is four miles long, beginning near the water tower near the airport, off Haugen Drive. Much of it is boardwalked, until you start the climb. Get up high enough, and you hit a Forest Service cabin, which offers unbeatable views. The **Blind River Rapids Boardwalk** is at Mile 14.5 on the Mitkof Highway, south of town. It's a mile-long walk through a nice muskeg area. Handicapped-accessible.

All these trails are difficult; allow at least six hours for the round-trip on the Petersburg Mountain Trail which, on a clear day, offers unparalleled views of the town and the surrounding mountains and glaciers.

Leave three hours for the Petersburg Creek Trail, which has excellent creek fishing and wildflowers. Trailheads are at Bayou Point, directly across the sound from town. You can probably catch a ride most days from someone down on the docks; there's a lot of traffic back and forth between the islands, but it will cost you a bit.

DON'T MISS: *Some of the best hiking isn't on the Petersburg side of things, it's over on Kupreanof Island. You can get a boat across the sound (ask around at the harbor to see if you can hire someone to take you across) and hike up Petersburg Mountain Trail, or take the Petersburg Creek Trail or the Petersburg Lake Trail, a bit over 10 miles, leading to a Forest Service cabin.*

Excursions to Glaciers

The hot destination for charters from Petersburg is LeConte Glacier, the southernmost tidewater glacier in North America. At least it's the southernmost right now – if the melt continues it won't be a tidewater glacier much longer.

STATIC GLACIER

Since 1994, the glacier has been giving itself a face-lift; in 1995 alone, it lost half a mile of ice, a greater loss in one year than in the previous dozen years. Since then, the shrink has continued. LeConte is falling back dramatically, even though the position of the face isn't changing much – the melt is matching the forward pressure of the glacier.

Because the water in the bay in front of the glacier is so deep – more than 800 feet – there is no real way for the glacier to advance, so it calves when it moves forward. This means that the area in front of the glacier can be absolutely full of icebergs and bergy bits. The channel back to the face is roughly nine miles from Frederick Sound, and the entire way can be choked with ice. It's absolutely spectacular to see the colors in the ice, and the sheltered waters protect a huge seal rookery. It's not unusual to see a couple hundred seals hanging out on the ice floes. The passage in offers great views of the surrounding mountains.

A trip to LeConte is probably your best chance in Alaska to see serious glacier calving. The glacier is about 25 miles southeast of town on the mainland and is a finger of the Stikine Icefield. John Muir visited here in 1879 and, although LeConte Bay had been providing San Francisco with most of its ice since 1853, it was not charted until 1887.

THUNDERBIRD

LeConte was long famous with the locals, who called it "Thunder Bay." Tidewater glaciers calve often, and the ice is constantly cracking and groaning. The Stikine Indians thought the glacier was the home of the Thunderbird, who made the sounds by flapping his wings. They considered the many glaciers splitting off the icefield to be children of the mountains: the mountains took care of their children by sheltering them with snow blankets in winter, and protecting them from the sun with rocks and dirt.

Adventure Outfitters

There's only one real choice for going to LeConte: **Kaleidoscope Cruises**. Others make the trip, but Kaleidoscope's is the one to take, simply for the quality of narration. We've gone all over Alaska and rarely found people who know their stuff as well as these guys. Trips to LeConte run $130. They've also got trips into Frederick Sound for whale watching, for $180.

Frederick Sound is one of the two great places in Southeast for whales (the other is Icy Strait, near Glacier Bay). According to the Forest Service, of the roughly 1,000 humpbacks that feed in Southeast each year, fully half of them come to Frederick Sound. The captain of Kaleidoscope's ship said his best day of whale-watching was 206 different whales sighted. If that's not enough, there are also orca, Steller's sea lions, harbor seals, and Dall's porpoise in the sound. It can be one of the best days out you've had, if your luck is running with you.

Fishing

Petersburg makes its living on fishing, so the odds are you can catch something in the area, too. Your best bets for charters are **Secret Cove** (☎ 772-3081) and **Screaming Reel** (☎ 772-3998). Figure on a full day running about $175 per person.

To process your catch, there's **Northern Lights Smokeries**, at 501 Noseeum St., ☎ 772-4608. Smoking runs about $2.80/pound. If you miss out on catching anything yourself, buy some smoked salmon at **Tonka Seafoods**, ☎ 772-3662, in Sing Lee Alley. It's way better than you're going to find anywhere else in Southeast. They also run tours of the operation, which are pretty interesting.

Southeast

Kayaking

Tongass Kayak Adventures, ☎ 772-4600, offers half-day trips around Petersburg Creek, for $55. They've also got longer trips available, including some that go whale watching in Frederick Sound.

If you've got your own kayak and have a couple days, charter a ride out to Thomas Bay, 20 miles north of town. There are several Forest Service cabins near the bay (the best of them is Spurt Point, near the Baird Glacier, but Swan Lake and Cascade Creek are not bad alternatives). The bay is huge, quiet, and very, very scenic, with waterfalls and glaciers coming into it. You'll have the place to yourself, and you'll never want to leave.

■ Food

 Petersburg has one of the best restaurants in Southeast, **Coastal Cold Storage**, ☎ 772-4171,downtown at 306 Nordic. It's Alaskan fast food – fish and chips, fish burgers. Doesn't sound like much, but it makes the trip to Petersburg worthwhile all by itself. They also have a large selection of fresh seafood you can buy and prepare yourself. Fill up here for under $10.

If you want a little more comfort, try **Northern Lights**, ☎ 772-4608, at the end of Sing Lee Alley. Good chicken and fish dishes, a nice view of the channel. From $10-15.

Helse Café at Sing Lee Alley and Gjoa St., ☎ 772-3444, has health food, natural drinks, soups and salads, from $4-10. There's a health food store next door. If you're not in a health food mood, try **Pellerito's Pizza**, ☎ 772-3727, directly across the street from the ferry terminal. Good, big pizzas with great crust, other Italian specialties and ice cream. Prices from $8-25. If you're in a hurry from the ferry, they do sell slices.

Kato's Kave, on Sing Lee Alley, has good Mexican food. Don't let the exterior scare you away. **Hammer and Wikun Convenience Store**, ☎ 772-4811, downtown, is open until 11 PM. You can pick up a sandwich here.

■ Accommodations

 One of the best room deals in town is at **Tides Inn**, 1st and Dolphin Sts., ☎ 772-4288. Just $85 gets you a nice third-floor-front room with a water view. A great bargain. When you're making a reservation here, try to avoid the rooms on the ground floor, which are pretty dark. **Scandia House**, 110 Nordic Dr., ☎ 772-4281, is convenient and comfortable, with rooms starting at $85. Includes continental breakfast. One of the nicest hotels in town, but it may be a little cutesy for some. **Narrows Inn**, Mile 1 Mitkof Hwy., is directly across from the ferry terminal. Basic rooms from $65. ☎ 772-4284.

Petersburg has a good assortment of B&Bs. Get a complete list from the Visitor's Bureau. **Water's Edge**, on Nordic Dr., north of downtown, is one of the nicer places in town. Rooms are $80 for a double. This is run by the same people who do Kaleidoscope Cruises, and you'll find the same fine attention to detail. ☎ 772-3736, or 800-868-4373. Book early: this place fills up fast.

Other good bets include the **Seafarer's Shack**, at 710 Rambler St., ☎ 772-3934, which runs $80 for a double. **Das Hagedorn Haus**, near downtown in a quiet neighborhood at 400 2nd St. N, ☎ 772-3775, has doubles for $90. The **Broom Hus** is in a 1920s house, nicely refurbished. Doubles are $80 for a nice, homey feel. ☎ 772-3459. The location is a ways out of town, but they'll pick you up from the ferry terminal or the airport. **Petersburg Bunk and Breakfast Hostel**, 805 Gjoa St., ☎ 772-2790, has bunks for $25. Basic, but it's cheap.

■ Camping

Camping near the city center in the summer is difficult. The only choices are **LeConte RV Park**, 4th and Haugen, ☎ 772-4680, $15/night; or **Tonka View**, Mile 2.2 Mitkof Hwy., ☎ 772-3345. They both offer little more than a gravel parking lot. LeConte does have a couple passable tent spots, if you can't get farther out.

Twin Creeks RV Park is another gravel lot about seven miles out of town – it's actually built in an old gravel quarry, and you wonder why the owners put the spaces there, with no view, instead of in the view lot across the street, which they also own.

Out of town, try **Ohmer Creek Campground**, Mile 22 Mitkof Hwy. You can choose from one of the shady green sites. There are pleasant trails in and around the campground. A little farther out is **Ernie Ogden Campground**, Mile 26.8 Mitkof Hwy. It has unimproved but very pleasant sites. Both campgrounds are free; make sure to bring your own water.

If you can't get out of town, you can pitch a tent in **Tent City**, between the airport and Shady Cove, about two miles from downtown. This used to be one of the biggest slums in Alaska, but it has cleaned up considerably over the past couple years. The super is careful to segregate fishery workers – not many now that the canneries all have new dorms – and families or travelers. There are 52 tent platforms, coin-operated showers, fire pits and firewood. Much nicer than everybody is going to tell you it is.

Finally, there are about 20 **Forest Service cabins** in the Mitkof Island region. Check with the Forest Service for availability and reservations.

Kake

In the 19th century, the tribe living in Kake was said to be the fiercest in Southeast. They couldn't even go on vacation well. During a visit to Puget Sound, they got into trouble, and a U.S. ship opened fire on them. One of the Kake chieftains was killed, and so the next year the tribe sent a canoe of warriors from Kupreanof Island to Whitbys Island in Washington – about 800 miles of paddling. They beheaded the first official they could find, who happened to be an ex-customs collector – another reason why wearing a uniform to work can be hazardous. Reports from the time suggest it might have been all right with other Whitbys Islanders if it had been a tax collector. This little Kake rebellion was not an isolated incident. In fact, the villagers caused so much trouble that, in 1869, General Jefferson Davis, commander of the U.S. troops in Sitka, ordered the destruction of Kake villages on Kuiu Island, across from what is now the village of Kake. This was in retaliation for the Kake Indians killing two white men; that killing was itself in response to the shooting of a Kake. John Muir recounts a visit to a Kake village where bones were laying about all over the ground. Kake has settled down since then. Today it's a fairly quiet fishing and logging village with a population of about 700.

■ Basics

Kake is served two or three times a week by the **Alaska Marine Highway**. You can also fly in with **Wings of Alaska**, ☎ 772-3536. The town has almost no visitor facilities and no chamber of commerce.

■ Attractions & Adventures

Kake is a working town and, other than the 132-foot totem pole built for the 1970 Osaka World Fair (turn left from the ferry and head up the hill), there isn't much to be seen here. Kupreanof Island has been heavily logged and there's little point in getting off to explore it. An exception might be for birders, who could go to Big John Bay (a Forest Service cabin) to watch the waterfowl. The Kuiu Wilderness, on the south side of nearby Kuiu Island, remains almost untouched, even though it is surrounded by clear-cut islands. It abuts the Tebenkof Bay Wilderness (on the west side of the island), a complex ecosystem within the larger Southeast. The bay is dotted with tiny islands and rocks, perfect nesting habitat.

Kayaking & Canoeing

The area is excellent for those with canoes and kayaks; pick up a copy of a map showing local routes at the Petersburg Forest Service office. The standard route through the wilderness area is to paddle from Kake along the Keku Islands. Passing Hound Island and Pup Island, you eventually hit Port Camden. Take the western side of the fork, following past Cam Island and great waterfowl areas. At the western end of Port Camden, you hit a 1.3-mile portage, ending at the Bay of Pillars. From there it's three miles (some of it open water) around Point Ellis to Tebenkof Bay. Come home up Alecks Creek, to Alecks Lake. You'll have a longer portage there, from the lake into No Name Bay, about 2.3 miles. This takes you back into the Keku Strait via Rocky Pass, which is a narrow and, yes, rocky area that makes for some interesting paddling; Kake is to the north, and before you get there, you'll pass the remnants of an old fox farm on Horseshoe Island. There are three Forest Service cabins along the way.

Don't even think about kayaking without proper charts and gear unless you're looking for an unusual way to die in the middle of nowhere. Contact the Forest Service office in Petersburg before heading out – file a float plan with them, and check on the trail conditions for the portages. For the whole thing, including plenty of time to get out and look around, figure on eight to 10 days.

> 📖 Pick up a copy of ***Kuiu Kisland/Tebbenkof Bay Canoe/Kayak Routes*** from the Forest Service office for $3.

■ Food & Accommodations

 In Kake, stay at the **Nugget Inn**, ☎ 785-6469, which also has a small restaurant. Or try the **Waterfront Lodge**, ☎ 785-3472. Openings may be seasonal, and both places may be full of loggers or fishermen. If you can get a room, figure on $90 for a double.

Juneau

It's the capital of Alaska – the most inaccessible capital in the United States – it's the biggest town in Southeast Alaska, and it's also one of the largest cities in the world, at least as far as area goes. Juneau incorporated an icefield into the city limits, just because they could. It's a town where the downtown area is considered liberal, the valley conservative. Once a boomtown for gold prospectors, it's now a boomtown for government – fully half of the city's workers show up at a government office of some sort each day.

The Juneau/Auke Bay area was originally settled by the Auk-Quon branch of the Tlingit Indians. They lived on Douglas Island, across the Gastineau Channel from what is now downtown Juneau, and an area 15 miles north of modern downtown, in the village of Ahnch-gal-tsoo (Auke Bay, where the ferry terminal is now). The bay was their winter home until the late 1880s.

The Auks were so powerful and so well entrenched in the area that they succeeded in chasing one of George Vancouver's expeditions all the way to Admiralty Island, in 1794. Of course, they had a reason for trying to get rid of him – the night before, one of his men had taken a potshot at an Auk canoe: "After passing the village... the boats were followed by many large and small canoes; and as the evening was drawing near, to get rid of such troublesome visitors a musket was fired over their heads, but this as before had only the effect of making them less ceremonious."

It's not the sort of thing you need to worry about now. Juneau today has something for everybody.

■ History

The city of Juneau was named after a prospector, Joe Juneau, who came here in 1880 with his friend, Richard Harris. They were led to huge gold deposits by Kowee, a Tlingit chief. The Tlingits themselves weren't all that impressed with gold, didn't have a whole lot of use for it.

Joe and Richard staked a 160-acre townsite near the beach of Gold Creek; the following month of November brought shiploads of prospectors to the town. The Alaska gold rush was on, a full decade before richer strikes were hit in Yukon. Miners flooded into the area, working to get their share of the 6.7 million ounces of gold that the Juneau fields produced between 1881 and 1944.

Although the mines shut down during the war, the gold supply was far from exhausted. A Canadian mining company that now holds rights to the A-J mine, the same mine area originally claimed by Harris and Juneau, is trying to re-open it. But there is much local opposition to that and the plan to re-open two other historic mines.

Southeast Alaska had a considerable population by the time of the first gold rush – the official transfer from Russian ownership to the U.S. had taken place in Sitka a dozen years before. The city of Juneau is considered to be the first town founded after the transfer. Juneau was named the territorial capital in 1906, and maintained its status with entry into statehood.

▪ Juneau Today

Juneau is Alaska's third most populous city and, with an incorporated area of over 3,100 square miles, one of the largest cities, area-wise, in the world. Yeah, all that ice is politically important. But Juneau isn't the hub of power in the state. Even though the state legislature descends upon Juneau regularly (and, according to locals, drops the city's average IQ by 50 points), the real moving and shaking still goes on up north in Anchorage.

There is a nearly perennial attempt in Alaska to move the capital closer to Anchorage and the center of power (Juneau is, perhaps, the most inconveniently located capital in the country). Juneau has notoriously bad weather in winter, which can cost lawmakers days of delays when flying in and out of the capital. Although a measure was passed to move the capital to Willow (a small town northeast of Anchorage) in the 1980s, money was never appropriated for the move, and Juneau held on. The peculiar balance of Alaska – half the population lives in Anchorage, the other half considers Anchorage to be "just 30 minutes from Alaska" – keeps the capital movement in gridlock.

There is a move afoot to make Juneau at least a little more accessible by punching a road through to Haines or Skagway. However, the expense of building through such rugged terrain would probably exceed the cost of building several new ships for the Marine Highway fleet. As you spend time in Southeast, you'll find that nearly every community dreams of building a road to somewhere, more to alleviate island fever than for any practical purpose.

And so Juneau sits, isolated and under attack from those who would move the capital. This dichotomy – being a capital with very little power – has left Juneau in the enviable position of being a very liveable city. And its location, with the Juneau Icefield, Tracy Arm, and Admiralty Island all nearby, makes it a paradise for those seeking the best of Alaska.

▪ Basics

i All cruise ships stop in Juneau. The town gets over 600,000 cruise ship passengers a year, and in summer, there can be seven or eight thousand people off the ships on any given day. Juneau's cruise ship dock is right downtown. When the number of ships overloads the enormous dock's capacity, the extra ones anchor off in front of the State Office building and the downtown area, bringing lighters ashore into the heart of town. So guess where all the tourist shops are in Juneau? Heavy cruise ship days are good times to go out on the road hiking or kayaking.

Southeast

The **Alaska Marine Highway** has daily service to and from Skagway, Haines, Sitka, and Prince Rupert, stopping at points en route. The ferry terminal is 13 miles north of downtown Juneau, in Auke Bay. The problem is, once you're at the ferry terminal, you're 13 miles from town, and there ain't no way in except to take a taxi – a $30 ride. Look for somebody willing to share.

There are two fast ferries that connects Juneau to Haines and Skagway: the **Haines-Skagway Water Taxi**, ☎ 888-766-3395, charges $90 for a round-trip; the **Fjord Express**, ☎ 800-320-0146, charges $99. Either will cut a lot of hours off the AMH running time. The ferry has a downtown office, at 12th and Glacier, that can answer most of your questions without you having to go clear out to Auke Bay.

With the legislature moving in and out, Juneau's airport is a busy place, but there's the usual **Southeast Alaska** airline monopoly: you fly Alaska or you don't fly a jet. There are also a host of small charter flights that can take you to Glacier Bay, Admiralty, or a choice of Forest Service cabins, as well as offering scheduled flights to smaller communities in the area. Check with **Wings of Alaska**, ☎ 789-0790; **Skagway Air**, ☎ 789-2006; and **L.A.B. Flying Service**, ☎ 789-9160 or 800-426-0543, for timetables and rates. The **Gustavus Ferry**, ☎ 586-8687 or 800-820-BOAT, runs twice-daily trips from Juneau to Gustavus, the base for trips to Glacier Bay. The basic round-trip is $85.

Juneau is the only city in Southeast with much of a bus service. Buses run between the downtown, Mendenhall Valley, Auke Bay and Douglas areas. A current schedule can be picked up at the Davis Log Cabin, or call **Capital Transit Bus** at ☎ 789-6901. Fares are $1.25 per ride.

There are three taxi companies, comparable in price and service: **Taku Taxi**, ☎ 586-2121; **Juneau Taxicab Co.**, ☎ 790-4511; and **Capital Cab**, ☎ 586-2772.

Juneau is one of the few Southeast towns where a car is a necessity. All the main rental car chains have offices in Juneau: **Avis**, ☎ 789-9450; **Hertz**, ☎ 789-9494; and **National**, ☎ 789-9814. There are several local dealers as well, the cheapest being **Rent-a-Wreck**, ☎ 789-4111.

Juneau's Information Center is at 101 Egan Drive, ☎ 586-2284 or 888-581-2201. Open daily from mid-May through mid-September, 8:30-5, and the rest of the year Monday through Friday, 9-5, they have the usual variety of handouts about the town and also show videos on Southeast Alaska.

    📖   Be sure to pick up the brochures *Free Things to Do in Juneau, Alaska,* and *Juneau Walking Tour*, which outlines an easy path through downtown's highlights.

They also have information on local B&Bs, city tours, and attractions in and around Juneau. There are smaller tourist information booths run during the summer season at the airport, the Auke Bay ferry terminal, and at the Marine Park Cruise Ship Terminal, in the heart of downtown.

The **Forest Service** office is at 8465 Old Diary Road, near the airport, ☎ 586-8751. They have details on Alaska's public lands, Glacier Bay, Tracy Arm, and they can make reservations for Forest Service cabins. This is the place to come to talk about Admiralty Island cabins and regulations for the Pack Creek Bear Reserve. Information is on-line at www.fs.fed.us/r10/tongass/districts/admiralty/.

    📖   The Forest Service sells some very good maps to Admiralty Island and other nearby locations, as well as a book called ***Juneau Trails***, $3, which outlines hikes in the region.

JUNEAU AT A GLANCE

QUICK TOUR: Take a ride on the tram for an overview of the town; close your eyes, plunge through the tourist hell of Franklin Street, and take a look at the sublimely beautiful Russian Orthodox Church.

DON'T MISS: Everybody who goes to Southeast says the same thing: walking on Mendenhall Glacier was the high point of the trip. Grab a helicopter flight, preferably with Northstar Trekking. Remember: the longer you're on the glacier, the more fun you'll have. Afterwards, head out whale-watching. Orca Expeditions has a bright purple boat. You know they must be good. Tracy Arm makes Glacier Bay seem positively dull. A day-trip to Tracy Arm offers up the most dramatic glacial scenery in Southeast.

BEST FREEBIE: I like the glacier trails – they don't make views like this back home.

In summer the Forest Service hold regular lunch-time lectures and cultural demonstrations, including Native dancers. Check for the current schedule of events. Finally, there's a small museum that gives you a quick look at the environment around Juneau. ☎ 586-8751. Another Forest Service information booth is at the Mendenhall Glacier. Fishing regulations and tips are available by calling ☎ 465-4116.

The ***Juneau Empire***, Juneau's daily paper, has daily listings in the Around Town section on page 2, with local events. Check it early in the morning for evening shows and lectures.

Southeast

There are several Internet cafés downtown. **Soapy's Station**, on Franklin St., uses the same time cards as the Ketchikan branches. To get Juneau information on the web, go to www.traveljuneau.com.

Juneau's zip code is **99801**; Ward Cove, a subdivision of Juneau near the pulp mill, is 99028; Auke Bay, 99821.

■ Museums & Attractions

MOUNT ROBERTS TRAMWAY: A good place to start touring Juneau is by taking a ride up the Mount Roberts Tramway, with its base right at the cruise ship dock, ☎ 463-3412 or 888-461-TRAM. It takes just a couple of minutes to go from the water to the 2,000-foot level on Mt. Roberts. Once you're up there, there's a huge gift shop, restaurant, craft displays and demonstrations, and a very good free film about Alaskan Native life. There are also occasional live performances in the auditorium. Once you're at the top, there are quite a few hiking trails that branch off – they're usually pretty boggy, so make sure you've got proper shoes.

A round-trip on the tram is $19.75 for adults. The price covers one day, so you can ride up and down as much as you want for the day you get your ticket. There are also package deals with the Tram and Trolley Tour, which adds on unlimited trolley rides for $29.75, or a nature tour package for $44. At the top of the mountain, just a quick boardwalk trot away from the tram, is the **Mount Roberts Nature Center**, which has a few small displays about local hiking and wildlife. They also have guided walks on the peak.

The tram is trying to make the ride a cultural experience, and they do a pretty good job at it. You'll learn a lot about local cultures by spending a half-day up there – an odd thing to say for a ride to a gift shop, but it's true. If you hike up the hill (access near the hostel, at 6th St., no parking anywhere near the trailhead), you can ride the tram down free, as long as you spend $5 in the restaurant or the gift shop.

TROLLEY TOURS: The Juneau Trolley Car Company, ☎ 586-RIDE, runs a circuit that takes in most of the downtown places a visitor will want to see, including the Governor's Mansion, St. Nicholas, the Log Cabin Visitor Center, the State Museum, and more. A day pass runs $12 for adults, or you can buy it with a tram ticket package, as noted above. Once you've got the ticket, you can jump on or off anywhere you want; the tram hits the stops about every 30 minutes.

ALASKA STATE MUSEUM: This excellent museum is at 395 Whittier, ☎ 465-2901. Open in summer, Monday-Friday, 9-6; Saturday and Sunday 10-6. The museum features a wonderful standing collection of Aleut and Tlingit artifacts, as well as general historical and wildlife exhibits.

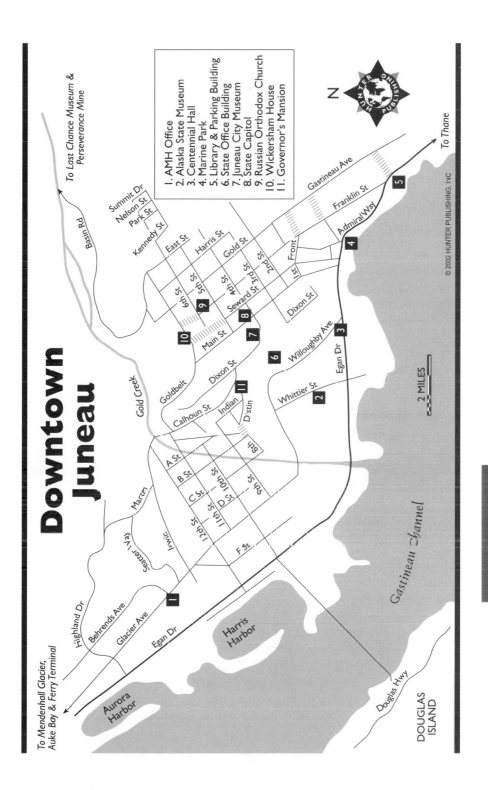

Downtown Juneau

Legend

1. AMH Office
2. Alaska State Museum
3. Centennial Hall
4. Marine Park
5. Library & Parking Building
6. State Office Building
7. Juneau City Museum
8. State Capitol
9. Russian Orthodox Church
10. Wickersham House
11. Governor's Mansion

© 2002 HUNTER PUBLISHING, INC

To Last Chance Museum &
Perseverance Mine

To Thane

To Mendenhall Glacier,
Auke Bay & Ferry Terminal

2 MILES

Gastineau Channel

DOUGLAS
ISLAND

Southeast

This is one of the best museums in the state; maybe only Sheldon Jackson in Sitka surpasses it. Although the downstairs exhibits could use better signage, this place is well worth a morning of your time. Don't miss the Eskimo whaling boat, or the startlingly beautiful collection of masks. The museum also regularly bring in traveling exhibitions. $4 per adult.

JUNEAU-DOUGLAS CITY MUSEUM: Another museum, this one on 4th and Main. It tracks Juneau's history from its early gold mining days to its current status of national importance. There are some touchable displays that kids love. The museum is open weekdays, 9-5, weekends, 10-5 in the summer. For more information, ☎ 586-3572. Admission is $1.

STATE CAPITOL: Also at 4th and Main is the Alaska State Capitol. Free tours are offered in the summer, every half-hour from 8:30-5.

CHURCHES: Although Juneau was never a Russian city, there is a Russian Orthodox church in town, **St. Nicholas**, at 326 5th St. (☎ 586-1023). It is open from 9-6, Monday-Saturday, for general visits and you can attend Sunday services (be aware that Russian Orthodox services are long, and nobody ever sits down). The church was built in 1894, and was rebuilt in the late 70s. While not as spectacular as the Russian Orthodox structures in Sitka, Kodiak, or Dutch Harbor, it does offer a good look at the Russian face of Alaska. The small size of it, and the quite beautiful paintings, make this place something special. They request a $1 donation for admission. Another popular church downtown is the **Episcopal Church of the Holy Trinity** at 4th and Gold, which was built in 1896.

The final scenic church is the **Shrine of St. Therese**, 23 miles north of downtown. The shrine, made of dark stone that seems to blend into the forest backdrop, is open daily. It sits on a tiny spit of land in a truly lovely location and is especially nice at sunset. Walk the stations of the cross and swat at mosquitoes.

 WATCHABLE WILDLIFE *There's a good chance of seeing whales or other sea mammals offshore by the church. Keep a lookout as you enjoy the scenery.*

WICKERSHAM HOUSE: This house at 213 7th St., ☎ 586-9001, features a marvelous collection of ivory carvings. It has been a longstanding labor of love, trying to get the house back into the shape it was when Judge Wickersham (Alaska's first territorial delegate to Congress) lived there, with storytelling and re-enactments of Juneau's history. It's three bucks to get in, open 10-12 and 1-5 daily except Wednesday.

NATIONAL MARINE FISHERIES LAB: In Auke Bay, ☎ 789-6000, the lab offers free self-guided tours on weekdays from 8-4:30. It's a great chance to see what's under the water of Southeast. Excellent aquariums.

GASTINEAU SALMON HATCHERY: A commercial hatchery that offers very brief tours for $3 (2697 Channel Dr,. ☎ 463-4810). Although they have some good aquariums inside, unless you're there at exactly the right moment – either when fish are returning or fry are being released – there isn't much to the tour that can't be seen from outside the building.

LAST CHANCE MINING MUSEUM: This museum gives you a glimpse of what built Juneau: greed. It's at 1001 Basin Road, ☎ 586-5338. Located in the Jualpa Mine Camp National Historic District, it's your best chance to see how a really big mining operation worked. Open 9:30-12:30 and 3:30-6:30 daily. The cost of admission is $3, and for that you get to see the world's largest Ingersoll-Rand air compressor. Wait till you get home and tell your friends. Seriously, big mines built much of Alaska, and you owe it to yourself to see how they worked – and to see the lengths people went to simply to pull small bits of rock out of larger bits of rock.

GLACIER GARDENS: A botanical garden located at 7600 Glacier Highway, ☎ 790-3377. Guided tours lead you up a mountain through the beautiful Southeast rainforest. And there's no strain on your legs – you're riding in a golf cart. It's a good chance to get a close-up look at the forest and its inhabitants. The guides know the plants, offering a detailed narrative of what you're looking at and how the Natives used the plants of the forest. Admission is $14.95 for adults. Open Monday through Saturday, 9-8, and Sundays, 9-6.

ALASKAN BREWING COMPANY: Juneau is famous for its local beer produced by this company, 5429 Shane Dr. (☎ 780-5866). Tours are offered from 11-5, Tuesday through Saturday. If you're a beer drinker, don't miss the ale, which compares with Europe's finest. Their amber was voted Best Beer in the Nation in 1986. All of the beers produced here are unpasteurized and contain no preservatives.

CONCERTS: During the summer, there are free concerts at **Marine Park** on Friday nights at 7 PM. The park is about a half-mile north of the cruise ship docks. ☎ 586-ARTS for more information. There are free organ concerts at noon (year-round) on Fridays in the State Office Building.

SALOONS & BARS: It seems as though every cruise ship passenger stops at the **Red Dog Saloon**, 278 S. Franklin, ☎ 463-3777, although it's difficult to figure out why. It is crowded, expensive, and the only bar in town with a gift shop bigger than the serving area. Ultimately what it proves is that cruise ship passengers really do listen to those on board "shopping experts." Why, we'll never know. Locals prefer **The Alaskan**, just down the road at 167 S. Franklin, ☎ 586-1000, which is in a lovely old building listed on the historic register.

EAGLECREST SKI AREA: Finally, if you're here in winter and find that everything has shut down, don't despair. Eaglecrest Ski Area, on Douglas Island, has some of Alaska's best snow. ☎ 790-2000 for reservations and opening schedules. Cross-country skiing near the face of

Southeast

Mendenhall Glacier under a full moon is an experience not to be missed. The lake freezes and is perfect for skating.

■ Mendenhall Glacier

 The town of Juneau is a great place, but it's not the shows and shops that draw people; ice is Juneau's biggest attraction. Mendenhall, the most easily accessible glacier in Southeast, is just a little finger of the enormous Juneau Icefields, albeit a 12-mile-long, 1½-mile-wide finger. When you consider that the icefields cover more than 1,500 square miles (bigger than Rhode Island), Mendenhall pales in significance. When you're standing there saying wow, think how much ice is back there that you can't see. Without exception, everybody who comes to Juneau says that the high point of their trip was going up on the glacier. Do not miss this.

Drive to the glacier along **Mendenhall Loop Road**, which leads directly to a hill overlooking the glassy blue-gray waters of Mendenhall Lake – the color is due to the meltwater dumped in from the glacier. Toward the south, even from more than a mile away, you can hear the roar of a waterfall pouring into the lake.

The glacier towers more than 100 feet above the surface of the lake and, as with an iceberg, there is a lot more below the surface of the water. Mendenhall Lake is as deep as 200 feet.

ADVANCING OR RETREATING?

The glacier is receding at a rate of about 25 feet per year and, by looking at the hillsides around the glacier, you can see the damage that the moving ice causes. Rock closest to the ice is stripped bare, while farther away from the retreating mass, plantlife starts to take hold.

There is a two-foot forward motion to the glacier each day but, with the larger retreat, melting, and breakage, the overall effect is of a diminishing glacier.

The **Mendenhall Glacier Visitor's Center**, ☎ 789-0097, open 8-5 daily (summer), sits on the hill above the parking lot. It offers films about the glacier, as well as some good displays on glaciation. Check with the rangers as to where the daily guided hike is headed.

Hiking Mendenhall Glacier

There are some good trails that get you closer to the ice. The **Photo Point Trail** is only .3 miles long and takes you to the edge of the lake. There's also a half-mile **interpretive trail**, pointing out the effects of a glacier on the landscape. The more ambitious should try the **East Glacier Loop Trail**. Although it doesn't offer great views of the ice, it takes you past several waterfalls into the high mountain rainforest above the glacier on a 3½-mile loop. The prettiest and most strenuous of all the hikes is the **West Glacier Trail**, with its starting point over near the campground, on the other side of the lake. This 3½-mile trail offers increasingly lovely glacial views – make sure you have plenty of film.

Helicopter Tours of Mendenhall

Like we said above, going up and walking on the glacier is what pretty much everybody lists as the high point of their trip to Southeast. There are a lot of helicopter tours up, none of them cheap. Our advice is this: get the trip that you can afford that spends the most time possible on the ice. Even Martha Stewart loved the glacier, although she refused to wear the red safety jacket her outfitter gave to all clients. Apparently it clashed, and she didn't get on the chopper until they found her a blue one.

On a busy day, the number of helicopters heading to and from the glacier make the skies over Juneau look like a scene from *Apocalypse Now*. But there's a reason: everybody loves it up there.

Take a trip to a Juneau glacier.

Southeast

With that in mind, that the longer you stay on the glacier the happier you'll be, the operator of choice is **Northstar Trekking**, ☎ 790-4530, www.glaciertrekking.com. For $380, you get a four-hour expedition, including a flyby of the icefields and about two hours on the glacier. You're fully outfitted with boots, crampons, ice axe, gaiters, and a very warm coat, then helicoptered up to the glacier, where you're given lessons in walking on thick ice. With guides, you trek the face of the glacier, up and down ridges, past beautiful blue sinkholes, alongside little streams that run on the glacier face, their water only about .2 degrees above freezing. Usually, you end up at a vertical ice face, learning how to ice climb, which is a lot of work and a lot of fun. You need to be at least vaguely fit to enjoy this trip to the fullest – Northstar says that you may end up walking as much as two miles on the glacier, and it is walking up and down hills, although with the crampons walking on the ice doesn't feel all that much different than walking on dry ground. What is different is the view. Nobody else in Juneau gives you such a good look at the glacier, or this much time up on the ice. The other great advantage to Northstar is that they take only a few people at a time; with some of the other operators, especially on a cruise ship day, the glacier landing areas can get as crowded as a downtown street corner. With Northstar, you're out there with, at most, a dozen other people, and nobody else in sight. This is quite simply the best thing you can do with your money in Juneau.

You can take shorter trips on the glacier, but they'll likely leave you wanting more. Northstar and **Temsco**, ☎ 789-9501, www.temscoair.com; **Coastal**, ☎ 789-5600, www.coastalhelicopters.com; and **ERA**, ☎ 586-2030, www.eraaviation.com, all offer roughly hour-long helicopter trips, which include about 20 minutes on the glacier itself. The helicopter lands and deposits you on the ice, where a naturalist points out some of the glacial features, but you don't really get to walk around and get a close look at things, as you do on the longer trip. On the way out, the chopper flies over the Juneau Icefields, getting close to pinnacles of rock in one of Alaska's most dramatic landscapes. These are the bread and butter helicopter trips in town, and you'll need to book a day or so in advance, as the cruise ships frequently have them full up. Figure around $175-200 for one glacier landing, $250 for a longer trip with two glacier landings.

Raft Trips on Mendenhall River

You can get down into the glacial waters with a float trip from **Alaska Travel Adventures**, ☎ 789-0052, or with **Auk Ta**, ☎ 586-8687. The 3½-hour tour starts near the base of the West Loop Trail. From there, you go across Mendenhall Lake and down the Mendenhall River, passing through a quick but fun Class III rapid. Trips offer you the chance either to sit while someone else does all the work, or to paddle the raft yourself. The scenery alternates between wilderness and luxury homes, with eagle nests dotting the tops of the trees. It's a lot of fun for $89. Be prepared to get wet and don't forget to bring dry socks. If you've never rafted before, you're going to enjoy this. If you have rafted before, it's probably not for you.

Heliskiing

It's reason enough to come to Juneau: tall mountains, endless snow. **Out of Bounds Adventures**, ☎ 800-HELL-YEA, or 789-7008, on-line at www.heliskialaska.com, runs trips into the deep back country. It's not cheap, but if you're a good enough skier or boarder to even think about this, you already know that. Prepare to gasp.

■ Adventures

One of the best things about Juneau is how easy it is to get out of the city and into the wild. There is excellent fishing, wildlife watching, canoeing, kayaking, hiking, and mountain biking, all within easy reach. Dozens of charter companies are ready and waiting to take you far from the bustle of downtown.

There are three one-stop booking agencies, **Orca Enterprises**, ☎ 789-6801 or 888-733-ORCA, on the Web at www.alaskawhalewatching.com – good people running a good business; **Juneau Sportfishing**, ☎ 586-1887, www.juneausportfishing.com; and **Goldbelt**, in the Seadrome Building, ☎ 800-820-2628, www.goldbelttours.com. One of the advantages of using these people is if you have a lot of things you want to do and don't want to run around making hundreds of stops or phone calls. Let them know what you want to do, then let them work out the sticky details.

Hiking

In addition to the aforementioned Mendenhall Glacier trails, you can hike to **Treadwell**, an old gold mine, now a ghost town, on Douglas Island. The trail starts from Sandy Beach. If you hike the **East Glacier Loop Trail** at Mendenhall, you'll also find a few remains of mining operations.

Among the most popular is the 2½-mile **Perseverance Hike**, an easy 2¼-hour hike that follows an old wagon road used by gold miners. There are still mining implements left by the prospectors along the trail. Also popular is the 3½ mile, three-hour **Mt. Roberts Hike**, which takes you up through mossy rainforest into the high alpine meadows above town (quite nice when the wildflowers are in bloom). On a clear day, you could not ask for more beautiful views of the sapphire Gastineau Channel and surrounding area. If you hike up Mt. Roberts, you can catch the tram back down for $5.

Salmon Creek is a bit more challenging. It's 3½ miles one way, and you can figure on six hours for the round-trip. The trailhead is at Mile 2.5 of Egan Dr., behind the Salmon Creek Powerhouse. The trail follows an old mining trailing; you walk on a fairly wide roadbed that is being allowed to grow back into forest. The last mile of the hike is up a fairly steep slope, leading to the reservoir. The lower reaches of the trail are a favored berry-picking area in season.

If you want a truly difficult trail, try the **Blackberry Ridge Route**, 3½ miles one way, a 10-hour round-trip. It's an unmaintained route that climbs 3,000 feet from sea level. The trail is undeveloped and not well marked, but you'll be rewarded by great views of the Lemon and Ptarmigan Glaciers. The trailhead is off Egan Dr., up the Salmon Creek exit. It starts, unmarked, from the end of Wire St. Be sure to go prepared for boggy, wet conditions.

Another very difficult but rewarding hike is the **Amalga Trail**. This is 7½ miles long, and will take 10-12 hours. While there is not much elevation gain – only 500 feet or so – it can be very boggy. The trail, which leads to the invisible remains of the old Amalga Mine and then up to Eagle Glacier, part of the Juneau Icefield, dead-ending at the moraine in front of the glacier, is one of Juneau's wilder hikes: bears are common, and even wolverines have been sighted. Pick up the trailhead at Mile 28.4 on the Glacier Highway.

Easier glacier views can be had on the **Herbert Glacier Trail**, a 4.6-mile trail that you should be able to do in an easy four hours. It's a good trail for seeing how the earth responds to a glacier's pullback – the closer you get to the glacial face, the more barren the ground is. The Herbert Glacier Trail is a good place to watch for bears, and check the surrounding mountains for goats. **Juneau Parks and Recreation**, ☎ 586-5226, run biweekly hikes of varying difficulty.

    📖   For more information on hiking, pick up *90 Short Hikes in Juneau*, or *Juneau Hikes*, both available at the Mendenhall Visitor's Center or in bookstores around town.

Kayaking

Juneau is kayaking paradise. Head north of town, put in, start paddling, watch for whales. It's that simple.

Alaska Discovery, 5449-4 Shaune Dr., ☎ 780-6226 or 800-586-1911, www.akdiscovery.com, one of Juneau's oldest operators, has been bought out by Mountain Travel-Sobek, so you know the kind of trips they run. They also have a lovely lodge in Glacier Bay that runs $100 a night for a double. Their kayaking trips include eight days paddling Glacier Bay for

$2,390, five days for $1,695. **Pack Creek** kayak/bear-watching trips are $475 for single days, or 2½ days for $895. They've also got shorter trips around Juneau.

If you're not familiar with kayaking, **Auk Ta Shaa** (☎ 800-820-2628) has introductory trips for $95. You'll be briefed on kayak safety and then, with no more than five paddlers per guide, taken out into the calm waters north of Juneau.

WATCHABLE

WILDLIFE

There's an excellent chance of seeing whales and seals when you're in a kayak – a much different experience than seeing them from the tall, noisy ferry.

For longer trips, **Alaska Discovery** runs 2½-day trips to Pack Creek, for bear-watching, at $895. You fly over, paddle Admiralty, and fly back. They also have a trip along Juneau's coastline, three days, $495. Finally, they can set you up with kayak rentals in Glacier Bay (guided one-day paddles there are $119).

AUTHOR TIP

Kayaks are smooth and easy to paddle, and you don't need to be an athlete to enjoy this great way of sightseeing.

Other places to rent kayaks in town include **Alaska Paddle Sports**, ☎ 789-2382; **Juneau Outdoor Center**, ☎ 586-8220; **Adventure Sports**, ☎ 789-5696; and **Auke Bay Kayak Rentals**, in the Auke Bay Harbor, ☎ 790-6545. Figure $40-50 per day for a single kayak.

For kayak drop-offs contact Auk Nu for Glacier Bay, ☎ 586-8687 or 800-820-2628; **Adventure Bound Alaska**, ☎ 463-2509 or 800-228-3875, for trips into the Tracy Arm; or **Kayak Express**, ☎ 790-4591, for custom trips.

Whale-Watching

Juneau is prime whale habitat, and you won't likely get a better chance to see these giants up close. The most eco-sensitive operator for whale-watching is Captain Larry's, booked through **Orca Enterprises**, ☎ 789-6801 or 888-733-ORCA, www.alaskawhalewatching.com. These people had the boat custom-made to ensure that it had the least impact possible on the whales – special set ups for running as quietly and clean as possible. From above, the boat is a bit unusual looking – it's bright purple, for starters – but the whales seem to love it, and they don't run from it the way they do regular boats. Another advantage is that the boat is fully handicapped-accessible.

Captain Larry (yes, that's his name) runs classes to teach boat captains how to act around whales, and the company is heavily involved in education and helping the biologists gather information on whales and orcas.

Southeast

These are the people to go with. The trips run 3½ hours, including transportation from your hotel, so you get about 2½ hours on the water. A bargain for $99. Trips run in summer at 9:30, noon, and 3:30. You will come off this trip with a huge smile on your face. Ask about their adopt-a-whale program.

THE IMPORTANCE OF BINOCULARS

On August 13, 2000, the *Juneau Empire* had the following front-page headline: "Faking it for Tourists: Man says he fooled thousands of visitors by using an old boat to simulate a whale."

The thrust of the article is that a man, whom we shall not name, and who was later fired by the people he worked for, took the Grinch theory of reindeer and applied it to whales: if he couldn't find one, he'd make one instead. According to the article, he took a 22-foot fiberglass skiff, flipped it over, painted the hull a mottled black, and scuttled the boat. He even checked this out with the Coast Guard, which didn't care as long as no oil pollution resulted.

"The result was near perfect, as the strakes of the hull closely resembled the forward end of a humpback, barnacles and scars were realistic looking, and the blowhole [water forced up by waves through a hole in the hull] worked astonishingly well."

The fake whale floated for a couple weeks, and appears as a small black dot on thousands of tourist photos. Finally the Coast Guard labeled the skiff a navigation hazard and made him get it out of the water.

Real whales move around. Lots. Half-sunk boats drift. Know the difference, know your operator.

Juneau Sportfishing, ☎ 586-1887, has a four-hour (on the water) whale-watching trip for $125. Two-and-a-half-hour trips are $90. **Dolphin Whalewatch Tours** runs similar trips, using a bright red jetboat. ☎ 463-3422. Less flexible is the **Gustavus Ferry**, ☎ 586-8687 or 800-820-BOAT, which runs twice-daily trips from Juneau to Gustavus, the base for trips to Glacier Bay. The basic cost is $85 round-trip; there's a whale-watching add-on that bumps the price up to $139. Or you can do the whale-watching and skip Gustavus for $78. They run you farther from Juneau, into Icy Strait, which is chock-full of whales in summer. The downside is, you're on a pretty big boat.

SELECTING A WHALE-WATCHING BOAT

If you can't get on an Orca trip, you've got to go out and find somebody else. There are a lot of whale-watching trips and excursions that run out of Juneau. One thing to watch out for is how the whales are approached. There are teams of boats that will surround the whales – this makes sure you get a good look at the whales, but it also really irritates the whales and disrupts their day. Before booking with anybody, ask how many boats, how many people, and what they do when they sight whales. Also find out how long you're actually going to be on the water – some will tell you it's a three-hour trip, but that includes ground time, which cuts dramatically into your watching time.

Fishing Charters

There are more than three dozen fishing charter boats in Juneau, offering everything from half-day to full-week excursions. For a complete list, you can check with the Log Cabin Visitor Center.

Orca Enterprises, ☎ 789-6801, has a roster of a dozen captains they can put you out with. The quality of your experience is their prime goal. The same high standards that they apply to their whale-watching trip go here, too. Prices are $135 for a half-day, $250 for the whole.

Another good place to call is **Juneau Sportfishing**, ☎ 586-1187, which maintains a large fleet of boats and can customize your trip. Prices will vary according to the ship you take out and where you want to go. Figure on $125 for a half-day, $205 for a full day for their basic fishing charter. This includes everything but the license, which you can purchase on board the boat ($10 per day/$15 for three days; $30 per month; $50 per year). Trips are limited to a maximum of six.

A company that does longer trips is **Adventures Afloat**. Their trips run two days or longer, with prices starting around $900. Visit them at 4950 Steelhead, or ☎ 789-0111. Other choices include **Anytime Cruises**, ☎ 789-0609, and **Bear Creek Outfitters**, ☎ 789-3914, which specialize in fly-fishing; **Wilderness Swift**, ☎ 463-4942, which runs a 32-foot boat on trips to Pack Creek and Tracy Arm; and **Juneau Sport Charters**, ☎ 789-2238; **Alaska Salmon Guaranteed**, ☎ 789-9345; and **Capital City**, ☎ 789-3871, all of whom can take you out for salmon or halibut. **Auke Bay Sportfishing/Charters** runs a fleet of boats and can customize your trip. ☎ 789-2562.

ABC Alaska's Yacht Rentals, ☎ 789-1239, can rent you bare boats if you've got the experience to head out on your own.

Southeast

SELECTING A CHARTER BOAT

For single-day charters, look for prices around $200-250. If anyone is considerably cheaper or more expensive than that, find out why. A charter should supply you with some kind of lunch or snack, all necessary fishing gear, and should at least help with the fish processing. There are also some good, lower-priced charters that simply avoid the deep water where the largest fish are, but still give you a good fun day on the boat. Ask questions and let the operators know your expectations before booking.

AUTHOR TIP *King salmon run from mid-May into October, peaking the last week of May and the first week of June. After that the coho start, followed by the chum salmon, through most of July and August.*

Flying Trips for Angling & Sightseeing

Another great way to get into the tiny communities around Juneau is by air. Contact the smaller airways listed above – Wings, L.A.B., Glacier Bay Airways – for charter rates. **Alaska Fish N' Fly Charters** runs trips to Pack Creek, to the icefields, or semi-customized trips, depending on what you want to see. Prices start around $140 per person, based on five people per plane. They'll also drop you off at Pack Creek (if you've already got the permit) for $200 per person, round-trip. If you can't get a Pack Creek permit, you can try their Bear Country Tour, where you fly over to Windfall Creek on Admiralty. From there, you head out on a 90-minute hike in great bear territory. The trip runs $400. For a chance to fly in to a remote lake, it'll run you $350 per person for four hours. Contact them at ☎ 790-2120.

Locals go with **Bear Creek Outfitters**, ☎ 789-3914 for fly-fishing. Top-notch service.

 DON'T MISS: *Save yourself the trouble of fishing and head out to eat the results of someone else's work at* **Taku Glacier Lodge**, ☎ 586-8258.

This is a great trip into Alaska's past. The lodge was originally built as a retreat for a Juneauite in 1923. It's a small cabin in a beautiful location, with the river rushing by in front and glaciers on view. To get there, you board a floatplane in downtown Juneau; the flight out is about 45 minutes, and there are great views of icefields and a good chance of seeing mountain goats on the peaks. Once at the lodge, you can pig out on salmon and watch the river flow by. There are some short hikes nearby.

It's a lovely excursion out of town for $198. You'll probably start wondering how you can buy a remote cabin for yourself.

According to the American Rivers Group, the Taku is one of the 10 most endangered rivers in the country – polluted by past mining, threatened by a proposed reopening of cold and copper mines near the banks. See it while you can.

AUTHOR TIP *Because of the smell of salmon roasting over an open fire, there's always a good chance of seeing bears – the bears can smell that salmon smoke for a couple of miles.*

■ Scenic Drives

The other great way to get out of town is to drive. All the drives to the end of the roads are nice, but especially recommended is the drive out beyond Auke Bay. The scenery is lovely; the wildflowers are out in June and the berries start to ripen in July. There are great places to walk along the beach, launch a kayak, fish, or just sit and watch the whales go by.

Another fine drive is to the north end of Douglas Island. You have a good chance of spotting a great blue heron or eagles along the Mendenhall wetlands, and there are some great views of the Mendenhall Glacier and the surrounding mountains.

If a car seems a little too modern, give **Breadline Horse Tours** a call, ☎ 790-6570.

■ Tracy Arm

Most well-traveled Alaskans will tell you that Glacier Bay is pretty, but Tracy Arm is gorgeous. Few people who've been to Tracy Arm ever see much reason to go to Glacier Bay again. It's one of the most popular excursions from Juneau.

Tracy Arm is nearly 25 miles long, but barely a mile wide. It's surrounded by cliffs towering up more than 2,500 feet above the water (which, itself, is often more than a 1,000 feet deep).

Two glaciers are responsible for the dramatic landscape (they used to be one – perhaps as recently as in the past hundred years or so – but have split as they've retreated). **North Sawyer** and **South Sawyer glaciers** are the highlights of a trip into Tracy Arm. Retreating glaciers (South Sawyer is retreating by about 300 feet per year), they are both more active than Mendenhall Glacier.

Southeast

WATCHABLE

WILDLIFE

The glaciers are surrounded by wildlife. Seals are so common that you may see a dozen of them sitting on an ice floe. Bears and mountain goats dot the shoreline and peaks, and you've got a good chance of seeing humpback or killer whales at the entrance to the channel. Porpoise are almost a sure thing, and some people go into the Arm for shrimping.

John Muir was here, of course, and he was impressed. There were already miners working the gold deposits in Holkham Bay, the entrance to the arm, when Muir arrived. There were also a few Natives left – a couple of dozen – the rest having been killed off by wars and disease.

Ships going in to Tracy Arm now face two challenges. First, there's a terminal moraine right at the entrance, barely under water. If you line your boat up wrong (there are markers), you're likely to run aground. The other problem is that there are big icebergs breaking off the glacial face. Really big. This is due, in part, to the quick retreat of the glaciers and also due to the dramatic tidal fluctuation. Those entering the Arm on their own should stay well away from the glaciers – a big enough calve can easily swamp a small boat a mile away.

Endicott Arm, a lesser-known part of the area, is equally dramatic – the retreating Dawes and North Dawes glaciers calve frequently into the water.

FORDS TERROR

If you've got your own boat or a customized charter, be sure to visit the small branch arm of Fords Terror, which was named in 1889 for a crewmember of the *Patterson,* who went ashore to duck hunt and missed the tide change. Ford dodged rough water and crushing icebergs for six hours, until the tide went slack again. At least he had good scenery to look at: cliffs, waterfalls, the narrow reaches of the fjord. It's still not a place to forget about tides: the flow can exceed 15 knots through the narrow entrance.

■ Adventures

Most of the charter outfits will run trips into Tracy Arm. It's about 130 miles, round-trip, if you're going to see everything, so plan on being out all day.

Auk Nu Tours, ☎ 586-8687 or 800-820-BOAT, runs full-day trips for $109. A light lunch is included, along with drinks and binocular use. Trips leave at 9 AM, return at 5 PM, and you travel in a 78-foot catamaran. It's a good, comfortable boat, but in the middle of the season, it can get kind of crowded. Stake out your spot early.

Adventure Bound Alaska, ☎ 463-2509 or 800-228-3875, takes a small and comfortable boat into the Arm, leaving daily at 8:30, returning at 6, for $99. This is the operator of choice for locals taking their relatives out.

Alaska Fly 'n Fish Charters, ☎ 790-2120, www.alaskabyair.com, does flyovers of the Tracy Arm for $550 – for this price, you're booking the entire plane for the nearly two-hour trip. The plane holds five people or 800 pounds, whichever comes first. Juneau Sportfishing takes you into the Arm in a 16-passenger boat. The trip runs $130. ☎ 586-1887.

■ Shopping

Most of Juneau's tourist stores are located downtown, on Franklin St. The large percentage of them are interchangeable – T-shirts, ulu knives, stuff for the relatives back home – particularly close to the cruise ship dock, but there are a couple of shops worth seeking out.

For high-quality art, The Raven's Journey, in the Senate Building, 175 S. Franklin, ☎ 463-4686, is your best bet. Beautiful whalebone carvings. Also try Portfolio Arts, across from the cruise ship dock, 493 S. Franklin, ☎ 586-8111. A wide selection of traditional and modern art, quite reasonably priced.

The Robert Service Shop, on Franklin at the intersection, doesn't look like much from the outside, but inside you'll find some of the best scrimshaw in Alaska. Also the only Juneau-made postcards you're likely to find. Spend the extra dime, buy local.

Peer Amid Beads has a huge assortment of Russian trade beads, both loose and strung. The Russians left millions of these things behind; they're even more beautiful now. Downtown, half a block off Franklin, at 213 Ferry Way, ☎ 463-4438.

William Spear Design, 174 Franklin (upstairs, above Heritage Coffee), ☎ 586-2209, www.wmspear.com, has the modern equivalent of trade beads: pins. Great designs with marvelous detail, from biological specimens to greyhound dogs.

For tourist fare with a twist, try Mt. Juneau Trading Post, 151 S. Franklin St., ☎ 586-3426. A good assortment of both high- and low-end items. They have one of the better assortments of affordable masks you'll find. Sourdough Pete's, 152 S. Franklin, ☎ 463-1226, has some great replica masks, if you can't afford the real thing.

The Observatory, 235 2nd St., ☎ 586-9676, features rare books about Alaska and a world-class collection of antique maps. There's a used bookstore around the corner, Rainy Day Books, 113 Seward, ☎ 463-2665. For new books, try Hearthside, 254 Front St., ☎ 789-2750.

Southeast

If you still need to pick up a few things before you head out into the wilderness, stop at the **Foggy Mountain Shop**, 134 N. Franklin, ☎ 586-6780. It has good camping gear and rough weather clothes (Patagonia, the North Face, Eagle Creek). There's also **Nugget Alaskan Outfitters**, in the Nugget Mall, out by the airport. Good selection of outdoor wear.

For a bit of to-go chow, try **Taku Smokeries**, next to the cruise ship dock, ☎ 800-582-5122. Smoked salmon of just about every description. Finally, if you're on your way to the ferry terminal, a stop at the **Boardwalk Bight** is worth the effort. Local art, and lots of stuff that might surprise you. 11806 Glacier Highway (near the Auke Bay Harbor), ☎ 789-2928.

■ Food

 For the state capital, the restaurant picture in town is surprisingly bleak. Everyone in the city eats at the same half-dozen or so places. Stray away from them and you're in terra incognita.

If you haven't tried a salmon bake yet, there are some good ones in Juneau. The most popular with locals is the **Thane Ore House Salmon Bake**, south of town, which has an all-you-can-eat deal for $20 per person, or $27 if you hang around and watch the play. They open at noon and, if you can beat the crowd, it makes for a great lunch spot. Free transportation. ☎ 586-3442. Also very popular is the **Gold Creek Salmon Bake**, nine miles north of town. Again, all you can eat for $22. They also run a free bus ride out to the bake site. ☎ 789-0052.

If you'd like a little more ambience, try the **Twisted Fish**, next to the Tram, in the Taku Smokeries building. The best fish you'll have in town, from $8. And you can't beat the view.

A cheap eating option where the locals flock is the **Channel Bowl Café**, 608 Willoughby, ☎ 586-6139. It's a five-minute walk from downtown. Part of the local bowling alley, they serve excellent soups and sandwiches at rock bottom prices.

If you're out at the end of town and want fast food, the **Hot Bite**, ☎ 790-2483, in the boat harbor at Auke Bay, is the place for a hamburger, and the only place in town for a serious milkshake. You'll fill up for under $6. The only problem is finding a place to park. Across the street from the Hot Bite is **Chan's Thai Kitchen**, ☎ 789-9777, which has a good vegetarian menu and dishes like Kong Tao Poh – a curry with lime leaves and tamarind juice. Prices $8-12. This is probably everybody's favorite restaurant in town.

The **Fiddlehead** is Juneau's most famous eatery – the restaurant even puts out its own cookbook. Located at 429 Willoughby, near downtown, ☎ 586-3150, they have a variety of largely natural dishes. A good place to go if you're looking for fairly healthy food. From $12.

On the Italian food front, the place to go is **Vito & Nick's**, 299 N. Franklin, ☎ 463-5051, near the airport. A fast-food place with great lasagna and pizza from $8. Lasagna that will make you cry with joy. Downtown is **Pizzeria Roma**, ☎ 463-5020, in the Wharf Building, downstairs. They've got a cheap lunch special with serious thin-crust pizza.

You've probably never had a real bagel. No, we mean a real one, with the dough boiled. Head to the **Silverbow**, 120 2nd St., and discover that bagels are not simply donuts that failed on the evolutionary ladder. Great food, great people. If you're more of a bacon and eggs sort, try the **Capital City Café**, at 2nd and Seward. Jammed in the mornings.

A favorite place to sit and watch Juneau go by is at the **Heritage Coffee Co.**, 174 S. Franklin, ☎ 586-1087. Most Alaskan coffee lovers won't drink the stuff unless it's one of Heritage's freshly roasted gourmet blends. Stop in for a cup, or for one of the light meals or pastries served. Cheap and delicious. Juneau also has the usual chain restaurants, most of which are readily evident downtown.

AUTHOR TIP *For lunch with a view, follow the lead of the local business people: get a take-out lunch and eat on the 8th floor terrace of the State Office Building. The view of the Gastineau Channel is unbeatable.*

To pick up your own lunch or breakfast, hit the **Silverbow Bakery**, at 120 2nd St., for genuine East Coast-style bagels, or pick up some health food at the **Rainbow Foods and Deli**, at 2nd and Seward.

■ Accommodations

Juneau has the widest variety of lodging in Southeast Alaska. Between the politicians and the tourists, though, it can sometimes be hard to find a room, and none of it is going to be cheap.

GHOSTS OF ALASKA, PART ONE

There are few things in life more fun than staying in a haunted hotel, and if the ghost is eccentric, all the better. There is at least one, probably two, and possibly three ghosts at the **Silverbow** (see below). The one most often spotted is that of Gus Messerschmidt, the man who started the place nearly a hundred years ago. Oddly enough, he only seems to haunt bakers and dishwashers. There are also a couple other possible ghosts in back nooks and crannies of the building.

Start with the Silverbow. They've put the same kind of care into their rooms that they do into their food at the bakery next door. In a world full of corporate monotony, it's great to find a place run by real people, with

Southeast

personality. Comfortable rooms, breakfast included, summer rates from $128 for doubles. This is the first place we call, although we haven't been lucky enough to see one of the ghosts yet. 120 2nd St., ☎ 586-4146, www.silverbowinn.com.

The **Goldbelt**, 51 W. Egan, ☎ 586-6900 or 888-478-6909, is owned by the local Native corporation. Huge rooms, many with water views. Prices start around $135. The **Baranof Hotel**, 127 N. Franklin, ☎ 586-2660 or 800-544-0970, is the local Westmark Property. Again, comfortable, and right downtown. Rooms start around $150. The **Prospector** is an easy walk from the center of town, at 375 Whittier St., ☎ 586-3737 or 800-331-2711. Comfortable doubles from $120.

At the bargain end of downtown, just down the street from the Baranof is the **Alaskan Hotel & Bar**, 167 S. Franklin, ☎ 586-1000 or 800-327-9347. Basic, but cheap. Rooms near the bar are a lot noisier. Doubles with a private bath run from $65.

The **Best Western Country Lane Inn** is at 9300 Glacier Highway, ☎ 789-5005 or 800-528-1234. Rates start at $99 for a double. Similar is the **Breakwater Inn**, 1711 Glacier Ave., ☎ 586-6303 or 800-544-2250. Doubles from $100. The **Driftwood Lodge**, 435 N. Willoughby, ☎ 586-2280 or 800-544-2239, has doubles with private baths from $85.

Juneau also has an abundance of B&Bs. The **Alaska B&B Reservation Service**, Box 21890, ☎ 586-2959 (offices at 369 S. Franklin, Suite 200), can set you up at any B&B in town, matching your personality to the property. They've also got listings in several other Southeast cities.

If you're in the mood to pamper yourself, try **Pearson's Pond Luxury Inn**, 4541 Sawa Circle, ☎ 789-3772. Huge comfortable rooms, a hot tub and a VCR in every room, and an available computer make it a great place for a longer stay. Summer rates start at $189. If you want the pampering to be in a more hotel-like setting, **Frontier Suites**, near the airport at 9400 Glacier Highway, ☎ 790-6600 or 800-544-2250, has huge rooms, some with Jacuzzis. Rates start around $100.

On Douglas Island, across the bridge from downtown, try the **Blueberry Lodge**, 9436 N. Douglas Hwy., ☎ 463-5886, which is conveniently located for skiers across the road from Eaglecrest. There's an eagle's nest right outside one of the windows. Big breakfasts and friendly hosts. Doubles from $100. **Grandma's Feather Bed**, 9300 Glacier Highway, ☎ 789-2818 or 888-781-5005, has rooms in a restored Victorian. Rates start around $90.

Juneau has a great **Youth Hostel**, 614 Harris St., ☎ 586-9559. A room in the dorm is $10. Make sure you're in by the 11 PM curfew, and know in advance that you're not going to find anywhere to park anywhere close.

■ Camping

The place to go is the **Mendenhall Lake Campground**, right by the glacier – enter from Loop Road and follow the signs. It offers 61 sites at only $10 a night for tents, up to $26 for full hookups. ☎ 800-280-2267 (a reservation costs an extra $8). Closer to the ferry terminal is the **Auke Village Campground**. Only 11 sites but just $8 a night. Nearby is the **Auke Bay RV Park**, at 11930 Glacier Highway. Full hookups for $22. ☎ 789-9467. No tent sites.

Even farther from downtown is the **Eagle Beach Camp Sites**. These are 29 miles north of town. There are no facilities except for the outhouses, so come prepared with your own water. The best thing about the sites is the price: only $5 a night.

   📖 The Juneau Visitor's Bureau offers a free brochure on what to do with an RV in Juneau's very limited spaces. ☎ 586-2201.

Hoonah

A stopping place on the run between Juneau and Sitka, Hoonah sits on Point Sophia, Chichagof Island. But the village has not been here long. Until the glacial ice in Glacier Bay advanced and pushed them out, the Huna tribe of Tlingits lived inside Glacier Bay. The village that's now Hoonah was finally settled by the Huna after they had ranged around the Icy Strait region for some time.

The Russians were fond of Pitt Island, in front of Hoonah, as an anchorage, and made frequent stops here, but they didn't stay long. The town got its first store in 1883 and since that time has grown very slowly, reaching its current population of just under 900. Most people make their living through hunting, logging, and fishing.

LOCAL LEGEND

There is an explanation for the advance of the ice. According to tribal custom, when girls reached maturity they became unclean, and had to go into a ritual seclusion for some months to a year. During this period they saw only their mother, who brought them food. One girl did not want to play by the rules; instead, she called the glacier down upon the village, forcing everyone to move.

What you're going to find in Hoonah is... well, not much. It's a quiet town where not a lot is going on, and there isn't a fantastic amount of scenery – the area around town has been devastated by clear-cut. Jokes in Southeast make it out to be something like the Cleveland of Alaska.

> ### BASKET WEAVERS
>
> Hoonah is home to some of the last truly traditional Tlingit basket weavers. This nearly dead artform involves boiling reeds and, while they're piping hot, stripping them with your teeth. Basket weavers who have been at it a long time have arch-shaped teeth. New Tlingit baskets made in the old style are now nearly impossible to find; prices start above $200 and go up rapidly.

■ Basics

The **Alaska Marine Highway** serves Hoonah four times a week. Local number is ☎ 945-3292. The stopover, usually two hours, is long enough to see the town. However, most of the runs hit Hoonah in the middle of the night. If you stop here in daylight, you'll notice every house in the town looks the same. The original village burned in 1944 and the U.S. government diverted a shipment of houses destined for military use in the Pacific theater. Fly into Hoonah on **Wings of Alaska**, ☎ 945-3275, and **L.A.B.**, ☎ 945-3661.

■ Local History

Stop at the old Hoonah cannery, built in 1912, which is about a mile north of town. There is also excellent berry-picking and fishing in and around the town. The only other standard attraction is the Hoonah Cultural Center, with a small museum open Monday through Friday, 10-3.

■ Adventures

Whale-Watching

The best thing about Hoonah is its location on the edge of Icy Strait, prime whale country. Humpbacks sometimes come right up to Hoonah's docks. Still, if you're looking for an Icy Strait ferry trip, you're probably better off taking the Pelican run – at the very least, you get more daylight to look for whales.

Hiking

The Forest Service office in Hoonah has a bit of trail and kayaking information on the district. They maintain three hikes nearby. There is only one Forest Service cabin near Hoonah, the Salt Lake Bay cabin, 10 miles southwest of town. Get in touch with the **Hoonah Ranger District** at Box 135, Hoonah, 99829, ☎ 945-3631.

Kayaking

Hoonah is often used as a stopping point in a grand kayak trip from Tenakee to Glacier Bay. You have to portage at the head of Tenakee Inlet, in a location the Natives called "Killer Whale Crossing Place." The name comes from a time when the land was a bit lower, and a group actually saw the orcas crossing from Tenakee Inlet into the waters of Port Frederick. The portage also features prominently in Louis L'Amour's book, *Sitka*. It's a pretty simple route to follow: northwest up Tenakee Inlet, past Long Bay and Seal Bay (chance to spot grizzly bears in both), past an area where Vancouver had trouble with locals trying to steal his anchor chains. If you hit the dead end of Tenakee Inlet, you've gone too far by about a mile. The portage is pretty obvious; once you've done it, simply follow the shoreline out to Icy Strait.

■ Food

 The **Huna Totem Lodge** has a restaurant, which is one of only four places in Hoonah to eat. ☎ 945-3636. If you don't like the food here, you can try **Papa Smurf's** for pizza and burgers. Alternatively, give **Spanky's Pizza & Deli** or **Mary's Inn** a shot. Mary's Inn Restaurant is a non-profit operation, benefitting Hoonah's kids.

■ Accommodations

 There isn't a wide choice of places to stay in town. There's the **Hubbard's B&B**, ☎ 945-3414; the **Huna Totem Lodge**, ☎ 945-3636, roughly 1½ miles from the ferry terminal; and **Snug Harbor Lodge**, ☎ 945-3636.

■ Camping

You are pretty much free to camp anywhere outside of town, but check before pitching your tent to be sure. Snuggle down and drift away.

Tenakee

Tenakee Hot Springs is one of Juneau's favorite weekend retreats. The upper crust of Juneau society has weekend houses here, and many even retire in this tiny town of about 100 permanent residents with no roads and no plumbing. Then the ferry comes through, dumps a load of tourists, and the town is overrun, up to their eyebrows in strangers. The permanent residents are people who moved this far into the boonies to be left alone, so it's easy to understand why Tenakee is one of the few un-friendly towns in Alaska. Unless you're planning to move here, it's not re-ally worth the effort to come to Tenakee; there are a lot of better hot springs around.

■ History

The town has always been a vacation spot, even before its offi-cial founding in 1899. The hot springs have long drawn people, including local Indians, to soak in the mineral waters. There are even some pictographs nearby, recounting a battle between warring bands. The victors went to soak in the hot springs, the losers lay decapi-tated on the beach.

The town was founded as a vacation retreat for fishermen and miners drawn to the waters. When an East Coast journalist visited the area in 1943, his only comment was, "Tenakee, as seen from the water's edge, consists of the Brunswick pool room, Snyder's grocery store, a salmon cannery, and a row of shacks built on pilings with Chic Sale annexes at the end of the piers." Those were the boom days.

■ Tenakee Today

Today, Tenakee survives on pensions and a very small income from tour-ism. Since there's so little for a tourist to spend money on, residents see tourists as a problem, not a solution. As with most small, remote, retreat towns in Alaska, the mood is considerably less friendly than you find elsewhere. Not hostile – but there's a definite sense among most of the lo-cals that they wish you'd just go away.

A few commercial fishing boats go out from Tenakee's harbor, and there are nearby logging operations that help keep the town afloat.

■ Basics

 The **Alaska Marine Highway** stops in Tenakee two or three times a week during its Juneau-Sitka run. You cannot unload a vehicle in Tenakee. There is only one road and it is off-limits to all traffic except the residents' own ATVs and bicycles. When the ferry docks, you'll see locals taking off their shopping in wheeled carts. Most people make a monthly trip to Juneau.

From Juneau, **Wings of Alaska** (☎ 789-0790) makes daily flights to Tenakee.

Tenakee's zip code is **99841**.

■ Adventures

There are really only three things to do in Tenakee: hike, fish, and soak in the springs. All of them are easily accomplished and you can do them on your own.

Hiking

The mountain behind the town is laced with hiking trails. A good one starts right by the boat harbor and follows the shoreline around the point. Along the way you'll pass by several bear dens, so take care. Make noise while you hike and stay away from loaded berry bushes.

Fishing

For fishing, the easiest thing to do is hike out with your pole and try your luck for salmon. With a boat, there's also good halibut fishing, crabbing, and shrimping.

Kayaking & Canoeing

If you're a kayaker or a canoer, the possibilities are endless on the smooth water of the inlet – see the Hoonah section, above, for one of the longer possible routes. You can transport your boat cheaply on the ferry; if you don't have your own, check the Juneau section for rentals.

WATCHABLE

WILDLIFE

There are lots of humpback whales, otters, and seals in the inlet. Keep a look out and maybe you be rewarded with seeing some.

Southeast

Tenakee Hot Springs

The hot spring itself is strictly segregated, and the pool is not really very big, measuring only 5 x 9 feet. Wash off fully before getting into the tub – it is for soaking only, not cleaning. The water runs about 106°, the temperature of a mildly hot bath. Hours for men are 2-6 PM and 10 PM-9 AM. Women can soak from 9 AM to 2 PM and 6 to 10 PM. Admission is free, but donations for the bath's upkeep are welcome at Snyder Mercantile. Don't wear jewelry in the tub – the metals react with the water.

■ Food & Accommodations

Much of Tenakee – including the only real hotel – burned down in the summer of 1993. Nobody ever got around to rebuilding a lot of stuff, so your choice of places to eat or stay is very limited: eat at the **Blue Moon Café** or prepare your own food, and camp or stay in one of the cottages rented by Snyder Mercantile.

Snyder Mercantile is the only store in town (which has amazingly cheap prices for such a small town) and the only place for food now that the tavern is gone. It's an old-fashioned general store in the best sense of the word, offering a little bit of everything, including some places to stay. The Mercantile rents out several very basic but very comfortable cabins in Tenakee. Some of these have porches right over the water. You have to bring your own bedding – there are beds, but no sheets or blankets – and the toilet is an outhouse some distance away. The cabins have full kitchens and are a bargain starting at $45. Besides, if you want a roof, this is what's on offer. Contact the Mercantile at P.O. Box 505, Tenakee, AK 99841. ☎ 736-2205. If they're full, try the **Patch B&B**, ☎ 736-2258, or the **Tenakee Hot Springs Lodge**, ☎ 736-2400.

■ Camping

You can camp outside of Tenakee. Turn right out of the ferry dock and head up the trail about three-quarters of a mile, where there are several tent campsites. Another three-quarters of a mile farther down you'll find a few more sites. Use all proper bear precautions here: no food in the tent and, if you don't have bearproof food storage with you, hang your food from a tree – not too close to the tent.

Angoon & Admiralty Island

Angoon, the only permanent community on Admiralty Island, draws more than its share of visitors looking for bears. Admiralty Island National Monument has its headquarters in Angoon, and the densest population of bears in Alaska – about four per square mile – is a draw for nature lovers.

The earliest charts show Admiralty as being attached to the mainland; it wasn't until Vancouver circumnavigated the island that its insular status was marked on the maps. In his endless attempts to suck up to power, he named the newly found island "Admiralty," after the group he was hoping would give him a better job and a more cooperative crew when he got home.

EARLY CONFLICTS

No matter how freaked out the early explorers might have been by the bears, Admiralty was such an obviously rich place that there were bound to be conflicts between the Natives and the European settlers. Much of the action took place on Killisnoo Island, three miles southwest of the present location of Angoon. There, the Northwest Trading Company built a whaling station and a herring reduction plant. Another whaling station was built on the southeast tip of Admiralty.

Relations between the Europeans and the Tlingit turned bad when a Tlingit shaman was killed in a hunting accident. The villagers seized a whaling ship, nets, and two settlers, and they demanded 200 blankets as compensation, plus two days off from their government-imposed corvee labor, to perform funeral rites. Ever reasonable, the Northwest Trading Company went to the military in Sitka and got them to shell the town on October 26, 1882. Most of the houses were destroyed and the town's winter supplies were wiped out. The villagers themselves had to pay out 400 blankets to make up for the trouble of getting the gunship here. Although the Navy has, for over a hundred years, managed to avoid demands for an apology, in 1973, the U.S. government paid out $90,000 to compensate for the bombing.

Angoon sits on the edge of Kootznahoo Inlet, on a mud flat that spurts with clam spit. Behind it tower the mountains of Admiralty, and the bears. But bears aren't the island's only attraction: it's estimated that more than 1,000 eagle nests are on Admiralty.

Southeast

Unfortunately, the natural wonders are not close to town. If you're just spending a couple of hours here, walk along the beach just beyond the ferry dock and look for the remains of a lovely old cemetery.

The Admiralty Island National Monument overlaps with the Kootznoowoo Wilderness. "Kootznoowoo" is the transliteration of a Tlingit word meaning "Fortress of the Bears." The Russians called the island *Ostrov Kutsnoi*, which translates to "Island of Fear." Their attitude was obviously a little different than John Muir's. When he came past looking for glaciers, he called the island "this foodful, kindly wilderness."

Residents will tell you that Angoon isn't the happiest town around, that it's always been a hard place to live, with lots of wars and disaster; those who grew up there think the place has a haunted feeling, as if there were oppressive spirits around. Or maybe it's just being outnumbered by all the bears.

■ Basics

Angoon is served by the **Alaska Marine Highway** three or four times a week, on the run between Juneau and Sitka. If the stopover isn't in the middle of the night, there's plenty of time to see the town – if you can catch a ride the two miles there – but no time to see the island. **L.A.B.**, ☎ 788-3500, and **Wings of Alaska**, ☎ 788-3530, fly into Angoon.

■ Accommodations

Most people who visit the island stay in a **Forest Service cabin** or camp. The Forest Service runs an office in Angoon, ☎ 788-3166, and offers information on local trails (none maintained) and kayaking routes.

In town, the **Favorite Bay Inn**, ☎ 788-3123, and **Kootznahoo Inlet Lodge**, ☎ 788-3501, offer accommodations for around $85. Both places can also help you rent a canoe or kayak, or get you out to where the bears are. There are no restaurants in town; get your food at **Angoon Trading**, ☎ 788-3111 (closed Sundays), or, better for your wallet, carry in supplies from Juneau or Sitka.

■ Pack Creek

The most popular viewing site for bears is Pack Creek, on the Juneau side of Admiralty – and trips here are easier to arrange from Juneau than Angoon. Some of the bears there are habituated to humans and go about their business as usual. This means they're not afraid of you – bears in the Pack Creek area have destroyed a lot of camping gear.

Pack Creek is one of Southeast's two best bear-watching spots (the other is Anan Bear Reserve, near Wrangell). In season (July and August), when the fish are in the stream, there will be bears at the platform. Big, brown bears. There's nothing quite like spotting a 600-pound bear ripping a salmon apart. Still, unlike a trip to Anan, where you can roll up in Wrangell in the morning and be watching bears in a couple of hours, a trip to Pack Creek requires advance planning: you're going to need a permit.

Most outfitters already have the permit required to go to Pack Creek between June 1 and September 10. If you're looking to get your own permit, contact the Forest Service office at 101 Egan Drive, ☎ 586-8751, in Juneau. Permits are $50 per person in the peak season (July 5 through August 25) and $20 in the shoulder season. Permits for seniors and juniors are half-price.

Permit numbers are very limited and they're hard to come by in the peak season. You can't simply show up the day before you want to go out. Applying three days in advance of your planned trip offers a vague hope, when a lottery is done for four permits. Every day a drawing is held for a permit for the third day following. Pick which day you want to go, count three days back, and apply on that day. Then cross your fingers and get out your rabbit's foot. Off-peak, you don't need to worry so much about advance reservations, but your chances of spotting bears diminish dramatically. Once the salmon are out of the stream, the bears don't have much reason to hang around.

You land roughly a mile from the observation tower. There are bearproof food containers near the landing, so be sure to use them. No food should be taken up the trail. On the trail, make noise, and let the bears know you're there. Talk loudly to each other, sing, call out "Hey, bear," at blind corners. We'll say it again: Never surprise anything that can swallow your head.

Once you get up to the observation tower, it's a matter of waiting. You'll have better luck if you're quiet, and don't use camera flashes when you see a bear. There is a maximum of eight people allowed in the tower at any given time, and if it's really busy, the rangers will kick you out of the tower after three hours. There is an alternative viewing spot, on the spit roughly a quarter-mile from the boat landing. This puts you at the mouth of the river, a bit less than half a mile from the observation tower.

You are restricted to these two areas at Pack Creek. Everywhere else is reserved for the bears, and the advantage of limiting people to these two places is that the bears know where to expect you.

Southeast

Remember at all times in bear country that a surprised bear is an unhappy bear. And you don't want to run into unhappy bears.

You can camp at the north end of Windfall Island, just across the water from Pack Creek. There is no camping allowed anywhere near the bear reserve on Admiralty. There's no water at the site, so bring your own.

No more than 12 people are allowed at the viewing area at any given time, and only 24 people per day. Pack Creek closes from 9 PM to 9 AM. Again, you are allowed only on the trails around Pack Creek and there is no camping permitted on the main island near the bear reserve. Although there are rangers at the creek, they are there for the bears, not you. There's no drinking water, no food, no toilets, nothing. For more details, contact the Juneau office noted above.

You can charter a trip to Pack Creek from Juneau quite easily. **Alaska Discovery**, 5449 Shaune Dr., #4, ☎ 780-6226, www.akdiscovery.com, in Juneau, leads guided trips of prime bear-viewing areas. $475 for single days, or 2½ days for $895. Check the Juneau outfitter listings for more options.

There are two unrestricted viewing areas near Pack Creek: **Swan Cove** and **Windfall Harbor**. The bears here are not used to humans and so can be quite unpredictable. Caution is necessary. Both areas are tideflats and they have no developed facilities. Best viewing seasons are in July and August, when the bears hit the streams for the salmon runs. Swan Cove is at the head of two rivers north of Pack Creek, a large tideflat jammed into a V-shaped area. Windfall Harbor, which does have a small shelter, is smaller, draining one river, south of Pack Creek. Nearby are two smaller flats where there are frequently bears. Charter into them from Juneau and keep in mind that it's illegal to approach bears from the water.

Bear Rules

- Speak softly.
- Don't use flashes. If you have a pocket camera with an automatic flash, put black tape over it. Startling a bear is rarely a good idea.
- Don't rush from one side of the viewing platform to another. The more slowly you move and the calmer you are, the less chance you'll have of spooking the bears.
- Before heading out here, particularly if you're going to camp, read the section on bears, pages 42-46. Even if you're camping nearby on a small island, guess what? Bears can swim, and they can smell food from miles away.

Pelican

The beauty of Pelican is not so much the town itself – even if it is the most scenic of the fishing villages in Southeast – but the ride into Pelican. The ferry from Juneau travels through Icy Strait, the best whale-watching channel in Southeast. The strait takes you around the lip of Glacier Bay and into Lisianski Inlet, a narrow passage lined by 3,000-foot mountains.

The ferry does not go into Glacier Bay at all, but the run to Pelican is as close as it gets. After passing Pleasant Island (named by S. Hall Young, who camped here with John Muir), the ferry goes right past Gustavus, past the Sitakaday Narrows, and south of the huge Brady Glacier, the southernmost glacier in the park. Turning south, the ship passes Elfin Cove, a tiny fishing village, rounds the Althorp Peninsula, and enters Lisianski Inlet, which nearly splits Chichagof Island in half.

"PELICAN"

The town of Pelican was founded in 1938 by Charles Raatikainen, who named the townsite after his boat. Now, in front of the state capitol in Juneau are some sculptured pelicans. Hired to make a sculpture that captured the real Alaska, the sculptor cast about for something that said "Alaska" without bringing up the Outside's stereotype of snow, ice and polar bears. He looked at a map, noticed Pelican, and didn't bother to check bird books to find there were no pelicans in Alaska.

With or without pelicans, Pelican thrives as a fishing village. The population doubles in the summer when the cannery fires up, and triples for the Fourth of July, when yachts from all over the world gather to celebrate. There's not much here, but it's a beautiful, beautiful spot.

■ Basics

i The **Alaska Marine Highway** serves Pelican twice a month, making a round-trip from Juneau. It's one of the best day-trips you can make from Juneau, and one of the cheaper ways into Icy Strait for whale-watching. It would be a near miracle of bad luck if you didn't spot a whale on this trip during the migration season. Contact the ferry office in Juneau; you'll never find any officials in Pelican. The ferry stays in Pelican two hours, which is plenty of time to walk the boardwalk and soak up the scenery, the real attraction.

Southeast

Pelican is also served by **Wings of Alaska** (daily flights from Juneau), ☎ 735-2284. There is no tourist information office in Pelican.

■ In Town

Pelican has only one road and one boardwalk. Neither goes anywhere in particular. Follow the boardwalk to the end and you'll come to the lone shop in town, next to **Pacific Seafoods**. Good souvenirs and food that might not be as expensive as you would anticipate.

The focus of Pelican's nightlife is **Rosie's**, ☎ 735-2265, an Alaska tradition. You're haven't seen anything until you've been here. Rose is no longer a daily presence – she used to hang out on the dock and harangue people as they walked by, providing some of the most interesting entertainment in town – but her establishment survives. It has a full-service bar, food and there are also rooms for rent. Turn right from the ferry.

■ Outside Pelican

 WHITE SULPHUR HOT SPRINGS: Near Pelican is White Sulfur Hot Springs. It's a 20-mile water trip, easily done in a kayak if you bring one in.

There's a very popular and usually booked **Forest Service cabin** at White Sulphur, but you can enjoy the waters and the scenery any time. People who have traveled all over Alaska consider White Sulfur to be the single prettiest spot in the state. You can book charter planes to the springs, but you'll lose out on a lot of scenery that way, and floatplanes can't always make the landing.

WEST CHICHAGOF-YAKOBI WILDERNESS: This wilderness is almost untouched by visitors. It's situated north of Pelican on the tip of Chichagof Island, and Yakobi Island. On Yakobi, anchor at Cape Bingham, where there's a good sandy beach. A trail leads from Soapstone Point – there was once a soapstone mine here – across the peninsula. You have a good chance of seeing wildlife here – whales, otters, bears, sea lions, and more. There are Forest Service cabins in the wilderness area at Goulding Lakes and Lake Suloia.

For all boaters, remember that, once you get out of Lisianski Inlet or Strait, you're in open water. The west side of Yakobi can get fairly wild, but the scenery is astounding, and there are a few sights of historical interest, including an abandoned settlement at Deer Harbor, Cape Cross, where Cook spent a few days watching sea lions (you'll probably see some, too). There's also the point where a Spanish expedition gave up heading north because the crew was so devastated by scurvy – by the time they hit this point, in the summer of 1775, after the long trip up from their California holdings, only three men were left who could work.

When Vancouver got here, he found an interesting trace of the local culture: his men "rested for the night in a small cave under a high hill, where a box was found about four feet square, placed on wooden pillars about six feet from the ground. This box contained the remains of a human body very carefully wrapped up, and by its side was erected a pole about twenty feet high, painted in horizontal streaks red and white; the colours were fresh and lively, and from the general neatness of the whole, it was supposed to be the sepulchre of some chief."

■ Accommodations

 If you want to stay in Pelican, you can try the **Otter Cove B&B**, ☎ 735-2259, doubles $95, for rooms quieter than **Rosie's** (doubles $75) are likely to be. That pretty much does it for accommodations, although you could always head out into the woods and pitch a tent. There's not a lot in the way of rules and restrictions here.

A few miles north of Pelican is the lovely **Lisianski Lodge**. It accommodates only eight guests; meals are included, and charters can be arranged. Prices run $260 a night for a couple. Box 776, Pelican, 99832, ☎ 735-2266. They'll also rent you a kayak.

Gustavus

The area around Gustavus (pronounced Gus-TAH-vus) is possibly the flattest land in all of Southeast. It wasn't always that way, though. Long ago there were mountains, as on the rest of the coast. The difference here was the glaciers – big ones. When they finished their rapid retreat only a couple of hundred years ago, they left the area that is now Gustavus not only flat, but with very rich soil. Gustavus is one of the best places in the region for farming – one of the only places in Southeast, in fact, where farming is practical.

The small community of Gustavus, originally known as Strawberry Point – the name Gustavus comes from King Gustavus II of Sweden, a bit of geographical sucking up by William Henry Dall – was started by a few homesteaders in 1914. Most of the large-scale farms – the cattle ranches, the endless acres of vegetables – slowly shut down over the years as shipping costs became prohibitive, but the town retains a quiet rural atmosphere and most people still have a little livestock and large gardens.

Southeast

There isn't much else in Gustavus. With only 220 people living there, need for services is limited. There's just a general store and a gas station that's open rather idiosyncratic hours. Oh yeah, and there are hotels. Lots of them, handling the visitors who come in the summer months, using the town as a base for seeing the better-known Glacier Bay.

Okay, so it doesn't sound like much. But it's a fantastic place to sit back for a few days, ride bikes on the long, flat roads, and watch eagles come and go. Gustavus has a feeling to it. Everybody who comes here falls in love with the place.

■ Basics

i The Alaska Marine Highway doesn't go to Gustavus. The town residents have voted down initiatives to bring in the ferry for years and, when they finally voted yes, the ferry system decided it didn't have enough money to build a dock. Most cruise ships skip the town and head straight into Glacier Bay.

However, that doesn't mean you can't take a boat to town. The **Gustavus Ferry**, ☎ 586-8687 (in Juneau) or 800-820-BOAT, runs daily trips between Auke Bay and Gustavus. It's $45 one way, $85 round-trip. There's also a whale-watching option on the run – for that, plus the round-trip, it'll cost you $139. Remember that the water between Juneau and Gustavus is Southeast Alaska's prime whale territory. To put your kayak on the boat for transportation adds $40 to the cost each way. The boat is wheelchair-accessible.

If you don't want to take the two-hour boat ride, you can easily fly from Juneau. The town is about 50 miles west of Juneau – a jet flight of about 12 minutes, or 20 minutes by one of the smaller planes that ply the route. In the summer there is daily service to and from Juneau – expect to pay from $130, round-trip. Flights also go between Gustavus and Sitka, Haines, and Skagway. **Air Excursions**, ☎ 697-2376 (in Gustavus) or 789-5591 (in Juneau), flies over all of Southeast and also does flightseeing tours of Glacier Bay. **Alaska Airlines**, ☎ 800-426-0333, has summer daily jet service. **L.A.B.**, ☎ 697-2470, or in Juneau 789-9181, runs flightseeing tours of Glacier Bay. **Skagway Air**, ☎ 789-2006, offers charters and excursions, plus some regularly scheduled flights, as does **Wings of Alaska**, ☎ 789-0790 or 697-2236.

Gustavus proper is about 10 miles from the entrance to Glacier Bay. Most lodges offer airport pickup and many include free bicycle rental with their rooms. A shuttle bus meets Alaska Airlines flights, but it costs $10 to get to Bartlett Cove from the airport. **TLC Taxi**, ☎ 697-2239, will get you around, or you can rent a car at **Bud's Car Rental**, ☎ 697-2403.

There is no visitor information center in town, but you can write for information to: **Gustavus Visitor's Association**, Box 167, Gustavus, AK 99826.

You can pick up a few souvenirs at the **general store** or try **Fireweed Gallery** on Rink Creek Road, which has a good selection of works by local artists. **Glacier Bay Lodge** also has a large gift shop.

Gustavus' zip code is **99826**.

■ Adventures

While most people use Gustavus as a base for visiting Glacier Bay, it is also a pleasant place to hike, fish, kayak, or view wildlife. There are a variety of tours, rentals, and charters offered in the area – most accommodations will make arrangements for you, or you can make them yourself. Kayak trips require little or no previous experience, but if you're going to venture out into Icy Strait, you'd better know what you're doing or you'll die wet and cold.

Hiking

There are few maintained hiking trails around town, but you can walk anywhere. Some pleasant places to go include **Bartlett Lake**, along the beach near the airport, and along the **Salmon** or **Goode** rivers.

Fishing

There is also pretty good fishing in the **Salmon River** for char, salmon, and trout. Rent or bring a kayak and glide through the calm waters in the area.

For charters, try **Mike Nigro,** ☎ 697-2233. Full day is $250 per person; a half-day is $135. He'll also do kayak drop-offs. **Explorations Northwest,** ☎ 697-3038, does full-day trips for $300 per person.

Whale-Watching

The town of Gustavus sits at one side of Icy Strait, the best whale-watching water in Southeast Alaska. During the migration season, you have to really work hard not to see a whale here. The cheapest way through the strait is the AMH ferry from Juneau to Pelican, 13 hours, round-trip. If that's too long, and you're in Gustavus, charter a boat. Don't pass it by just to spend all your time in Glacier Bay. The **Auk-Nu** has regular whale-watching trips – you can combine them with a ferry ride in from Juneau. $140 gets you the ride to Gustavus from Juneau, and a trip across the Strait to Point Adolphus, where the whales really like to hang out. ☎ 800-451-5952 or 586-8687.

Gusto Charters in Gustavus does much longer trips out to see the whales – you leave at 8 am, return at 5 pm from Gustavus, and you don't spend much time traveling, as Point Adolphus is so close. Prices are $180, if you want to use one of their kayaks to get a better look at the whales, or $160 without. This includes a small lunch. ☎ 697-2416.

If you've got your own kayak and just want to get to the other side of the strait to go whale watching on your own, Mike Nigro, ☎ 697-2233, does drop-offs for $150.

Kayaking

Your first and best choice is to go kayaking inside Glacier Bay itself. You need to know what you're doing, take all proper food and equipment, but it will be the paddle of your life. To get into the bay, you book space on the *Crystal Fjord*, run by the Lodge and Glacier Bay Cruises, ☎ 800-451-5952 or 586-8687. There are specific points in the bay where the Park Service allows kayak drop-offs. It's $167.50 for a round-trip, where they'll pick you back up at a pre-arranged time and place. There's also a good deal with their pass, for $187.50, which lets you arrange multiple times and places – so you can paddle one area, have the ship pick you up and drop you somewhere else, and then paddle there for a while. There are three specified pick-up and drop-off points: Sebree Island (near Tlingit Point, where the East and West Arms divide), Geikie Inlet, or Queen Inlet. You're probably best off choosing the Sebree Island drop-off so you can get away quickly from the cruise ships. The ship leaves Bartlett Cove daily at 7 AM and returns at 4 PM. Spread this out over a few days, and you've had a very, very good time.

There are plenty of operators in town ready to take you paddling. **Alaska Discovery**, in Juneau, ☎ 780-6226, www.akdiscovery.com, has eight-day trips up the bay for $2,390; five days for $1,695.

Spirit Walker Expeditions, based in Gustavus, ☎ 800-KAYAKER, www.seakayakalaska.com, has day-trips for $125; it's $487 with an overnight. Trips across to Point Adolphus to watch whales run $319 for a day; $681 for two days; $794 for two days/two nights.

Glacier Bay Seak Kayaks, ☎ 697-2257, has rentals, from the lodge, for $40 a day for singles. They also do overnight trips into the Beardslee Islands, nearly as pretty as the bay, and with no permit hassles. **Sea Otter Kayak** also rents from town. Singles are $40 a day. ☎ 697-3007.

Flightseeing

Any of the charter operators in Gustavus, Haines, or Skagway do Glacier Bay overflights. **Mountain Flying Service**, ☎ 766-3007 or 800-954-8747, www.flyglacierbay.com, has hour-long flights up the East Arm of the bay for $115 from Haines; $149 from Skagway; slightly longer trips up the West Arm are $159/199. A two-hour flight that takes you over Glacier Bay, and on to the Fairweathers and the Pacific Ocean, is $259/289.

■ Food

 Bear Track Mercantile, ☎ 697-2358, is the town's general store. Stock up here on camping and fishing supplies as well as trail goodies, but be prepared to spend a lot more than you would on the same items in Juneau.

If you can get in, it's worth having dinner at the **Gustavus Inn**, ☎ 697-2225, but call early. If the inn isn't fully booked, they make a few meals available to non-guests. Well worth it, for their fresh local menu.

For vegetarians, try **Bear's Nest Restaurant**, ☎ 697-2440. It's just up Wilson Road from the intersection.

Many of the lodges and B&Bs have their own dining rooms, feeding only their own guests. There's also a café out at the **Glacier Bay Lodge**.

If you're planning to stay in Gustavus, the limited food options are something to keep in mind when you're booking your place to stay. If they're not feeding you, your choices are really limited.

■ Accommodations

Accommodations fall into three basic categories in Gustavus: deluxe, basic, and camping. Most places can also arrange various tours in and around Glacier Bay and will pick you up from the airport. Reservations are even more essential here than in the rest of Southeast due to the extremely high influx of summer tourists. The town and most inns are about 10-13 miles from the Glacier Bay Park Headquarters.

The deluxe places generally include three gourmet meals in very comfortable quarters. They differ a little in ambience, but they're all quite lovely and more luxurious than you can imagine. They can also all put together activity packages for you – ask about rates when you book your room, as it can save you quite a few phone calls.

Annie Mae Lodge, ☎ 697-2346 or 800-478-2346, has doubles with a shared bath for $215; $255 for private. This includes all meals and transfers. The place has great beach views, and a good down-home feel to it.

Glacier Bay Country Inn, ☎ 697-2288, offers singles from $144, and doubles from $228. There are also cabins at $380 for a double. These rates include all meals. The same people run the **Whalesong Lodge**, where doubles are $170. Closer to town, but only breakfast included.

The **Gustavus Inn**, ☎ 697-2254 or 800-649-5220, charges $140 per person. Right near the intersection, this inn was built in the town's original homestead. Great atmosphere, amazing food, and fully handicapped-accessible rooms available.

The **Bear Track Inn**, ☎ 888-697-2284 or 697-3017, is probably the swankiest place in town. For a two-day, one-night package, including airfare from Juneau, rates are $432 per person. They can also bring you in from Skagway, Haines, or Sitka. The inn is quite a ways out of town, but it's in a beautiful spot, and they'll shuttle you in to town or back to the lodge. Quite stunning gourmet meals are included in the price.

Glacier Bay Lodge, ☎ (206) 622-2042 or 800-622-2042, built in 1966, has the convenience of being next to park headquarters, but meals are not included in their rates, and you're 10 miles from town. Singles start at $130; doubles run from $155. Dorm space will cost you $28. Due to its location, it's considered the best place to stay in town and it fills first.

Alaska Discovery runs a nice lodge near the intersection. Doubles are $100/night, but it's frequently booked up with people who are on paddling tours. ☎ 780-6226.

Salmon River, ☎ 697-2245, has cabins for $70 apiece. **Good River B&B**, ☎ 697-2241, has rooms from $95 for a double, or a cabin with no running water or electricity for $85. You do have to share a bath.

The **Tri B&B**, ☎ 697-2425, charges $90 for a double, and that includes pick-ups and drop-offs to get out there. Lastly, free camping is available at **Bartlett Cove**, by the entrance to Glacier Bay. The sites are very nice. Bear-proof food containers are supplied (use them – lots of bears around) and there are coin-operated showers. Best water views in town.

Glacier Bay

The Little Ice Age that created Glacier Bay began in the 1400s and lasted approximately 300 years. The ice has been affecting people's lives for centuries.

■ History

Tlingit Indians once lived on the Beardslee Islands, 10 miles north of the mouth of Glacier Bay. When a glacier suddenly advanced in the mid-1700s, covering the islands in ice, the people moved across Icy Strait – the passage between Gustavus, the mainland and Chichagof Island – and formed the village of Hoonah.

HIDDEN BY GLACIERS

When Capt. George Vancouver explored and mapped the coastline of Icy Strait in the late 18th century, he saw and charted only a small indentation, about five miles long, where Glacier Bay now exists. The rest of the bay was still covered by glacial ice sheets over 4,000 feet thick. The tiny bay was blocked by "compact and solid mountains of ice, rising perpendicular from the water's edge."

John Muir visited the bay in 1879 with missionary Hall Young – they traveled from Wrangell into Glacier Bay by canoe. Muir and Hall stopped in Hoonah for supplies and guides, and were offered warnings about the danger of the Glacier Bay area. One of the chiefs asked Young to pray for the ice to leave. Sure enough, eight years later the glaciers started to retreat, greatly increasing Hall's credibility. Hoonah Indians told Muir of "vast masses of floating ice and a constant noise of thunder as they crashed from the glaciers into the sea," and also of the "fearsome bays and passages full of evil spirits which made them very perilous to navigate." Muir found the landscape vastly changed from most of the earlier records of the bay – the glaciers had retreated 48 miles since the last European visitors had written about their trips. The glacial retreat left the forests stunted, stripped bare, and even now, a hundred years later, it is just beginning to start the slow process of regrowth.

FIRST SIGHT

In *Travels in Alaska*, Muir writes of his first view of Glacier Bay: "I reached a height of fifteen hundred feet, on the ridge that bounds the second of the great glaciers. All the landscape was smothered in clouds and I began to fear that as far as wide views were concerned I had climbed in vain. But at length the clouds lifted a little, and beneath their gray fringes I saw the berg-filled expanse of the bay, and the feet of the mountains that stand about it, and the imposing fronts of five huge glaciers, the nearest being immediately beneath me. This was my first general view of Glacier Bay, a solitude of ice and snow and newborn rocks, dim, dreary, mysterious."

Muir's visits and reports on Glacier Bay were soon made public, mostly through their publication in the *San Francisco Bulletin*. By the 1890s, Muir Glacier was probably the most famous glacier in America. Hordes of tourists flocked to Alaska by steamship to see the wonders for themselves. The ships went very close to the glacial face, and then let the passengers disembark by a boardwalk that had been built on the beach near the glacier. A porcelain sign announced "Muir Glacier." The boardwalk al-

Southeast

lowed people to get out onto the more stable surfaces of the ice, listen to geology lectures, and see the legendary ice worm. This early cruise ship traffic continued until about 1904, when the glacier began retreating so rapidly that it was too dangerous for ships to go within four or five miles of its face.

 DID YOU KNOW? *Glacier Bay was proclaimed a National Monument on February 26, 1925 by President Calvin Coolidge, though the boundaries of the park were a little less than half of those today. In 1939, the park was enlarged to its current size.*

■ Glacier Bay Today

Glacier Bay now encompasses 3.3 million acres, 600,000 of which is water. About 300,000 visitors come here each year, that number being roughly double what it was less than a decade ago. There is a fair amount of debate about how they come here – in the 1970s, attempts were made to limit the number of cruise ships going into the bay, as the ships were scaring off the whales. The number of ships allowed in dropped from 103 to 79; this held for quite a while, but by 2001, it was back up to two per day during the three-month summer season – more than 180 total – and they were back to causing serious problems. One of them is a rather astounding amount of pollution when the exhaust stacks' effluvia mix with air coming off the ice; the smog gets held down just like a bad day in L.A. To deal with this – at least to try and limit the damage – the Park Service keeps the big boats out of the East Arm. Now at least only half the park is getting trampled to death.

In the summer of 2001, as we were working on this book, a cruise ship whacked and killed a whale. The Park Service suddenly decided that they'd been reading the law wrong all these years, and they didn't have to let that many ships in after all. Quite abruptly, they cut nearly a third of the available up-bay trips out from the cruise ships. Suddenly, a number of cruise lines were having to explain to their passengers why they were not going to Glacier Bay after all. There are still too many ships going up bay; there's no question of that. But there's more attention being paid to the problem now.

And, ultimately, we must have faith that nature will win. The seasons keep coming and going, and the park is in a constant state of change. As the glaciers retreat, the land is springing back up, currently at a rate of about one foot every eight years. Over the past 200 years, the glaciers have retreated 65 miles. Farther up the bay, advancing glaciers litter the sea with gleaming icebergs. There are an average of 17 tidewater glaciers in the park – the number fluctuates with glacial movement – giving the area the highest concentrations of tidewater glaciers in the world.

As you head up the bay, the process of glacial retreat and the changes it makes on the land are evident. The land closest to the glaciers has been deeply gouged by the ice and is barren of all life, while closer to the entrance the forests have returned.

WATCHABLE

WILDLIFE

Wildlife is abundant in the park: huge grizzly bears, moose, wolves, mountain goats, wolverines, lynx, humpback whales, orcas, seals and sea lions, as well as a good variety of birds, including cormorants, pigeon guillemots, murres and murrelets, and the ever-popular puffins, both tufted and horned. Visit in the spring if you're a bird watcher – many spring migration routes pass through the area, with over 200 species having been spotted in the park. Icy Strait seems to be a kind of boundary point for Dall's porpoise and harbor porpoise; the Dall's don't seem to come up here very often.

June and July is the best time to see the abundant wildflowers growing on the mountain slopes. Late summer is the perfect time to go berry and mushroom picking.

Make sure that you keep a sharp eye out for bears – they have first harvest rights and are protective of them.

Glacier Bay is Southeast in a nutshell. If you don't have time to see the rest of Alaska, this is the place to come.

■ Adventures

Boat Charters

The most popular way to enter the bay is on the ***Spirit of Adventure***, a high-speed catamaran that travels to the end of the West Arm of Glacier Bay. The ship stops along the way to offer views of glaciers, small islands, and wildlife, and to drop off and pick up campers and kayakers. There is a Forest Service naturalist on board to point out the attractions and to answer questions. The fare (including lunch) is $156. See the Gustavus section for information on getting kayak transport and drop-off into the bay (page 262).

You can book two-day trips from Juneau into Glacier Bay via the *Spirit of Adventure*, with overnights at the lodge: it'll run you $399 from Juneau; $534 from Haines; or $556 from Skagway. Two-day trips are $481 from

Juneau; $617 from Haines; and $639 from Skagway. There are one-day trips for $312 from Juneau; $397 from Haines; or $416 from Skagway. You'll have a lot more fun on the two-day trip, though, and the extra cost isn't that much more than a night's hotel stay.

If you want to bring your own (motorized) boat into the bay in the summer, you must write or call ahead for permission 60 days prior to your expected arrival. Contact: Superintendent, Glacier Bay National Park, Gustavus, AK 99826, ☎ 697-2230.

Backcountry Travel

Perhaps the best way to see Glacier Bay is to go out into the backcountry for a few days. There is currently no permit required to camp, kayak, or hike in the park, but there is a voluntary check-in and orientation meeting at the headquarters. (Park officials say this will probably become mandatory soon.) It's insane to head off into the backcountry without telling somebody where you're going, so take advantage of the Park Service, where you can also check out conditions. You are given bear-proof storage containers at park headquarters before heading out.

Glacier Bay is open year-round. While visitor's services are open only mid-May to mid-September (7 AM-7 PM daily), the park headquarters and offices are open year-round, 8-4:30, Monday through Friday.

Hiking

There are two maintained trails in Bartlett Cove. The **Bartlett River Trail** is a pleasant half-day hike. It's three miles long and is not difficult. Use all proper bear cautions, and also watch for moose. The **Forest Trail** is an easy one-mile nature trail through the rainforest. Check at park headquarters for information about off-trail and ranger-led hikes.

■ In the West Arm

By law, most ships go up the left fork, or West Arm of Glacier Bay, following a path that shows the history of the land's change and regrowth in reverse. The bay as a whole has risen 18-21 feet since the ice began to melt and the glaciers started to retreat 200 years ago. The land closest to Bartlett Cove has been out from under the ice the longest and is covered by forests of spruce and hemlock. **Willoughby Island** housed a fox farm in the 1920s. To the west of **Francis Island** you may see the remains of an older forest that was covered by ice – the fossilized tree stumps are all that survived. To the east lie the **Marble Islands**, so named for the marble deposits found there.

WATCHABLE

WILDLIFE

The southern island is covered with bird colonies – watch for kittiwakes, cormorants, and murres. The north island has a harbor seal haul-out at its northern tip. Watch also for tufted puffins and humpback whales in this area.

Past the Marble Islands, you can see **Tlingit Point**. A gigantic glacier once covered everything down to the mouth of the bay with an ice wall 15 miles long and about 250 feet tall. During its retreat, the glacier was split in two by the land mass at Tlingit Point – the western portion became the **Grand Pacific Glacier**, which carved the West Arm, while the eastern portion formed **Muir Glacier** and, eventually, the East Arm.

Muir Glacier was named for John Muir, who set up one of his camps on Tlingit Point during his second trip to the bay in 1890. Cruise ships turn left at this point and go up the park's West Arm, also known as Reid Inlet, which means that most kayakers turn right and head up the East Arm, or Muir Inlet, toward Muir Glacier. As you continue up the bay, notice the change in the water color. The sea has a milky aquamarine hue caused by the high amount of glacial silt in the water. As the ice melts the silt is carried off the glaciers and icebergs in fresh water. Because fresh water is lighter than salt water, the silt sits near the surface and refracts the light. Whales tend to stay away from the heavily silted water, although seals don't seem to mind it much.

Fairweather Range, in the West Arm of Glacier Bay.

Southeast

The high misty peaks to the west comprise the **Fairweather Range** – the highest coastal range of mountains in the Americas, except for the Andes. Mt. Fairweather towers over the range at 15,300 feet. If you're very lucky you may even see the range in its entirety, but some cloud cover is to be expected.

THE WAVE OF 1958

The Glacier Bay/Fairweather area has not only been sculpted by ice, but also by the fault lines that lie under the high mountains. In 1958, a major earthquake between Glacier Bay and Yakutat triggered a huge rockslide into Lituya Bay (on the west side of the Fairweather Range). The slide created a tidal wave 1,720 feet high that traveled at an estimated 100-120 mph and washed away over four square miles of forest.

At the head of Tarr Inlet, only a mile or so from the Canadian border, tour ships stop near the base of the advancing Margerie Glacier to watch huge chunks of ice calve from the glacial face. The water this close to the glacier is dark gray with silt.

WATCHABLE *Watch the ice floes – they are a favorite haul-out and pupping spot for harbor seals. The seals favor the ice because it offers safety from land predators. Even the orcas stay out of the very murky water of* **WILDLIFE** *the upper bay.*

Only a few hundred yards away is **Grand Pacific Glacier**, which stretches for more than 25 miles. Grand Pacific is one of the more mobile glaciers around. In the 1920s, it had retreated behind the Canadian border, moving back so far that the Canadians drafted blueprints for building a seaport at the glacier's base. The glacier had other plans though, and by 1966 the ice was well back in U.S. territory. But that wasn't the glacier's most dramatic move. Between 1860 and 1880, Grand Pacific Glacier retreated 20 miles from its position in Geike Inlet to the mouth of Tarr Inlet, near Russell Island. It has retreated yet another 10 miles since then, making it perhaps the fastest-moving glacier in the world. Note that the recently exposed rock in this area is covered with a bare sprinkling of lichens – this is the beginning of a new forest. Closer to the ice, the rock is barren of all life.

Grand Pacific, of course, caused frequent headaches for the bean counters in both the U.S. and Canada. Remember, these are the people who thought clear cutting a strip of trees all along the U.S.-Canadian border made sense. How could they know who owned the glacier – and a big chunk of Glacier Bay – if it kept moving around? Finally, in 1936, the International Boundary Commission put the glacier in the U.S. Just for fun, that same year President Roosevelt opened the area up for mining, and in the 1940s, Excursion Inlet was home to a secret base that was planned as part of the campaign to take back the Aleutians from the Japanese.

Mining (didn't quite pan out), war, and even plans to dig tunnels under glaciers to get at ore deposits were never the bay's biggest threat. Despite its natural beauty, vast size, and protected status, not even the pristine waters of Glacier Bay are safe from the worries of environmental impact. As mentioned above, the park is being loved to death, much like Yellowstone and Yosemite. Several years ago, after the numbers of whales spotted decreased dramatically, hydrophones were placed at various spots to measure the impact of motorized ship noise on the whales. Current motorized traffic levels are tightly regulated, though there has been heavy pressure from the cruise ship industry to greatly increase the numbers (since they've got money and that's what Congress runs on, the number of ships was rising until the summer 2001 clampdown). Periodic spot checks are done on the ships' emissions, but you can hit a smoggy day even this deep in the wilderness.

Here's a little look at the numbers: the first cruise ship went up bay in 1969; that year, about 15,000 people came to Glacier Bay. By 1981, that number was 86,500 people, most on cruise ships. For 1997, 336,226 people entered the bay, fully 306,216 of them on cruise ships.

MINING PLANS SHOT DOWN

An outside threat to the park was finally shot down in 1993. There were plans to mine Windy Craggy, at the headwaters of the Tatshenshini and Alsek Rivers, which pour into Glacier Bay. Two open pit copper mines were planned for the top of the mountain and the tailings were to have been contained behind a dam. This would not be a problem unless leakage occurred, which would've gone straight to the bay, polluting the two wild rivers along the way and destroying millions of acres of wildlife habitat and bird nesting grounds. Fortunately, the Canadian government, much to the dismay of Alaska's pro-development then-governor, Wally Hickel, declared the river and the surrounding area a National Park, stopping this development.

■ In the East Arm

If you don't have a motor, this is the direction to come. Scenically, you've got essentially the same drill: big mountains, big glaciers, lots of wildlife. But you've got it largely to yourself, with no huge ships carrying a thousand people passing by you.

Southeast

The first part of the trip is the same as described above, as far as Tlingit Point. That's where the East and West Arms split off. You pass Muir Point on the right, which is where Muir had a cabin during his 1890 stay here. He was all over the place, heading out at 2 AM or so, not getting back until after dark (which, in summer, means he was out on the glaciers for 18-20 hours a day), when signal fires from his Native friends would guide him back to camp. Part of his project in 1880-1890 was to erect stone cairns, which served as baseline markers for where the glaciers were – what you need to know before you can determine how fast the glaciers are moving.

WATCHABLE

WILDLIFE

*Around the corner from Muir Point is **Adams Inlet**, a nesting ground for Canada geese. It's a nice side trip if you have time.*

The **Muir Inlet**, the main channel in the East Arm, dead-ends in the face of **Muir Glacier**. Before you get there, you'll pass the face of the **Plateau Glacier** (you can paddle up the Wachusett Inlet, along the Plateau, to a favored sealing area), at Rowless Point, and see the Burroughs Glacier, to the left, and the Casement Glacier, to the right.

📖 Get a copy of Margaret Piggott's ***Discover Southeast Alaska with Pack and Paddle*** before heading up the Bay in your kayak.

Across from **Westdahl Point**, Muir had a few problems: "I had not gone a dozen steps toward the island when I suddenly dropped into a concealed water-filled crevasse, which on the surface showed not the slightest sign of its existence.... Down I plunged over head and ears, but of course bobbed up again, and after a hard struggle succeeded in dragging myself out over the farther side. Then I pulled my sled over close... made haste to strip off my clothing... and crept into my sleeping bag to shiver away the night as best I could."

CAUTION

*Muir escaped **hypothermia**, but he was lucky. Remember when you're out here that hypothermia is your biggest enemy. Take all precautions. The other danger is calving ice. A good berg coming off a glacial face can kick up waves plenty big enough to capsize a kayak. Keep your distance.*

Sitka

itka is located on Baranof Island in one of the most beautiful spots in Southeast Alaska. The waters of Sitka Sound are dotted with hundreds of tiny islands. Off to the west there is a clear passage to open water, and to the northwest is Mt. Edgecumbe, a 3,201-foot volcano that looks much like Japan's Mt. Fuji. Once the Russian capital of Alaska, it's now a town that has managed to reverse its economic collapse in the mid-80s by becoming the destination of choice for Californians looking to kill off part of Alaska by putting up over-sized, inappropriate vacation homes that are empty 51 weeks of the year.

■ History

Sitka's history is the most important in Southeast. It's the blue-print for what happened everywhere else, with a few twists and turns thrown in for fun.

The Tlingits

Tlingits lived for centuries in the Baranof Island area, finding the riches of the waters, streams, and mountains more than attractive. Except for the Aleuts far to the west, these people were probably the most skilled builders of canoes, which were used for fishing in the waters of Sitka Sound. They called the area "Shect' ká" – the land behind the islands.

Arrival of the Russians

The Russians first came to Baranof Island in the 1740s. Vitus Bering, commanding the Russian Great Northern Expedition, a 10-year trip to map out Russia's arctic, first hit the North American coast at Chichagof Island in 1741. He sent 15 men ashore, and they never came back – either they drowned or the Tlingit made an early statement about their feelings toward intruders. While he left his men to die, Bering went blithely off to explore the Gulf of Alaska with naturalist George Stellar. It was on this trip that Stellar first found the now-extinct Steller's sea cow.

But Bering did go back with tales of furs. While their overhunting in Southcentral Alaska had started the decline of the natural resources there, Southeast was still rich with otters and seals. The Sitka area was first settled in 1799 by Alexander Baranov. He built a fort, which he called Mikhailovsk, and left 200 settlers behind at the original Russian town site, New Archangel, which was situated near the present-day ferry terminal. Like Bering before him, Baranov then left. For two years, thanks to the same natural resources in the Sound that had drawn the Natives, the Russian town flourished. In his *Notes on Russian America*, K.T. Khelbnikov, in the early 1800s, listed the advantages of Sitka as: 1) Landmarks at the Entrance – Mt. Edgecumbe, particularly, served as an early navigation beacon; 2) Tides – the tide in Sitka is much more gentle than in a lot of other places along the coast, with a variation of only about

15 feet at most; 3) Construction timber – the Russians built a shipyard in Sitka, and Khelbnikov wrote, "We can use these forests for another century without the supply becoming exhausted"; 4) Good potato harvest; 5) Fish catch, mountain sheep, raising pigs and chickens; and 6) Trade with foreigners.

Tlingits Strike Back

However, the local Tlingits soon tired of Russians cleaning out of their prime hunting and fishing grounds (Khelbnikov lists "Dangers from indigenous people" as the number three disadvantage to Sitka's location, behind dangers from "civilized" enemies and the problems of starvation if regular supply shipments were stopped).

Baranov's Revenge

The fun didn't last for the Russians. In 1802, the Tlingits raided New Archangel and torched the town, killing every settler they could find. Baranov himself was away at the time and, when he came back two years later, survivors who had fled to the woods told him the harrowing tale of the last days of New Archangel.

Once he did finally arrive on the scene, Baranov was not slow to retaliate. He called in the troops and moved his base of operations right into the center of the Tlingit village, Shee Atika. This forced the Tlingits to move to the mouth of Indian River (now inside Totem Park). Quite a few skirmishes followed, until the Russian ship *Neva* shelled the Tlingit settlement. Soldiers moved in to torch it and, as the Russians themselves had done at New Archangel, the Tlingits fled to the forest. The Russian hold on Sitka was complete.

That's not to say the Tlingit were entirely complacent about this. They waged a kind of guerilla campaign for years, as Khelbnikov wrote: "The most vicious of them make plans every year to attack our fortress." In almost a tone of puzzlement, he stated that "the fact that we killed several hundreds of them must have left the seed of vengeance in several thousands of them."

Still, despite the fact that they were vulnerable to being picked off by Natives as soon as they left the fortress, the Russians went out to waste the otter population. The hunting started up in earnest. Statistics from the years 1842-1860 showed that the Russians took out the furs of "25,602 sea otters, 63,826 'otters,' probably river otters, 161,042 beavers, 73,944 foxes, 55,540 arctic foxes, 2,283 bears, 2,536 ursine seals, [and] 338,604 marsh otters."

The Territorial Capital

Sitka, so close to the open water and more temperate than many Southeast locations, was the natural choice for the Russian territorial capital when it was moved from Kodiak, which was, by the beginning of the 19th century, too remote from all Russia's American riches. Sitka grew in leaps and bounds, feeding off the fur trade, basking in the status of officialdom.

The U.S. Takes Over

The Russian presence came to an end at the price of about two cents an acre. The Russian flag came down and the U.S. Stars and Bars was raised. It was in Sitka, on October 18, 1867, that Alaska was officially transferred from Russian ownership to the U.S.

Because it was such a hardship post, the first thing the U.S. did was build a couple of 10-pin alleys (although some experts on Russian Alaska will tell you there were already alleys in town, along with everything else a distant outpost needs: brothels and bars).

And then Sitka was forgotten.

From 1867 until 1884, the territory of Alaska had no government. The United States had bought this huge chunk of land – primarily in the hopes that it would make annexing British Columbia easier – and then didn't have a clue what to do with it. Sitka, robbed of its base of power, facing seas stripped almost bare of marine mammals, like the rest of Alaskan settlements in this lawless period, went on the decline. There was a brief upsurge when, in 1884, the territorial capital of Alaska was placed in Sitka. But in 1906, the offices of power were moved to Juneau and Sitka was left to languish in its scenic setting.

What kept Sitka alive for so many years was the land and the sea. The timber industry moved in and canneries flourished on the yearly salmon runs into the rivers feeding Sitka Sound. The federal government established a hospital in town and the Bureau of Indian Affairs (BIA) started a school that drew Native kids from around the state. There was a quick spurt of activity around World War II, when Sitka was part of the last line of defense against a Japanese invasion of Alaska, but that faded quickly, leaving only concrete behind.

■ Sitka Today

Today, Sitka is the single largest town in the United States – over 4,000 square miles of land have been incorporated into the city boundaries. Its population of about 9,000 makes it the fifth-largest city in Alaska.

Southeast

Sitka is, however, suffering the same fate as many Alaskan towns, finding that it can no longer depend on the fisheries and the timber industry for support. In 1993, the pulp mill, the largest single employer in the town, closed. Declining catches have left more fishermen searching for fewer fish and prices are dropping.

Thanks no doubt to the beautiful location and the active cultural life, Sitka has become the place in Alaska for rich yuppies to build second homes. This has squeezed many locals right out of the market – a standard middle-class house can sell for upwards of $400,000 – and left the town landscape with mansions looming over trailer parks. Meanwhile, the local economy – except for the building sector – is down. Cruise ships have almost stopped coming to Sitka, as it's a little too far out of line with the other towns, and because it's the only major town in Southeast where the ships have to bring their passengers on shore in small boats. There have been plans bandied around for a cruise ship dock, but so far, nothing has happened.

The only town in Southeast that can compete with Sitka for pure scenic beauty is Pelican. Sitka looks like no other place along the coast: the wide mouth of the sound, dotted with tiny, tree-covered islands, the cone of Mt. Edgecumbe the only thing between the town and the open sea. It makes most of the rest of Southeast's towns look dowdy. It was once known as the "Paris of the Pacific," and modern Sitka is trying to reclaim the title with its natural beauty, historic importance, and cultural importations.

■ Basics

i Sitka is served almost daily by the **Alaska Marine Highway**. The most ready connections are to Juneau and Haines. The Juneau run stops at several smaller villages en route. The ferry terminal is seven miles north of town, almost at the end of the road. Local AMH number is ☎ 747-8737. Cruise ships anchor off Crescent Harbor; lighters bring passengers ashore in the harbor, next to the Centennial Building, or at the lighter dock under the bridge that connects Sitka to the government town of Mt. Edgecumbe, on Japonski Island.

Alaska Airlines connects Sitka to other Southeastern communities, and to Seattle and Anchorage. The airport is on Japonski Island, across the channel from Sitka proper. For charter flights, try **Harris Aircraft**, ☎ 966-3050. Another company, **Coastal Helicopters**, ☎ 747-5557, charters chopper flights.

For taxis, there's **Arrowhead Taxi**, ☎ 747-8888, and **Sitka Cab**, ☎ 747-5001.

Car rental options are: **A&A**, ☎ 747-8228; **Allstar**, ☎ 966-2552 or 800-722-6927; and **Avis**, ☎ 966-2404 or 800-478-2847.

There's a shuttle bus in the summer season, the **Visitor Transit Bus**, that runs from Crescent Harbor to Sheldon Jackson, Totem Park, the Raptor Center, O'Connell Bridge, the Sitka Tribe Community House, and downtown. An all-day pass is $5, and the bus hits the stops every half-hour.

Another shuttle bus meets ferry arrivals. It's $5, one way, $7, round-trip for transportation to downtown. You are dropped off and picked up at the Centennial Building. Usually there are quick tour shuttles meeting the ferries as well, with tour prices running $12.

Bicycle rentals are available at **Southeast Diving and Sports**, 203 Lincoln St., ☎ 747-8279.

The **Visitor's Center** is in downtown, catty-cornered from the back of St. Michael's Cathedral, on the second floor of the Lahmeyer Building, 303 Lincoln. It is open 8-5, Monday through Friday. ☎ 747-5940. During the summer months, they also run a booth in the Centennial Building and another at the O'Connell Bridge Lighter Dock when there are cruise ships in. They have a video of the town available for $7.95.

Sitka is actually made up of two communities: Sitka itself, and Mt. Edgecumbe, which is across the bridge on Japonski Island (don't confuse the town of Mt. Edgecumbe with the volcano of the same name, over on Kruzof Island). Mt. Edgecumbe is primarily a government installation, including a Public Health Service hospital. The airport and the local community college are also in Mt. Edgecumbe.

Internet access available at **Highliner Café**, behind the She-atika.

Sitka's zip code is **99835**.

SITKA AT A GLANCE

QUICK TOUR: The Sheldon Jackson Museum is the best museum in the state – flat out; the Russian Bishop's House is the best-preserved Russian building in Southeast. Stop in to see how the original colonists lived.

DON'T MISS: After you've taken in the museum and the Bishop's House, get out of town. Hike the Salmon River trail, or get really ambitious and hump over the mountain for three days to get to Baranof Warm Springs. Just plan your trip so when you come back, you can catch one of the music festival concerts.

BEST FREEBIE: Hike from Totem Park across to the Indian River trail. You can take an hour or two, or take all day. Stick with it until you peak out, and you'll get views of Sitka Sound that will haunt you for the rest of your life.

Southeast

■ Museums & Attractions

 Sitka, unlike many towns in Southeast, is very, very compact. Once you get downtown, most of the attractions are within easy walking distance.

CENTENNIAL BUILDING: The majority of tours of Sitka start at the Centennial Building, right at the edge of Crescent Harbor, where the cruise ship lighters dock. The Centennial Building is Sitka's cultural center and home of the **Isabel Miller Museum**, which gives a good look at Sitka's history. Admission is free (donations requested); the museum is open daily 8-6 in summer (10-5, Monday through Friday in the winter). If you're interested in any special aspect of Sitka's history, this is the place to come. They maintain a huge photo archive of historic pictures of Sitka, quite a variety of specialist publications, and they have a staff that really knows the town.

In summer months, the Centennial Building's stage – backed by a window that looks out over the harbor – is used in the day by the New Archangel Dancers, who perform **traditional Russian dances**. The schedule depends on cruise ship arrival. Admission is $6. ☎ 747-5517 for times.

For three weeks in June, the Centennial Building is turned into a world-class music hall with the **Sitka Summer Music Festival**. Musicians from all over the globe – one year the festival drew Horowitz himself – come to play a series of chamber music concerts that should not be missed. The Centennial Building seats only 500, though, so get your tickets as early as possible. It's worth scheduling a trip to Sitka just to attend the festival. ☎ 747-6774 or 688-0880 for more information. If you're there at the time of the festival, but can't get tickets, try hanging out around Sheldon Jackson College, where you can often listen in on rehearsals.

ST. MICHAEL'S CATHEDRAL: The most photographed of the Russian churches in Alaska, St. Michael's is right in the center of downtown. The main street splits around it, and you can see the onion domes from the Centennial Building, only one street over. The current building was erected in 1967, after a fire completely engulfed the original 1840s structure, which was built by Finnish shipwrights, the only people around who could handle wood properly. While the church burned, locals broke in through the main doors and formed a human chain to pass out the icons. All were saved, and it's worth coming in to look at one of the finest collections outside of Russia.

On Sundays, services are held in three languages: Slavonic, English, and Tlingit. The liturgy is more or less sung while one priest swings a censer about the room and another blesses the parishioners. It's quite moving.

Be sure to look at the music stands by the piano for transliterations of hymns into Tlingit. The church is open daily; admission is $2.

CASTLE HILL: Heading toward the water from St. Michael's, you pass Sitka's shopping district and come to the old Post Office building; just next to that is a stairway leading up to Castle Hill. The hill, the highest spot of land in the downtown area, is where the official transfer of ownership from Russia to the U.S. took place back in 1867. There isn't much up there any more: a few low brick walls mark the boundaries of the old mansion known as Baranov's Castle (erected 1837), and a couple of cannons point toward the sea. The Alaskan, U.S., and Russian flags fly over the hill, which offers good views of Sitka Sound. A recent archeological dig, which combined with various renovations of the hill to make it more accessible, found more than 80,000 artifacts under the old concrete. Many of these were simply astounding finds: organic materials, such as leather shoes, feathers, and hair, things that ordinarily are eaten up by the wet Southeast climate. Some of these artifacts are on display at Totem Park. Unfortunately, most of them are headed to the state museum in Fairbanks.

Although it is now associated only with the Russians, Castle Hill had strategic importance long before they showed up. The Kiksadi clan of the Tlingits had the hill fortified and pestered the Russians from its heights for quite a while. When Baranov took over the hill around 1804, he built himself a log cabin so he could watch over his town from the heights. This was followed by a larger house and, ultimately, Baranov's Castle, a huge two-story building with what may well have been the first lighthouse on the Pacific coast of North America. Baranov left Sitka in 1818, at the age of 72. He never made it back to Russia – he died April 16, 1819, en route, after 30 years of ruling Alaska. His castle burned to the ground in 1894.

There is an interesting sidelight to Castle Hill. The Tlingit sold it to the Russians, outright. There's even a receipt of sorts. But now there are claims that, because it was the only part of Alaska actually signed off to the Russians, it's the only part they had any right to sell. Fun things lawyers think up while you're sleeping.

THE RUSSIAN BLOCKHOUSE: There are a few other Russian remains downtown. The Russian Blockhouse, near the corner of Marine St. and Seward, is a replica of the original structure. A few Russian graves dot the hillside around it.

KATLIAN STREET: The blockhouse originally served to separate the Native village from the Russian settlement. If you walk toward the ocean from here, you'll find yourself on Katlian St. For years this street – even extending into the early U.S. settlement in Sitka – was an almost completely segregated Native area. Katlian still maintains a strong native presence and, after years of neglect, a kind of renewal is going on as the old buildings are fixed up, some painted with traditional Tlingit designs. On the ocean side of the street are the fish processing plants. To the land side it's easy to imagine what the original village once looked like.

There has been a cultural renaissance among the local Tlingit, and it's centered around the **Sheet'ka Kwaan Naa Kahidi Community House**, at 200 Katlian St., across from the ANB Harbor, ☎ 747-7290 or 888-270-8687. The house is built more or less on traditional clanhouse plans, with a few additions to allow for the stage. It's quite a lovely building, and worth coming in just for a look around. The backdrop screen on the stage – a traditionally carved house screen – is one of the most beautiful re-creations in Alaska. There are regular programs of traditional Tlingit dance, which run $6. The presentations last about an hour, and are a good deal, with a lot of history mixed in to the presentation. Recommended. Also stop and see if Tommy Joseph is there. An astounding Native carver. If you're looking for the real deal, give him a call, ☎ 747-3451.

They also put on some special affairs. In odd-numbered years, there are canoe races held at the end of April; in even-numbered years, there's a celebration – think all the clichés of a powwow – in June.

Right at the edge of Katlian St., next to the Community House, is the **Pioneer Home**, built in 1934. The land it now occupies was once the parade ground for Russian troops. The building serves as a retirement home for "sourdoughs" – the real Alaska old-timers. If you get a chance, stop in to talk to some of the residents, if you can find one in the mood to chat. No telling what stories they've got. There's also a gift shop.

GHOSTS OF ALASKA, PART TWO

Just across Marine St. (access is actually from Seward), is the grave of the Russian Princess Maksoutov. She and her husband were the last residents of Baranov's Castle, but there's no judging her importance from the gravestone: it's just a flat marker stone with Cyrillic writing. The princess does, however, live on in Sitka legend. More than a few people have claimed to see her ghost walking the hill by the blockhouse, looking for her people to come back. When we went to high school here, checking out the graves in the middle of the night was one of the standard weekend entertainments. Never had any luck seeing the ghost, though.

RUSSIAN BISHOP'S HOUSE: Head back through downtown, back past the Centennial Building, up Lincoln Street, for the other half of Sitka's attractions. The first one you come to is the Russian Bishop's House, which was recently restored to its full glory from what was a tottering wreck by the Sitka waterfront. In fact, the building had decayed so much by the late 1970s that there was some talk about just tearing the thing down and removing the blight from the town. Hard to believe, looking at the beautiful structure as it stands now.

Completed in 1843, the building actively served as the apartments for the Bishop of the Russian Orthodox Church until 1969, when it was closed due to its condition. The structure, originally built of spruce, had rotted over the years. According to the National Park Service, which has done a masterful job of restoration, over 75% of the south wall and 25% of the north wall had rotted away. Still, the building is the oldest complete – or nearly so – Russian structure in Alaska.

Restoration took more than 16 years. Much of the work that went on was not visible from the outside, but bit by bit the house was returned to its full 1853 glory. And, thanks to the care of the restorers, over 70% of the original structure remains. On a tour of the building's first floor, some sections have been left partially unrestored to show the restoration process and to illustrate Russian building techniques, which include ingenious insulation, essentially sealing off each room and each floor. High thresholds kept out both drafts and evil spirits (in Russia, they're traditionally thought to haunt doorways).

Other displays on the first floor show the history of Alaska's Russian years, and there is an original Russian territorial marker – one of only 20 known. There are also a lot of ecclesiastical items, and pictures of the house during its prime, including a great photograph of the priest and his students (the building served as a school) standing in front of a row of beehives.

The second floor has been redone to resemble the Bishop's living quarters, with as much original furniture from the time of Father Ivan Veniamnov as possible. Father Ivan (later Bishop, later Metropolitan) was one of those great polymaths that the 19th century seemed to produce. He ran the church, ran the school, did ethnology at a time when the field was entirely undefined, and compiled a Russian-Aleut dictionary.

Note the map and books in the study and the original bed – barely five feet long – used by a man well over six feet tall. There was a reason for this besides voluntary infliction of pain: it was thought that sleeping in a sitting position would help prevent tuberculosis.

DID YOU KNOW? *Notice that there are curtains that can be drawn over most of the icons; the reasoning behind this is that icons are not paintings, but were windows to the heavens, and windows can be seen through both ways. Sometimes you need some privacy, even from God.*

The final stop on the tour is the **Chapel of the Annunciation**. This is the oldest Russian Orthodox chapel surviving in the Western Hemisphere. Clean and ornate without being fussy, it's a beautiful room, and it is still consecrated for service. The Russian Bishop's House is open daily in the summer, 9-1 and 2-5; the last tour (you can't go upstairs unless you're on a tour) starts at 4:30; admission is $3.

ST. PETER'S BY-THE-SEA EPISCOPAL CHURCH: Continuing to walk along the waterfront past the small boat harbor, you'll pass the St. Peter's by-the-Sea Episcopal Church, which was built in 1899. Note the rose window – there's a star of David in the middle of it, due to a bit of confusion at the stained glass factory. Rather than wait another two years for a replacement, the congregation decided to ride with it.

SHELDON JACKSON COLLEGE: A bit farther along you come to Sheldon Jackson College. Sheldon Jackson was a Presbyterian missionary who traveled Alaska and northern Russia from 1877 until his death in 1909. A tireless traveler and proselytizer, Jackson tramped the state building schools, helping teach modern farming methods and introducing reindeer as a new food staple for the Eskimo (herds of reindeer, descendants from those Jackson introduced, were wandering the state as late as 1937). As his hobby, Jackson spent considerable time collecting artifacts from tribes whose way of life his well-meaning efforts were destroying.

Don't miss the **Sheldon Jackson Museum** on the college grounds. Jackson was an inspired collector, interested in everything. The museum was first erected in 1889; it assumed its present shape in 1895, when his collection became too big for the original building. The new structure was the first concrete building in Alaska and one section displays a chunk of that wall. Although it has undergone a few changes over the years – and a lot of cleaning up, as you'll see from pictures – it retains the shape of the 1895 building, and it still houses the finest collection of Eskimo artifacts in the state. There are examples of each kind of kayak made by the Natives, hunting weapons, ceremonial implements, and simple tools and dolls from daily life.

AUTHOR TIP *Much of the display is in glass cases, but a lot more of it is in drawers, which you can open. Most of the really amazing stuff is found in these drawers, so don't pass them by.*

It doesn't look like much on the outside, but there is nothing anywhere in Alaska to compare with the Sheldon Jackson Museum. Don't miss it. Open 8-5 daily. Admission is $3.

TOTEM PARK: A little farther up the road is Totem Park or, as it is officially known, **Sitka National Historical Park**, where a one-mile walking path takes you past Tlingit totems surrounded by forest, the site of the decisive battle between the Tlingits and the Russians, and Indian River – absolutely jammed with salmon in season. A recent spruce needle blight has ravaged the forest. It used to be one of the prettiest spots in Southeast as the light filtered through the needles to the undergrowth. But the totems are still particularly fine examples, and the paths are still filled with locals jogging or walking their dogs.

Totem Park is the oldest federally funded park in Alaska. It was established in 1910 to commemorate the battle between the Russians and the Tlingit, who fought from behind the massive Kiksadi Fort. Nothing remains of the fort but its outline in a meadow within the park. The Tlingit's fort held up amazingly well against the guns of the battleship *Neva* and three other gunboats. When the smoke from the shells cleared, little damage had been done; an attempted storming of the fortress was even less successful. Only on the seventh day of the siege were the Russians able to move in; the Tlingits had abandoned the place in the middle of the night when they'd run out of ammunition.

The park's original totems were brought here in 1905, taken from villages around Southeast to be used in the 1904 Louisiana Purchase Exposition. Rather than put them back where they came from, Territorial Governor John Brady chose Sitka as their new home. There are about a dozen totems now, almost all in the first quarter-mile of the trail, starting on the ocean side.

In the Visitor's Center there is a good display of Tlingit history and also a variety of craftsmen – from totem carvers to beaders – working at their traditional arts. There's also a small display of artifacts recovered from Castle Hill. The center is open daily. They have a historical film that offers a pretty good overview of Russian-Tlingit interaction, but it's done in rather cheesy watercolor paintings that makes it a little hard to watch.

The trails in Totem Park lead back to the Indian River and beyond. Cross the bridge, and there's another network of trails, which lead to an old gravesite and not much else. Still, it's a nice place for a walk.

ALASKA RAPTOR REHABILITATION CENTER: Located on Sawmill Creek Rd. about a mile from Totem Park, the center was established in 1980 to care for sick or injured eagles and other birds of prey. The center has grown to the point where it now fills the buildings of the old community college. About 40 eagles a year pass through the center, being treated until they are ready to go back to the wild or, more likely, end up in a zoo somewhere. Quite a number of hawks, falcons, golden eagles, and owls come here, too; the center may handle a couple of hundred birds a year. According to the center, more than 80% of the injuries these birds receive are from brushes with humans: running into power lines is the most common injury, but a lot of birds are injured by coming into contact with fishhooks and line, poison, and about 10% – despite federal protection – end up with gunshot wounds. Approximately 30% of the birds are returned to the wild; the others go to captive breeding programs or educational programs. The center sends birds to schools around the country.

The Raptor Center is an interesting combination of medical clinic – they do serious research here on avian problems like feather fungus – and zoo. Even in the aviaries, most of the birds are chained down. When you walk into the center, you walk past several bald eagles, all chained to stumps. The eagles don't seem to be that happy to be only a few feet away from walking tourists, but the tourists are amazed.

Perhaps the most interesting thing at the center is to watch the reactions of people to these birds. When an eagle is brought in during the lecture, most of the visitors look like little kids at Christmas. People come away genuinely touched by these birds, and the center gets people who come back every year to volunteer their time, money, and resources (a doctor sent them a new X-ray machine, for example) to keep the work going.

Eagles are endangered in the Lower 48, but almost as common as crows in Alaska – in fact, there used to be a bounty on them. This has caused some controversy about the Raptor Center, wondering if, in their effort to do good, they hadn't simply thrown another wrench into the workings of nature while disguising a bird zoo as something worthwhile. Does one kind of intervention balance out another, or is it all simply intrusion? There is no doubt that they help a lot of these birds; quite a number go back to the wild. The question is, do the birds really need the help? For the ones that aren't returned to the wild, is this any kind of life at all?

The director of the center says she'd like nothing more than for the place to be no longer needed. No more human-injured birds needing care. But the fact is, that isn't going to happen, and in the meanwhile, they're doing their best. New aviaries are under construction to give those birds that can still fly more room to do so. There's also a nice trail that leads past aviaries and into the muskeg.

The Raptor Center is open 9-5, Monday through Saturday, 12-4 on Sundays. Admission is $10 for adults, $5 for kids, but the center has a few open house days when admission is free. Check the *Sitka Sentinel* newspaper for the current schedule.

MOUNT EDGECUMBE: You can cross the bridge to Mt. Edgecumbe, site of the Coast Guard station, as well as the airport. A walk around the perimeter of Edgecumbe (which sits on Japonski Island – don't confuse the town of Mt. Edgecumbe with the volcano, over on Kruzof Island) will turn up a number of old installations from WWII: there are a few bunkers, mostly collapsed, and some gun emplacements. There was a genuine fear, around the time the Japanese were invading the Aleutians, that mainland U.S. was just a few leaps away. The defensive structures in Sitka are part of the same burst of energy that built the Alaska Highway, all to protect the Lower 48. With its location on the outer edge of the archipelago, Sitka was a prime location for deep-water anchoring – there is, on the other side of the airport, the remains of a rough harbor – and in an emergency, it could have served as a base for anything short of an aircraft carrier.

The other Mt. Edgecumbe is the volcano, over on Kruzof Island. If you're lucky enough to be in town on a clear day, it's a thing of beauty, although Vancouver wasn't terribly impressed by it. But there aren't many volcanic cones as perfect as this one.

■ Town Tours

If you're going to see the town, you might as well do it with the people who were here first. **Tlingit Cultural Tours**, ☎ 747-7290 or 888-270-8687, shows you both the Russian and Native hot spots. The tour includes a dance performance at the Community House.

Sitka Tours, ☎ 747-8443, runs a variety of programs around town, including the Ferry Stopover Tour, which picks you up at the terminal and gets you back in time for sailing, for $12. They also have a longer program, which includes the New Archangel Dance performance, for $25; $12.50 for kids.

■ Adventures

Sitka isn't as easy to get out of as many of the other towns in Southeast. There are no glaciers or fjords to visit. But **Sitka Sound** gets regular migrations of whales (humpback and minke), and **Baranof** has a good supply of bears, too.

Hiking

Sitka is a hiker's paradise. Trails range from the relatively easy Harbor Mountain trip – you can drive almost to the top of the mountain, and then take a semi-steep trail up through an alpine meadow for great views of Sitka – to the torturous Verstovia Hike, which challenges all but the most experienced mountaineer.

The **Gavan Hill Trail** is a moderate three-mile hike that leaves from downtown. Head up Baranof St., and you'll find the trailhead. It goes up Gavan Hill, offering good views of town, gaining 2,500 feet of elevation in three miles. From the peak, the trail links with the Harbor Mountain Trail, leading to the only subalpine area in Southeast that you can reach by road – which, if you don't want to hike down Harbor Mountain, also gives someone a place to come pick you up. Figure four to six hours for the entire six-mile hike. You can pick it up from the other direction by driving up Harbor Mountain. The trail, which used to lead straight up the slope of the face, now starts to the left of the parking lot, easing its way up to the ridgeline.

The popular **Beaver Lake Trail**, trailhead at the Sawmill Creek Recreation Area, is only 30 minutes from the road to the lake, which is a well-frequented picnic site. It's a mile-long hike, and a pretty easy one. Nice muskeg fields. Another good lake hike is the **Thimbleberry/Heart Lake route**. The trailhead is at Mile 4 on Sawmill Creek. Thimbleberry Lake is about a 20-minute hike from the road, Heart Lake another half-hour or so beyond that. The trail between the lakes can be hard to follow.

The **Indian River Trail**, which begins just past the State Troopers' office on Sawmill Creek Road, is an easy walk from downtown. It's a 5½-mile trail, pretty flat for the first four miles, then uphill to a waterfall. The flats can get fairly boggy, and in season there are bear risks, as the river is full of fish, but it's a really nice, easy hike in the woods that you can break off and turn around on any time. If you're just looking to get into the forest, this is probably the hike for you.

The most difficult trail in town is up **Verstovia** – the name comes from the Russian word "verst," which means a mile and refers to the mountain's height. It's a two-mile track to the summit, beginning at Mile 2 on Sawmill Creek. If you manage to stay on the trail, you're rewarded at the end with absolutely unbeatable views. Verstovia is a very easy trail on which to get lost – it's not well maintained, there are a lot of switchbacks, and we can tell you from experience that once you lose the trail you're looking at hours of bushwhacking through devil's club to get back down. There is also a steep altitude gain, so take care.

Right next to the ferry terminal, Sitka has been working hard to turn **Starrigavan Bay** into a recreation paradise. There are three loop trails: one through marsh, one through forest, and one through prime fishing area. If you've got a ferry lay-over and don't want to go to town, just leave the terminal and turn left; you'll be right there. There's an easy **boardwalk trail** that takes you out over the estuary and into the forest and muskeg regions. This links up with a slightly hilly **three-quarter-mile trail** through forest and muskeg. These are very popular walks with locals out to stretch their legs. The third trail at Starrigavan is the **Mosquito Cove Trail**, which leads along the shoreline, giving views of the Starrigavan River estuary, the ferry terminal, and the north end of Sitka Sound.

Starrigavan Bay is the location of Old Sitka, the first area the Russians tried to settle. An 1802 map of the region shows only a few buildings there, but the names were distinctive and showed what the Russians had in mind: virtually every name was some variation of a term for "treasure." Nothing remains of the old town but the ghosts that haunt it.

At the other end of town, **Blue Lake** is a popular picnic and recreation site. Drive to the end of the paved road and, at the now-defunct pulp mill, take the gravel road up the hill. A pretty spot.

WATCHABLE
WILDLIFE

There's a good chance of spotting mountain goats on the peaks around the lake. Keep a sharp eye out and you may see one.

Right before that on Sawmill Creek Road, you are in **Whale Park**, which offers views of Silver Bay and the Eastern Channel, a common spot for humpbacks to pass through. There's a steep staircase down to the water, where there are a few explanatory signs and a nice spot to sit for a bit of a picnic lunch.

Bears are extremely common around Sitka – high school students often see them nosing around the parking lot at the base of Gavan Hill – so take all proper precautions. Make noise while you hike and stay out of berry bushes.

For more information on Sitka area hikes, check with the **Forest Service office**, just off Katlian St. at 204 Siginoka Way, ☎ 747-6671. They can also help get you reservations for one of the Forest Service cabins in the area, all of which require access via charter plane or boat. There are three cabins on Kruzof, under the shadow of Mt. Edgecumbe. Another good choice is the cabin at the head of Redoubt Bay. It offers great scenery and is a perfect fishing spot. Lake Eva is probably the most popular of them all, but requires booking well in advance.

The **Sitka Conservation Society**, ☎ 747-7509, has guided walks through the rainforest during the summer months. There are guided walks four times a week on the Indian River trail, for $5; and on Sundays, there are free guided hikes on one of the town's other trails. Difficulty ranges from easy to moderate, and the guide will point out a lot of things you'll miss on your own. Check with them for their current schedule.

Wildlife-Watching

Right on the edge of the open ocean, Sitka is a great place for wildlife. Every November, the town hosts the **Whalefest**, three days of educational and fun events. Sitka is a little unusual in that it has whales that stay nearby all year round, not bothering with the long trip to Hawaii. For information on the Whalefest, ☎ 747-7964, www.sitkawhalefest.org.

The rest of the year, the best way to see wildlife around Sitka is to take one of the **Wildlife Quest** tours. This may be the most professionally run wildlife tour in Alaska. There's a naturalist on board every boat, and you are guaranteed to see an otter, whale, or bear, or they'll refund half the cost of your trip. The tour lasts two hours and costs $49 for adults, $30 for children under 12. Contact Allen Marine, P.O. Box 1049, or ☎ 747-8100. The trip includes a spin past St. Lazaria, a great birding area.

Sitka has one of the more unusual ways to get out and see animals: a **semi-submersible**, which lets you sit below the water and look out at the tremendous amounts of life on the rocks and swimming about. If you don't scuba dive, this is the closest you're going to come to seeing what divers get. Trips vary in schedule, but there's usually one every Saturday, about 90 minutes long. Price is $65. ☎ 966-2301.

If you're looking for something a little more intimate, call **Raven's Fire**, ☎ 747-5777, www.ravensfire.com. They've been doing this longer than just about anybody else around, and you'll get a quality trip.

The Visitor Center has a handout of other wildlife tours, if you can't get on one of these.

Kayaking

Sitka Sound is perfect for kayaking. Despite being relatively open, it has some of the calmest waters in Southeast and the hundreds of islands dotting the bay make for nice resting points.

Sitka Sound Ocean Adventures, ☎ 747-6375 (or find them in the blue school bus in the Centennial Building parking lot), offers two-hour guided tours for $50. Groups are very small – five or six people at most – and there are several options. You can go out to where there may be whales, or head for more open water. The trailing seas coming back are great fun for paddling. Ocean Adventures also rents kayaks for $40 per day, and they have several floathouses in Camp Coogan (about six miles from town) that start around $130 per day – a great place to get away from town and enjoy the deep wild. Nice people, a great operation. See accommodations, below, for details.

Baidarka Boats, next to the Shee-Atika, ☎ 747-8996, were the first to bring sea kayaks to Sitka. They'll customize most any trip you want to take around town, with a sliding fee scale for how many people are going out – one person runs $100 for a half-day, while a group of six pays only $30 per person. Kayak rentals start at $35 per day for a single. Get drop-offs from **EZC Transfer**, ☎ 747-5044.

Boat Charters

If you want to let somebody else do the propelling, there are plenty of outfitters ready to take you onto the water. **Whale of a Tale Charters**, ☎ 747-5085, takes you out fishing or sightseeing. Trips start at $210 per person, with a minimum of three on board, for a full day.

Sitka's Secrets, ☎ 747-5089, puts a biologist on every trip and will drop a hydrophone in the water if there are whales about. Prices start from

$100 for a half-day. The tours are run by former wildlife refuge managers – these people know the outdoors.

Other good charter operations include **Berry Island Adventures**, ☎ 747-5165; **Alaska Fantasy Charters**, ☎ 747-0574; **Jolly Roger Charters**, ☎ 747-3530; and **Palco Charters**, ☎ 747-7119. Half-days with any of these are going to run in the $150 range.

There's a good fishing supply shop at the foot of the bridge, on the Sitka side. **Fly Away Fly Shop** has got more than you ever thought you needed. ☎ 747-7301.

CHOOSING A TOUR OPERATOR

As with all charters, let the operator know what you want before you sign up. Some prefer fishing, others wildlife viewing. Find out what's included before booking. A complete list of operators is available from the Visitor Center; it changes fairly often, so check for latest information.

These are a couple of the prime spots for getting away, if you're looking at customizing a charter: **Goddard Hot Springs**, south of Sitka; **Kruzof Island** to get a good look at the volcanic peak of Mt. Edgecumbe; or, if you're interested in WWII history, out to the end of the airport causeway, where there are extensive bunkers, an old hospital (never used) and, for the nature lover, some great tide pools. If you decide to look in the old hospital – it's open at both ends – take a flashlight, and be aware that there are huge holes in the floor just waiting to swallow you up and break your leg, at the very least. It's dark, it's creepy, and it's very dangerous.

For a longer charter, try the fishing village of **Port Alexander**, on the far end of Baranof Island. Port Alexander is a good place to see how a small village survives when contact with the outside world is largely cut off. There's no scheduled service into the town at all, so you'll have to charter.

Only 17 miles from Sitka by land, but a full day away by sea, is **Baranof Warm Springs**, on the back side of the island. Eleven residents live here year-round, but the town booms to nearly two dozen in summer. There are warm springs – follow the boardwalk trail – and the town itself sits in a lovely little spot, dominated by a huge, rushing waterfall. Even by Southeast Alaska standards, it's an unusually pretty spot.

■ Food

Bayview Restaurant, upstairs in the Bayview Trading Company, 407 Lincoln St., ☎ 747-5440, has excellent burgers and sandwiches, as well as a cappuccino bar out front. One of Sitka's most popular lunch spots, with prices starting around $7. Fancy dinner fare starts at $20.

Chinese food is available at the **Twin Dragon Restaurant**, 210 Katlian, ☎ 747-5711. Standard specialties, from $8-12.

The **Raven Room** in the Westmark Shee Atika, 330 Seward St., ☎ 747-6241, has good breakfasts from $6.

For splurge nights out, Sitka has some particularly fine spots. **Van Winkle & Son's**, 228 Harbor Dr., ☎ 747-3396, has warm salads, steak, seafood (including a famous old fish and chips recipe) and, occasionally, venison. Lunch from $8, dinners from around $15-20. The **Channel Club** is the other Sitka institution for fine dining. It has a salad bar that shouldn't be missed. Located at 2906 Halibut Point Rd. Reservations are suggested. ☎ 747-9916. There's free transportation out to the Club from town.

The **Backdoor Café** is the local hang-out. You're as likely to meet fishermen killing a few hours before heading back out to sea here as you are the movers and shakers of Sitka. It serves gourmet coffee (much of it from Heritage Coffee Co. in Juneau), and has an excellent location right behind Old Harbor Books. Also downtown, and the cheapest place in town to eat, is the **Lane 7 Snackbar**, next to the bowling alley at 331 Lincoln. You can fill up for under $7. Finally, in the downtown area, is **Victoria's**, in the Sitka Hotel, 116 Lincoln St. Very popular for breakfast, prices start at $8.

The other notable place of color is the **Pioneer Bar**, at 212 Katlian St. It's worth going in just for a look at the ship pictures that cover the walls.

■ Accommodations

 In summer, Sitka's accommodations fill to the brim. Early reservations are important, otherwise you might have a few unexpected cold, wet nights in one of the campgrounds.

The town's premier hotel is the **Westmark Shee Atika**, 330 Seward St., ☎ 747-6241. Right downtown, rates start around $115. Also downtown, and on the other end of the luxury scale, is the **Sitka Hotel**, 118 Lincoln St., ☎ 747-3288. Basic, comfortable, recently renovated, and cheap, with rooms starting around $55.

There is a **Super 8** at 404 Sawmill Creek Blvd., ☎ 747-8804, about a five-minute walk from most of the town's attractions. A standard chain motel, with rates starting around $80.

Finally, there is the **Cascade Inn**, small but comfortable, at 2035 Halibut Point Rd. Rates start at $100 ($125 with a kitchenette), and every room has an ocean view. ☎ 747-6804.

If the motels are filled up, try the B&B's, which are becoming more numerous by the day. There is no central booking service in town, but the **Bed & Breakfast Association**, ☎ 789-8822, on the Web at www.wetpage.com/bbaaip/, in Juneau, books some Sitka properties.

Biorka Bed & Breakfast, 611 Biorka St., ☎ 747-3111, is in a good part of town, with attentive service and thoughtful amenities. Doubles from $70. **Alaskan Ocean View B&B** is a bit away from town, but they make up for it with amenities, including a spa. Rooms from $65. ☎ 747-8310. **Karras B&B** is near downtown, with four rooms available. ☎ 747-3978. Rates start at $50. **Seaview B&B**, ☎ 747-3908, has a room with a private entrance, kitchen, and bath available, from $55.

Helga's B&B, 2827 Halibut Pt. Road, ☎ 747-5497, is right on the water's edge. Rooms have a private entrance, and the ferry shuttle stops nearby. Rooms from $65. Only a little farther out from town is the **Shoreline B&B**, 3301 Halibut Pt. Rd., ☎ 747-8508 or 800-327-5131 ext. 8508. Great views, from $50.

If everything is full, you may be able to find a room on the campus of **Sheldon Jackson College**. There is an Elderhostel there and occasionally other rooms are opened up (no telephone). It's no bargain at $60 a night, but it's nice to have as a last resort. There is also a **Youth Hostel** in town, operated only in summer, at 303 Kimshan St. ☎ 747-8356. The Sitka Convention and Visitor's Bureau has a handout on accommodations in town.

If the hustle and bustle of a town with nearly 10,000 people in it is getting to be too much, head out to one of **Sitka Sound Ocean Adventures' floathouses**. These are anchored in Camp Coogan, about six miles from town; you can paddle back and forth in the sheltered waters if you've got a boat, or they'll transport you for $20. There's a floathouse for four that starts at $150 a night, and another starting at $130 that's a lot more basic and holds up to eight. You'll never get better scenery.

■ Camping

There are two campgrounds at the north end of Halibut Point Road, in **Starrigaven**, about a mile beyond the ferry terminal. They're both quite nice, with sites for $8. Almost never crowded, and you're right at the Starrigavan Recreation Area. ☎ 747-4216. There's another campground out Sawmill Creek Road: go past the pulp mill, then head up the hill toward Blue Lake. This puts you about eight miles from town, but the lake is nearby, and so is the Beaver Lake Trail. Weekends, you may have to share the area with teenagers who come up here to make out. Sites are free. ☎ 747-4216.

Southeast

None of these campgrounds have facilities for RVs. If you need hookups, try the **Sealing Cove RV park**, over on Japonski Island, where hookups are $21 (☎ 747-3439); or **Sitka Sportsman's Association RV Park**, right next to the ferry terminal, where sites are $18 per night. ☎ 747-6033.

Haines

The Alaska Marine Highway connects up easily to the Alaska Highway in two places: Haines and Skagway. Most people on the run up from Bellingham are headed to one of these two towns. The trick is deciding which one you want to see.

The town of Haines offers scenery and proximity to the best country in the state; Skagway gives you a different kind of scenery, and some of the more interesting history you'll find. The Haines Highway, connecting the town to points north, is, quite simply, the most beautiful road we've ever been on, anywhere in the world. If you're going to drive, Haines is your only sane choice.

On the other hand, although there's a ton of stuff to do in Haines, it doesn't have the gold rush history and the restored downtown that Skagway offers. Although the bulk of the gold rush went through Skagway, there are a few traces of it in Haines. The Chilkat Pass, a longer but less steep alternative to the Chilkoot, had its trailhead here, as did the Dalton Trail. Both trails saw so many hopeful miners trekking their length that the paths are still etched into the stone a hundred years after the gold rush faded. Finally, Skagway can get 6,000 or more cruise ship tourists in town on any given summer day. They all leave at night, but if you're looking for peace and quiet, Haines is the way to go.

The best solution? Go to both. They're less than 20 miles apart, and a fast ferry connects them.

■ History

Haines was almost always a way to get somewhere else. The Chilkoot and Chilkat Indians lived in the Haines area, using it as a trading base. Its position on the coast gave them access to groups in the interior, as well as to the riches of the coast and the islands. The modern Haines airport is on the site of the old village of Yendestakyeh. Other major Native settlements were along the Chilkat River (Klukwan survives today) and on Chilkoot Lake.

The Russians passed Haines by, and it wasn't until 1881 that Hall Young, a missionary who had first seen the region two years before when traveling with John Muir, established a mission in the area. Although the locals called the mission Dtehshah, or "end of the trail," the new settlers chose the name Haines, after Mrs. F.E. Haines. Although she was never actually in the city that bears her name, Mrs. Haines was an important fundraiser for the mission.

The mission settlement grew quickly. With the base population stable, canneries were built and, during the years of the gold rush, Haines was an alternative to the more popular (and crowded and lawless) Skagway. When the gold petered out, the military moved in. In 1902, construction began on Fort Seward. During World War II, the presence of the base and the large contingent of soldiers made Haines an important point on the planned supply route to the Aleutians and the interior, in case of Japanese attack. The Haines Highway was built to connect the coast with the Alaska Highway and the interior, so as to further ease transport of supplies.

■ Haines Today

Since the war, things have calmed down. The town survives on tourism, lumber, and fishing, and on its convenience as a middle point between other destinations. It thrives on its beautiful location. Haines is one of the most attractive towns in Alaska and also the fastest growing – *Outside* magazine named it as the place to live if you've just won the lottery and don't have to worry about making a living. The next few years will reveal how growth and beauty mix in this spectacular setting.

■ Basics

The **Alaska Marine Highway** (☎ 766-2111) stops at Haines six times a week in the summer, with direct runs to Skagway and Sitka and connections to all points south. The route to and from Haines is simply lovely, as the ferry travels along the Lynn Canal, with great views of Davidson, Garrison, and Ferebee glaciers and the Eldred Rock Lighthouse, which looks like the prototype for all lighthouses.

Most cruise ships skip Haines and dock in Skagway; however, the towns are so close that a lot of the activities the ships book are actually in Haines.

 DID YOU KNOW? *The Lynn Canal, at 1,600 feet deep and more than 50 miles long, is the longest and deepest fjord in North America.*

If you want to park or camp in Haines and still see Skagway without driving the long haul back (360 miles by road, 15 by water) or getting back on the AMH, the **Haines-Skagway Water Taxi** offers an alternative to the ferry. The taxi makes two daily round-trips between the towns and takes no vehicles (except for bikes; an extra $5 charge). A one-way trip takes a little over an hour; reservations are strongly recommended – call at least a day in advance. Fare is $35 round-trip, $18, one way. Call ☎ 766-3395 or 888-766-3395 for schedules and information. There are also trips to Juneau – it's only two hours, as opposed to 10 or so on the ferry. That'll run you $90 round-trip, or there's a $110 deal that takes you to Juneau, gives you a quick tour of town and a stop at the glacier, and gets you back in Haines (dinner on board the boat) before evening.

Chilkat Cruises runs the same basic trip, Haines to Skagway, $36 round-trip. To Juneau is $90 round-trip. ☎ 766-2100. Of course, if you've got your own kayak, this is a great paddle.

The Haines Highway connects the town with the Interior of Alaska, British Columbia and the Yukon. The 160-mile road was built by the Army Corps of Engineers in 1943, shortly after the completion of the Alaska Highway. It passes through one of the prettiest concentrations of scenery in the state. It's a hard highway to drive, because you're gawking so much.

AUTHOR TIP

Canadian Customs, at Mile 42, is closed between 11 PM and 7 AM, but you can smile at the camera and pass through any time – just follow the directions posted at the customs house. You must have proof of insurance for your car at Customs. Officers can also ask about your finances: you must have $50 per person for 48 hours in Canada, $200 for a longer time period. Plastic is okay. Check in Haines for any changes before you try to cross outside regular hours. Security changes mean it's important to get up-to-date local information.

It's about 3½ hours from Haines to the nearest town, Haines Junction, on the Alaska Highway. There are some lovely campgrounds along the way, as well as a few lodges. See the *Alaska Highway* section at the end of this book for more details.

Skagway Air, ☎ 766-3233; **L.A.B. Flying Service**, ☎ 766-2222; and **Wings of Alaska**, ☎ 766-2030, all fly out of Haines to Southeast, and offer charter flights as well.

If you fly, boat, or bus to another city, you can still leave your vehicle in town and pick it up on the way back. **Bigfoot Auto**, ☎ 766-2458; **Haines Hitch-Up**, ☎ 766-2882; and **Piedad Mini Storage**, ☎ 766-2563, all have outdoor storage. Prices start from $3 per day, depending on the size of your vehicle.

Haines Shuttle & Taxi, ☎ 766-3138, runs $5 tours of town. The 45-minute trip includes the harbor, Fort Seward, Dalton City, and a stop to see totem pole carvers. For a slower pace, try the **Haines Carriage Company**, ☎ 766-2665, located in front of the Visitors Center, which offers horse-drawn carriage trips.

The **Tourist Infocenter** is at Second Ave. and Willard. It's open 8-8 daily, except for Sunday (11-6) and Wednesday (8-11). ☎ 766-2234.

Internet at **Northern Lights Internet Lounge**, 715 Main St., ☎ 766-2337.

The zip code for Haines is **99827**.

HAINES AT A GLANCE

QUICK TOUR: Head out to the Chilkat River; take a look at Fort William H. Seward.

DON'T MISS: Raft the Chilkat; fly out to one of the tiny valleys behind town and be intimidated by the size of the state; if you've got a car, drive up on the Haines Highway. You'll never think of driving in the same way again.

BEST FREEBIE: In fall, Haines has the largest concentration of bald eagles in the world. Even if you're there too early in the season for the eagle gathering, just a look at the river will amaze you. It's the quick tour, it's the best thing to do: head out and get a look at the Chilkat.

■ Museums & Attractions

In summer months, many of the shops and attractions may be closed if there isn't a cruise ship in town. If there is a cruise ship, the whole place can be too crowded to deal with and, unless you're after something in a specific gift shop, cruise time is a good time to go hiking.

SHELDON MUSEUM AND CULTURAL CENTER: A good first stopping point in town is this center, on Main Street near the boat harbor. The museum is open Monday through Friday in the summer, 8:30-5, and admission is $3. Check for other opening times, which can be slightly irregular. The small but excellent museum shop has a good selection of Alaskana books. Haines was a center for the Tlingit Indians, and you can see their local history illustrated beautifully here. Don't miss the blankets on the second floor. Make sure to pick up any of the free historical sheets on topics that interest you. ☎ 766-2366.

FORT WILLIAM H. SEWARD: The Alaska Indian Arts Workshop, ☎ 766-2160, downtown by the totem village, lets you see Native carvers and artists at work making totem poles, masks, and blankets. It's open 9-5 weekdays. The workshop is housed in what used to be the recreation hall for the old Fort William H. Seward. The fort was built just after the turn of the century, after the Protestant mission deeded 100 acres of land to the government to establish a base. Fort Seward was used as a training base in World Wars I & II. After World War II, the fort was decommissioned, and it lay vacant until it was purchased by five World War II veterans in 1970, and declared a National Historic Landmark.

📖 Pick up a walking tour map of the fort at the visitors center and explore the old barracks and other areas.

Most of the buildings have been taken over by private concerns and are now shops or hotels. There are also quite a few private residences among the fort buildings. If in doubt, ask.

CHILKOOT SLED DOG ADVENTURES: This is next to the Parade Ground at the fort. Demonstrations are held nightly for $3; they also have a drawing for a dog sled ride. ☎ 766-3242.

CHILKAT BALD EAGLE PRESERVE: The highlight of Haines is this 48,000-acre preserve, which each winter hosts the largest gathering of eagles in the world. The birds generally come here from November through February to feast on the late chum salmon run. There can be almost 4,000 eagles along the river at peak times. There are few sights as impressive as a bald eagle swooping down for a fish (it's also a lot of fun to watch them miss).

EAGLE ERROR

When eagles are hitting in the rivers after fish, an interesting fact of eagle biology can take over: They can't unlock their claws on the upswing. This means, if they're trying to gain altitude, whatever is in their claws is stuck there (there's some debate about this, but it's still widely accepted). If the bird has grabbed something too big and can't take off, it ends up doing a header into the water; from there it either has to swim to shore (they're very good swimmers, using their wings as you use your arms in the water) or sometimes they get dragged down and drown. No wonder Benjamin Franklin wanted to make the turkey the national symbol.

Take a good camera, fast film, and warm clothes on your eagle-watching expeditions; in winter months the sun is up only from about 10 AM to

2 PM in December and January, and there's likely to be rain or snow. About 200 eagles live in the area year-round. Haines has started an annual **Bald Eagle Festival**, held in November, with educational talks, films, tours, Native dances, and more. ☎ 800-246-6268.

There are a few rules to obey when you're looking for eagles. First, remember the birds have better civil rights protections than you do. Hassling the birds can get you a $10,000 fine. When you're in the preserve, stay off the flats – that's where the birds are, so it's where you shouldn't be. The parks people want you between the river and the highway, which gives the birds a nice buffer zone. This does not mean stop your car on the roadway. There are turnouts. Use them, or keep your insurance company phone number handy. The best views are usually somewhere between Miles 18-21 on the highway.

Alaska Nature Tours, ☎ 766-2876, has guided hikes along the Chilkat Valley for $50. **Keet Gushi Tours**, ☎ 766-2168, does a tour of the eagle preserve, along with a visit to Klukwan, where you can see the totems and the fine screen. The 2½-hour trip runs $65.

CHILKAT CENTER FOR THE ARTS: Nightlife in Haines is not as eventful as it was in the early gold rush days, but there are still a few things going on. At the Chilkat Center are the incomparable Chilkat Dancers, who offer a rare chance to see traditional dancing, as well as Chilkat blankets. Shows on Monday, Wednesday, and Saturday nights; admission is $8. There's also a dinner deal with a salmon bake. ☎ 766-2000. Look for it on Ft. Wm. Seward.

Tsirku Canning Company has tours of a small-scale salmon canning operation. The good thing here is that they've still got the can maker working – probably your only chance to ever see one of these, as most canneries order their cans from down south. The tours are only $10, are held daily at 1 PM, and it's worth it to see what fueled the Alaska economy for so long. And, oh, yeah, you get a chance to buy fish at the end. They're at 5th and Main, ☎ 766-3474.

SOUTHEAST ALASKA STATE FAIR: During the second week of August, Haines plays host to the Southeast Alaska State Fair, featuring pig races, logging shows, 60-pound cabbages from the Matanuska Valley, games, rides, and contests. Book your hotel well in advance.

■ Adventures

There's enough stuff to do around Haines to keep you busy for months. The trick is narrowing down the list. **Portage Cove Adventure Center**, ☎ 766-3800 or 877-766-2800, www.portage.klukwan.com, on the street at 142 Beach Road, is a central booking service for a lot of expeditions around town. Some good packages include a round-trip to Skagway on the water taxi, with a ride on the White Pass & Yukon Route Railway for $109. They also book Glacier Bay trips, and lots of fishing and boating on the Chilkoot.

Hiking

Haines has some pretty good hikes. There's the **Mt. Ripinsky Trail**, a four-mile hike up the mountain. From there you can walk along the ridge before heading back down. If you do the ridge walk, figure on overnight camping. The trailhead is off Young St. – keep left when the road forks. The first 1,600 feet are relatively easy, but it gets steeper at the end, peaking out at 3,650 feet, where you've got killer views of Haines, the Lynn Canal, and more snow-covered mountains than you can imagine. Obviously, with the elevation gain, this is not an easy hike, so go prepared, and figure it might be 10 hours round-trip. There are other trails up the mountain at Piedad road and Seven Mile, on the Haines Highway. At Seven Mile, the trailhead leads up to the **Seven-Mile Saddle**, a 2,400-foot mountain pass, below the peak of Ripinsky. Go prepared for mud. This isn't a hike for beginners; figure five hours just to get to the saddle.

Mt. Riley is a little easier. Pick up the trail head on Mud Bay Road, and hike just over two miles to the summit. Figure three hours or so. Good views of the river and the canal. There are alternate ways up the mountain via Lily Lake – 2.8 miles each way. The trailhead is off the FAA Road behind Officer's Row in Ft. Seward. The trail is more gradual than the Mud Bay alternate, plus you get a lake along the way. Finally, you can get up from Portage Cove, a four-mile hike one way. There's only one steep section on this trail, which leads you to a muskeg meadow a few hundred yards below the summit.

Seduction Point is 6.8 miles to where the Chilkoot and Chilkat inlets meet. Figure on 10 hours or so, but it's a fairly easy forest and beach walk, with good views of Davidson Glacier, and a great chance to look at both inlets. The trailhead is at the Chilkat State Park Campground.

Kayaking

If you've got your own canoe or kayak (or have rented one), head to the Chilkat River. It's a relatively sedate Class I, with excellent animal-watching; look especially for eagles and bears. The best place to put in is at Mile 19 on the Haines Highway, then you can paddle back to town.

Deishu Expeditions, ☎ 766-2427 or 800-552-9257, has a nice introductory paddle on a lake near town. Half-day is $85; full days are $120. They're also the people to call if you want to rent a kayak.

Bikes

Sockeye Cycle, ☎ 766-2869, in Ft. Seward, rents bikes for $6 an hour; $30 for eight hours. They've also got quite a variety of tours. Best of all, you can rent a bike here and take it over to Skagway, returning it to their office there, giving you a chance to peddle in both towns. It's only an extra $5 to load a bike onto one of the fast ferries.

If you've got a car, you can get your bike up to the edges of the **Tat-Alsek park**, where there are a lot of old mining roads that make for good mountain biking. Try the trailhead at Parton River, Stanley Creek, or about a mile and a half above the Selat Viewpoint, where you can ride on the original Haines road. Remember, weather conditions change quickly. Go prepared.

Flightseeing

For a look at an incredibly remote part of the world – and only a few minutes away from Haines – take the day tour with **Glacier Valley Adventures**. You fly back from Haines to the Tsirku Valley, a landscape that looks like the glaciers only pulled back yesterday. It's about a half-hour flightseeing trip back, and you land at Nugget Creek Gold Mine, which was an operating mine early last century. The most impressive thing about the operation is how obsessed these miners were at finding gold – digging 30 and 40 feet into hardscrabble, just hoping for a glimpse of color. There's still a lot of mining equipment around, and it gives you a good chance to see how gold mines worked. After you've looked around, there's a quick airboat ride up the Tsirku River to the Deblondeau Glacier Cabin. This cabin sits at the foot of a glacier in a little spike of land surrounded by wilderness: look one way, it's Glacier Bay; look the other, it's part of the Kluane-Wrangell-St. Elias Wilderness area. It's an astounding spot. You end up back at the mine for lunch and gold panning, and then get a flight back to town. It's quite a day, and the scenery is quite different from anything else you're likely to see on your trip. It's a stunning spot. It's $310 per person, ☎ 767-5522, www.akcrosscountry@wytbear.com.

Chilkat River Trips

All through the gold rush, the goal for the miners was to get up the river. They were missing the point; it's a whole lot more fun to come down. It's not a whitewater river; what you're in for is an incredibly beautiful float, with mountains ranging both sides of the river, and wide flats, where there are almost always eagles, and where you also stand a really good chance of seeing moose, and maybe the occasional bear. There are few sights quite as beautiful as a mother moose and calf walking across the flats.

Chilkat Guides, ☎ 766-2491, www.raftalaska.com, takes you out to Klukwan, then brings you back to town in a raft, for $82. The trip takes about four hours. **Eco Orca**, ☎ 766-3933, www.alaskafloattrips.com, has a similar program, for $62.

■ Tatshenshini-Alsek Wilderness

There are three great transboundary rivers that end in Southeast Alaska: the Stikine, near Wrangell, the Taku, near Juneau, and the Tat, here near Haines. The west side of the Haines Highway, from the Yukon border to Customs, travels along the edge of the Tatshenshini-Alsek Wilderness Provincial Park. This park, which is contiguous with Kluane and Wrangell-St. Elias parks, forms part of the largest protected wilderness area in the world, a UNESCO World Heritage Site.

The Tatshenshini-Alsek wilderness area was set aside in 1993, in response to a particularly stupid mining plan. The proposed mine would have dumped tailings and poisons into the Alsek, and threatened the entire area's wildlife. There was a huge public outcry – part of the complication being that the mine was going to be in Canada, with most of the damage downstream in Alaska – and this beautiful park was the result. For once, the good guys won.

Rafting & Kayaking

Because it is a wilderness area, no motorized vehicles are allowed. Experienced rafters can shoot the Tatshenshini or the Alsek, both of which have Class III-IV whitewater and both of which are increasingly popular. Outfitters from Haines can easily be booked; it's a lot harder to get on the river yourself, as the number of boats allowed is controlled by a permit system. Only one launch a day is allowed on the upper Alsek, and half of those permits are reserved for commercial companies. You also need overnight camping permits for the stretch in Kluane National Park & Reserve. ☎ 867-634-2345 for more information. If your trip is going to go all the way down to Glacier Bay, you'll need a permit from Glacier Bay National Park too (☎ 697-3341) – and it'll cost you $25 just to get on the waiting list. Don't expect to get off the waiting list any time soon.

If you do get a permit, make sure you know what you're doing. The currents in the canyons are very tricky, and the water is cold enough to give you hypothermia in a matter of moments. You'll also be as deep in the wild as you have ever been in your life, which means help is a long, long way away. This is not a solo trip for the novice. If you're in a hurry, you can do the Alsek in five days, but it's kind of pointless. Better to take 10 and enjoy yourself. This is one of the best river trips in the world, a marvel of scenery. Campgrounds with 20 glaciers visible become old hat after a few days. People who have run both the Tat-Alsek and the Stikine can rarely make a choice as to which they prefer – either trip is the trip of a lifetime. You need to make your choice on available access.

Trips on the Tat usually cover about 140 miles; on the Alsek, you go closer to 200 miles. About half of each trip is run below the confluence, where the rivers meet. Higher up, though, they have rather different characters. If you're after bear, take the Alsek; that's also the choice for those looking to get as remote as possible, and who aren't as worried about fast water. The Alsek is like traveling through the last ice age: this is what the world looked like right after the ice pulled back. The Tat has much more lush scenery – the land has had more time to recover from the last round of glaciers – and lots of moose, but not so many bears.

Alaska Discovery, 5449 Shaune Drive #4, Juneau, ☎ 780-6226 or 800-586-1911, has a 10-day trip on the Tat, which includes Class III water through the Tatshenshini Gorge. Price is $2,450. Twelve days on the Alsek – rougher, more remote than the Tat, water up to Class IV – runs $2,750, including an airlift past Turnback Canyon, which is pretty much unrunnable in a boat.

Chilkat Guides, in Haines, ☎ 766-2491, www.raftalaska.com, has 10-day trips on the Tat for $1,975; 13 days on the Alsek for $2,400. They've got a video of their Tat trip available for $15, which gives you a pretty good idea what you'd be in for.

■ Other Rivers

 Chilkat Guides also takes trips on even more remote rivers. If you don't have time for a full trip on the Tat or Alsek, and you're looking for something a little more remote than the Chilkat, check into trips on the Tsirku or the Kleheni.

■ Serious Adrenaline – Mountains

 If even the thought of rafting the Alsek is a little too tame for you, there's still plenty for you to do in Haines. Give **Alaska Mountain Guides** a call, ☎ 766-3366, www.alaskamountain-guides.com. Start off with their two-day mountaineering course, where you'll take a ski plane somewhere north (depends on conditions) and then get to learn ice conditions, hiking, ropes – in short, everything you need to know at altitude. The two-day course is only $380; longer courses, up to a full three weeks, are also available. This will get you ready for one of their peak assaults – Denali, say, or Mt. Bona. They also lead international climbs – little jaunts in Greenland, Patagonia, or perhaps a job up Aconcagua, peaking out just below 23,000 feet.

This is also the place to learn ice climbing. Some of the best ice in the world is in their neighborhood. Three days, $540; five days, $860. Rock climbing is two days for $380.

Skiing your thing? Five days backcountry skiing in Glacier Bay for $860; three days of hut-based skiing for $540. Finally, they've got a 10-day combo trip, mountain climbing and sea kayaking, for only $1,980. This company offers some of the best ways to get where no one else is. Good people, good programs, good deals.

■ Shopping

 Since Haines doesn't get the number of tourists that Skagway does, downtown is more for locals than travelers. Still, there are a couple things worth checking into.

Form and Function Gallery, 209 Willard, ☎ 766-2539, has beaders and carvers working in the shop, and a great selection of nice pieces – particularly the masks and boxes. **The Far North**, just around the corner on 2nd Ave., has lovely ivorywork, walrus whiskers, and other items from Inuit lands.

Buy some fish for the road ahead at either the **Tsirku Canning Company**, at 5th and Main – see above, for info on their tour – or at **Dejon Delights**, in Ft. Seward. Buy some wine to go with your fish at **Great Land Wines**, ☎ 766-2698. They're a ways out of town, but the grocery stores will have their local wines, made from, among other things, rhubarb, onion, "porcupine carrot gold," and a wide variety of berries.

Finally, just because you can, check out the **Lost Coast Surf Shop**. It's a block up from the fast ferry dock. Really. We're not making this up. It's really a surf shop.

■ Food

 Some of the best places to eat in Haines are a ways out of town. The **Thirty-Three Mile Roadhouse**, ☎ 767-5510, is out past the Chilkat Bald Eagle Preserve, nearly to Klukwan. Try it for steaks, seafood, and the view. Dinners start at $14. For true gourmands, try **Weeping Trout's** Saturday night dinner. For $47.50, you get an astonishing meal at the resort, which is located on the edge of a lake well outside Haines – it takes two boat rides to get there. The basic price includes transport from the first boat landing; if you need a ride all the way from town, it's $74 for the trip and the meal. Go early, play a round of golf at the resort. A chance to do something really different.

Local choice in town is the **Bamboo Room**, open all day, right downtown. Burgers from $6, steak for $21.

The **Fort Seward Lodge**, ☎ 766-2009, makes a good night-out dinner. Steak and seafood from $9, and all-you-can-eat crab dinners for $25.

The **Port Chilkoot Potlatch Salmon Bake** is open from 5 to 8 PM (except Thursday). All you can eat for $21.75, served in a replica of a Native house. The **Chilkat Restaurant and Bakery**, at 5th and Dalton, has the town's best baked goods. Also soups, sandwiches, and salads.

The **Mountain Market**, at 3rd and the Haines Highway, is the town's health food store. They've also got a deli inside. Finally, **Howsers Supermarket**, on Main St., has a deli next to the groceries that offers sandwiches, chicken, and ribs, cheap.

■ Accommodations

In Haines, much of the lodging is located in or around Fort Seward, and thus many of the buildings are historic sites. Nothing is really cheap. Try the picturesque **Hotel Halsingland** for historic accommodations; you may get a room with a claw-foot tub. Doubles from $85. There are also some cheaper rooms with shared baths. ☎ 766-2000 or 800-542-6363.

Another lovely old house turned into a hotel is the **Fort Seward B&B**. On the National Register of Historic Places (it used to be the surgeon's living quarters), it's very small, so book early. Doubles from $85. They'll pick you up at the airport or ferry terminal in a vintage Lincoln Towncar. ☎ 766-2856.

Fort Seward Condos offer one- and two-bedroom apartments complete with full kitchens year-round, from $85 a night. There's a two-day minimum, and longer-term stays receive extra deals: a free night with a week stay, or a monthly rate of only $850. ☎ 766-2425.

Downtown there is slightly more generic lodging. Nicest is **Captain's Choice Motel**, ☎ 800-247-7153 (in Alaska, 800-478-2345), with rooms from $85 to $175. Nearby are the comfortable **Thunderbird**, ☎ 766-2131 or 800-327-2556, with doubles from $70, and **Mountain View**, ☎ 766-2131, with rooms from $64 (plus a few bucks more for a room with a kitchenette).

There's a lovely option out of town, the **Weeping Trout Sports Resort**. It's about 90 minutes from town, on Chilkat Lake – you can only get there by boat. Packages, including boat use, start around $200 a day. It's rustic – no hot water in the very comfortable cabins – but how many other places have you been where you can play a round of golf and fish without going more than a hundred yards from where you slept? ☎ 766-2827; www.weepingtrout.com.

Southeast

As in most towns in the North, B&Bs come and go. Some that have been around awhile are the **Summer Inn**, at 117 Second Ave., ☎ 766-2970, with doubles from $80; the **Chilkat Eagle** in Ft. Seward, ☎ 766-2763, with doubles from $75; and **Sheltered Harbor**, at 795 Beach Rd., ☎ 766-2741, with doubles from $80.

The **Dalton Street Cottages** are quite nice, close to downtown. Doubles start at $110, and there are kitchenettes, so you can save a few bucks on food. 116 6th St., ☎ 766-3123. **Pyramid Island BB**, a mile and a half out Mud Bay Road, has a courtesy van, killer views, and doubles from $95.

The cheapest place to stay in town is the **Bear Creek Camp & Hostel**, Box 1158. They offer cabins from $40, as well as tent ($8) and dorm ($14) space. ☎ 766-2259. Really quite nice, and they'll pick you up.

■ Camping

There are four lovely state park campgrounds in Haines: **Chilkat State Park**, seven miles south of town on Mud Bay Rd.; **Chilkoot Lake**, 10 miles north of town off Lutak Rd.; **Portage Cove** on Beach Road, just under a mile out of town; and **Mosquito Lake**, at Mile 27 on the Haines Highway. All of them have water and toilets along with good fishing. Sites cost $6 to $8 a night.

If you require hookups, there are several choices: **Alaskan Eagle RV Park**, on Union St., ☎ 766-2335, and **Haines Hitch-up RV Park**, at Main and Haines Highway, ☎ 766-2882. There are also spots at the **Hotel**, ☎ 800-542-6363. Farther from town, Mile 27 on the Haines Highway, is the **Swan's Rest RV Park**, ☎ 767-5662.

Skagway

A "ton of gold" was carried off the docks into the small town of Seattle in July 1897. A full year had passed since the stuff of dreams had been discovered in the Klondike, on Rabbit Creek, a tributary of the Yukon River; but it was only when the ship hit Seattle, wallowing gold-heavy in the light swells of Puget Sound, that the rest of the world had its first news of the gold strike.

The very next ship heading north from Seattle was overflowing with hopeful prospectors. The rush was on, and it all channeled through Skagway, the northern port for the would-be rich.

■ History

Skagway became one of the most famous cities in the world in 1897. There was hardly a newspaper printed in the continental U.S. that year that didn't have an article on the gold rush and the trip north. It was from Skagway that thousands headed up the murderous **Chilkoot Trail**, bound for the gold fields of the Yukon, 600 miles to the north. The Chilkoot actually started in nearby Dyea, which would have been the boomtown if ships could have gotten to it more easily, but a huge mud flat meant ships stayed well away. Miners would disembark from their ships in Skagway and head over to the trailhead as quickly as possible, getting ready for the arduous climb over the mountains.

CAPTAIN WILLIAM MOORE

Captain William Moore, anticipating the gold rush by almost a decade, had staked claim to 160 acres at the mouth of the Skagway River nine years before the first strike and begun construction of a wharf. When the first load of miners arrived in his would-be village of Mooresville, a group including surveyor Frank Reid forced Moore and his claim aside, drew up a new town plan, and renamed the town Skaguay, after the Tlingit "Skagua," or windy place. Moore never did make his fortune, though, after years of court battles, he finally received a small part of the value of the land.

Skagway was the largest Alaskan town during the gold rush years, with a population between 10,000 and 20,000. It also had a reputation as lawless and dangerous. Many stampeders never reached the gold fields but instead lost everything to one of the myriad conmen waiting at the docks. Many more lost everything in the mud, on the trail, or they simply came to their senses – not many in this last category – and headed back home. One estimate is that a grand total of 100,000 people started off for the gold fields. Half made it to Alaska. Maybe fewer than 50 actually got rich.

During the first year of the gold rush alone, about 20,000 to 30,000 gold seekers headed up the Chilkoot Trail from Dyea. After starting from the port in Skagway, the trip took an average of three months. As the Canadian government required that each person carry a year's supply of food and necessities – the Canadians weren't that interested in finding a lot of dead hopefuls on their land – a lot of hiking back and forth between Skagway and the top of the pass was required.

Figuring that a miner's gear – 350 pounds or so of flour, 150 pounds of bacon, 100 pounds of sugar, another 100 pounds of beans, 70 pounds or so of coffee and tea, plus clothes (all wool, remember, in those pre-synthetic days), bedding, shovels, picks, etc. – cost a total of roughly $500-2,000, you know there were plenty of people waiting and hoping to sell stuff. It was the only sure way to get rich off the gold rush (one estimate says that within two weeks of the first ship of gold docking in Seattle, local merchants sold $325,000 worth of mining gear). Along the way, boomtowns sprang up, some considerably bigger than modern Skagway. Atop the pass, miners built rough boats on the lakes and floated the Yukon River up to the gold fields.

Later in the rush, an alternative route at the **White Pass**, first charted by Frank Moore, came into its own. The trailhead for this route was practically in the center of Skagway. Nicknamed "Dead Horse Trail" for the 3,000 or so animals that died (according to Jack London, "like mosquitoes at the first frost") hauling packs along its length, the White Pass was considerably less steep but longer than the Chilkoot. There was no shortage of miners who took a look at the steep slopes of the Chilkoot and then decided the slow route might be the better one to take, and so the White Pass saw more than its share of stampeders trying to get their gear up to where it could be approved by Canadian Customs. Within two months, the trail had become almost impassable from overuse.

In 1898, construction began on the **White Pass & Yukon Route Railway** (WP&YR), which still operates today. The line didn't get finished until June 8, 1900 – after the bulk of the rush was past (all those pictures you see of miners hiking straight up a hill – the "Golden Stairs" – in the snow come from the winter of '98-'99; and remember they probably each went up and down that hill close to 50 times). Getting the line through meant the trip to the gold fields was cut from six months to six days, but the traffic was already thinning.

■ After the Gold Rush

The railroad was leased by the U.S. War Department in 1942 for the duration of World War II, and used to transport supplies and men for the construction of the Alaska Highway. Everything arrived by barge, was transported to the army's base camp in Whitehorse, and then moved out to the work sites along the highway. During the months of construction, the line moved 15 tons of freight every two weeks – more than it had moved in the 40 years previous. There were up to 17 trains a day running through the pass. It was on this railroad that the idea of container shipping was first tried. Truck trailers came off barges, were loaded onto the train, then transported north to the road. Now used worldwide, the idea started right here.

Glacial pools in Skagway.

📖 There are two excellent books on the gold rush and the White Pass, detailing the early history of Skagway and the trials of the miners: *The Klondike Fever*, by Pierre Berton, covers the gold rush; *The White Pass*, by Roy Minter, is a fascinating history of the WP&YR railway.

■ Skagway Today

Except when the cruise ships are in, Skagway is considerably calmer than it once was (and even then, as one long-time resident put it, "In the gold rush days, we had 20,000 people walking the streets with guns; now we just have six or seven thousand tourists"). This sleepy town of 850 year-round residents faces more tourist jams than guns now. From 9 AM to 9 PM, there can be as many as 7,000 cruise ship passengers on the street – yeah, there's really only one – of Skagway, all of them come to see a town that's being restored to its full 1898 glory. Don't let the numbers put you off. Skagway is a beautiful city in one of the most dramatic settings in Southeast. During ship hours, head for the mountains; when the ships are out, come in and walk around the beautiful town.

Southeast

There are those who complain that Skagway is becoming a kind of Disneyland of the far north – an unreal town living only for the tourist trade – but few visitors go away disappointed.

■ Basics

i Skagway and Haines are the only places where you can switch from the Alaskan road highway to the Alaska Marine Highway for trips south. The ferry terminal is located about half a mile from downtown. See the Alaska Highway chapter at the end of the book for details on linking up to the road system. Local phone for the **AMH** is ☎ 983-2941. Do be aware that the road from Skagway into Canada isn't anywhere near as beautiful as the road from Haines. Cruise ships dock right at the edge of downtown. Head inland. You'll strike shops.

Rent a car from **Avis**, ☎ 983-2247 or 800-331-1212; or **Sourdough Car Rental**, ☎ 983-2523. **Sockeye Cycle** rents mountain bikes, ☎ 983-2851; **Sourdough Car Rental** does as well. Check at their office on 6th, off Broadway. Rates start at $10/hour.

Charter a helicopter from **Temsco**, ☎ 983-2900, which also has heli-flightseeing tours of the local glacier area. **L.A.B.**, ☎ 983-2471; **Wings of Alaska**, ☎ 789-0790; and **Skagway Air**, ☎ 983-2218, also charter and run similar tours in fixed-wing planes, as well has having regularly scheduled runs to nearby towns.

Haines-Skagway Water Taxi, ☎ 888-766-3395, offers a good way to take a day-trip to Haines, get some good views of the Lynn Canal and possibly some wildlife, and still be back in Skagway in time for dinner. The trip takes roughly an hour each way; the taxi makes two round-trips per day. Fare is $35 round-trip. $90 puts you on the fast boat to Juneau.

The Fjord Express, ☎ 800-320-0146, also runs fast ferries to Juneau, for $99 round-trip.

To take a bus to the Interior, call **Alaskon Express**, ☎ 800-544-2206. It'll run you about $200 from Skagway to Anchorage.

AUTHOR TIP

The Canadian border is open from 8 AM to midnight from November 1 to March 31, and 24 hours a day the rest of the year. If you're traveling in winter, remember that these are Canadian times – an hour ahead of Alaska. See the Alaska Highway *section (page 427) at the end of the book for more details. Also, be sure to check locally before you head out. The world is changing pretty fast right now, security-wise. Get the latest info.*

The **Information Center** is right downtown, in the old AB Building. You'll recognize it because of the herd of tourists out front taking pictures of its beautiful driftwood exterior. It has the usual assortment of stuff and a map of the Skagway walking tour – Skagway is one of the most beautiful towns in Alaska to walk around in. If you're doing the tour, though, take a good look at the map first and check for shortcuts to the places you're really interested in. Nothing is very far away in Skagway. The Info Center is open daily 8-5 in the summer, 8-12 and 1-5 the rest of the year. ☎ 983-2855.

The **National Park Service Visitor Center** is in the old WP&YR offices, right in the center of downtown. They're open daily 8-7 in summer; 8-6 in May and September; and 8-6, Monday through Friday, the rest of the year. ☎ 983-2921. See below for more details.

Access the Internet at **Skagway Cyber Café**, next door to the Great North Hotel, on Broadway.

The zip code for Skagway is **99840**.

SKAGWAY AT A GLANCE

QUICK TOUR: Skagway is four blocks wide and 12 long. Use your imagination.

DON'T MISS: Rail buffs, here's your chance to ride the White Pass & Yukon Route; if you're looking for something to do with your feet, head over to Dyea and hike the Chilkoot. You'll appreciate the train all the more.

BEST FREEBIE: People-watch. There's nowhere in Alaska so perfect for it. Find a comfortable place to sit, and sooner or later, every tourist in the state will walk by. When you're done with that, take the five-minute hike out to Yakutani Point and watch the ocean to remember why you came to Alaska to begin with.

▪ Museums & Attractions

 Skagway's attractions are all pretty close together, and you can walk to everything. It's a great town for walking, too, because ocean and mountain views come out and surprise you around the edges of Victorian houses everywhere you turn. Despite the maddening crowd, Skagway is a fun place to hang out. Even if the ships sometimes make downtown look like an old fraternity gag – how many people can you stuff into a VW Bug? – don't let it get you down. There's no way around it, the town is still a blast, and on the off chance there's no ship in, most of the attractions will be closed anyway.

Southeast

KLONDIKE GOLD RUSH NATIONAL HISTORICAL PARK: Located at Broadway and 2nd, open 8 AM to 8 PM, June through August; 8 to 6 in May and September. Once the depot for the WP&YR, it's now the forest service and park headquarters and marks the beginning of a seven-block corridor that houses many restored buildings dating to gold rush days. The center has daily film shows, and it's the starting point for free guided walking tours of the town. The tours take about an hour and are well worth joining. The film, 30 minutes long and shown on the hour, is way above average for this kind of thing, and not a waste of time. There are daily ranger talks at 10 AM and 3 PM, as well. They've also got some great displays of old mining items. Finally, this is the place to begin planning your hike up the Chilkoot.

📖 Be sure to pick up a copy of the ***Skaguay Alaskan***. The **Skagway Trail Map** is also invaluable if you plan to do any hiking. ☎ 983-2921.

WHITE PASS & YUKON RAILROAD: The WP&YR is next door to the old depot; the new depot becomes a hive of activity when the train pulls in to start the trip up the White Pass. All the publicity shots show a steam train on this run; sorry, it's not gonna happen. They only use the steam train for special occasions, and odds are high that all you'll see moving is a diesel. Still, the carriages are either originals or beautifully made replicas, the scenery is simply astounding – there's no feeling quite like looking out the train at places where miners wore paths down into bedrock as they hauled their gear – and it's a must-do for train buffs (and everybody loves a choo-choo train, right?). The four-hour trip up to the summit and back is a great way to spend the afternoon. Nobody comes off this ride without a smile on their face. Tickets are $82 for adults; $41 for kids age three through 12. There's also connecting service to Whitehorse. For more information, ☎ 983-2217 or 800-343-7373. The train does have wheelchair access.

AUTHOR TIP

The railway climbs more than 2,800 feet in only 20 miles, and because the line follows the curves of the mountain, there are some great chances to lean out the windows and get pictures of the train even when you're on it. If you want to shoot some pictures of the train as it goes by, stand along Spring Street. Back in the old days, the tracks actually ran down the center of State Street; the train yards are still there, to the north of town.

Train fans should check out the **Train Shoppe**, inside the depot. It's got a large selection of train stuff, from whistles and books to videos and models.

Other White Pass excursions include the **Chilkoot Trail Hiker's Service** – the train picks you up at Lake Bennett – for $30, and a nice long ride up to Carcross in Yukon, for $90 round-trip, including lunch. You can even charter an entire car for yourself and your friends at only $650 for a caboose or $2,500 for a luxury railcar from the days when people had more fun with their money than they seem to now.

RED ONION SALOON:
Coming out of either the Park Service building or the WP&YR station, you'll see the saloon right across the street – a lively place with music and crowds until late in the evening. Once a brothel, it's now a restaurant with the best food in town and a very interesting atmosphere. There are also (somewhat dubious) rumors of a ghost.

White Pass & Yukon Route, Skagway.

GHOSTS OF ALASKA, PART THREE

Reports of the ghost in the Red Onion are iffy, but there's not much doubt about the one in the town's oldest hotel, The Golden North, built in 1898. Guests regularly spot the ghost, and there's always a chance of it wandering through the dining room. Stay the night and try your luck with the ghost. Even if you're not staying there, stop to look around the lobby. ☎ 983-2289. But that's not the only ghost in Skagway. Across the street in the Eagles Hall (not open to the public), we've got very reliable reports of another ghost. The building has lots of odd nooks and crannies, and it's a natural place for a haunt.

THE TRAIL OF '98 MUSEUM: In the old City Hall, the museum displays artifacts pertaining strictly to Skagway and its history and the gold rush. Among the various attractions is a display of early gambling equipment dating from the time when Skagway was at the very edge of the Wild West.

Open daily in the summer; admission is $3. The Old City Hall is on 7th St.; turn east off Broadway. The old City Hall building was the first granite building in Alaska, and you should take a look even if you're not interested in the museum. It was renovated, and over the next few years it will be fascinating to watch the new stone blend in with the old.

CORRINGTON MUSEUM: Yes, it's inside a gift shop, but that's not what's important. This museum has a nice collection of Aleutian baskets and ivory, with good model displays. Also some of the best scrimshaw you're going to find. The museum is open daily in the summer. 5th & Broadway. Well worth stopping in.

GOLD RUSH CEMETERY: The cemetery is the final resting place for, among others, two people who made Skagway history: Soapy Smith, a gang leader who held the town under his thumb for years, and Frank Reid, the man who killed Soapy on July 8, 1898. Soapy had just enough time to shoot back, and Reid died 12 days later. Two miles north of town, near the WP&YR lines. Sadly, they've put up replica stones next to the real ones – mostly too aged to read – and it ruins a lot of the effect.

KLONDIKE GOLD DREDGE TOURS: ☎ 877-983-3175, lets you see just how far people would go in their search for gold. They've taken a huge dredge – one of those machines that ate rivers whole – and opened it up for tours. For $25, you get a movie (try to stay awake if you can), a tour of the dredge, and you get to try some gold panning yourself. Best for those who like big machinery, but the gold panning is always a hit.

DYEA: Eight miles on a bumpy gravel turnoff leads to the ghost town of Dyea. Once almost as big a boomtown as Skagway, living off the miners headed north, the town collapsed when the WP&YR was completed. All that remains are the skeletons of buildings, a wharf, and Slide Cemetery. However, the drive out is lovely, there's a good chance of seeing seals in the bay, and Dyea is the trailhead for the Chilkoot (see below).

Dyea had been the end of a trading trail for centuries, part of the extensive trade network the Tlingit operated in Southeast, connecting them with the interior. The first trading post was built in 1880, and seven years later, there were nearly 200 people in town. Right after the news of gold got out, though, the town boomed to nearly 8,000 people. As with any boomtown, though, this didn't last long. As a port, Dyea sucked. Literally – the mud flats exposed at low tide swallowed more than one miner's gear, and ships couldn't get anywhere near the town. If the trail hadn't been there, nobody would have come near the place, and after an avalanche in April 1898 killed more than 60 wannabe miners, even more of the traffic moved over to Skagway and the White Pass Trail. By 1900, only two years after the gold strike, the town was back down to 250 people. By 1903, there were all of three people rattling around what had once been one of the largest towns in Alaska.

The site is now a National Historical Park, with all the protection thereof. There's lots of stuff under the brush and grass, but leave it there. The Park Service has daily walks of the townsite at 2 PM in the summer. Meet at the parking lot in Dyea.

DAYS OF '98 SHOW: For more than half a century, the Fraternal Order of the Eagles has been putting on the Days of '98 Show in the Eagle's Hall at 6th and Broadway. The show gives a good, entertaining history of Skagway – complete with the fight between Soapy Smith and Frank Reid, plus a few chorus girls. The evening show features "mock gambling." Daytime shows are at 10:30 AM and 2 PM; the evening performance has gambling starting at 7:30, with the actual performance beginning at 8:30. It's a good way to spend the evening. ☎ 983-2545.

■ Tours

With the cruise ship market requiring maximum scenery with minimum effort, there are plenty of town tours available. If you've only got a few hours, these are a good idea. They're all going to do pretty much the same thing: take you past some of the Victorian houses, the Gold Rush Cemetery, and up to the White Pass summit, stopping at a couple of the spectacular waterfalls along the way. The number of operators out there selling these tours keeps them all pretty nice – good buses, with a pretty nice budget price of around $35.

Klondike Tours, ☎ 983-2075, **Frontier Excursions**, ☎ 983-2512, **PB Tours**, ☎ 983-3385, and **M&M Brokerage**, ☎ 983-3900, all have the same basic program. **Southeast Tours**, www.southeasttours.com, or stop at their office on 5th and Broadway, has the usual summit trip, but also books a 5½-hour horseback trip, for $130, or a dogsled trip for $84.50. They've also got a half-day mountain bike trip for $82.

■ Adventures

If you are an experienced kayaker and have your own boat, you can easily paddle the 15 miles to Haines, getting a good look at both the Lynn Canal and the Taiya Inlet.

Rent a kayak from the **Mountain Shop**, at 5th near Broadway. **Klondike Water Adventures**, ☎ 983-3769, has introductory paddles on Lake Bernard.

AUTHOR TIP *The best paddle is probably over to Haines, or turn up the Lutak Inlet and paddle for the old town of Chilkoot.*

Skagway Float Tours, ☎ 983-3688, has a really nice combination hike/float, for $75. You hike a bit under two miles on the Chilkoot Trail (not the steep part, but there is a pretty good uphill portion), and then load into rafts for a nice float back downstream on the Taiya River. The trip takes about four hours, and it's a lot of fun – plus you get to claim that you've hiked at least part of the Chilkoot Trail. If the hike is more than you're in for, just the float runs $65.

Packer Expeditions has a great trip that gives you the best of Skagway – you helicopter up over the Juneau Icefields to Glacier Station; once there, you do a five-mile hike along the Skagway River, over to Laughton Glacier. Finally, you return to town on the WP&YR train. The trip runs $299. They've also got a cheaper full-day hike up the Denver Trail; you take the train six miles to the trailhead, then hike back to the head of the valley, past waterfalls and into the old growth forest. You're going to need to be in shape for these hikes, but you'll have the time of your life. ☎ 983-2544, or stop in at the Mountain Shop, on 4th Ave. just west of Broadway.

Alaska Sled Dog Adventures, ☎ 983-3392, has dog demos, where you get to ride around on a wheeled cart. Sled dogs are as much – more – a part of Alaskan history than the greed for gold. There's nothing quite like watching a half-dozen huskies blast off. The ride, demo, and getting to play with puppies runs $78.

Hiking

The best hiking is obviously on the Chilkoot (see below), but there are a lot of other options that aren't quite so strenuous. There's a quick viewpoint hike out to **Yakutani Point**. Take the footbridge past the airport and head left. Good place for a picnic.

The easiest hike is the **Lower Dewey Lake Trail**, only .7 miles. You go from 2nd Ave. and head east. There's no way to miss the signs. From Dewey Lake, you can hook up with the **Northern Bench Trail**, another mile that takes you back toward town. The trailhead is at the northwest corner of the lake. If you want to see **Upper Dewey Lake**, it's only another 2.3 miles. It's pretty steep at first, but levels out, ending up in a muskeg meadow.

The more ambitious should try the **Denver Glacier Hike**, three miles at Mile 6 on the WP&YR, or seven miles from the Gold Rush Cemetery. You go through spruce and hemlock forests typical of Southeast Alaska's mid-latitudes rainforest, then climb up the mountain along the banks of the East Fork Skagway River, through an area covered with alder and devil's club.

A hike up **AB Mountain** will kill a full day. It's 10 miles round-trip, and it has an elevation gain of around 5,000 feet, so you'll be hurting by the top. Pick up the trailhead on the Dyea Road, but make sure you don't lose the trail once you get above the treeline. The **Lost Lake Trail** leaves from Dyea, climbing 1,400 feet over a 2.9-mile route. You can camp up at Lost Lake, a nice spot most of the way up the mountain.

📖 Pick up a **Skagway Trail Map** at the Infocenter or at the Forest Service Office.

The Chilkoot Trail

Not to be attempted lightly, the Chilkoot is still open for hikers. It takes three to five days to hike this historic route, and it can be a bit crowded in the summer. About 3,000 people hike the trail each year. At the end of the trail, you'll be given a certificate by the Canadian Park Service documenting your accomplishment.

Before setting out, stop by the National Park Visitors Center (in the old train depot) for mandatory registration, and for their useful handouts on the trail. They'll also know the latest trail conditions. Parks Canada now requires $40 (Canadian dollars) for a permit to hike the trail; only 50 people a day are allowed on the trail. Call well in advance of your planned trip for reservations: ☎ 800-661-0486.

Go fully prepared, taking all necessary camping gear, food, and personal items, keeping in mind that the weather can change dramatically and quickly. There are no shelters on the trail. Bring your own tent. There are 10 designated camping areas along the way; Canyon City, Sheep Camp, Deep Lake, and Lindeman are especially nice.

None of the water is safe for drinking, so be sure to boil it first. All camps are in bear country, so keep the camp clean.

📖 There is a good guidebook specific to the trail, *A Hiker's Guide to the Chilkoot Trail*. You can pick it up in town, or order it in advance of your trip from the Alaska Natural History Association, ☎ 274-8440, www.alaskanha.org.

ARTIFACT ETIQUETTE

Along the way, there are many artifacts that were dropped by the tired miners: Do not touch these. Nearly a century of being exposed to the elements has left them extremely fragile, and they are part of a living museum protected only by state law and your courtesy. Take all the photographs you want, and leave the objects untouched for other hikers and the researchers, who are putting back together a picture of life on the trail.

Southeast

The trail goes from sea level to a peak of 3,000 feet. At its base, you are in a rainforest; at the top of the pass, you've entered an alpine tundra zone, which means that for quite a stretch you're above the tree line and there's no protection from the elements at all.

Pick up the trail right before the Taiya River bridge at Dyea. The first dozen miles or so are a fairly gentle climb followed by a long flat, but then you hit the famous steep climb to the pass – this is the section you've probably seen in photos. During the gold rush, steps were carved into the ice on the slope, but it didn't help that much when you were hiking up the trail for the fifth time that day with 60 pounds of bacon on your back. There's nothing too difficult about the last portion of the trip, unless the weather turns bad. The Park Service actually considers it easier to go up this slope than down and they try to discourage people from hiking the trail in reverse for fear of injuries here.

You can make reservations to ride the WP&YR back to Skagway from Lake Bennett (daily service in the summer) if you don't have a ride waiting for you at the end or don't have the time to hike the trail round-trip. It's a memorable hike, and not a terribly difficult one if you're fit. The trail is well marked, well traveled, and hard to miss. For the first two or three miles, you may well end up sharing the trail with a cruise ship tour, but they tend to fall off quickly. Just follow the rules, talk to the Park Service first, and prepare for every contingency. If you'd rather do the trail with a guide, talk to **Packer Expeditions**, in the Mountain Shop, or ☎ 983-2544.

■ Fishing Charters

Not many people come up the Lynn Canal to go fishing; as with Haines, there simply aren't a lot of charter operators working. **Dockside Charters**, ☎ 877-983-3625, has been working in town for years. Half-days, $135, full days, $225. If they're booked, try **Choctaw Charters**, ☎ 800-764-7670, or **Chilkoot Charters**, ☎ 983-3400.

■ Shopping

It's a small town, designed for handling masses of cruise ship passengers in a very short time. You're not going to have any trouble finding the stores.

The **Mountain Shop**, on 4th Ave. just west of Broadway, has a full line of outdoor gear, a lot of it at prices cheaper than you're going to find down South. ☎ 983-2544. **Gold Vein Designs**, on Broadway near 6th, has beautiful trade beads – one of the best selections in the state.

Corrington's Alaskan Ivory, at 5th and Broadway, is worth stopping in for the free museum; they've also got the standard tourist fare, but with some interesting twists.

The Miner's Cache, at 6th and Broadway, has some really nice works on paper, and good knives.

For a taste of Alaska, try **Teas and Mysteries**, on 3rd Ave west of Broadway. Outstanding huckleberry tea.

The **Skaguay News Depot**, on Broadway between 2nd and 3rd, can take care of your reading needs for books on the town's history.

■ Food

You can eat very, very well in Skagway. The **Skagway Fish Company** and the **Stowaway Café**, both on the east side of the boat harbor, are the places to go for the best food in town. Try the halibut and brie at the Fish Company, or one of the Cajun specialties at the Stowaway. You're not going to be sorry. Entrées start around $15.

The **Red Onion Saloon**, mentioned earlier for its possible ghost, has burgers, and steaks priced under $12. Lots of atmosphere.

The **Corner Café**, 4th and State, has great lunches and big breakfasts, and is quite cheap. Ten bucks or so fills you up.

There are two places for Italian food: the **Portobello**, at 1st and Broadway, or **Northern Lights Pizzeria**, at 5th and Broadway.

The **Sweet Tooth**, Broadway and 3rd, is a converted saloon that now serves up a great breakfast for only $5: eggs, sausage, and excellent hash browns. It gets crowded here around 7:30 in the morning.

The restaurant in the **Golden North Hotel** has a good selection, reasonable prices, a microbrewery, and there's always the chance of spotting the hotel ghost.

■ Accommodations

There are no bargains in Skagway. Early reservations are a must. The **Golden North**, ☎ 983-2451 or 983-2294, at 3rd and Broadway, is the town's oldest hotel. Doubles run around $100. **Sgt. Preston's Lodge**, ☎ 983-2521, is also a good bet. Centrally located on 6th, a block west of Broadway, with rooms from $75. They've got a courtesy van, too. It's off Broadway, so a little quieter. The **Gold Rush Lodge**, ☎ 983-2831, 6th and Alaska, has 12 rooms from $65. Good and comfortable.

Smaller but quite nice is the **Skagway Inn B&B**, 7th & Broadway, ☎ 983-2289, with doubles in an 1897 Victorian house from about $70.

The **Mile Zero B&B** is one of those lovingly run places that just amaze you when you stay. Rates start at $70, all rooms have private entrances, and, rarity of rarities, soundproof walls. At 9th and Main, ☎ 983-3045.

If everything else is full, try the **Westmark**, which has more rooms than the rest of the town combined. Be aware it's often filled with package tourists. ☎ 983-2291.

The **Forest Service** runs one of the nicest places to stay: a converted caboose, five miles up the train line. As with any Forest Service cabin, bring your own gear. Reservations on line at www.reserveusa.com.

■ Camping

Skagway has recently increased its camping facilities, so your chance of finding a spot is much greater than it used to be. Still, things can get really busy when a ferry arrives, full of people who don't want to start the drive into Canada for another day. So check in early. **Pullen Creek RV Park**, ☎ 983-2768, is down by the ferry terminal. Full hookups are available for $20, dry sites are $10.

More scenic are the RV and tent sites at Broadway & 14th, in **Hanousek Park**. It's also the best place for watching the steam engine of the WP&YR go by. Phone for reservations, ☎ 983-2768. Hookups, $16, dry, $8; but the place is often full of summer workers.

Garden City RV Park, ☎ 983-23RV, 15th & State, has full hookups for $16, dry for $8.

If you want to get out of town, drive to Dyea and stay at the **National Park Service Campground** there. Camping is free. The road to Dyea is not recommended for RVs, and this makes the campground a haven for tenters. There are 22 sites, and you just need to show up and see if there are any spots available.

Southcentral

Southcentral is what most people think of when they think about Alaska: a land of extreme temperatures, earthquakes and, more recently and unfortunately, oil spills.

Those are the images. The truth is rather different. The weather is milder in Southcentral Alaska than it is in Vermont. Earthquakes happen, but they're relatively rare. There was only the one big oil spill (plus, like anywhere else on the U.S. coastline, lots of little ones you'll never hear about), still in the process of being cleaned up – yes, even now, more than a decade later.

The region is more politically charged than most of Alaska – the oil spill polarized the communities between the conservationists and the pro-development people. To an extent, Southcentral's smaller towns all live in the shadow of Anchorage, the state's power base. Unlike Southeast, which is showing definite conservationist inclinations, Southcentral has a different mind-set. The pipeline and the fisheries have made people rich here; the oil spill made some of them even richer.

Politics aside, Southcentral is really a land of vast and diverse beauty, with massive fjords, rivers draining glaciers and icefields the size of counties in the Lower 48. For the traveler, Southcentral has some of the finest sportfishing in Alaska and, if you only want to watch wildlife, the largest bears in the world live here.

With all these attractions, Southcentral is a kind of Alaskan playground. Roads link most of the towns and the Alaska Marine Highway serves as the final stitch in the tapestry.

Come into Southcentral and you'll find a land that defies all clichés.

The Spill

You can't go through Southcentral without hearing about the spill, What you hear depends on who you talk with. We're putting it right up front here to give you an idea of some of the history and issues, but it should be remembered that you're almost certainly going to see nothing of it. You'll hear about oiled beaches, but the oil has sunk in, and, while it's still there, it's invisible unless you're on the beach digging for it. The Prince William Sound area is still stunningly lovely. The sad thing is that it used to be so much better. The spill was a betrayal of innocence.

To understand what's going on in Coastal Alaska, why people are so angry about roads being built to reach the Sound, and how much fear there is over another spill, you need a little background on one of the greatest disasters in Alaskan history.

■ The Contingency Plan

On March 24, 1989, Alaska suffered its first big oil spill – the largest ever in United States history – when the *Exxon Valdez*, an oil tanker heading south after taking on a full load of crude, ran aground on Bligh Reef in Prince William Sound.

Although an extensive plan had been previously laid out as part of the Alaska pipeline system's emergency procedures in the Alaska Regional Contingency Plan, planning and reality separated drastically. The plan was for a tiny oil spill, one that could be contained by a couple of booms. The *Exxon Valdez* was putting thousands of gallons an hour into the waters of Prince William Sound.

One example of how the official plan was grossly inadequate for the size of the *Exxon Valdez* oil spill was demonstrated by Exxon's attempts to fly in chemical dispersant to treat the spill. The commissioner of Alaska's Department of Environmental Conservation, Dennis Kelso, estimated that the stockpiles called for in the contingency plan were only 9% of the chemical dispersant needed to treat a spill of this size on the day of spill. It was like throwing paper towels at the ship and hoping they'd soak up the mess.

And so, while the federal, state, and Exxon authorities fumbled over a workable plan of action and tried to assess blame – there was a lot of that going on – very little was done to actually contain the oil flow into the Sound during the three calm days after the spill. The days following were not so calm, and as the wind and the waves kicked up, the oil spread rapidly, heading south.

In the end, 11 million gallons of crude poured from a gash in the ship's side. Legal battles were more furious than the efforts to save the Sound's wildlife (Exxon lost an appeal in the summer of 2000, 11 years after the spill, to try and avoid paying reparations to fishermen). Was the captain drunk? Was he even awake when the ship struck the reef? Why were there no containment booms in place for more than 24 hours after the spill? Why was Exxon being allowed to measure damaged coast in straight linear miles, instead of following the contours of the shoreline (which meant 10 times more coast was damaged than the news was reporting)? Because of the failure to contain the oil immediately, more than 1,500 miles of coastline were affected by landed oil, which spread southwest from Prince William Sound into the Gulf of Alaska and along the Alaska Peninsula.

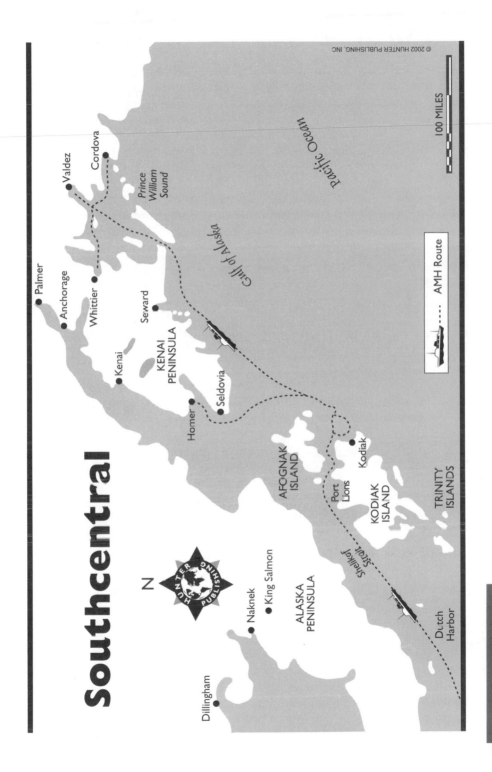

Southcentral

100 MILES

AMH Route

Pacific Ocean

Gulf of Alaska

Prince William Sound

Palmer

Anchorage

Whittier

Seward

Valdez

Cordova

Kenai

KENAI PENINSULA

Seldovia

Homer

AFOGNAK ISLAND

Port Lions

Kodiak

KODIAK ISLAND

TRINITY ISLANDS

Shelikof Strait

Dutch Harbor

ALASKA PENINSULA

King Salmon

Naknek

Dillingham

N

HUNTER PUBLISHING

■ The Effects

The ecology of Prince William Sound was devastated. The spill, which happened at a critical time of year from a wildlife reproductive stand-point, immediately killed an estimated half-million marine birds, 4,000-5,000 sea otters, 600 bald eagles, 200-300 harbor seals, and an unknown number of other marine and land animals, including bears, deer, mink, river otters, whales, and orcas. While an extensive animal rescue program was funded by Exxon and got a lot of TV time, the number of animals helped was comparatively small. Only 1,589 sea birds and 344 sea otters were brought to treatment centers (about one-third of the otters died after release). Meanwhile, the beaches were littered with corpses. It wasn't just the animals in the water, the otters and the birds, that were affected, but the animals that fed on them, too. The entire food chain became slick and greasy.

For the towns near the spill – Valdez, Cordova, Kodiak, and quite a few native villages – fishing catches were dramatically down, and the fish caught were feared to be dangerous for consumption. How could they be edible when they'd been swimming in an oil can? Hatcheries were threatened by the advancing slick, and damage to them could have ruined the entire fishing industry.

Clean-up efforts were difficult at best and the results were often uncertain. Three days after the spill, the weather turned windy and stormy, whipping the oil into a hard-to-clean froth. Even in the best of circumstances, only a fraction of oil can ever be recovered in a spill. Methods of recovering or treating spilt oil range from chemical aids such as dispersants or sinking agents, to mechanical helpers, such as skimmers, pumps, dredges, and containment booms. Some slicks may be burned, and oil is often washed from beaches using high-pressure hot water or by the use of chemical dispersants. Not much of this worked in Alaska.

A handout you can pick up in Valdez on the spill says, "The actual cleanup process was time consuming and ineffective in many ways. Workers would wipe down a beach, the tide would change, and oil-laden water would cover the rocks with a new coating of oil. Clean-up crews sprayed rock faces with steam hoses and manually wiped smaller rocks clean. By mid-summer new techniques and technologies were employed. Microorganisms that 'ate' crude oil were sprayed onto some of the beaches, and new materials were used in wiping operations."

A lot of money was thrown at the problem. The same handout says that "On average it cost Exxon $1,000 each day to support one worker on a beach cleanup crew." There were about 10,000 people out there cleaning at the height of the efforts, but, and forgive the pun, it was all just a drop in the bucket. A somewhat more objective source, the Oil Spill Recovery

Institute, says that in the three years after the spill, cleanup cost more than $2 billion. However, "oil is still present.... A casual scan of the shoreline reveals little evidence of oil but weathered oil remains trapped beneath rocks and in the subsurface of the more heavily oiled beaches." This is a way of saying nicely that they tried, but in many ways failed to clean up after the spill.

The causes and results of the spill are still being debated. Meanwhile, there are still polluted beaches – turn over rocks on many small islands in Prince William Sound and you'll think you've struck oil. The only lesson learned may be that red tape conquers all. More than 10 years after the spill, there is no evidence that it can't easily happen again. Retrofitting oil tankers with double hulls would cost too much and raise oil prices more than people are willing to pay. In September 1990, the *Exxon Valdez* – renamed the *Exxon Mediterranean* – was back at sea. And, in an odd publicity coup, a division of Exxon bought Anchorage's major newspaper, squashing a fair amount of reporting on the downside of the spill.

In August of 1993, a report was issued from the General Accounting Office, saying that nearly 15% of the money Exxon paid out for the clean-up had gone to reimburse government agencies *and Exxon itself*. That meant, for Exxon, a tax rebate of over $40 million! At almost the same time as the financial dealings were being disclosed, fishermen blocked the oil terminal for three days, protesting Exxon's failure to abide by the clean-up deal. Catches had declined steadily since 1990, and five years after the spill, in a meeting with Interior Secretary Bruce Babbitt, Valdez fishermen laid oil-covered rocks out on the conference table. Before the spill, to buy a salmon seine license for commercial fishing would have cost you about $300,000; now it's worth about $30,000. A lot of fishermen went bust. Exxon is still in business.

Now, a decade-plus after the spill, the effects are still being felt and are still debated hotly throughout Alaska. Chambers of Commerce and pro-development people try to paint a rosy picture, but those people making their living in the waters of the Sound present a different viewpoint. Fishing catches have been noticeably down, although there is some debate as to how much of this can be attributed to the spill, and how much is simply a matter of overfishing.

Bird populations have yet to recover. So many species were wiped out right before hatching that the young which did manage to hatch had no adult birds to teach them proper behavior. That practically wiped out the species in the region, creating an entire population of baby birds starving to death. The murre population is never expected to recover, nor is the short-tailed shearwater. It's estimated that 96% of these species in the Sound region were killed by the oil. The numbers are nearly as high for the fork-tailed stormy petrel and the tufted puffin. Overall, an estimated

64% of birds in the Kodiak region were killed by the spill. More than a quarter billion birds died from oil.

A report compiled and published as part of the Dark Waters project says that 10 years after the spill, "Harlequin ducks, three species of cormorants, pigeon guillemots, killer whales from the AB pod (the largest family group of killer whales in PWS prior to 1989), and the common loon are among species listed as 'not recovering.' "

The same report notes, "The population of PWS Pacific herring collapsed. None of the seven seabird species injured by the spill has been declared recovered. Recreation, tourism, and subsistence activities also are still affected by the presence of residual oil on some beaches, or the reduced availability of fish/wildlife in parts of the spill region."

That's not the end of the bad news. Other areas of the ecosystem that were immediately affected by the spill still show long-term effects. At the most basic level on the food chain, zooplankton, the tiny animal food of the larger animals, are highly vulnerable to dispersed and dissolved oil. All the way up the food chain, animals have been affected in a variety of ways by the oil; many are mutated, while others simply ingested the oil and died. Larger animals eating those contaminated by the oil suffered poisoning or disruption of their thermal regulation.

In most intertidal zones, the oil has caused decline in the populations of plants and animals. Some oil is still visible pooled under mussel beds and beach sediments. Heavily oiled mussel beds are thought to have contributed to continuing reproductive problems of harlequin ducks, sea and river otters, and pink salmon ("higher than normal egg mortality for pink salmon in oiled streams continued through 1994").

Some animals, such as the bald eagle, appear to be recovering. Harlequin ducks, which suffered a near reproductive failure the year after the spill, are also recovering slowly. However, many other species are not. The sea otter population is still well below normal and unusually high mortality rates continue. Terrestrial mammals, such as river otters and brown and bears, and Sitka deer, which feed in the intertidal zone, have been observed with oil-patched coats, indicating that they have been exposed to the oil hydrocarbons. The short- or long-term effects of the spill on these animals are uncertain.

Ten years after the spill, there was not a single additional double-hulled ship in Alaskan waters. Only $1.5 billion of the $6.5 billion in fines had been paid.

In 1999, Captain Joseph Hazelwood began serving his sentence: for ramming an oil tanker onto the rocks. Captain Hazelwood spends one month a year for five years, picking up trash in Anchorage.

In the summer of 2001, a research project at Snug Harbor, 55 miles from the site of the spill, still found surface oil under the rocks.

Official estimates – and these numbers get really interesting – are that about 70% of the oil from the Spill either evaporated or somehow magically disappeared – leprechauns, perhaps. They go on: all those famous clean up crews got maybe 14% of the oil. This leaves, even at oil company estimates, 13% of the spill – 1.4 million gallons – still in the Sound. Exxon's comment was "Of course there are places in Prince William Sound where, if you look hard enough, you can find *Valdez* oil."

How do you hide a million gallons of oil? Close your eyes real tight.

■ How Will the Spill Affect You?

Still, all is not doom and gloom. While the murre, marbled murrelett, harbor seal, sea otter, Pacific herring, and sockeye salmon in the Kenai and Akalura systems are showing no signs of post-spill recovery, sockeye at Red Lake are making a comeback, as are the bald eagle populations, black oystercatcher birds, mussels, and the orca pods.

As a traveler in the Sound, you're not likely to see any outward effects of the spill at all. Obvious signs have been removed, and you'd have to walk fairly remote beaches to find blatant traces of the spill. That's not to say your trip won't be affected. Because of the spill, you're missing what Prince William Sound once was. It remains a startlingly beautiful place but, as you travel through it, picture how much better it used to be when there was abundant wildlife here.

■ Alternative Viewpoints

The Spill demonstrates two unfortunate features of human behavior. The first is that you can find someone willing to justify anything. The second is that when there are too many people justifying, too few functioning, the result can be disastrous.

For the other side of the picture, see the story in the June 29, 1997, *Anchorage Daily News*, which suggested that the breakdown of oil molecules into simpler carbon molecules and the fact that carbon is the basis of life on this planet has encouraged fish reproduction, and that dumping all that hydrocarbon into the ocean was "somewhat like fertilizing your yard." Most biologists would agree the newspaper may be dumping fertilizer on the issue.

For the last word on the spill, in August 1992, the U.S. Fish and Wildlife Service made the frozen carcasses of more than 35,000 birds and 900 otters, all killed by oil, available for "scientific" study. This made a Dave Barry column, bringing in requests from around the world, but in the end

Southcentral

only about 3,000 bodies got dished out, mostly to scientists and museums. Fish and Fur officials acknowledged that, once thawed, the carcasses would pretty much be rotted beyond recognition. There was also the complication that, for some reason, the heads had been cut off all the otters.

Nobody claimed the frozen poodle that had found its way into the giveaway.

■ And Finally, A Good Thing

Out of disasters sometimes comes triumph. A man named Phillip McCrory was watching news photos of oiled otters after the Spill. McCrory worked with hair for a living, and he had the sudden idea that if otter hair was that good at soaking up oil, wouldn't human hair do almost as well? He got some sweepings from his barber shop, stuck them in nylon stockings, and tried soaking up a can of motor oil. It worked brilliantly. With some refinements, tests have shown that McCrory's hair cure gets up oil at a cost of about $2 per gallon, as opposed to $10 per gallon for more traditional methods. It's also more effective and less hazardous. NASA has picked up on the idea, and it may soon become the standard for oil cleanup world wide.

Cruising Southcentral

The Alaska Marine Highway makes a monthly trip, connecting Juneau to Yakutat (sometimes), Valdez, and Seward. If you're planning to move a car from Southeast to Southcentral, and don't want to drive the Alcan, this is how to do it. It's a two-day run, which is about equivalent to the time it would take to drive from Haines or Skagway to the Kenai Peninsula.

The trip is on the *Kennicott*, the most uncomfortable of the line's ships, and the run is made far enough out to sea that the scenery isn't all that great for most of the trip. If you've got clear days, there are good views of the Fairweather range, but the mountains are still a long way off. You do get a good look at Prince William Sound, however.

Cruise ships frequently make this same run, heading for Seward, where many passengers hop on the train to go up to Denali or other points in the interior. It's a long stretch of mostly empty coastline. It's as beautiful as anywhere else in Alaska, and it's reassuring to see its size.

Once you're in Southcentral, things get a little closer – Seward is, for example, only three or four hours by car from Homer, the opposite point on the peninsula. Southcentral offers many of the same attractions as Southeast – mountains, glaciers, rivers, incredible wildlife – but in smaller chunks, with the major sites much closer together.

Southcentral can be divided into three areas: the eastern area, with Valdez and Cordova; the central area, on the Kenai Peninsula; and finally, the far reaches, with Kodiak Island.

The eastern area and the far reaches are pure scenery: you are in the deep wild in these places. Cordova and the Copper River offer one of the biggest migratory flyways in the Americas. Kodiak has bears.

The Kenai section of Southcentral is the playground for much of Alaska. On weekends, the roads from Anchorage to Seward or Homer are jammed. But there's a reason why: this part of Southcentral is so much fun.

Yakutat

Yakutat has historically been one of the few refuges for vessels along this part of the coast, but it's only since 1998 that the AMH has come here – and now only a few times a year, as part of the cross-Sound run that the *Kennicott* makes in the summer months. If you're planning to visit, schedule your trip carefully; miss the ferry and you either stay for another month or you'll have to fly or charter a boat out (really expensive). If you want to get around after you're in Yakutat, you run out of road real quick and end up having to take a plane. There's not a whole lot around, but there are some serious glaciers, and a tiny chance of spotting a glacier bear.

Yakutat Bay was the principle winter village site of the local Tlingits. It's really no more than a big indentation on an otherwise solid bit of coastline between Cross Sound and Controller Bay. The city, the northernmost in the Southeast, lies just 40 miles southeast of the majestic Mount St. Elias; the mountain, 18,008 feet high, looms over the town, dominating most views – Vancouver was able to use the mountain as a landmark from more than a hundred miles away. The bay is a true fjord and has mountains of 2,000-3,000 feet rising up straight out of the sea. It is notable for having been visited by more geographical expeditions than any other place on the Alaska coast, due to its unusual glacial action; the nearby Hubbard, LaPerouse, Fairweather, and Grand Plateau Glaciers are perfect places to study the last Little Ice Age, which occurred roughly 600-1,000 years ago.

■ History

The explorer Malaspina (for whom one of the ships of the AMH is named) came to this area in 1791. He didn't care for it much, and bitterly named it *Puerto del Desengano* (Port of Disenchantment), as it was not the passage to the Northwest that he and most of the rest of the sailing world was seeking. The name of the place changed several times during the 18th century, as other Spanish, English, and French explorers came through.

Then the Russians showed up in search of sea otter pelts. While they were sending natives out to bop seals, they also found time, in 1795, to build a penal colony on the southeast shore of the bay. Although the local Tlingit were the first to officially defect to the Russians, about 1803, they changed their mind pretty quickly, and the colony was bombarded by repeated native attacks and eventually abandoned in 1804 (you may still be able to see a cellar hole or two in the area). Later, gold seekers came to work the black sand beaches, and in search of a new and easier route to the gold fields of the Yukon.

The area was first thoroughly mapped in 1890 by Lawrence Martin, and the first salmon cannery was built here in 1904. Today salmon, black cod, halibut, and crab fisheries are the mainstays of the economy. The Malaspina Glacier, the largest on the North American continent, covering an area of roughly 850 square miles (bigger than Rhode Island), with ice up to 2,000 feet deep, is fed by more than 25 tributary glaciers. It is located just northwest of town, but you'd need to hire a helicopter or hike through some serious bush to get to it.

RECORD-BREAKING WAVE

Yakutat is the town closest (close is a relative term – it's about 10 hours away by ferry) to Lituya Bay, home of the largest wave ever recorded. In 1958, an earthquake caused a massive rockslide – essentially an entire mountain fell from 3,000 feet. This kicked up a wave that, on the opposite side of the bay, stripped trees from the mountain to an altitude of 1,720 feet. Meanwhile, another branch of the wave headed toward the open mouth of the bay at upwards of 100 miles per hour. This was not good for the three fishing boats that were working the bay that day. In all, four square miles of forest were stripped right off the mountains, and two fishermen died.

■ Basics

i As mentioned above, there's not a lot to recommend. Yakutat has daily jet service and charter aircraft. For charters, get in touch with **Gulf Air Taxi**, ☎ 784-3240.

For taking care of other business in the town, there are two gift shops, a bank, two grocery stores, two hardware stores, a café, clinic, post office, and gas station. To get around, call **Sunset Taxi**, ☎ 784-3612.

Yakutat has a nice website at www.yakutat.net.

Cruise ships don't stop here. Ever.

The **Alaska Marine Highway** makes Yakutat a whistle stop on the cross-Sound trip. As mentioned above, plan carefully, or be prepared to pay big time to get out.

In other words, Yakutat is a quintessential Alaskan small town.

■ The Ferry Stop

If you're on the *Kennicott* for its brief stop, you've got about enough time to leave the dock, turn left, and walk down to **Mallott's General Store** and go back. Stock up on food for the rest of the trip, but don't expect any good postcards of the Fairweathers.

■ Adventures

If you don't surf, there are really only two reasons to come to Yakutat: to see glaciers, or to see the glacier bears. You'll have to hop a charter to reach the glaciers, which are really more interesting to scientists than the average visitor. If you just want to see some ice, many places offer easier access than this.

Glacier bears don't live on the glaciers; they live in the surrounding forests, and this is the only place in the world where they're found. Somewhat like the kermodie bears down around southern British Columbia, glacier bears are a subspecies of black bear; but their color is actually a kind of silver gray. Quite beautiful, quite rare, and quite frankly you can tromp around in the woods for weeks with little chance of spotting one. But if you're determined, they're out there, and they are gorgeous. Ask around town if there have been any recent sightings, and head out, fully prepared – obviously remembering to take all proper bear precautions. Charter a flight to the glacier from Gulf Air Taxi, ☎ 784-3240.

Southcentral

Fishing

Most people in Yakutat make their living off fish one way or another. If you're looking for someone to take you out, try **Yakutat Charter Boat Co.**, ☎ 888-317-4987, where full-day charters run $185 per person. Another good alternative is **Tidewater Charters**, ☎ 784-3650. See the accommodations section, below, for a lodge deal.

Surfing

Yes, really. Yakutat has more than 70 miles of beaches, and thanks to a long, low sandbar surrounded by reefs, you can surf south of town. You'll need a dry suit and good advice. Check with the **Icy Waves Surf Shop**, which you can contact through the people at the Mooring Lodge, ☎ 888-551-2836. Think of the bragging rights next time you're surfing down south. Catch a 51° curl. That's water temperature, not angle of attack.

■ Accommodations

 You shouldn't have any trouble finding a place to stay – although late in the season, things can get busy – but it's going to cost. The **Bay View Lodge**, ☎ 784-3341, runs $150 a day, or $400 per day per person, if you want guide service and your choice of fishing, glacier tour, or a float trip thrown in. The **Mooring Lodge**, ☎ 784-3300 or 888-551-2836, has two condos for rent, which start around $300 per night and hold up to four people.

Yakutat B&B, ☎ 784-3413, has rooms for $60/person, with breakfast. The **Blue Heron Inn** is also a good choice, with rooms from $120 for a double. ☎ 784-3287. **The Glacier Bear Lodge**, ☎ 784-3202, has doubles for about the same price.

The **Yakutat Lodge** has some nice fishing packages – four days and three nights are only $725 per person. ☎ 800-YAKUTAT, or 784-3232.

■ Camping

Camping is available at the **Cannon Beach** (picnic facilities only), or at one of the cabins along the **Russell Fjord Wilderness Area** (there are 13 cabins; none of these are on the fjord or at the glacier). There is a USFS office at the airport, but advance reservations are suggested.

Cordova

Located at the mouth of the Copper River, Cordova is one of the most unusual, beautiful spots in Southcentral Alaska, with Prince William Sound on the shore and the riches of the Copper River Delta toward the mountains. Five glaciers are easily accessible from Cordova.

Cordova has also been, over its long history, one of the more controversial towns in Alaska. While the town itself is largely insular and conservationist in mood – it elected the nation's first Green Party mayor – forces around the town keep dragging it out to meet the rest of the world.

■ History

The area was first settled by Eyak Indians, who fished and hunted in the Copper River Delta. Using some of the copper from which the Delta has gotten its name, they traded copper "shields" as far south as Sitka.

The first European explorations were in the late 1880s, part of the U.S. attempt to figure out what they had bought from Russia. A cannery was built in 1889, but Cordova's early prosperity had to wait another 20 years for the railroad: the town served as the port city for the massive Kennecott copper mines to the north, near McCarthy. The ore was hauled by rail down to Cordova, where it was transferred to ships. The line was laid from 1907-1911, over the strong objections of Valdez residents, who'd hoped to have the terminus port. (For more on the mines, see the *Kennecott* section, page 336.) For 31 years, Cordova needed nothing else: the railway and the riches from the mine kept the town fat and happy.

When the mine closed in 1938, fishing moved in to fill the hole in the economy and has remained there ever since. After the spill, residents worried about Cordova becoming a ghost town. Valdez got all the press, but Cordova was actually impacted more heavily. In the months before the spill, people were leaving good jobs because, without staying in tents, there was simply nowhere to live in town; within days of the spill, dozens of houses were for sale. There were those who made money off the spill – captains with masters licenses could charge several grand a day for use of their boats during clean up – but the fishermen knew they were royally screwed.

While the effects of the spill – as well as of overfishing – are still being debated, Cordova did not dry up and blow away, but the future of Southcentral's fishing industry remains uncertain. The only other possibility for growth in Cordova was a road that former governor Wally Hickel tried to push through the Delta along the old railroad right of way.

Southcentral

This would have linked Cordova to the rest of the state, but the plan was stalled when Hickel and his bulldozers didn't get re-elected.

Then Cordova, needing something to spur the town, decided to try something different. There were plenty of cruise ships along this section of the coast, moving from Glacier Bay to Seward. In 1998, the first one stopped in Cordova, dropping 800 passengers in the town's three-block-long downtown.

Things have been changing fast since then. Get out into the Copper River Delta while you still can.

■ Basics

i Cordova is served three times a week by the **Alaska Marine Highway**, with connections to Valdez and Whittier. **Alaska Air, ☎** 424-7151, makes daily flights into town. **Cordova Air Service, ☎** 424-3289, has charters.

The **Chamber of Commerce** offers basic tourist information at 622 1st St., next to the bank. Write to them at Box 99, or **☎** 424-7260. They're open Monday-Friday, 8-4.

Cordova's big party is **February's Ice Worm Festival**, held the first full weekend of the month. It's full of parades, booths, and general carousing. You'll find it all but impossible to book a room in town at this time; people come from all over the state for this one.

The **Forest Service** office is on 2nd, between Browning and Adams. Open Monday-Friday, 8-5, they've got handouts on hiking and you can make cabin reservations here. There are 14 cabins in the area, all in gorgeous locations. **☎** 424-7661.

Rent a car at the **Reluctant Fisherman Inn, ☎** 424-3272. Cordova's attractions are out of town, so you'll need transportation. Rent a kayak, skiff, or bicycle from **Cordova Coastal Adventures, ☎** 424-3842.

Internet access is at the **library**, Adams and 1st.

The zip code in Cordova is **99574**.

CORDOVA AT A GLANCE

QUICK TOUR: The town itself is tiny; if you've only got a couple hours, you don't have time to get out, so enjoy one of Alaska's nicer small towns.

DON'T MISS/BEST FREEBIE: The Copper River Delta. Drive out to the Million Dollar Bridge. Be amazed. Be very amazed. Best of all, it's free.

■ Museums & Attractions

CORDOVA HISTORICAL MUSEUM: A small, but good museum on 1st St. between Adams and Browning, next to the library. They try hard here, and there are some good displays on the Delta, as well as excellent displays of Russian artifacts and a fine three-man baidarka. There's a well-done local history film shown daily. There is no charge for admission, and the museum is generally open in the summer from 1-5 PM, Tuesday-Saturday.

While you're there, it's worth thinking about taking the cassette tour of town. For $9, the museum rents you a tape and a player, which guides you on an hour's walk.

That about does it for attractions in town. If you're still scrambling, the **U.S. Forest Service Visitor Center**, in the old courthouse on 2nd, has some nice wildlife displays. Open 8-5. The **airport** has some stuffed birds in the lobby and offers the best chance to see just how big a trumpeter swan is. Most days, you can watch **sea otters** near the ferry terminal.

■ Adventures

Hiking

For an overview of the town, hike **Mt. Eyak** above the town. The trailhead is at the end of 6th Ave., and if you're in the mood, you can keep going once you hit the top of the hill, all the way back to **Crater Lake**. In winter, you can ski here, and that, of course, means there's a ski lift. This one was once used in Sun Valley, so you might be sitting where Marilyn Monroe once did. Summer rides up the hill – with great views – are $7. The lift is run on Monday, Friday, and Saturday.

Once you've gone over the hill to Crater Lake, you've got quite a few choices. The usual access to the lake is not over Mt. Eyak, but from **Eyak Lake Road** (if you're at the lake in late winter, early spring, check out the melt pattern on the mountain behind: it looks like a bear). It's a steep, 2.4-mile climb to the lake, and you've got killer views once you're there. Another option for the trip down is to head over the ridge to the **Alice Smith Cutoff**, another 5½ miles of hiking, where you meet the **Powder Ridge Trail**. It's a 12-mile loop, so go prepared.

Out the Delta Road, at Mile 21.6, is the trailhead for **McKinley Lake**. A 2½-mile hike takes you back to the ruins of the Lucky Strike mine. The two Forest Service cabins on the trail are among the easiest to reach in the delta.

Southcentral

Fishing

In June, fish the Eyak River or the Slough for red (sockeye) salmon. Take your catch to **Eyak Packing**: they'll can it right in front of you. Smoked fish also available. It's worth a stop just to see the process – take one of the tours for additional information. ☎ 424-5300. The plant is located just past the hospital.

Since the spill, boat operators have been looking for ways other than commercial fishing to make a living. The number of charter operators over the past few years has skyrocketed. Expect daily rates starting around $150 per person. Ask what you're getting before you book. Operators include **Auklet Charter Services**, ☎ 424-3428; **Cordova Fishing Charters**, ☎ 424-5467; and **Winter King Charters**, ☎ 424-7170.

■ Copper River Delta

While Cordova has no standard tourist attractions, it does have the incomparable Copper River and the Copper River Delta, home to some of the best birdwatching in the world.

The Spanish were the first to send an expedition up the river, in 1779. The truth is, they were the first because none of the other expeditions that had come this way – including one headed by Captain Cook – had noticed the river. The first European expedition headed up the river in 1783, led by a man named Nagaief. They got into looking for metals, which might explain why the local Eyak were not that thrilled to see more Europeans in 1796; the Eyak stopped this batch before they got up the river. The Copper River dumps into an area named Puerto Cordova y Cordova by the explorer Caomaño in 1792, a name published in Cook's report of the region in 1798.

No matter how many raids the Eyak made, the European tide was unstoppable in the long run. Throughout the Prince William Sound region, they moved in, the natives died or moved out. One estimate put the entire native population of Prince William Sound at only 300 by 1898. By 1901, Abercrombie wrote, "the entire valley, embracing the main and subdrainage of the Copper River, was as well known as that of most any mining district in Montana."

The delta itself is a vibrant landscape, always changing. The rivers drop tons of silt into the delta daily and Mother Nature herself occasionally spurs some faster changes. The '64 earthquake raised the land level up to a dozen feet and more, drastically changing the plantlife and drying out much of the old marshland, while new marshland was created in areas that were formerly underwater.

Head south out of town; the road curves around to the east, skirting **Eyak Lake**. The lake offers excellent trout fishing off the bridge, below the weir; during the salmon run you can't fish above the weir. To the left, you can see the **Scott Glacier**; its meltwater pours into the Scott River, which helps form the massive delta complex. To the right, all along the road, is the delta, a maze of lakes, bogs, ponds, mosquito breeding areas, and glacial waters pouring down from the icefields. No roads lead into the delta itself. To preserve the habitat, the area has been closed off to traffic.

WATCHABLE *Trumpeter swans nest in the ponds around Mile 10.7 on the Copper River Highway. You can often see these huge birds here, spots of white among the sea of green marsh grass, swimming peacefully in* **WILDLIFE** *the water. They share their habitat with beavers – dens dot most of the ponds – bears, and moose.*

Cordova Airport has had a lot of trouble with moose on the runway, but moose are a relatively recent addition to Cordova. The first moose showed up in the late 1940s; most of the ancestors of the current population were brought to the delta in the 1960s, after the '64 quake raised the level of most of the land in the delta anywhere from two to 12 feet. This changed the area from being swampy, too wet for moose, to being marshy, absolutely perfect for them. The airport, not far beyond the nesting area, is the last facility on the road. From here on out, it's wilderness.

Glacial ice has been largely responsible for the shape of the area and the easiest glacier to reach is **Sheridan**. An access road (turn off at Mile 13.7 on the Copper River Highway) takes you within 100 yards of the ice. Walk to the right (the left path ends up at a hill, difficult to get over) and you can step right up onto the frozen water. The glacier here is hilly, full of melt ponds and deep blue crevasses. Hiking on the glacier is possible, but it is somewhat dangerous. Crampons are very useful.

The road crosses the Copper River just past Mile 25. For the next 10 miles, it runs along the bank of the wide river; actually, the road is on an island in the river's mouth. The water is choked with glacial silt, fallen trees, waterbird nests and more.

It's worth driving to the end of the road and the base of the **Million Dollar Bridge**. The bridge, which once connected Cordova to points north, was damaged in the 1964 earthquake. Boards have been laid across it, and it is possible, though not advisable, to drive across. The road becomes impassable about two miles beyond the bridge.

Two glaciers are visible from the bridge: **Miles Glacier** to the northeast; **Childs Glacier** to the northwest. You can take the little spur road down to the river's edge in front of Miles Glacier, which is very active and calves regularly. Some of the ice floes are big enough to make standing on the beach dangerous; one local resident has a video of a berg calving off the

Southcentral

glacier sending up a wave big enough to lift and overturn the van the cameraman was in. A covered viewing platform now prevents you from getting that close.

Childs Glacier makes its first appearance in western history in 1850, when C. Grewingk stumbled across it. Abercrombie (see the *Valdez* section for more on him) ran the rapids in front of the glacier in 1884. At that time he estimated that it delivered 8,160,768,000 pounds of ice per year to the river. Numbers are useful when filing official reports; it's not clear how he came up with a figure this precise.

The delta area is laced with 21 miles of maintained **hiking trails** – see the hiking section, above, for details. Popular trips are to **McKinley Lake** and **Crater Lake**, for the views. There's a good hike along **Eyak River**; trailhead is at Mile 5.8, the head of Eyak Lake.

AUTHOR TIP

Eyak River is the best place to fish for silver salmon in July and August; there's another good spot near the ferry terminal.

For **canoers**, **kayakers**, or those with **Zodiac-type boats**, there's a pleasant float trip from Wrongway Creek, Mile 22.9, to McKinley Lake, and then back down to the road along McKinley River. The creek gets very shallow at points and there are a lot of snags and beaver constructions in the water.

WATCHABLE

WILDLIFE

*Traveling on **Wrongway Creek** is an excellent way to see the local waterfowl and, possibly, moose or bears. The only known nesting area of the dusky Canada goose is in the delta. Eagles, owls, jaegers, cranes, geese, sandpipers, snipes and more feed off the rich waters.*

There are four **Forest Service cabins** in the delta – three are along the Alaganik Slough, the prime bird-nesting habitat, the other is in the hills to the north side of the road.

To get out on the Copper River, try **Copper River/Northwest Tours**, ☎ 424-5356.

■ The Kennecott Mines

It would have taken the world a long time to get around to noticing the Copper River if it weren't for the incredibly rich copper strike – the richest ever – that started the Kennecott Mines.

The mines got their start in 1900, when a couple of miners looking for gold found copper instead. They weren't that thrilled, but they headed back south to see if anybody else was interested. In 1901, Stephen Birch was sent to the area to see how much copper was there, and what it would take to get it out. His report caught the eye of some rich bigwigs (the Guggenheim family and J. P. Morgan). They figured out a way to get a whole lot richer, and the Kennecott Copper Corporation was formed.

"KENNICOTT"

The first problem was that the rich guys didn't know how to spell. It's the Kennicott River and the Kennicott Glacier, both named after Robert Kennicott, an early explorer who traveled through here. But if you've got more money than anybody else, those around you are usually afraid to point out your errors. Hence the utter mediocrity of Microsoft Word as a computer program. By the same light, it's the Kennecott Mines on the Kennicott River.

There was a problem as to how to extract the copper. In the spring of 1908, construction began on the Copper River Northwestern Railway. The railway started in Cordova and stretched 196 miles to the mines. Over the years, it hauled out more than $200 million in copper ore. It was not, however, just a matter of going in and laying some track. On the first try at putting in a route, everything got swept away by floods. Guggenheim and company poured some more money into the problem, and Michael Heney found a way to build a four-span bridge across a glacier face; he sank pilings more than 150 feet into the streambed, his crew working in freezing water. It took three years to finish the line, and it ended up costing $23,500,000, a huge amount of money in those days. But it did pay off. In only a few years, more than $100 million worth of ore had been taken out of the mines.

The mines closed in 1938. The railway, with nowhere to go, shut down at the same time. The railway line was donated to the federal government in 1941 – it was thought that the government might build a road along the right of way, but the area ended up protected in the Copper River Delta area. More recently, there has been considerable controversy over this right of way. Ex-governor Walter Hickel (a man who never met a patch of concrete he didn't like) decided that there should be a road through here, and damn the wilderness. Wally's road, of dubious legality, was started; the logic was that, since there was once a right of way along the river, he was just bringing it back, not building anything new, which would have been forbidden by federal regulations. Luckily, before too much damage could be done, Hickel was voted out of office. It's the classic battle in Alaska between pro- and anti-development forces. Hickel was classically pro, although he had served as Nixon's Secretary of the Interior in the early 1970s. When he became governor of Alaska in the 1980s, he actually received fewer votes (it was a split ticket) than the initiative to legalize marijuana. He never stood a chance for a second term.

Southcentral

If you want to get out on the river, you really need to go up into the Interior to Kennecott and McCarthy, the ruins and the town that service the ruins. To do that, first you need to get to a road connection, which means leaving Cordova for, most conveniently, Valdez.

Alaska Wilderness Rafting, ☎ 522-1978 or 800-523-4453, offers trips on the Kennicott, the Nizina, and Chitnas. A 10-day trip from McCarthy to Cordova is $2,300, which includes getting you to Anchorage at the end of the trip. A trip down the Copper River is worth every penny, but if that's out of your budget, they've also got overnights into the Nizina Canyon for $275, plus quite a few other trips.

 If you head out onto the waters by yourself, keep in mind that the rivers change rapidly here; rain a considerable distance away can affect the waters where you are. Be prepared.

For details on Kennecott and McCarthy, see our other book, ***Adventure Guide to the Alaska Highway***.

■ Food

 There's no gourmet dining in Cordova, but you're not going to starve, either. After a glorious day in the delta, everything tastes good. **Baja Taco**, on Nicoloff Ave., has fast, cheap Mexican food and fish tacos. **Ambrosia Pizza** is the place for inexpensive pizza and simple Italian fare (on First St.). For something a little healthier, the **Killer Whale Café**, inside Orca Book and Sound, has soups, salads, sandwiches, good desserts (and a great selection of books in the rest of the place). The café is also a good spot just to have a cup of coffee with a great view of the harbor. Moving upscale, the **Powder House**, Mile 2 on the Copper River Highway, is the place for shrimp and sandwiches and a view over Eyak Lake. Check out the **Cookhouse Café** next to the ferry terminal – the seafood dinners and Sunday brunch are especially nice. Cordova's finest dining is at the **Reluctant Fisherman**, downtown above the harbor. It offers steak and seafood, along with great views of the eagles on the beach.

For years, the Reluctant Fisherman restaurant threw fish garbage outside onto the beach, to attract eagles. Then Fish and Wildlife made them stop. It turns out that dumping the garbage is not illegal, but feeding eagles is. The restaurant kept tossing the garbage, but erected a sign that said, "Attention eagles: it is illegal for you to eat here." There are no laws on the books requiring eagles to be literate.

■ Accommodations

Cordova used to be a nightmare for those in search of a bed for the night, and in-town accommodations are almost always filled with fishermen in the summer. That's changed a bit and, with a bunch of new B&Bs opened, you shouldn't have too much trouble finding a place to stay. Advance reservations are still a good idea, though.

The primary address in Cordova is the **Reluctant Fisherman**, 407 Railroad Ave., ☎ 424-3272. It is the nicest hotel in town, with a good restaurant on the premises and diving eagles behind in the water. Doubles run from $120. **Prince William Sound Motel**, at the corner of 2nd and Council, ☎ 323-3201, has doubles from $85. Cheaper is the **Alaskan Hotel and Bar**, on 1st St. ☎ 424-3288. Rooms start at just $40 without bath, from $60 with bath, but the odds are the place will be entirely booked with fishermen.

Like everywhere else in Alaska, there's boom and bust in the B&B market. A good choices is the interesting **Cordova Rose Lodge**, which is actually a converted barge, brought ashore in the mudflats of Odiak Slough. Quite a spot. Doubles from $75. ☎ 424-7673.

King's Chamber, ☎ 424-3373, is on 4th St. It's the place for big groups – they've got three- and four-bedroom apartments available. Basic rooms start at $75 for a double.

The **Blue Heron Inn** is 1½ miles north of town, with good water views. Figure around $75 for a double. ☎ 424-3554.

■ Camping

Camping is surprisingly limited around Cordova. There's the **Odiak Camper Park**, which is primarily a gravel pit for RVs out on Whitshed Rd., next to the old city dump (there is a small tenting area). The views are good, though, and it's only six bucks for tents, $12 for RVs with an electric hookup. ☎ 424-6200. There's also a small campground across from the airport, at **Cabin Lake**. No services, just show up and look for a spot.

You can pitch a tent pretty much anywhere outside of town. The ski hill is fairly well used during the summer, as is the bluff behind the ferry terminal. Make sure you're not on private property, watch for bears, and obey all common camping courtesies.

Valdez

Valdez, terminus of the Trans-Alaska Pipeline, is not the town it once was. The original site, like an old lurking ghost, is located three miles outside of what's now Valdez. In the old or new location, Valdez is one of the most beautiful spots in Alaska.

Valdez has made world news twice. The first time was on Good Friday in 1964, when a great earthquake struck Alaska. The town was leveled by the quake and the resulting tidal wave. The old town site was deemed unrecoverable, so everyone packed up and moved down the coast. The second time Valdez made headlines was 25 years after the first, when the tanker Exxon *Valdez* ran aground on Bligh Reef in Prince William Sound. (For the details of the spill and it's effects, see *The Spill* section, pages 319-326.)

Oil never came near the beaches of Valdez; tides and wind pushed the huge oil slick south. What the spill meant for Valdez was boomtown status. While the world gasped in horror at pictures of oiled otters and birds, workers here made upward of $16 an hour for aiming hoses at beaches; boat captains got several thousand dollars a day for the use of their boats. There was not a hotel room to be found in town, and the Alaska Highway was jammed with travelers headed for Valdez. The population of Valdez rose from its usual 4,000 to more than 12,000 people (no more than half of which were news crews) hoping to strike it rich from the ecological disaster. Rumor has it that truckloads of kitty litter were being brought up by one entrepreneur, in the hopes it would soak up the oil. But the spill and the earthquake were only two bad moments in an otherwise peaceful history.

■ History

Captain Cook sailed into Prince William Sound, mapping out the land in 1778. He named it Sandwich Sound, after his patron and the inventor of the hoagie, the Earl of Sandwich. By the time Cook got back to England, however, Sandwich had fallen out of favor (the earl, not the food), and the area name was changed to Prince William Sound.

The name of the town came from Don Salvador Fidalgo, one of the Spaniards trying to grab up land in Alaska before the British and Russians took all the good bits. Fidalgo was also responsible for Cordova's Spanish name. The area was first settled in the winter of 1897-98, when prospectors came looking for a route into the gold fields through only U.S. territory. Both the Chilkoot and the Chilkat Trails crossed Canadian territory, and the Mounties imposed heavy taxes and restrictions on miners. About 4,000 would-be miners passed through the budding town of Valdez, some staying behind to sell to other would-be miners. But, of course, as mentioned above, nobody made it to the gold fields.

An 1898 government survey of the region, completed before the rush, showed a small village called "Valdes" at a time when what's now Anchorage didn't even merit a blip on the map. The surveyors reported that when they landed on April 7, snow was six feet deep and "the reindeer counted on for transportation had not been brought." They went on to say, "about a dozen white men have married into the native tribes and have become residents there, being engaged in trade or some other industry, such as blue fox raising." The official government description of Prince William Sound was quick and to the point: It had "the topography of a submerged coast."

The fortunes of the town rose and fell with mining and the railroads. Cordova was chosen as the railhead for the Kennecott mines, and Valdez languished, interrupted only by the earthquake. This was the situation until the late 1960s, when the town was chosen as the port for the Trans-Alaska Pipeline. (For details on the engineering marvel of the pipeline, see pages 343-344.) And, except for the year of the spill, Valdez has remained a quiet town of about 4,300 people making their living off oil, fish, or tourism. Despite its two moments of bad luck, Valdez is a nice little town – especially once you get away from the small downtown area. Most people stop by just long enough to see the pipeline and the Columbia Glacier, but Valdez is a good place to stay for rest and recuperation.

▪ Basics

i Valdez is served by the **Alaska Marine Highway** six times a week, connecting the town to Cordova and Whittier and, in the summer only, to the Southeast once a month. (To get around to Seward from Valdez, see the end of this section.) Local number for the ferry is ☎ 835-4436. If you're looking to get out of Valdez without getting back on the ferry, hop on the **Richardson Highway** and head north into the Interior (details below).

Not many cruise ships dock in Valdez. If they do, the usual dock is north of town, and you'll need to catch a bus to get in.

Valdez is served by **Alaska Air** via the sub-carrier **ERA**, ☎ 835-2636. Charter operators include **ERA Helicopters**, ☎ 835-2595, and **Ketchum Air**, ☎ 835-3789.

The lovely Richardson Highway connects Valdez with the rest of the state. Even if you're traveling exclusively by boat, it's worth your time to drive out the road to Thompson Pass, 26 miles outside of town. The scenery on a clear day is unbeatable and the alpine wildflowers in summer are gorgeous. The pass, at 2,678 feet, regularly receives some of the state's heaviest snowfall (see below for more).

The **Visitor Information Center** offers daily films about the pipeline and the great quake. Located on Fairbanks, off Hazlett, it's open 8 AM-8 PM in summer. ☎ 835-INFO.

Rent a car from **Avis**, ☎ 835-4774, or **Valdez-U-Drive**, ☎ 835-4402.

Taxis are available from **Valdez Yellow Cab**, ☎ 835-2500.

Internet access is at the **public library**, across from the museum.

The zip code in Valdez is **99686**.

VALDEZ AT A GLANCE

QUICK TOUR/BEST FREEBIE: Go look at big machinery at the pipeline terminus. And while you're in town, look at the mountain behind: the horizontal lines are the scoring of glacial action, as the ice moved back and forth on the mountainside.

DON'T MISS: Drive out of town. It's one of the prettiest roads in the state; kayak Prince William Sound and pretend you're an oil tanker; head to the museum for the cool fire truck;charter a chopper and scare yourself to death in the most extreme skiing in the world.

■ Museums & Attractions

VALDEZ MUSEUM: Start your visit at the museum, corner of Tatitlek and Egan (☎ 835-2764), open daily. It houses an interesting collection of objects, including the first fire engine in Valdez, a 1907 Ahrens Steam Fire Engine. There's also a reconstruction of a miner's cabin, a bar, and the lens from a lighthouse dating to 1840. Admission is $3, under 18 enter free.

ALASKA CULTURAL CENTER: 300 Airport Rd., ☎ 834-1690. The center has nice displays of traditional Eskimo boats; also a good assortment of Native arts and crafts. The collection has as its base the Jeese and Maxine Whitney collection; these people traveled Alaska for 50 years, and they had both money and taste.

OLD VALDEZ: The old town site of Valdez is beyond the Alyeska complex. There's not a whole lot to see out there, just fragments of a ghost town. You can also tour the **Solomon Gulch Fish Hatchery** for $2, but you need to give advance notice. Talk to the people at the Visitor Information Center for arrangements.

THE PIPELINE

The Trans-Alaska Pipeline stretches from Prudhoe Bay to Valdez, crossing 800 miles of tundra, mountains, permafrost, and caribou migration trails. It's an engineering marvel, completed in 1977 for about $8 billion, to take North Slope crude on a long journey south to the marine terminal at Valdez. Although much of the pipeline is buried, it does come above the ground near Valdez. At the northern end of the state, along the Dalton Highway, it is nearly always visible above ground because the permafrost prevented the its burial. Oil in the pipeline is 145° Fahrenheit, which would turn the permafrost into a bog, bending and ruining the pipes.

In its above-ground sections, the pipeline is made up of sections of 48-inch diameter pipe, elevated on special supports, which carry heat up through the structure to finned radiators, above the level of the pipeline. The supports are located about every 60 feet, and the pipeline can move on the support, so it can react to earthquakes or expansion and contraction due to heat variations. The zigzag path the pipeline follows also helps it adjust to movement; at one point (on the Denali Fault), the pipeline's design allows up to 20 feet of horizontal and five feet of vertical movement. Every 800 to 1,000 feet, there is an "anchor" to help prevent uncontrolled movement. Where the pipeline is buried, it lies at a depth of between eight and 35 feet, on an insulated bed, and is covered with gravel padding and soil fill. At three points along the pipeline it was necessary to bury the pipe under permafrost, to allow the highway and the caribou migration to cross. At these points, the buried pipe is refrigerated. Loops of pipe carrying chilled brine circulate around the oil-bearing pipe. The pipeline itself is insulated with 3.75 inches of fiberglass throughout its length and is jacketed in galvanized steel.

Construction of the pipeline was preceded by five years of study on the fragile Arctic terrain and wildlife, the climate, and the impact of the pipeline. The entire route was surveyed by archaeologists. On November 16, 1973, construction began, and by August of 1975, 21,600 workers were on the project. The first oil was pumped on June 20, 1977; it was loaded in tankers headed south by August 1. About two million barrels of oil a day are now pumped through the pipeline.

Southcentral

Despite all this technological marvel, and the fact that the pipeline has flowed smoothly for 20 years, there are subtle things to undermine your faith. A brochure passed out by Alyeska titled "What to do in case of a pipeline-related emergency" explains how to recognize a leak ("a pool of dark liquid") and offers useful tips if you do spot a leak ("Do not create sparks, light matches, start an engine, switch on a light, use a camera flash or a cellular telephone.") For more info on the pipeline, write to Alyeska Pipeline Service Company, Public Relations Department, 1835 South Bragaw St., Anchorage, AK 99512.

PIPELINE TOUR: You can take a two-hour tour of the pipeline terminal, getting a full view of what Alyeska – the company that runs the pipeline and the shipping terminal – does with all that oil, and how they're trying to keep more of it off the ground. The pipeline is one of the best examples of the balancing act that goes on continually in Alaska. People move here for the vast tracts of untouched wilderness, but they still have to make a living somehow. More than 30% of Valdez's workforce is employed by the pipeline in some respect. And, despite the cries of environmentalists, the U.S. is not a country likely to give up driving. Come here to decide for yourself if the cost of the oil is worth it. ☎ 835-2686 for tour reservations. Cost is $15 for adults, $7.50 for kids age six to 12. The tour is best for the environmentally curious or those who really like to look at big machines and are fascinated with statistics. The Alyeska Terminal does have a history prior. It was once the site of Fort Liscum, which operated from 1900 to 1923. The fort was established to provide security for gold miners and to see what could be done about punching a road into the interior. At its peak, 172 men were stationed there.

Outside of Valdez, in **Mineral Creek Canyon**, there is an interesting old stamp mill. The mill was used to crush ore; while the crushing was going on, water was mixed in and then the mixture was placed on amalgamation plates, where the gold mixed with mercury. After the excess mercury was removed, the mixture was heated, melting and separating the purified gold and the mercury. An efficient method, if the mercury poisoning doesn't bother you. Mineral Creek is a great place for berry picking, and the scenery is lovely.

■ Adventures

Hiking

 There's a lot of good hiking in the Valdez area. The most popular trails are the Solomon Gulch and Goat Trails. **Solomon Gulch Trail** is 1.3 miles toward Solomon Lake. The hike is not an easy one, but it offers panoramic views of the town. Pick it up off Dayville Road. Part of it goes by the pipeline. It's about two hours round-trip.

The **Shoup Bay Trail** is a more challenging 6½-mile hike. Pick the trail up at the west end of Egan St. The first part of the hike is easy, with boardwalks, but once you head uphill, you'll know you're working. You do have to cross a couple of small streams on this trail, but at the end, you're up where gold miners once played.

Goat Trail begins in Keystone Canyon and follows the road that was once the only connection between Valdez and the interior. The hike is about a five-mile round-trip, and after the first very steep incline, it levels out some and gets easier. An offshoot of the trail takes on a part of the original gold rush trail. Somewhat easier is the **Mineral Creek Trail**, a bit under two miles, which picks up on the end of Mineral Creek Drive and follows the creek valley. The trail ends at the old stamp mill.

Dock Point Trail is quick – a half-hour or so – and easy. Start across from the boat launch ramp on Kobuk Drive. You head right up the hill, and then drop into a lovely meadow. Take the boardwalks for views.

 Any hikers on any trail should be very wary of bears. Valdez, with its salmon runs and berry bushes, is prime bear country.

Because the original mining trail north to the gold fields, to put it bluntly, sucked (see hike below), the military put in an alternate route. Head out the **Richardson Highway Loop** to Mile 12.5 where you'll find the trailhead. Nice views of the canyon and the Low River; after a bit of hiking, you end up in Horsetail Falls Valley. It's a fairly easy hike, one of the prettier around. Figure two hours for the trip.

This hike actually links up with the **1899 Trans-Alaska Military Trail** – as does the Goat Trail hike. One of the original builders of the trail wrote "The effort of climbing over, under, and through this brush on a side hill so steep as to scarcely afford a foothold; falling stumbling, grasping at devil clubs; bruised and beaten by the stout alder branches, and, at the same time, endeavoring to blaze out a line with a uniform grade or on a level is simply inconceivable to one who has not tried it." The trail is still undergoing restoration, but at least this bit of hiking gives you an idea of what it was like during the gold rush.

This trail will, eventually, link up with the **Eagle-Valdez Trail** – a trail from the coast to the gold fields, far inland. Until roads were built, this was one of the only ways into the interior – and the only way that didn't involve entering Canada. If you follow it (figure on a couple of weeks and some serious bushwhacking, plus some unpleasant walking along the side of the highways), you'll more or less follow the path of the Richardson and Glenn highways before heading across wild territory north of

Tanacross (just west of Tok). Know what you're doing and go prepared – or be prepared to die. Rough maps are available in Valdez, but you'll need serious topo maps for this one.

📖 When you're in the Valdez Museum, pick up a copy of their brochure on Valdez trails – worth it for the *Hiker's Bible*, which features wisdom such as: "Mosquito dope or spray will keep the demons of the air off thee."

Scenic Drives

If you've got a car, you owe it to yourself to get out of town. The road out of Valdez is one of the prettiest in the state. **Keystone Canyon** is, quite simply, a dazzling spot in a land where you've already run out of superlatives. The canyon walls are mossy green, and there are lots of waterfalls; Bridal Veil Falls and Horsetail Falls are close enough to the road to mist your car as you drive by. The canyon was once fought over by nine different companies, each hoping to get a railway line through. This came to a head when someone was killed fighting over turf, culminating in a spectacular murder trial, a turn-of-the-century O.J. circus. All nine companies went bust, and the railway never did get through. Mile 3 (the mile markers are not entirely accurate, as they measure distance from the old city site) is the turnoff to the pipeline terminal and the Allison Point Fishery (see above for details).

Keystone Canyon was part of an alternate route from Valdez to the gold fields. In 1898, Captain William Ralph Abercrombie, hearing rumors of a possible way to bypass Canada on the way to the gold fields, came up to the Copper River area to look for a route. He spent a year mapping the territory, but by the time his maps were ready, the anxious prospectors had already passed him by, trying a route that involved climbing the Valdez Glacier, then dropping down the Klutina Glacier onto the Klutina Lake and River. This was tried by about 6,000 people. Only 300 of them survived. None of them made it to the gold fields.

The prospectors weren't exactly the brightest people on earth. Greed had brought them into a territory they knew nothing about, and as anyone who has walked in the Alaskan bush can tell you, it's not a forgiving territory. If you know what you're doing, it's the gentlest land in the world, full of things to eat; for the unfamiliar, it's a death trap.

The prospectors showed up, treated the land like it was some cakewalk back east, and dropped like flies. One of the biggest problems was snow blindness. When prospectors got up on the glaciers, reflected light burned their corneas. This is an astoundingly painful condition – blinking feels like someone raking nails across your eyes – and, of course, stumbling around blind on a glacier is not the best thing in the world to do. By the time Abercrombie showed up in Valdez in 1899, he found a

Glaciers make a stunning backdrop for photographs.

huge graveyard and a lot of would-be prospectors talking about a "glacier demon" that prevented people from getting north.

The 1939 Federal Writer's Project guide to Alaska sums this up as "Many had gone mad and talked of a 'glacier demon,' an unearthly being that threw men off the glacier." Abercrombie wrote, "Many of these people I had met and known the year before were so changed... that I do not think I recognized one of them. Some were more or less afflicted with scurvy, while not a few of them had frost-bitten hands, faces, and feet... the saliva and breath of those afflicted with scurvy gave forth a stench that was simply poisonous as well as sickening to a man in good health, and sure death to one in ill health." The few surviving miners were crammed into cabins the size of single-car garages, up to 20 men waiting for someone else's death to open up a little more space. Abercrombie fed everyone able to eat, shipped most of them back down to Seattle, and added a few of the healthier ones to his exploratory expedition. Nobody got to the gold fields this way.

The road climbs to **Thompson Pass** and the nearby **Worthington Glacier** (Mile 29), home to some of the worst weather in the state. The record snowfall for Thompson Pass is five feet, two inches in 24 hours. Worthington Glacier is a study in glacial blue on a sunny day; take some time off to peer into its crevasses and to listen to its slow melt. The glacier has three fingers leading off the main body of ice. Ten years ago, when we did the first edition of this book, you could drive right up to one of them. Now it's a fair hike up the hill and over a moraine. From the parking lot – where there's a small gift shop and some outhouses – you can hardly see the thing now. The glaciers are going fast, and it's difficult to describe how it feels to us, watching them get smaller year by year. Once you hit the intersection, straight ahead takes you to Tok, and eventually to Dawson City and Canada; turn left for Anchorage and points in the interior.

Kayaking, Fishing, Rafting & Boat Charters

While Columbia Glacier is Valdez's main attraction – more people come to see it than anything else – there is lots of other beautiful wild territory in the area. If you're good with a boat, you can run the rivers – the one-hour runs through Keystone Canyon or on the silty Love River are great – or kayak with **Keystone Raft & Kayak Adventures**, ☎ 835-2606. They've got day-trips and grand 10-day adventures, from floats down the Tosina (which hits Class IV whitewater) to serious trips on the Talkeetna.

Anadyr Adventures, ☎ 835-2814, runs guided kayaking trips into Prince William Sound. Just a quickie half-day trip will run you $59; as with any trip of this sort, you're better off taking the full-day version, because you get a chance to get away a bit more. A day paddling near Gold Creek will run you $89; going out to the Shoup Glacier by ship and then picking up the kayaks there will cost you $139. Trips out to Columbia Glacier or Galena Bay run $169. Kayak rentals are available from $45 per day. Anadyr Adventures will also arrange drop-off and pick-up. **Pangaea** (☎ 835-8442) is the town's other kayaking outfitter. They're newer than Anadyr, and run about $10 cheaper for similar tours. Nice people.

Kayaking Valdez is not really kayaking Prince William Sound, unless you head out for several days. If you want to kayak the Sound, take a ferry from Valdez to Cordova, where things are less crowded and considerably more open (and where the Copper River Delta offers prime wildlife viewing, birding, and rafting in glacial waters – see above), or go around to Whittier to put in – just be ready to get out of Whittier quick (see below).

Charters

If you're interested in the Spill, get a custom charter and head out to the beaches to see what effects linger. Most charter captains in Valdez were part of the cleanup efforts so they know where to go.

There are three central charter booking outfits in town: **Fish Central**, ☎ 835-5090, 888-835-5002; **Harbor Reservation**, ☎ 800-430-4302; and **One Call Does It All**, ☎ 835-8373, 877-835-8374. Any one of these can hook you up with a good boat. Call a week or so before you get to town, tell them what you want – fishing, sightseeing, whatever – and let them worry about the details. If you want to go direct, try **Northern Magic Charters**, ☎ 835-4433 (they'll also do kayaking drop-offs); **Ivory Gull Charters**, ☎ 456-2551; **Goodhand Charters**, ☎ 835-4333; or **Popeye Charters**, ☎ 835-2659. These places have all been in business a long time and will take good care of you. Figure a full day of halibut fishing will run $175-225, or a half-day of salmon fishing for $100 and up. For something a little different, you can charter a sailboat for the day (up to six people) at around $500 from **Raven Charters**, ☎ 835-5863. They also run overnight trips.

COLUMBIA GLACIER

Most people go to Valdez for one reason: to see Columbia Glacier. Part of the same icefield that includes the Matanuska Glacier, Columbia is famous for its towering wall of ice, calving into the open ocean. The cheap way to see the glacier is to take the ferry to Whittier. The drawback of this way is that you don't get that close, so you'll need a good pair of binoculars. In fact, over the past few years, with the retreat, you're not likely to see much at all except for some bits of ice floating around the shore. If you really want to see the glacier, you're going to have to spend money, and there are quite a few tour companies and countless boats for charter. These allow you to get considerably closer in, and you may even see seals basking on ice floes as the new icebergs plunge into the ocean around them. Expect to pay around $100 and up per person for a trip to the glacier. Many people feel glutted on glaciers long before getting to Columbia, but the sight of a house-sized block of ice dropping into the ocean is unforgettable.

In addition to the charter operators listed above, all of whom can get you to the glacier, specialists include **Stan Stephens Cruises** (☎ 835-4731), which runs nine-hour tours of Columbia and Mears glaciers. A shorter, six-hour trip only runs $69, but you're better off with the longer trip. They can also arrange longer packages that include a stay at the Growler Island Camp. The **Glacier Wildlife Cruise/*Lu-lu Bell*** is a bit shorter – around five hours, but a lot of fun. Not so slick as the other operators, and church services are held on board on Sundays. ☎ 800-411-0090. It's the choice of locals taking friends or relatives out. **ERA Helicopters** will fly you out over the glacier. A one-hour tour goes for about $175 per person, and it includes a landing at the face of Shoup Glacier. ☎ 800-843-1947. **Ketchum Air Service**, ☎ 800-433-9114, takes you out in a floatplane for a flyby of the glaciers, including a water landing at Columbia.

Southcentral

Skiing

In winter, Valdez hosts the world **Extreme Skiing Championships** in Thompson Pass. Downhillers zigzag and jump on slopes most folks wouldn't even think of attempting. Valdez and Cordova are bases for the nutcases who do "extreme" skiing – if you can't handle a 50-degree slope, don't even think about wasting the time of the helicopter operators who take the skiers out.

Ice Climbing

In February, the **Ice Climbing Festival** is held. Valdez is justly famous as a mecca for ice climbers, and the waterfalls in Keystone Canyon serve as great big frozen monkeybars. Check with the Visitor's Center for details, ☎ 835-4636, and dress warm.

■ Food

 Overall, food prices in Valdez are high, but so is the quality. **Mike's Place** is the night-out spot, with steaks, pasta, and seafood, from about $15. Almost next door is **Oscars on the Waterfront**, on Harbor Drive. Dinners from $10 and up. Oscars also has an all-you-can-eat barbecue for $15 – come early if you want to sit down and don't like waiting in line.

For faster seafood, try the **Alaska Halibut House** at the corner of Meals and Pioneer, where you can get fish and chips from $7. Get Chinese food at **Fu Kung**, on Meals Ave.: lunches from about $7. **Pioneer Drive Pizza** has Italian specialties and good Greek pizzas from $8.

If you're heading out hiking, kayaking, or camping you can get vacuum-packed fish at **Peter Pan** – it's cheap, and it's good. The perfect pick-me-up for a night around the campfire. In late summer, there's a **farmer's market**, with lots of organic veggies, next to the post office.

■ Accommodations

 There are no bargains here. Expect to pay upward of $120 per night at the **Westmark** (☎ 835-4391 or 800-544-0970). A bit cheaper but in the same ballpark are the **Pipeline Inn** (☎ 835-4444) and the **Keystone Hotel** (☎ 835-3851; 888-835-0665).

If this is not your idea of a good time, try one of the many B&Bs, but you're still looking at $100 per night. These go in and out of business, as people with spare rooms open and close. You can check out the stacks of brochures in the **Visitors Center**, or try the reservation center for B&Bs, which will help you find who's in business; dealing with them usually assures a reasonable place to stay. Phone **One Call Does It All** (☎ 835-4988); they also arrange glacier trips and charters.

There is also a small association of B&Bs in town, with only eight members, but some good networking. Try **The Headhunter's Inn**, ☎ 835-2900; **Alaska Woolybugger** (worth it just for the name (☎ 835-8505); or the **Copper Kettle** (☎ 835-4233). The **Valdez Hostel** (☎ 835-2155) has dorm rooms for $22 per person; bring your own bedding.

■ Camping

A quick drive through downtown Valdez makes you think of the elephant graveyard: there are so many RVs parked, white butts facing the ocean, that you've got to think this is where they limp off to die. The RV parks in Valdez are very central, very crowded, and very ugly, with the usual charm you expect from a parking lot.

There are several campgrounds in Valdez. **Bear Paw Camper Park**, near the small boat harbor, has full hookups for $22; dry camping for $15. It's a good spot and, unlike most RV parks, they have a tent sanctuary a couple of blocks away – down by the ferry terminal at the end of Hazelet Avenue. Here you'll find 15 sites nestled among trees and berry bushes for $15. Of course, there's still a huge line of RVs between you and the water, but at least the showers are hot and it's only a few minutes' walk from the center of town.

If that's full, try the **Sea Otter RV Park**, on South Harbor Drive, or **Eagle's Rest**, just off the Richardson Highway and Pioneer Drive – probably the best place for tents. Finally, try the **Valdez Glacier Campground**, behind the airport. This is also a great spot if you're in a tent. There is unofficial camping along **Mineral Creek** or along the dirt road that leads up to the water tower. Just be inconspicuous, and don't start any fires.

Whittier & Prince William Sound

Up until the summer of 2000, the only way into Whittier was by boat or train. If you look at the map, it's a long, long way around the Kenai Peninsula from Anchorage to Whittier – the nearest ice-free deepwater port – by sea; however, the peninsula is only a few miles wide at Portage, and so the train was a quick and easy, although somewhat surreal, trip. You loaded your car onto a flatbed, and off you went. When the trains weren't running, you couldn't get in or out of Whittier. This system worked surprisingly well for a very long time. And then Wally Hickel became governor of Alaska. As such, he realized that he could play with as many bulldozers as he wanted to. Being a man who never met a patch of concrete he didn't like, and frustrated by the opposition to his attempts to build an entirely illegal road to Cordova, he said, hey, let's build an entirely senseless road to Whittier. Easy enough, right? The road is less than 10 miles long. There's one bridge. Should be the kind of thing a good road crew can do over a long weekend.

But it didn't work out that way. Surveyors came in, everybody chipped in with an idea, and only $90 million later (the original budget was $15 million, and in a sick piece of irony, the money was to come from the *Exxon Valdez* settlement), the road was finished. Along the way, nobody seems to have noticed that a trolley car could have been run for a fraction of this cost. No, this is America, and dammit, we drive.

The main part of the expense was converting the railway tunnel to dual use. If cars were going to go through the tunnel, there had to be huge exhaust fans, so people wouldn't keel over from carbon monoxide poisoning. There also had to be guards and information booths to keep people from driving through the tunnel when the train was coming. And then there were about $70 million of just-for-fun cost overruns.

So what did the town of Whittier get out of all this?

Well, they can now leave town more or less whenever they want to – or at least every hour, when the tunnel is open. If you've never lived on an island or in a remote community, you can't realize what a relief it is to know you can go somewhere. Whittier is also now easily accessible for tourists who want to see Prince William Sound. These could be seen as good things.

But there is a large downside. Remember the line from Hunter S. Thompson's *Fear and Loathing in Las Vegas,* where he says Vegas is what the whole free world would be like if the Nazis had won World War II? Whittier is what the whole world will be like when tourists from Des Moines take over. You've got a town of 300 people that's so crowded they had to put in parking meters. You've got traffic jams. You've got a cloud of pollution from bus exhaust. You've got crowds of people standing around wondering where the scenery is. In 2000, the sockeye fishery in the region was closed, and the arrival of more people is not going to decrease the stress on the fish. You've got the entire population of a city trying desperately to be the first to think of new ways to fleece tourists. And those who can't fleece, resent.

Welcome to a little suburb of hell.

And that's a shame, because it used to be a gorgeous town, and it's still the easiest way to get into Prince William Sound. It's the classic traveler's lament, best summed up by a couple of former British spies we met on a bus in Kathmandu: "Oh, you should have seen Albania before they ruined it."

Oh, you should have seen Whittier before they ruined it.

■ The Tunnel

If you want in or out of Whittier, and you don't want to get on a boat, you have to go through the tunnel. It's almost worth it, just to see how desperately wrong planners can go if they really try. The tunnel is now as much an Alaskan sight as a glacier, so live it up: if you don't have a car, hitchhike through – it's easy to get a ride, since everybody knows right where you're going. Before you can go in the tunnel, you have to stop and get the tunnel brochure from the guardpost. This poor guy sits in a concrete bunker all day and watches cars line up.

There are lots of statistics about the tunnel. It's the longest highway tunnel in Alaska (technically, in North America, but it's hard to call this stretch of road a highway, and there are lots of longer tunnels on blue highways down south), and the first tunnel with computerized traffic control. It's built to work fine at temperatures of 40 below and with the wind blowing 150 mph. The tunnel opens at specific times – about once an hour, each direction – so you'll likely end up sitting in line with other cars for a while.

Once you're inside the tunnel, the idea is to keep a steady speed, and keep your distance from the car in front of you. Headlights on at all times. Inside, it's cold, it's wet, it's dank – hey, it's a tunnel – and keeping your car steady is not entirely easy, with the rough railroad bed, ties, and rails to contend with. Again, keep your distance from the car in front of you.

If you're claustrophobic, you will not enjoy this, but you're out faster than you think.

The tunnel was free for the first year. It's not anymore; it's a toll tunnel. They've got to pay for that $70 million in cost overruns somehow.

For complete information on what's on the other side of the tunnel, and how that can get you to points all over the state, see our other book, *Adventure Guide to the Alaska Highway*. The roads here link to the entire peninsula, up to the interior, and to points in Canada.

■ History

 Whittier started off as part of a portage route for Chugach Indians who were traveling from Prince William Sound to fish in the Turnagain Arm. The city itself dates back to WWII, when it was an army camp, the primary debarkation point for the Alaska Command.

Southcentral

The port is ice-free, and the armed forces made the most of it until 1960. Today about 300 people call Whittier home. Considerably more bears live in the area – in 1999, a black bear got into the grade school and wandered around for 45 minutes, before he curled up and went to sleep in the gym. During his ramble, he actually figured out how to open doors using the pushbars. Now that the RV crowd has taken over town, though, and a quiet backwater has turned into a boomtown, the bears are heading into the deeper woods.

■ Attractions

Assuming you didn't take a look, gasp, and get back in line to drive through the tunnel, or immediately leap back onto the ferry, you'll quickly find that the best thing to do in town is leave – head into the mountains, or into Prince William Sound, but don't linger in town.

There's not a lot there. Whittier is dominated by the Begich Towers, part of a 1,000-room apartment complex, a leftover from military days, when it also housed a hospital, theater, pool, and virtually the town's entire population. Today, it's got the post office and the library, and it's still got most of the town's people. It's kind of hard to look at the building now without shifting your gaze to the glacier on the mountain behind – it looks like the Blob coming down to eat the diner Steve McQueen is hiding in.

The town itself doesn't have a lot to offer. The **Visitors Center** is in an old railway car across from the small boat harbor. There's a **historical museum** in the first floor of the Begich Towers, open 1 to 5, Wednesday through Friday, which displays historical photos and some marine stuff.

■ Adventures

Hiking

The main reason to go to Whittier is to get out of Whittier. That's even more true now that the town itself has become unbearable. For hikers, there's the trail to **Portage Pass**. This is the old route used for thousands of years by Natives and for 100 years or so by hopeful miners. The trail took them from Prince William Sound to the Turnagain Arm. You can't take the whole route anymore – Portage Glacier has put itself in the way – but you can hike to the top of the pass in about an hour. You can camp at Divide Lake, or keep hiking along the side of the stream (the trail disappears and you're on your own) down to the glacier. Getting onto the glacier itself is a very bad idea, unless your idea of fun is falling into a crevasse and freezing to death while stuck head first in a hole. The trailhead is at the foot of Maynard Mountain, about a mile behind Whittier Station. It's a great day-trip.

Kayaking

Despite the hiking attractions, most people come to Whittier to get into the water. Whittier is heaven for kayakers – the only thing to watch out for are a couple of channels where you'll have to dodge cruise ships. The payoff is incredible scenery and endless wildlife, including otters, seals, Dall's porpoise, orca, and bald eagles.

Launch from the Whittier Small Boat Harbor. A $13 launch fee is required at the Harbor Office, where you can pick up tide tables. Tell the people in the office where you're going. You might also want to stop in at the Harbor Office when you get back as well. It has a fire-hose-caliber hot shower available for only $3.

An eight-mile paddle east through **Passage Canal** brings you to **Decision Point** (there's a nice camping spot near here, in Squirrel Cove, if you're putting in late in the day). From here, you can head north toward **Port Wells**, or south into **Blackstone Bay**. Most kayakers head to Blackstone Bay. It's about 10 miles east of Whittier and offers great views of tidewater glaciers in a relatively protected bay. Come bundled up, because the wind blows cold off the ice.

Port Wells leads north at the end of the Passage Canal to the biggest attractions around – the **calving tidewater glaciers** (the Coxe, Barry, and Cascade) of College (home to the Harvard and Yale glaciers) and Harriman Fjords.

CALVING GLACIERS

When a glacier calves, chunks of ice the size of houses can come off. It's not smart to get too close – kayaking in a 10-foot wave is never a good idea – but sitting back at a reasonable distance gives you a view of the ice crashing into the water and lets you hear the popping of the ice – it sounds like rifle shots – as it weakens in the warmer water. It's more than amazing, and the only drawback is the number of tour boats sharing the water with you.

Turn southwest at Point Doran, and the **Harriman Fjord** continues another eight miles to the Surprise and Harriman glaciers. The several days of paddling it takes to see this area are definitely worth it. Dip your hand in the water and pick up a piece of glacial ice that could be 1,000 years old.

Southcentral

There are some cautions to remember if you're in the water here:

- Camp only above the high-water mark. Find where the color of the beach changes, and then move even farther back.

- Bears are everywhere. Obey all proper bear precautions and stay out of the berry bushes.

- Wind comes off the glaciers, causing cold and choppy seas, which can make paddling difficult.

- Stay well back from a calving glacier – at least half a mile. We were at a glacier one summer when a burg calved; we were a mile away; chips of ice hit the boat, and we were rocking in waves for at least three or four minutes. The calve wasn't a particularly big one.

- Finally, remember that cruise ships always have the right of way, because they're not paying a bit of attention to you.

If you're looking for kayak pickup or drop-off, try **Honey Charters** (☎ 472-2491). They've been working the area for a decade and can put you in at prime paddling spots. They also run day cruises that are a good value if you just want to sit back and enjoy the scenery.

You can rent kayaks from Honey Charters or **Sea-Kayakers** (☎ 877-472-2534). Both also have guided kayaking tours. Standards are trips out to Shotgun Cove for a full-day paddle, or a half-day birding expedition. Day-trips out to Blackstone Bay and back will run about $250.

■ Cruises & Charters

 As mentioned above, Honey Charters (☎ 472-2491) has good day-trips into Prince William Sound from Whittier. Options include a three-hour cruise to Blackstone, four to six hours in the Barry Arm to watch glaciers calve, or an all-day whale-watching trip. The trips allow a maximum of six people, so you get a much better view of things than you would crammed onto a 70-foot ship with 100 other people. Honey Charters can also arrange fishing trips – all day for $165.

Prince William Sound Cruises and Tours (☎ 800-992-1297) has a one-way option on this trip – Valdez to Whittier or vice versa – for $119. And starting for about $700, **Cruise West** (☎ 800-770-1035) will put you on a three- or four-night cruise of the Sound, starting in Whittier, taking a sidetrip to Cordova, and ending up at Valdez before the boat heads back to Whittier.

If you're looking for shorter trips into the Sound, there are options. Prince William Sound Cruises and Tours has a six-hour trip out of Whittier for $109; **Major Marine Tours** (☎ 800-764-7300) has similar trips for $99.

On either of these trips, they'll take you out from Whittier and down to Blackstone and Beloit Glaciers – great views, plenty of icy scenery.

■ Food

 For food, there are the hotels, plus the **Tsunami Café** for great pizza, or **Irma's Outpost** for burgers. To get your own food for a trip into the Sound, head to the **Harbor Store**, which has food and almost anything else you may need. If you've never seen a real general store, this is your chance.

■ Accommodations

If you're looking for a room, try the **Anchor Inn** (☎ 472-2394), with doubles from $75. The **Sportsman's Inn** (☎ 472-2352) is about the same price. Both hotels have loud bars and restaurants, so if you're looking for something a little more peaceful, try **June's Whittier B&B** (☎ 472-2396), with rooms from $75, moving up in price if you want a view. It's in the tower. **Camp** behind Begich Tower in gravel for $7. There's a cooking shelter and the sites are okay, but you're better off taking your tent to **Salmon Run**, a free campground which is rather nicer, a mile east of town. This is an unofficial campground – the signs say no camping near the picnic area – but if you go back down to the gravel area past the picnic tables, it should be okay. Same with anywhere else outside of town – pitch your tent in the bush, and as long as you're not starting campfires, you'll be fine.

Seward

Seward, located near the head of Resurrection Bay, is one of the oldest communities in Southcentral Alaska.

■ History

The first community here was founded by Alexandar Baranov in 1781, when he came into the bay on Easter Sunday looking for shelter from a storm during his passage from Kodiak to Yakutat. Resurrection Bay came to serve the Russians as a shipbuilding port. The first ship launched here – the *Phoenix*, in 1793 – was probably the first European-built ship launched on the West Coast of North America.

The U.S. history of the town begins in the 1890s, 20 years or so after the purchase of Alaska, when Captain Frank Lowell, along with his wife and children, settled in the area. They had the place pretty much to themselves until 1903, when the town of Seward proper was founded by John Ballaine, as an ice-free port terminus city for Alaska's then growing railway. Ballaine and his partners saw Seward as the future location of Alaska's major city, an easy route into the interior, and a perfect port, surrounded by stunning scenery. By 1904, the town's population was around 350.

The railroad was officially completed in 1923, when President Harding drove the golden spike. The railroad never turned out to be the cash cow Seward's founders had hoped for; except for a brief time during WWII, the railhead was largely neglected. In fact, the war sealed Seward's fate to remain a small town when the military developed the town of Whittier, much closer to Anchorage, as an alternate port. Seward was forgotten.

Historically, Seward also serves as a footnote to Alaska's most famous institution. The official story of the Iditarod dog sled race tells of mushers taking diphtheria vaccine to Nome; what's never mentioned is that the heroic mushers followed an existing trail, one that began in Seward. The trail was carved out by miners headed toward the Iditarod Mining District. It was used until 1928, with as much as a ton and a half of gold being hauled out by teams of 46 dogs.

BALTO THE DIPHTHERIA DOG

As an interesting oddity, the last of the dogs that actually made that famous diphtheria serum run was named Balto; several dog foods were named after him. He spent many of his later years exhibited in a carnival, until a man from Cleveland purchased him for $2,000. Balto died in the Cleveland Zoo, then was stuffed, mounted, and displayed at the Cleveland Museum for years.

Seward made the news in 1926, when local resident Bernie Benson, just 14 years old, won a contest sponsored by Governor George Parks to design the state's (then territorial) flag. Bernie's design of Ursa Major on a field of blue is one of the most eloquent state flags in the U.S.

Seward was almost wiped out in the 1964 earthquake, which was centered just 95 miles from the town. Seward's shoreline dropped nearly six feet. Since that time, the town has moved along quietly, prospering as a terminus city, a vacation area for Anchorageites, and a fishing community. The current population of 2,700 gives the town a quiet, pleasant air, without the tourist wildness of Homer. It's one of those towns where you have a really, really good time just hanging out and watching the world go by.

■ Basics

ⓘ The **Alaska Marine Highway**, ☎ 224-5485, connects Seward to Homer, Kodiak, and the Aleutians to the south and west, as well as Valdez to the east. The office is on Railway Ave., at the end of 5th Ave. The terminal building was once the Alaska Railroad Depot, but the 1964 earthquake wiped out the tracks and dropped too much of the right of way under water. The dock itself is at the end of 4th Ave.

Seward is the final stop for many cruises. From here, passengers take the train up to Denali, or to Anchorage, for the flight home. Cruise ships dock just north of the northern half of town, an easy walk to all attractions.

The **Alaska Railroad**, ☎ 224-2494 or 800-544-0552, still stops in Seward. The line heads north to Anchorage, via Portage. The depot is at the small boat harbor. There is no passenger service between late September and mid-May; during the summer, departures are daily. The fare is $50 one way. There's a package deal where you can get from Anchorage to Seward by train, visit Exit Glacier, do a two-hour cruise in Resurrection Bay, and take a two-mile dogsled trip, all for $209. Check with the Alaska Railroad for more details.

The Seward Highway connects town to the rest of the Kenai Peninsula and points farther north. The road passes through the **Chugach Forest** and your chance of seeing wildlife along the way, especially moose, is quite good. It's just over 125 miles to Anchorage. See our other book, *Adventure Guide to the Alaska Highway,* for full details. You can also take a bus from Seward to Anchorage via the **Seward Bus Line**, which offers daily departures. ☎ 224-7237.

The town has two **information centers**: the larger is on the main road, which you'll see to the right as you drive into town (☎ 224-8051). There's also the **Information Cache**, at Third and Jefferson, at Mile 2 on the Seward Highway, inside an old Alaska Railroad car. In either you'll find the usual variety of helpful flyers. Both are open daily in summer.

If you're planning ahead for the off-season, write to the **Seward Chamber of Commerce**, Box 749, Seward, AK 99664. Be sure to get a copy of the town's walking tour – Seward is a place best explored on foot.

The town can easily be broken down into two pieces: there's the **downtown area**, where the SeaLife Center is, and there's the **harbor area**, where most of the other attractions in town are.

The **Seward Trolley** – a little bus, actually – runs between downtown and the harbor. You can get a day pass for $3, but it's only a mile or so from the SeaLife Center, at one end of town, to the harbor, at the other, and it's a nice walk.

Southcentral

AUTHOR TIP *If you're going to park your car for the day, do it at the harbor side, in one of the big lots – $3 gets you a spot all day, or the first two hours are free. It's easier to park here than in downtown.*

On the harbor side, the **Chugach National Forest Service** office (☎ 224-3374) is at 4th and Jefferson. Stop in for current information on local hiking, fishing, and camping.

Headquarters for **Kenai Fjords** is at 1212 4th Ave. (☎ 224-3175; park infoline 224-2132), near the boat launch. Open daily mid-May through mid-September from 8 am to 7 pm, and Monday through Friday 8-5 in the winter, they offer slide shows that give you an idea of what the depths of the park are like. They've also got a small bookstore.

Rent a car at **Seward Rent A Car**, ☎ 224-7185; **Payless**, ☎ 224-8993; or **Hertz**, ☎ 224-6097.

Taxis are available from **Yellow Cab**, ☎ 224-8878, and **Independent Cab**, ☎ 224-5000.

Internet access is at the **public library**, 5th and Adams, or at **Harley's Hogs and Dogs** – go there, just for the atmosphere.

Seward's zip code is **99664**.

SEWARD AT A GLANCE

QUICK TOUR: If you've only got a couple hours in town, and you're mobile, head out to Exit Glacier. Great scenery, one of the most accessible glaciers along the coast; if you're stuck without a car, do the SeaLife Center.

DON'T MISS: One way or another, you owe it to yourself to get to Exit Glacier. It's worth the trouble; if you've got the time and the money, a kayak trip around Fox Island will be a highlight of your trip.

BEST FREEBIE: Seward is a town made for walking. Head south, along Resurrection Bay. You'll pass the whole town, and then, on the dirt road, have the bay to yourself. If you're not in the mood for water, hike Exit Glacier, and see what global warming is doing to us all.

■ Museums & Attractions

Seward is rapidly adding to its list of visitor attractions. The challenge city boosters face, with Kenai Fjords so near, is getting people to look at the town instead of the scenery.

SEWARD MUSEUM: The museum (☎ 224-3902) is across the street from the Info Cache, on 3rd and Jefferson. Unusual for anything on the coast, there's a good Iditarod display here, plus a slide show of Seward's history and another of the Iditarod. There's also a good earthquake display and a collection of Native baskets. Don't miss the cow raincoats or the basket made out of porcupine quills. Open daily May 1 through September 1, 10 to 5; for off-season hours, phone before you go. Admission is two bucks.

SEWARD MARINE EDUCATION CENTER: The University of Alaska maintains the center on Railway Ave., next to the ferry terminal. The many aquariums give you an underwater look at the local wildlife, plus there are films and educational displays, including the skull of a minke whale. Admission is free, and the center is open from 10 am to 4 pm, Tuesday through Sunday. ☎ 224-5261 for current programs.

ALASKA SEALIFE CENTER: Seward has also built this massive marine attraction, which is now the town's biggest draw. Funded in large part by a post-spill settlement from Exxon, the Alaska SeaLife Center is right next to the Seward Marine Center. With the seven-acre site split about evenly between research and visitor facilities, the center has rookeries for otters, sea lions, and seals that have been rescued and deemed unfit to return to the wild, and they hope to draw in large colonies of sea birds (they've got a few inside so far).

Design for the center was intended to recreate the natural world outside for the animals inside – including privacy areas where the animals can get away from people. There are also tanks where you can see salmon, a display where you can try to force-feed a model otter (really), and a small petting tank.

The bigger areas include seals and sea lions – what's on view depends largely on what's been rescued recently, or what they haven't been able to rehabilitate. There's also a nice bird area, where you can see puffins swimming underwater – worth the price of admission just for this. The center also offers films and other programs.

All that said, visitor opinion on the center seems to be fairly divided. It's a research facility, but you aren't likely to see much research going on; and as far as the animal viewing goes, it's pretty sparse for your $12.50. We've talked to some people who found this the highlight of their trip; others have wandered through, looked at the bored seals swimming in loops, and wished they'd gone somewhere else. Our take on it is this: if you don't have a lot of time to go out on the water, and if you haven't seen what you wanted to in the way of animal life, give it a look. If you've been pretty lucky with your sightings, pass it by. The center is open daily in summer from 8 am to 8 pm. ☎ 800-224-2525.

Southcentral

ST. PETER'S EPISCOPAL CHURCH: Built in 1906, this is one of the oldest churches on the Kenai Peninsula. Open by request (ask at the visitors center), the church is on the corner of 2nd and Adams.

■ Shopping

If you're out to shop, walk along 3rd and 4th avenues for a nice assortment of galleries and gift shops. If you need charts for a trip out, head to **Northland Books and Charts**, at 234 4th Ave. You'll find all the hiking maps and navigational charts you need.

■ Adventures

Kayaking

There's a lot going on around Seward. It's an ideal spot for kayakers. You can go from Resurrection Bay out to the glaciers, if you're experienced enough and have enough time.

If you want a guided trip, **Kayak and Custom Adventures** (☎ 800-288-3134) offer a variety of programs suitable for all levels of experience, from one-day guided trips to three- and five-day excursions. On the short trips, what you'll likely do is head out from town to Lowell Point Cairns Head State Park, a nice paddle of 10 miles or so. This will run about $100 for the full day, $55 for the half.

Kayak and Custom Adventures and **Sunny Cove Kayaking** (☎ 800-770-9119; www.sunnycove.com) do trips into Kenai Fjords. Sunny Cove caters a little more to the cruise ship audience, but for about $250, what you get is a cruise into the fjords and then a paddle around glaciers. Both also run trips to Fox Island, for about $150, which offers great wildlife watching potential. Kayak and Custom Adventures also has beginning and intermediate classes in coastal kayaking. Rent your kayaks from them or from **Kayakers Cove**, ☎ 224-8662. If you haven't kayaked anywhere else, this may be the perfect place for it. (See the *Kenai Fjords* section, page 364.)

Resurrection Bay offers exceptional sailing conditions – the best in the state. The yachting club here is very active and holds races and regattas throughout the summer. Take a picnic down to the beach and watch them man the mizzenmast. If you want to get onto one of the sailboats yourself, **Whale Song Sails** (☎ 224-5437) has full-day cruises out to Fox Island for $75. You can learn to sail from **Sailing, Inc.** (☎ 224-3160). They've got four-day packages for $750; when you're done, you should be reasonably able to take a boat out. They've also got more advanced classes.

On Land

You can rent a bike from the **Seward Bike Shop** (☎ 224-2448) for $32 a day for a mountain bike with suspension. Or if you want somebody else to provide the motor, **Bardy's Trail Rides** (☎ 224-7863) has horseback trips down to the edge of Resurrection Bay. Finally, **Ididaride Sled Dog Tours** (☎ 800-478-3139) gives you a chance to play with the puppies and ride in a wheeled sled dog cart.

If you're after wildlife viewing, head into Resurrection Bay. Six miles south of town is the **Cains Head State Recreation Area**, an old WWII base, where there are still bunkers, a subterranean fort, and great beaches. You can't drive there; you've got to hike or boat in. Before the Alcan was built, Seward was the main transportation hub for the Alaska Command, and here's a bit of what was left behind.

Seward has one of the biggest **Fourth of July** bashes in the state, with games, parades, fireworks, and general madness. Plan ahead or you won't find a place to stay. In winter, there's cross-country skiing at the **Snow River** area – get to it via the Primrose Campground, at Mile 18 on the Seward Highway or at **Glacier Creek** (see *Exit Glacier*, below). If you're in town in the winter, try the **Polar Bear Jump Off** in January. This is when insane people dress up in costumes, have a parade, and jump into the bay.

▪ Exit Glacier

 People come to Seward to see the glaciers in Kenai Fjords, but the glacier closest to Seward is the Exit Glacier, with a 150-foot-tall glacial face. You can drive to it from Seward by following **Exit Glacier Road**. The road is paved up to the Ranger Station at the foot of the glacier; if you continue north instead of turning off, you can reach several Forest Service cabins. This part of the road follows the river, and there are great views of the glacier up ahead, the silver water flowing from it. The road past the Exit Glacier turnoff is dirt and can be hard on low-clearance vehicles. The glacial face is about half a mile from the parking lot.

You can hike all the way out to the main icefield from Exit Glacier, but allow yourself all day for the trip. It's only 3½ miles out, but there's little maintenance on the path, so it's steep, rough, and often slippery. Much of the time the upper portion of the path is covered with snow.

If that's a bit much, there's an easy half-mile **Upper Loop Trail** that gives great views and takes you right up to the glacier's face. For the less ambitious hiker, the Ranger Station runs nature walks and hikes in and around the icefield. Check for current list of programs. For more on hiking, see page 366.

Southcentral

Among the most interesting things about Exit Glacier are the signs along the walkway: these show where the glacier was in the past. Like every other glacier in Alaska, Exit is on the way out. Thirty years or so ago, the glacier was where the parking lot is now; today, it's shrinking at a rate of about six inches a day.

Up at the top of the loop trail, you can get a good look at the glacial face, and by paying attention to the trail on the way in, you can see how glaciers impact the landscape. First, they obviously strip it all bare; then, over time, the forest returns. You can match up the date signs with the forest to see just how long it takes everything to return to full-growth.

■ Kenai Fjords

 Kenai Fjords is the reason most people go to Seward. The park, which extends far enough south to abut Kachemak Bay State Park outside Homer, is most easily reached from Seward. All that separates town and park are a couple of 5,000-foot mountains.

Kenai Fjords are dominated by the **Harding Icefield**, one of the largest icefields in North America, from which 23 named glaciers flow. The icefield is approximately 35 by 20 miles; until the early 1900s, it was thought to be one huge ice system.

WATCHABLE

WILDLIFE

The Fjords themselves are an excellent place for wildlife watchers. More than 30 species of seabirds are seen in the area, including both tufted and horned puffins, and the waters are full of marine mammals.

If you don't want to take a kayak out (see above), there are plenty of people ready to take you out in ships.

Ship charters run out of Resurrection Bay, around Aialik Cape, and finally into the fjords themselves, usually for a stop at the Holgate Glacier or, depending on the trip, the Northwestern Glacier. In total, Aialik Bay has three glaciers flowing into it; McCarty Fjord has two, including the dramatic Dinglestadt Glacier. McCarty Fjord also has a major seal pupping haul out. On any trip, you're likely to see seals and sea lions, as well as more puffins than you thought possible – they're everywhere. On a good day, you might be lucky enough to see a whale or two.

There is a caveat to these trips: if you've come up through Southeast Alaska, or if you've been to Glacier Bay, this will probably seem a little bland to you. It's a nice introduction to Alaska's coast for people who've never traveled it before, but, although it's pretty, there are better places around. So, if they're on your itinerary, this might be a skip.

If you're going out, remember that the water can get rough here; if you're prone to seasickness, take pills before you get on the boat. Even on a calm, clear day, the sea can be pretty bumpy when they're taking you around to see the haul-outs. Also remember that, even on a bright, sunny day, it's cold on the water. Dress accordingly. For your trip with the big outfitters, you'll get a spot on a large ship, narration from a naturalist, and lunch.

To get into the fjords for a tour, try **Kenai Fjords Tours Inc.** (☎ 224-8068 or, 800-478-8068). Full-day trips (six hours) start at $109. There's an 8½-hour trip that takes the same route and then detours to Fox Island for $119.

Renown Charters and Tours (☎ 272-1961; 800-655-3806) offers a six-hour cruise for $109; they also have short, 2½-hour trips through the fjords for $44 with breakfast; $49 with lunch. You're not going to get into the best part of the scenery with the short tours, though, so we'd suggest you plan on a full day if you're going out. **Major Marine Tours** (☎ 224-8030 or 800-764-7300) has the eight-hour standard trip for $99; add on another $10 for the all-you-can-eat buffet.

Finally, there's **Mariah Tours** (☎ 800-270-1238) which has a 10-hour, 150-mile trip through the fjords for only $115. Other companies will pack you on huge ships with as many as 100 other people, but Mariah runs 43-foot boats, with a maximum of 22 passengers.

All of these places have offices down by the harbor; stop by and talk to the staff, so you can pick one you like. It's not usually a problem getting a seat on one of the bigger ships. There are dozens of charter operators running smaller boats with customizable itineraries. See the charter section, below.

To fly over the fjords, you can go with **Kenai Fjords Air Tours** (☎ 362-1060), or **Scenic Mountain Air** (☎ 288-3646 – located in Moose Pass). Trips around the Harding Icefield start around $120.

Fox Island

One of the big sites in Kenai Fjords is Fox Island. There was a fox farm run here around the turn of the century, but the island's real claim to fame is that Rockwell Kent – perhaps the most famous illustrator of the early 20th century (his woodcuts for *Moby Dick* are amazing) – worked here. Kent had failed as an artist and was suffering from a crisis of confidence. He went to Alaska to get away from the pressures of down south, and he and his son were on the island for nearly a year, from the summer of 1918 to the spring of 1919. It would seem that their favorite activity while on the island was to sunbathe naked in snowdrifts and listen to the lady who ran the fox farm tell tales about her life – she was, from all accounts, quite a character.

Southcentral

Kent wrote of his time on the island that "So huge was the scale of all this that for some time we looked in vain for any habitation, at last incredulously seeing what we had taken to be boulders to assume the form of cabins."

That's how big it is up here.

Hiking

Just off the Exit Glacier Road, as you cross the bridge over the Resurrection River, is the **Resurrection River Trail**. This trail, which is 16 miles long, connects to the **Russian Lakes Trail**, which in turn connects to the **Resurrection Pass Trail** – about 70 miles of hiking in all. There's a cabin 6½ miles in on the Resurrection River Trail.

Other good hiking includes **Devil's Pass**, which connects to the Resurrection Pass Trail. The trailhead is at Mile 39 on the Seward Highway. **Johnson Pass** is a 33-mile hike that starts and ends on the Seward Highway – at Miles 33 and 64, respectively. Along the way, it passes excellent fishing lakes, but watch for avalanches along the trail.

For a shorter hike, try the **Carter Lake Trail**, which starts at Mile 32 on the Seward Highway and is only two miles long. It's steep in places, but it takes you up to an alpine meadow.

 Everywhere around Seward is serious bear country. Act accordingly. Take all proper precautions and keep your eyes open.

Charters

All around Seward you'll find outstanding fishing. The nine-day **Silver Salmon Derby**, held each year in August (book your hotel room well in advance), offers a $10,000 prize for the heaviest fish, but silver aren't the only game in town – head out for king, Dolly Varden, halibut, and more.

We're working on a mathematical formula that measures the relationship between the number of Subway sandwich shops in town and the quality of the fishing. Judging by this measure, the fishing in Seward is very good indeed.

There are dozens of charter operators working in town. You can get an idea of how their luck is running by going down to the docks around 5 pm, and seeing what the catch of the day has been. Figure a day of salmon fishing is going to run you around $175; halibut will usually go about $25 more. Try to book at least a few days in advance if you can.

The **Charter Option** (☎ 224-2026, 800-224-2026) runs more than 30 boats. Whatever you want, they've got the boat to handle it; they're also a good choice if you're looking for a sightseeing charter.

The **Fish House** (☎ 224-3674, 800-257-7760) has full-day trips for salmon or halibut; they run almost as many boats as the Charter Option does, and they have a full-service tackle shop, across from the harbor.

Those are the big guys, but there are plenty of well-qualified charter captains running a single boat. Try **North Star Charters** (☎ 224-5406); **Quarterdeck Charters** (☎ 224-2396); the **Saltwater Safari Company** (☎ 224-5232); or **Backlash Charters** (☎ 800-295-4396).

■ Food

Seward has one absolutely killer restaurant, and then an assortment of dining attractions that are fairly run of the mill – except for the seafood, of course, which is wonderful almost everywhere – with most places serving entrées for $10 to $20.

For one of the best meals you'll have in Alaska, head to **Ray's Waterfront** (☎ 224-5606), 4th Ave., by the Coast Guard Station. They've been written up in all of the food magazines, and their cedar-planked salmon is something you will not soon forget. Dinner from about $20, and worth every penny. Make reservations, or be prepared to wait a while.

Peking (☎ 224-5444), 338 4th Ave., has all the standard Chinese favorites, plus Kung Pao halibut. From $10. For Italian, try **Apollo**, near the ferry terminal. Dinners start around $12.

The **Harbor Dinner Club**, 220 5th Ave., is a good place for burgers and seafood. Figure on a complete dinner running about $20.

The **Resurrection Roadhouse** is a local favorite. It's .7 miles up the Exit Glacier Road, and dinners of steak, seafood, or chicken start at $10.

Smoke'n' Alaska's Fish and Chips is down by the harbor. Fast, if you can get their attention, and cheap, with halibut and chips for $7.

For breakfast, **Marina**, across from the boat harbor, is the place of choice. If you can't get in there, try the **Breeze Inn**, just a couple doors down. Either place will fill you up for under $10.

If you want to eat healthy, check out **Le Barn Appetit** (☎ 224-8706), a health food store/bakery/B&B, at Mile 3.7 on the Seward Highway, the first right off Exit Glacier Road.

■ Accommodations

The **Van Gilder** (☎ 224-3079 or 800-204-6835), 308 Adams (Box 2), is Seward's landmark hotel. Built in 1916, it's seen it all over the years, including a restoration. This is a registered National Historic Site, with doubles starting at $60 for a shared bath; private baths start at $85.

The **Best Western Hotel Seward** (☎ 224-2378 or 800-478-4050) is at 221 5th Ave. Doubles start at $100 in the shoulder season and run to $160 in high. Next to the Best Western is the **Seward Hotel** (☎ 224-8001 or 800-478-1774). Doubles here start at $96. The **Breeze Inn** (☎ 224-5237), by the small boat harbor, has doubles from $105. **Murphy's Motel**, 911 4th Ave., is popular and nice, with doubles from $90.

Take a look at the brochures in the Info Center, and you'll get the impression that half the town is running B&Bs. The percentage may actually be higher on that. Figure on around $90 for a double in a local B&B, and if the day is looking crowded, staff at the Info Center will help you find a place – vital during Salmon Derby days.

Just as a quick sampling, there's **Alaska Nellie's Inn**, which is part of an old homestead. You're a ways out of town with this – closer to Moose Pass than Seward – but it's a fun, historical place, with rooms around $75.

In town, there's the very nice **Bay Vista** – especially good if you've got a group, as you rent out one of two two-bedroom suites. Killer views from the one upstairs. Rates start at $80. ☎ 224-5880. Easy walking distance to the harbor.

Le Barn Appetit is also a Seward landmark. They're on Old Exit Glacier Road – which is a sidestreet on the Exit Glacier Road – about 3½ miles from town. They've got a room built around a tree ($100), an efficiency apartment for the same price, or a three-room suite that can be rented whole for $200, or in parts for less. But the real reason to stay is the food: gourmet, and healthy. There's also a small health food store here.

The cheapest place to stay is **Moby Dick Hostel** (☎ 224-7072). About halfway between the harbor and downtown, you can get a night here for under $20.

■ Camping

RV facilities are available at **Bear Creek** (☎ 224-5725), Mile 6.6 on the Seward Highway. **Kenai Fjords RV Park** (☎ 224-8779) also has full hookups, at Mile 1 on the Seward Highway. Campgrounds spread out regularly along the Seward Highway, if you've got a car. You'll find sites at **Mile 17.4**, **Mile 23.2**, and **Mile 24.2**.

There are also 12 tent-only campsites at **Exit Glacier**. There's potable water on site and a cooking shelter, but not much else. Killer views. Come well prepared with lots of bug goop, because the flies are just nasty here. Sites are free, and they're all well hidden; check for a rock placed on top of the site number to show if somebody's already claimed the spot.

Closer to town, try the **Forest Acres Campground**, at Mile 2. Tents only for $6.

Finally, there is the huge **Beachside Camping area**, across from Ballaine Blvd. – take a right from the ferry terminal and walk along the shoreline. You can't miss it, because there are hundreds of RVs parked here. It's managed by the Parks Department, and most of the spots have been graveled for RVs, but there are some grassy tent areas. Tents are $6; RVs are $8; hookups are $15. It's very convenient for quick overnights.

Homer

At the tip of the Kenai Peninsula, Homer bills itself as "The End of the Road." Stores sell a certificate of completion to people who have driven all the way out to the end of the Spit, as far as you can go south of Anchorage by road. Popular radio figure Tom Bodett started here and still lives here, broadcasting his NPR series, "The End of the Road." It's no wonder he's stayed even after hitting the big time. (Homer's other claim to fame, pop singer Jewel, grew up here, fled and now lives in Texas.) Homer is one of the great places in Alaska; it's got character to spare, and because almost all of the tourist activities are down on the Spit, the town itself stays safe, a charming little place that reveals its attractions only to the long-term visitor or resident.

■ History

Some of the finest fishing in Alaska is around Homer, and the Natives knew this for centuries before the RV crowd moved in. The Kenaitze Indians, an Athabascan group, had villages all along Kachemak Bay, their territory extended as far north as Cook Inlet.

Captain Cook claimed the Kenai Peninsula for England in 1778. Just seven years later, Grigor Shelikof sent an expedition to the Kenai Peninsula, and the Russian presence began. The first Russian settlement was at Alexandrovosk, or English Bay, south of present-day Seldovia. By 1787, the Russians had laid claim to the entire Cook Inlet area. They took hostages – mostly women and children – from the Kenaitze to ensure the cooperation of the Native men when it came to hunting and gathering sea otter pelts.

This method of hunting was so successful for the Russians that, by 1800, the once huge sea otter population had been pushed to the brink of extinction. Unperturbed, the Russians packed up and moved to Sitka. The population of the Kenai, estimated at about 3,000 in 1805, had dropped to 160 by 1880.

Homer got its start in the 1890s, when the English ran a coal mine at Bluff Point, just up the beach from the Spit. Although the mine closed in 1907, it was prosperous enough to inspire the building of a railroad from the mine to the dock at the Spit's end.

There was a brief heyday of gold mining in the Homer area, but what has kept the town going through booms and busts is the Spit, the tourists, and fishing. If you want to catch a 200-pound halibut, this is the place. Today, about 4,000 people call Homer home. Most visitors never venture far from the Spit, but downtown Homer is not short on charms itself.

OLD BELIEVERS

In Homer, you'll often see women in floor-length dresses and long head scarves. They come from the Russian villages south of Homer. The largest of the two villages, Nikolaevsk, is a town of "Old Believers," most of whom left Russia in the 1930s to escape persecution. (The schism between old and new believers dates back several hundred years, though; it was caused by a reformation in the rules of the Russian Orthodox Church. Old Believers didn't like the new rules. Today, there are about 1,000 Old Believers in Alaska.). The village of Nikolaevsk, founded in 1968, is a place where Russian is the de facto language and Russian culture thrives. The residents wear traditional Russian peasant garb and use old-fashioned tools. You can visit the village, but the residents do not seek or encourage tourists or attention. If you go, treat the people with respect.

■ Basics

i Homer is served by the Alaska Marine Highway's **M.V. Tustemena** three or four times a week, connecting the town to Kodiak, Seldovia, and Seward. ☎ 235-8449. The terminal is at the end of the Spit. Cruise ships don't come here.

Alaska Airlines flies into Homer almost hourly in the summer, using **ERA** as the subcontractor. ☎ 235-5205. Charter flight operators in Homer include **Southcentral Air** (from Anchorage), ☎ 235-6172; **Beluga Float Planes**, ☎ 235-8256; **Cal Alaska Helicopters**, ☎ 235-2844; **Gulf Aviation**, ☎ 235-7959; **HomerAir**, ☎ 235-8591; **Kachemak Air**, ☎ 235-8294; **Maritime Helicopters**, ☎ 235-7771; and **South Central Air**, ☎ 235-6172.

Homer Bus Lines has daily service to Soldotna, Kenai, Seward, and Anchorage. ☎ 235-8280 for current schedule and rates.

If you've got your own car and want to drive, Homer is the end of the road. Everything is north from here. See our other book, *Adventure Guide to the Alaska Highway* for details.

If you want to get off the Spit, you'll need transportation. Rent a car at **National**, ☎ 235-5515. Taxis are abundant, but expensive. Airport to ferry terminal, less than three miles, runs at least $8. Try **Lynx Taxi**, ☎ 235-5969; **Maggie's Taxi**, ☎ 235-2345; and **Chux Cab**, ☎ 235-CHUX.

Jakolof Ferry Service runs back and forth to Halibut Point, on the edge of Kachemak Bay State Park. The ship leaves the harbor below the Salty Dawg three times a day; ☎ 235-2376 for departure times.

There's a small **Tourist Information Center** annex on the Spit, about a mile from the ferry terminal. It may or may not be open, though. The main center is north of the Spit, on the ocean side, right at the crossroads as you're coming into town (next to the Ocean Shores motel) ☎ 235-5300. Off-season, write to **Homer Chamber of Commerce**, P.O. Box 541, Homer, 99603.

Internet access is available at the **Kachemak Bay Café**, 5941 East End Road.

The zip code for Homer is **99603**.

HOMER AT A GLANCE

QUICK TOUR: The ferry stops right at the end of the Spit. You've got plenty of time to look around and walk the tideline.

DON'T MISS: Get into Kachemak Bay: kayak, take a water taxi, something. It's some of the nicest scenery in South-central. Oh, yeah, the fishing's not bad, either. The Pratt Museum is one of the finest in the state. It is well worth your time.

BEST FREEBIE: Hang out at the Fishing Hole. Freak shows were a noble tradition in the circus world for years. Here's a different kind, but the same idea.

■ Museums & Attractions

THE SPIT: Homer's tourist action is on the Spit, a 4½-mile sandspit that projects into Kachemak Bay. The Spit is a glacial moraine – a deposit left behind by a retreating glacier – and, until the 1964 earthquake, was considerably larger. The quake put nearly half of it under water. An official guide to the city says that the Spit is "a source of artistic energy, a place to relax and get in touch with the rhythm of wind and water."

Southcentral

Maybe. But you'd have to ignore the chaos to do any relaxing. And that's the fun of the Spit.

Come down about 5 PM and watch the charter boats bring in the day's catch. This also gives you a chance to see the operators at work before you book. Or just hang out in front of the Salty Dawg and watch the people come and go. It's like a parade every day.

THE FISHING HOLE: If you want to fish and don't mind basically fishing in a barrel, try the Spit "fishing hole." Salmon fry are released here in a dead-end inlet right off the Spit. When they're mature and suffering from the salmon instinct to return whence they came, the fish end up in this tiny pool – dazed, confused, and suffering from hormonal derangement while they look for freshwater to spawn in. There isn't any, but there are eagles waiting to pounce and "fishermen" snagging and casting for them. If dynamiting a stream is your idea of fun, this might be the place for you. On the other hand, to be fair, if you've got small kids, or for whatever reason can't get out on the boats, this is your chance to catch a big fish. It is wheelchair-accessible. Despite the side-show aspect, you'll still need a fishing license here, just like everywhere else you drop a line. There is a special deal where kids under 16 don't need the license. If you haven't brought gear, you can rent poles in the store next to the hole.

Walking along the beach on the Spit at low tide can be interesting, or you can stay up higher above the waterline on the new paved trails that are popular with bikers and joggers. While you walk, watch for sea otters, which have made quite a comeback since the Russians left. There's also a wide variety of shore birds and a good bivalve community: butter clams and steamer clams on the east side of the Spit, razor clams on the inlet side and farther up along most of Homer's beaches. Tide tables are available everywhere. Remember, clamming requires a fishing license, too. The rest of the Spit itself is an assortment of charter operations, souvenir shops, and restaurants. See below for details.

One of the fun things about the Spit is that most places where you see brochures, there's also a bright orange flyer on what to do in case you're on the Spit when a tsunami hits. Homer, surrounded by volcanoes, is prime earthquake territory, and that means there is always a tiny chance of a big wave. If you see the water suddenly disappear and hear a siren blasting for several minutes, head for higher ground. No, this will not happen to you.

PRATT MUSEUM: In town, the Pratt Museum is at 3779 Bartlett St. The $4 admission gets you into one of the better museums in Alaska, featuring the usual historical displays, some excellent wildlife exhibits, and a selection of modern art. Their exhibit, "Darkened Waters," on the Exxon Valdez oil spill, won awards, spawned a traveling show, and made Exxon very unhappy. Lots of interactive displays.

ALASKA MARITIME NATIONAL WILDLIFE REFUGE: The refuge maintains a visitors center at 451 Sterling Highway, next to the Ocean Shores motel. The AMNWR, which stretches from Forrester Island in Southeast to Attu Island in the Aleutians and north nearly to Barrow, totals more than 2,500 islands and three million acres of vital wildlife habitat. AMNWR claims that 80% of all seabirds in Alaska nest in the refuge. In addition to the visitors center in Homer, AMNWR also maintains an office in Adak, and puts naturalists onto the ferries to Seldovia, Kodiak, and Dutch Harbor.

At the center, there are films, a computer program that helps you identify birds, and a small bookstore. The center has guided bird walks every Sunday and Wednesday from 1-2 PM, and there are sometimes beach walks, too.

HERITAGE TOURS: The Kachemak Heritage Land Trust offers a variety of summer programs, including nature walks, archaeological lectures, and more. Contact them at Box 2400, or ☎ 235-5263.

PIER ONE THEATER: In summer, Pier One Theater stages live weekend performances on the Spit. Past programs have ranged from performances by the Boston Pops Orchestra to productions of Woody Allen plays. Tom Bodett is a standard. Check the newspaper for current schedule, or ☎ 235-7333. Most shows are $11.

FESTIVALS: Homer's Halibut Derby runs May 1 through Labor Day. Entering for a day costs $7, and prizes start at $250, working up to a $32,000 jackpot. There are prizes for the biggest fish (the 1994 winner was 346.7 pounds) and for specially tagged fish. Check with the Chamber of Commerce for more information.

May 10th through the 12th is the **Kachemak Bay Shorebird Festival**. More than 100,000 birds pass through the area in the first two weeks of May. There's a birders' hotline for the latest sightings: ☎ 235-PEEP. The Tourist Info booth and the AMNWR office have a sheet with a checklist of local birds. In August, there's the **Summer String Festival**, with a concert series and classes. Check with the Kenai Peninsula Orchestra (☎ 235-6318) for the year's programs.

■ Booking Agencies

 Homer is activity central; sooner or later, everybody ends up here looking for stuff to do. Because of that demand, the town has three central booking agencies: one call to any of these can get you kayaks, fishing charters, bear-watching trips, excursions over to Seldovia, and nights in one of the town's countless B&Bs. If you don't want to run around and track this stuff down yourself, let these people do it for you.

It's an especially good idea to let them handle the details for you if you're coming into town on short notice in the high season. There are many days in summer when you have your choice of fishing boats to go out on, but there are also times when there's not a boat to be found for two or three days at a time. Calling one of these places early can save you a lot of frustration.

Central Charters (☎ 235-7847 or 800-478-7847) is the town's original one-stop shop, with a huge office on the Spit. Newer are **The Bookie** (☎ 235-1581 or 888-335-1581) and **Homer Alaska Referral** (☎ 235-8996).

We'd highly recommend letting one of these people get you a B&B if that's what you're going to want in town. Homer has more B&Bs per capita than any place in the North; let the booking agencies figure out which one is right for you.

■ Adventures

Skiing

 Any time of year, take the drive out East End Road for great views of the bay and the rolling hills around Homer. In winter, you'll find excellent **cross-country skiing** on Baycrest-Diamond Ridge, above town, on the Homestead Trail, and all around town. Get the free flyer on skiing from the Chamber of Commerce, or contact the **Kachemak Nordic Ski Club** (☎ 235-6018).

Kayaks

Kachemak Bay is kayaking paradise, as long as you're careful to stay out of tidal rips. If you're going out on your own, check around before you pick a spot to paddle.

True North Kayak (☎ 235-0708) offers rentals and guided excursions around Homer. Their day-trip takes you over for a paddle around Yukon Island, where there are plenty of otters to watch, for $125. They've also got overnight trips available, and best of all, unlike most guided paddles, you have a viable option of taking a single kayak out, rather than getting stuck in a double. **Seaside Adventures** (☎ 235-6672) has similar trips, as does **St. Augustine Charters** (☎ 235-6126).

If you've got your own boat, or are renting one for the day, there are several choices for drop-off. **Tutka Bay Taxi** (☎ 235-7166); **Bay Excursions** (☎ 235-7525); and the **Jakolof Ferry Service** (☎ 235-6384) – the town's original water taxi – all run water taxis, rent kayaks, and can arrange for drop-offs and pickups.

Water Tours

Coastal Outfitters (☎ 235-8492 or 888-235-8492) runs day-trips for whale watching and birding.

Danny J Tours operates the Kachemak Bay Ferry, which is the best way to get over to Halibut Cove (see below). The boat leaves daily at noon, and along the way, you'll pass Gull Island, where serious birders can usually add a species or two to their life list. You're back in town by 5 PM. Book through Central Charters, or direct at ☎ 296-2223.

Bears

The growth industry in Homer the past few years has been charter flights over to Katmai to see bears. Homer is the town closest to Katmai – sometimes referred to as the "Land of 10,000 smokes," reflecting it's highly active volcanic past – and sometimes just called "the place you saw on TV where all the bears are." When you see the pictures of bears lined up at a waterfall, waiting for the salmon to jump, you're looking at Katmai.

There are tons of bears in Katmai, and they're fairly used to people, so they just go on about their business – trying to get fat before the weather turns – while you have plenty of chances to get pictures. These are some of the biggest brown (grizzly) bears in the world, and the chances of not getting the best bear-watching you've ever imagined are remote. You will be amazed.

Now for the downside: a day-trip out to watch the bears will run you around $500. Yep, that's for the day-trip. You fly from Homer to the park, and then hike in to a bear-watching spot. You'll want a good camera (don't even think about wasting your time with a little pocket camera), a better lens, and lots of film.

Bald Mountain Air Service (☎ 235-7969); **Hughes Float Plane Service** (☎ 235-4229 or 888-299-1014); and **Emerald Air Service** (☎ 235-6993) – all offer similar trips. Flying time is about 90 minutes each way.

If spending this kind of money on a bear-viewing trip is a bit much for you, for around the same price you could fly or take the ferry down to Wrangell or Juneau, and then get a trip to Anan or Pack Creek, where the bear viewing is equally amazing – plus you get to see another part of Alaska. If your time is short, though, these trips to Katmai are unforgettable.

If a day-trip isn't enough, **Katmai Coastal Tours** (☎ 800-478-7131) runs four-day trips, basing out of a comfortable ship, for $3,250.

Southcentral

Power Trips

Finally in the tour department, there are some nice trips you can take around town. **Trails End Horse Adventures** (☎ 235-6393) has half-day rides for $65; full-day for $110. If that strikes you as a little sedate, **Wilderness 4-Wheeler Tours** has four hours of bashing around in ATVs for $99; eight hours for $159. ☎ 235-8567.

For flightseeing, there's **Maritime Helicopters** (☎ 235-7771) and **Kachemak Bay Flying Service** (☎ 235-8924), which flies a beautifully restored 1929 Travel Air 6000. Flying didn't always have the ambience of a fast food wrapper.

Hiking

For hikers, the **Bishop Beach Hike** starts at Bishop Park. The full hike is 11 miles and passes a seal rookery and Diamond Creek. All along you'll have great views, but check a tide table before you set out. You can also pick this trail up at the Ocean Shores Motel – just head down the hill to the beach. It's not exactly a trail you're on here, just the beach, but it's a great walk, and as long as you're watching the water, you get great views and the place to yourself. Just be out of there when the tide is coming in. The British have a lovely term – embayed – that describes what happens when beach walkers get stuck by the tide. You could, maybe, climb the steep sand bluffs to get away from the incoming water, but you wouldn't really want to try.

The **Homestead Trail** is a bit over 6.6 miles, starting on Rodgers Loop Road. You climb through meadows and get great views of the bay. Walking the length of the Spit along the beach is also a great stroll – about five miles from the airport to the ferry terminal. You'll have the tideline to yourself.

■ Kachemak Bay State Park

Homer's most famous attraction takes a little getting to: Kachemak Bay State Park. With over 350,000 acres, the park has a little something for everyone. It's located directly across Kachemak Bay from Homer and is accessible by boat. Many of the charter operators will offer drop-offs, or you can take the Jakolof Ferry, which runs back and forth to Halibut Point on the edge of the park. The boat leaves the harbor below the Salty Dawg three times a day; ☎ 235-2376 for departure times.

Kachemak Bay State Park varies between quite settled – Halibut Cove – and wild, with huge glaciers and strangely shaped rock cliff formations that are home to thousands of birds. Expect to see eagles, puffins, and more than 15,000 nesting seabirds on Gull Island.

The park has a variety of hiking trails. You'll recognize their trailheads by the large orange triangular signs at the water's edge. Some of the better ones are to **Grewingk Glacier**, a 3.2-mile, flatland hike that takes you to the glacial outwash. You can get to the glacier itself, but it's difficult and dangerous. Another good hike is the **Lagoon Trail**, 5½ miles from the Halibut Creek trailhead; it connects with the **China Poot Lake Trail**, 2½ miles along three lakes below China Poot Peak. You can climb the peak itself from the lake – the two miles will take at least three hours, round-trip.

Fishing throughout the waters of the park is good. Salmon run in the rivers (some are also stocked behind Halibut Cove, but this is just a bigger version of the Spit's Fishing Hole), and in the deeper waters you'll find halibut, cod, flounder, and red snapper.

There's only one cabin in the park, and it's usually booked. **Campsites** are at the foot of the Grewingk Glacier Trail, the Lagoon Trail, and the China Poot Lake Trail. There's also a ranger station near the China Poot Lake Trail. There is no safe drinking water in the park; boil or treat before use.

In the park, be aware that the tides in Kachemak Bay are tremendous. The vertical difference between high and low tide can be as much as 28 feet, with an average of 15 feet. Some of the passages get so narrow the tide flows in like a rapids, so take all proper boating precautions and stay off the mud flats. Don't kayak unescorted out here unless you really know what you're doing. And when you beach your boat, make sure you pull it up a lot farther than you think you need to.

Charters

Okay, let's get to the reason why you came to Homer: serious fishing.

Homer is charter operator's paradise. An evening on the Spit will make you think more boats leave Homer than the rest of the state combined. And they're all here for good reason. If you're a serious fisherman, Homer is the place to find salmon, halibut up to 200 pounds and more, cod, and flounder. If you're after the really big fish, you'll need an all-day charter. The biggest halibut are out around the point, in open water. It gets rough out there, so be prepared. If you're prone to seasickness, it will be a day in hell.

Southcentral

The three booking agencies listed above – **Central Charters** (☎ 235-7847 or 800-478-7847); **The Bookie** (☎ 235-1581 or 888-335-1581); and **Homer Alaska Referral** (☎ 235-8996) – are the places to start calling about charters. These agencies are linked with dozens of boats, and they're your best chance of getting exactly what you want. Take some time, talk to them, tell them what kind of fishing you're looking for, and let them match you up to the boat that will give you the best time.

Homer has so many independent charter operators that choosing one yourself can be a bewildering experience. Going down to the docks the night before you want to charter and talking to people coming in is one good way to pick a ship. The **Homer Charter Association** has certain standards that must be maintained, and membership is usually a sign of a good operation.

All the fishing charters are going to run about the same services. They'll provide you with the boat and fishing gear; you bring your own lunch. Beyond that, check what you're in for. Most operators will help you process your catch. Expect prices to start at $175 a day or so; if someone is drastically cheaper, find out why. They may go to a different area, stay away from the deep water, or offer fewer services.

Most charter companies will clean your fish, but getting it home is your problem. **Coal Point Seafood Company**, 4306 Homer Spit, ☎ 235-3877, can vacuum-pack, freeze, and ship your fish. Flash-freezing runs $1/pound. They'll FedEx your fish home at a rate of $43.35 for 20 pounds.

■ Shopping

 Homer claims a number of local artists, and downtown you'll find galleries stuffed with their work. There are five galleries on Pioneer Ave. alone, and a couple more nearby. Exhibits change, and so do the tastes of the gallery owners.

Alaska Wild Berry Products (☎ 235-8858), 528 E. Pioneer, has all the standard tourist fare, plus candies and jams made from local berries. Shipping is available. **Inua** and the **Roadhouse** – across from each other on the Spit – have good assortments of Native crafts.

■ Food

 Homer has a great array of excellent, reasonably priced eateries for such a small town. The Spit is jammed with seafood places, offering cheap, very fresh fish. **Land's End**, at the end of the Spit, has a good lunch special, starting at $6. The **Cactus Café**, also on the Spit, has wraps from $6 and is the only place in town for Mexican food.

Nearby is **Whales Cove Fish and Chips**, with a good, cheap lunch of halibut and fries for $8.

Café Cups (☎ 235-8330), 162 W. Pioneer, is the place for breakfast (they also serve lunch and dinner), with excellent coffees and teas and homestyle cooking from $8. They sport an art house décor, and their eggs Benedict will be a highlight of your trip.

The **Fresh Sourdough Express Bakery**, on Ocean Drive just off the Spit, serves great breakfasts with fresh-baked goodies, plus sandwiches for lunch. It's crowded and very popular – hard to find a place to park early in the morning. Lunch specials include spinach and cheese croissant turnovers and falafel burgers; for dinner, don't miss the lemon pepper-crusted halibut. Lunch from $8; dinner from $15. They've also got their own line of organic cocoa and coffee – buy a few jars to take home.

Smoky Bay Co-op, on Pioneer, has vegetarian specialties and a health food store. Lunch runs around $7.

The **Homestead Restaurant**, 8.2 miles out East End Road, is the nice night-out place. Prime rib, microbrews, and seafood that will make you start pricing property in Homer for your retirement. Good idea to have reservations. ☎ 235-8723.

Young's Oriental Restaurant, 565 Pioneer Ave., has all-you-can-eat buffets, $6.50 for lunch, $9 for dinner.

The **Salty Dawg** was named one of the best bars in America by *Men's Journal* magazine. Yeah, maybe they were having a slow day in the editorial office, but the place does have atmosphere.

Finally, if you've got some spare cash and want a night out you won't soon forget, head to the **Saltry** in Halibut Cove (☎ 296-2223). You have to figure round-trip water-taxi fare into the price of the meal, but even with that, it's a deal. The place serves incredible seafood, caught fresh and prepared with an expert touch. With transportation, figure on at least $80 for a couple. This is a great place to eat.

If you're heading out to more remote areas, remember that Homer is the last town to shop in. Several grocery stores are convenient to downtown.

■ Accommodations

 If you're determined to sleep in a hotel in Homer, call well ahead. In summer they are booked up. There are some good choices, though. The **Ocean Shores Motel** (☎ 235-7775) has a nice décor, water views from all rooms, and is newly renovated. Rates start at $105 for a double.

Land's End (☎ 235-2500) is at the end of the Spit. Doubles start at $99; if you want a view, figure around $140.

The **Heritage Hotel** (☎ 235-7787), 142 E. Pioneer, has doubles with a shared bath from $80; private bath from $90. It's clean, but it can get noisy with the bar. It has a great log cabin décor, though.

The **Beluga Lake Lodge** (☎ 235-6144), 984 Ocean Dr., is basic but fine, with doubles from $90. The **Pioneer Inn** (☎ 235-5670), 244 Pioneer Ave., has pleasant rooms from $70.

A quick look at the Visitor Center, and you'll think the entire economy of the town is supported by B&Bs. There are more of them here than you can even imagine. Talk to the **B&B Network** (☎ 800-764-3211); or **Central Charters** (☎ 235-7847 or 800-478-7847); **The Bookie** (☎ 235-1581 or 888-335-1581); and **Homer Alaska Referral** (☎ 235-8996), and let them do the work of finding one for you. There's also **Cabins and Cottages** (☎ 235-0191), which has nearly 20 properties around town where you can rent out cabins complete with kitchens and amenities. Whatever you're looking for, somebody is going to have it.

We'll just list a couple of the more interesting options here. **Katchemak Bay Lynx**, 6½ miles out East End (☎ 800-295-LYNX) has rooms and golfing with the occasional moose hazard. Doubles from $86.

Honey's Place is actually on the Spit, so you've got great views of all the comings and goings in town. What you're getting for your $150 a night is a two-bedroom beach house, so it's a good deal for small groups. ☎ 235-279-5055. **Homer Floatplane Lodge and Cabins** is on Beluga Lake, where the Spit meets the town. You get a small cabin and can watch the float planes come and go. ☎ 235-4160 or 877-235-9600.

Some of the best places to stay are not even in the town. Over across the bay there are quite a few cabins you can rent out for a night or a week. **Porter's Alaskan Adventures** (☎ 776-3626) has cabins on Hesketh Island in the bay. Rates start at $125, plus the trip out by water taxi. You can also check with the **Jakolof Ferry office** on the Spit; they book a wide assortment of cabins, with prices starting from $65 for a bare bones, bring-your-own-bedding deal, to considerably more for cabins nicer than your house back home.

There are two hostels in town. The **International Backpackers Hostel/Inn** is at 304 Pioneer Ave., ☎ 235-1463. It's $18 per night, and there's no curfew. **Seaside Farm Hostel** is five miles out East End Road. A room in the bunkhouse is $15; a private room is only $40. ☎ 235-7850.

■ Camping

 Camping on the Spit is bleak, windy, and barren, and you'll be surrounded by fishermen who haven't bathed in weeks. It's not as bad as it once was, though; since the cannery burned down, the number of permanent residents has decreased, and with them went much of the wildness.

There are a couple of private campgrounds on the Spit, and the one run by the city. Spots are only $7, and you're right in the center of the action. Much nicer than anything on the Spit is the **city campground**, above the ballfield off Bartlett and Fairview Ave. It has 33 nice sites, water, restrooms, lots of trees and privacy, and some good views of the bay. Sites run $6 per night for tents; $10 for RVs.

The **Driftwood Inn RV Park** is right above the beach, so you get great views, and you're within walking distance of town. Full hookups are available. ☎ 235-8019.

If all the camping is full, drive back up to **Anchor Point**, where there are several campgrounds.

Seldovia

O nly 13 miles from Homer, Seldovia seems a world apart. Once a bustling seaport, modern Seldovia is now a sleepy town of around 400 permanent residents living in a lovely setting under high mountains and ice-capped peaks. Enjoy it while you can. There are some really frightening development plans afoot, and just over the past five or six years, the growth in day-trippers coming to town from Homer has been exponential.

■ History

The name "Seldovia" dates back to the Russians. It comes from the Russian word *seldovoi*, or herring. An 1898 description of Saldovia [sic] and its people reads, "a village of 100 or more Kodiak natives and a few whites and Russian creoles [who] live by hunting and fishing." The town's fortune was made first on furs, then on shipping, and it was the major stopping point for ships headed to or from Anchorage. The entire Kenai Peninsula did most of its business through Seldovia – in the early 1900s, the town was bigger than Homer. The proximity of the first coal mine strike in Alaska didn't hurt the town either – the entire area in and around town has lignite coal beds running under it.

The '64 earthquake dropped the waterfront here by four feet, which caused the tides to wipe out much of the town's frontage. Further disaster struck with the completion of the highway to Homer, where business and prosperity quickly relocated. But the glory years of Seldovia have left it looking good – it's among the most scenic of Southcentral Alaska's villages, with friendly people. A good place for an escape.

■ Basics

 The **Alaska Marine Highway** is the cheapest way to reach Seldovia. The 13-mile run takes an hour and offers wonderful views of Kachemak Bay. The ship is docked long enough so you can see the entire town. Going back to Homer, the views of the cone-shaped Mt. Ilaimna, 10,017 feet, are spectacular. Contact the AMH Homer office, ☎ 235-8449.

AUTHOR TIP *Several Homer tour operators run trips to Seldovia, but the ferry is cheaper. Check with one of the trip booking offices in Homer – this run is their bread and butter now. A day-trip will run about $45.*

Flights into Seldovia can be chartered with **Homer Air**, ☎ 235-8591.

Seldovia is plenty small to walk, but, if you need a taxi, use **Seldovia Taxi**, ☎ 234-7859.

Rent a **bike** from the **Buzz Coffee House**, ☎ 234-7479.

Rent kayaks from **Kayak' Atak**, ☎ 234-7425. There are some good paddles – a lot of otters hang out around Yukon Island, and there's a cool natural arch on the far side that you can try to shoot your boat through – but remember that tides in Kachemak Bay can be very mean, and very fast. Know what you're doing.

The **Chamber of Commerce**, ☎ 234-7479, runs a small information drop inside Synergy Artworks (turn right from the ferry).

> Pick up the *Seldovia Otterbahn Trail Map* for details of a good hike through the center of town. Their city map points out longer hikes into the mountains.

■ Museums & Attractions

Seldovia's main attraction is the town itself. And there isn't much here in the way of excitement, just a bit of local history in the church.

RUSSIAN ORTHODOX CHURCH: The Russian church (turn right from the ferry), St. Nicholas, sits on a hill that offers views of the whole town. It was built in 1891. Unlike most Russian Orthodox churches, this one has no onion domes; it looks almost like a New England Protestant church. There is also a Russian cemetery in town. Go up the driveway of the Crow Hill B&B; it's to the left, and it's open most afternoons.

ALASKA TRIBAL CACHE: On Main. It has a small assortment of Native and Russian artifacts. So does the **Seldovia Historical Museum**, on Anderson Way. These are worthwhile if you're hard up, but the scenery around town is a lot more interesting.

BOARDWALK: The boardwalk, once the site of all Seldovia's action, can be reached by walking around the point to the right of the ferry terminal. There's not much there today, but Seldovia Slough is a good place for bird watching.

■ Adventures

The bushes in and around town are prime berry-picking areas: blueberries and salmonberries are all over, as well as some raspberries, cloudberries, and highbush cranberries. Just keep in mind that much of the land around you is private. Check in at the **Seldovia Village Tribe** building and see if you need permission first (generally, this is no hassle). One of the favorite spots is Blueberry Hill, right by the slough. Or you can just buy a jar of wild berry jam from one of the gift shops.

Hiking

There's nothing in town to compare to the trails back on the Kenai, but if you've got time to kill, there are some nice walks. The **Otterbahn** is a mile and a half long. Pick it up behind the high school, and it will lead you along the slough. Go at low tide. There's also the **Seldovia Outdoor Museum**, an easy walk that stops at a dozen points of local history. You can pick up a map at the Chamber of Commerce or at the Historical Museum.

For something more challenging, head down **Jakolof Bay Rd**. The beach hike is great – but as with hiking any Kenai beach, know the tides, or you're screwed. If you walk out toward **Seldovia Bay**, you can link up with logging roads that can take you even farther into the backcountry.

■ Food

Eating can be difficult, unless you fend for yourself at the grocery store. The **Mad Fish Restaurant** is the fancy place in town – you're going to need reservations (☎ 234-7676), since a lot of people come over here from Homer for the seafood specialties and the wine list. It's on Main, at Fulmore. Your other two real options are right by each other. For basic barbecue and Oriental food, try **Pumi's Seldovia Barbecue**; have your breakfast at the **Buzz Coffee House**, which is on Main, in front of the barbecue place. Good soups, too.

■ Accommodations

Most people only come to Seldovia for a day-trip. There are plenty of places to stay, though, and if you want to spend the night, you shouldn't have any trouble getting a room.

The **Seldovia Boardwalk Hotel** is right on the waterfront; doubles start at $88. They'll also arrange package tours of the area. ☎ 234-7816 or 800-238-7862. They've got a $129 bargain that includes the boat ride over from Homer, and a glacier fly-by on the plane ride back. Hard to beat the deal.

Dancing Eagles B&B is down by the old boardwalk. Doubles from $85, or $55 per person. ☎ 234-7627.

The **Seldovia Rowing Club**, ☎ 234-7614, is nearby, and offers a huge gourmet breakfast with a lovely view of the harbor; double rooms from $90. **Gerry's Place** is on Fulmar, a block from the harbor. ☎ 234-7471.

■ Camping

Tent and RV camping is available at **Wilderness Park**; tents only at **Outside Beach**. Both areas are north of town, a 10-minute walk from the ferry terminal. ☎ 234-7643. RV spots are $8; tents, $5.

If you take Anderson Way past Wilderness Park, you'll get to Jakolof Bay. If you head out the road from the Jakolof Ferry dock, you'll hit **Across the Bay Tent and Breakfast Adventure**. Stay in one of the tent-cabins (from $48, or $75 with meals included), or arrange for a kayaking trip or a bike rental. ☎ 235-3633. You're a ways out of town, but that can be a good thing.

Kodiak

Kodiak. The word is synonymous with the largest land predator in the Americas, the biggest carnivore since the last ice age: the Kodiak bear. Kodiak, the city, sits on a tip of Kodiak, the island, a fortress surrounded by 1,500-pound bears. You won't see the bears anywhere near the city; you probably won't even see them anywhere on the road system. But they're out there. And that's a big part of the charm. The atavistic thrill of knowing there's still something that could eat you whole. It's what the first men must have felt when they climbed out of the trees. We're talking bears with claws as big as serving platters here.

Technically speaking, Kodiak is closer to the Aleutians, both geographically and culturally, than it is to the rest of Southcentral Alaska. But politically, it's closer to Southcentral; still, since it's so far from anywhere, Kodiak has always existed much in a world of its own.

The island, dubbed "The Emerald Isle," is incredibly lush and green – though this is mostly low shrubs and bushes, as opposed to the rainforests of Southeast and the thick forests of Kenai. You run out of superlatives pretty fast when you're talking about Alaska's scenery, but Kodiak Island has a beauty that is different from every other stop along the ferry route. With rolling hills covered in a hundred shades of green, ending dramatically in rocky cliffs, you could easily think you'd somehow ended up in Ireland by mistake.

■ History

 The city of Kodiak has a long and checkered history. The island was known to Native populations as one of the prime hunting and fishing spots in all of Southcentral Alaska.

 DID YOU KNOW? *The Alutiiq people have occupied Kodiak Island for more than 7,000 years, and archeologists have found evidence of many village sites around the islands.*

It's estimated that the Kodiak archipelago supported as many as 20,000 people before the Russians arrived; however, the native population plummeted after the Russians moved in.

According to G.L. Davydov, who made a trip through the islands around Kodiak in 1802-1807, perhaps the best account we have of a by-then doomed culture, the native people were healthy, although there weren't many old men. "They have round, flat and long faces, but in both sexes there are few of attractive appearance... the women pierce their nostrils through at the bottom and wear there bones, beads, or coral." Like any good European, Davydov wasn't that thrilled at local decorative habits, and he goes on to relate, in great, shocked detail, that they also pierced their lower lips and "sew themselves beards" by rubbing a thread in soot and sewing a design into their chins.

Back on track, Davydov goes on to describe the local bird skin parkas, infinitely more practical than anything the Russians had, and how animal intestines were used for making waterproof clothing.

While he was a typical colonialist, sure he was dealing with subhumans, Davydov did recognize some of the Koniags' strengths. "They travel about the sea with such self-assurance that they might as well be on dry land," he wrote, considering that the Koniags had developed their senses to "a point of perfection unknown to Europeans."

Davydov came in when the fun was pretty much over. The Russian history of Kodiak began when they first discovered the island in 1673. They called the island *Kykhtakh*, their version of the native name (the word just means "large island"), but despite a string of expeditions, all of which reported on the incredibly rich possibilities of the fur trade, they did not settle into the area until 1784, at Three Saints Bay. In 1792, the settlement was moved by Alexander Baranov to the location of modern Kodiak, where a trading post was established. For 20 years, the town thrived as the Russian capital of the Alaska territory and the center of one of the richest hunting grounds in the world. It seemed as if you could walk across the ocean on the backs of the sea otters, there were so many. While the Russians were going great guns, kidnapping native women and children and holding them ransom until their male relatives brought in otter pelts and other prizes, the native population was dying out through disease and starvation due to the loss of hunting grounds.

It took the Russians fewer than 20 years to so deplete the animal population of the Kodiak archipelago that hunting was pointless and starvation imminent. They then packed up and moved to Sitka, leaving the native population behind to cope as best they could. By the mid-1830s, there were fewer than 7,000 natives on Kodiak and the surrounding smaller islands (Afognak, Tugidak, Sitkhinak, and others).

Say what you want about the Russians, they knew how to pillage and how to have a good time once they had defeated and demoralized local populations. An incredible amount of wealth was taken out of the islands in an alarmingly short time, leaving behind little but a devastated landscape and tales of Russian soldiers testing their guns by lining up natives and seeing how many they could kill with a single shot.

Without the lure of the fur trade, and without the Russians bringing in supplies to keep the tiny population alive, Kodiak languished, and it took more than a century to recover. In 1897, 30 years after the U.S. purchase of Alaska, the town had 317 residents.

To spur some activity, a sawmill was built around the turn of the century; however, there were too few trees here to make this a feasible venture. Kodiak is an island of brush and shrubs, not good milling trees like the rest of the coast. Fishing is what brought the town back to life. Between 1880 and 1890, 10 canneries opened.

The town had a major setback on June 6, 1912, when **Novarupta Volcano** erupted; Mt. Katmai, the defining feature of the area, actually collapsed into the volcano. Earthquakes preceding the eruption were felt 130 miles away and towns a hundred miles away were buried under ash. The sound of the eruption, one of largest ever, was heard more than 750 miles away and the eruption is responsible for the topography of the entire Katmai National Park area. For two days after the eruption the people in Kodiak could not see an object held at arm's length, there was so much ash in the air. The Ukak River valley was buried under more than 700 feet of ash, just a fraction of the seven cubic miles of debris spit up by the volcano. The ash was still in the air a year later, and the earth was covered with ash dunes. The bears had even gone temporarily bald, after the lye in the ash ate away their fur.

The lush landscape of Kodiak was turned into a sand dune; but that, in turn, helped fuel the lush brush as it grew back. By 1960, the town had fully recovered, and a new boom started. Kodiak was calling itself "King Crab Capital of the World," with a crab fishery whose output peaked at 90 million pounds in 1966.

But the recovery of the land portion of Kodiak's economy faced another setback on March 27, 1964 when the **Good Friday earthquake** that rocked Southcentral Alaska triggered a series of tsunamis that destroyed most of Kodiak's waterfront and central business district and heavily damaged area villages. The largest wave crested at 35 feet above low tide – residents evacuated up Pillar Mountain. According to Kodiak's local paper, the town has never quite recovered from the earthquake. Thirty years later, they're still blaming the quake for the fact that, physically, Kodiak is an incredibly ugly city. Post-quake Kodiak rebuilt quickly, without much thought. There were too many fish out there to pay attention to the town itself. From the 1960s into the 1980s, the fishing industry grew and grew, while the town itself got uglier and uglier. In the 1980s, Kodiak was the busiest fishing port in the U.S., in terms of dollar value. The town made a fortune on salmon and king crab. A huge shrimp fishery opened and it looked as if the money would never stop flowing.

But Kodiak failed to learn from its own history. Just as the Russians hunted themselves right off the island, Kodiak fished itself into a depression. The catches dried up and switching to new species quickly did more damage to the ocean harvest. The most recent switch has been to bottomfish. It's worth noting that Dutch Harbor has replaced Kodiak as the richest fishing port in the world over the past few years. Kodiak remains more than busy, but there's a sense that the end may be near.

■ Kodiak Today

There was a new boomtown impetus with the *Exxon Valdez* oil spill. The beaches north of Kodiak were heavily damaged. Sensing opportunity, the town raised prices sky high and tried to suck everyone dry before the oil dried up. Even now, things haven't yet settled back down to normal and Kodiak still seems to expect someone to come in and rescue the town from its splurge of self-destruction. The town expects tourists to help, without bothering to treat travelers the way most Alaskan communities do.

Southcentral

The Coast Guard Station keeps the town afloat for now, and there is talk of developing more tourist attractions, but Kodiak can be adequately seen in an afternoon. The best thing to do is get out of town to where the bears are.

▪ Basics

 The **Alaska Marine Highway** serves Kodiak between four and six times a week, connecting it to Homer and the Aleutian chain. The M.V. *Tustemena* leaves from the dock right at the edge of downtown. The ride into Kodiak is a beautiful one: towering cliffs coated with thick green brush. It looks more like Ireland than Alaska, until you notice the fin whales and puffins. Local phone number for the AMH is ☎ 486-3800.

The island is also served by **Alaska Airlines** through their subcontractor ERA, ☎ 486-4363 or 800-426-0333. Charter operators include **Island Air**, ☎ 486-6196; **Kodiak Air**, ☎ 486-4446; **Seahawk Air**, ☎ 486-8282; **Wilderness Air**, ☎ 486-8101; and **Uyak Air**, ☎ 486-3407. All five of these operators also offer bear-watching trips and they guarantee you'll see a bear.

AUTHOR TIP

 Because of Kodiak's weather – it can turn on a dime and always changes for the worse – flying can be a bit tenuous at times. Always allow for delays.

Rental cars are available at the airport through **Budget**, ☎ 486-2220, and **Rent a Heap**, ☎ 486-5200.

MONEY SAVER: *If you're going to need a round-trip taxi to the airport from town, it's almost cheaper to rent a car. Kodiak's taxi services think the oil spill people are still in town.*

From town to the airport, less than five miles, a taxi runs $14 and up. For the Airport Shuttle, it costs $5 dollars per person from the ferry terminal or selected hotels to the airport. ☎ 486-7583.

Rent a kayak from **Mythos Expeditions**, ☎ 486-5536.

Kodiak's Visitor Center is in the ferry terminal, part of the Chamber of Commerce office. Lots of brochures, open from 8 AM to 5 PM. ☎ 486-4782. On line at www.kodiak.org.

Internet access is at the **library**, 319 Lower Mill Rd., or at the **Treasury**, 104 Center Ave.

Kodiak's zip code is **99615**.

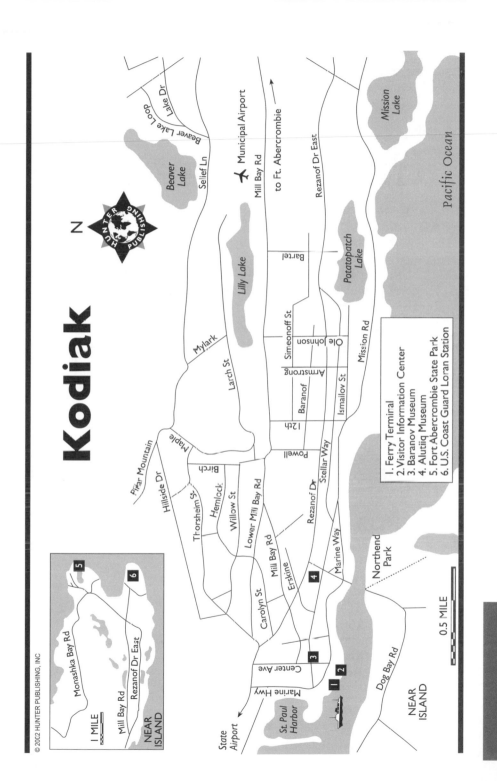

Kodiak

N

Beaver Lake Dr

Beaver Lake Loop

Selief Ln

Beaver Lake

Municipal Airport

Mill Bay Rd

to Ft. Abercrombie

Rezanof Dr East

Mission Lake

Pacific Ocean

Lilly Lake

Bartel

Mylark

Larch St

Simeonoff St

Ole Johnson

Armstrong

Baranof

Ismailov St

Mission Rd

Potatopatch Lake

Pitar Mountain

Maple

Birch

Hillside Dr

Trorsheim St

Hemlock

Willow St

Lower Mill Bay Rd

Mill Bay Rd

Erskine

Rezanof Dr

Stellar Way

Powell

12th

Marine Way

Northend Park

1. Ferry Terminal
2. Visitor Information Center
3. Baranov Museum
4. Alutiiq Museum
5. Fort Abercrombie State Park
6. U.S. Coast Guard Loran Station

Carolyn St

Center Ave

Marine Hwy

State Airport

St. Paul Harbor

Dog Bay Rd

NEAR ISLAND

0.5 MILE

© 2002 HUNTER PUBLISHING, INC

Monashka Bay Rd

Mill Bay Rd

Rezanof Dr East

1 MILE

NEAR ISLAND

5

6

3

2

1

4

KODIAK AT A GLANCE

QUICK TOUR: Kodiak has great Russian stuff. Hit the Baranov Museum and the cathedral right next door.

DON'T MISS/BEST FREEBIE: Bears. Why else would you come here?

▪ Museums & Attractions

i **BARANOV MUSEUM:** The house is the oldest one of only four structures to survive completely unscathed from Russian times. It was built in 1808 by Baranov, originally as an otter pelt warehouse, and has served over the years as residence, store, and warehouse. When the Russians moved out, the building was taken over by the Alaska Commercial Company. It's located directly across from the ferry office in Erskin House, at 101 Marine Way.

The museum houses a good assortment of Russian colonial artifacts and native prehistoric items. It's interesting to see how the natives made everything they needed from the land around them, while the Russians brought in samovars, elaborately painted icons, gold coins, trade beads, and more, making Kodiak, for the short glory days, as close a copy of St. Petersburg as possible. The museum also has some mementos of Alaska's territorial days, as well as WW II memorabilia. There is a nice museum shop here – Kodiak is the prime place to buy the rare deep blue trading beads. In the yard outside the house are some whale rib bones. They provide a good chance to see how big these animals really are. The museum is open 10-4 weekdays, noon to 4 weekends in summer. Admission $2. ☎ 486-5920.

HOLY RESURRECTION RUSSIAN ORTHODOX CHURCH: The museum's yard slants uphill slightly, rising toward the blue onion domes of the still-active Holy Resurrection Russian Orthodox Church. Perhaps the most lasting legacy of the Russian era is the Russian Orthodox religion. The church is a prominent fixture in downtown Kodiak. It houses the reliquary of St. Herman, who was canonized at the church in 1970. Nearby are St. Herman's Theological Seminary, the Veniaminov Museum, and a log chapel commemorating the bicentennial of the Orthodox Church of America, in 1994.

The current building dates to 1943, but the first church on the site was built in 1869 with classic Russian lines. A small cemetery sits behind the church. Inside the chapel are the ever-important icons. If the interior is not open, you can call the priest at ☎ 486-3854 to see about arranging a tour.

ALUTIIQ MUSEUM: This museum, at 215 Mission Road, is open 9-5 daily. The $2 admission gets you in to see a nice collection of Aleut artifacts. It's especially worthwhile for the masks. ☎ 486-7004. This is your best chance to see what the world of Alaska was like before the Russians came in like the comet that took out the dinosaurs.

KODIAK TRIBAL COUNCIL: In summer, there are Native dances held here daily at 3:30, near the high school. Admission is $15, and it's a good deal – and probably your only chance to see Aleut dances. ☎ 486-4449.

FORT ABERCROMBIE HISTORICAL PARK: There's history of a different kind at Fort Abercrombie Historical Park. Fort Abercrombie was one of the larger U.S. installations in Alaska during the Second World War. In 1938, Congress appropriated $350 million to build defenses in Kodiak, Sitka, and Dutch Harbor. Dutch Harbor and Sitka's defenses are in ruin; Fort Abercrombie is a remarkable memorial to a bad time. Four miles west of town, out Rezanof Drive.

In 1941, 780 acres of land were set aside for defending Kodiak and the Gulf of Alaska. Named Fort Abercrombie in 1942, the site got two eight-inch guns soon after Pearl Harbor. The guns, originally designed as battleship weapons, weighed 103,000 pounds each and had to be rotated regularly to keep them from sinking in their own tracks.

Although the fort saw no action – actually, the war was over before planned construction was anywhere near complete – big things were in mind. The main mess hall could handle 170 people at a time; quonset huts dotted the landscape. There are bunkers carved into the hillsides and the ammo reserve included three rooms each 15′ x 30′, holding enough ordnance to blow up the island.

Most of the structures have been swallowed up by the surrounding woods now, but you can pick up a walking tour map at the office that points out the highlights. It's worth going to the park for the view from the gun emplacements: the cliffs drop steeply down, with seabirds the only threat. Fort Abercrombie also has the nicest campground in Kodiak.

KODIAK NATIONAL WILDLIFE REFUGE: The bulk of Kodiak Island is part of this refuge. The visitor center for the refuge is at 1390 Buskin River Road, near the airport. Open 8 AM to 4:30 PM weekdays, noon to 4:30 on weekends, the center has good displays of the area's topography and wildlife. They can also book you into one of their eight cabins in the refuge, as well as point out what parts of the island are private land and should be avoided. ☎ 487-2600.

The most popular of the cabins is at O'Malley River. You'll need to book this one as far in advance as possible. When there, take all bear precautions. In late summer the bears are thick on the ground here, gorging on salmon headed up the O'Malley. Drawings for the cabins in the refuge take place on January 2 for April through June dates, and April 1 for July through September reservations. In winter, when access is more difficult and there few bears or tourists, a reservation drawing is held July 1 for October through December, and October 1 for January through March. Applications must be mailed ibefore the date of drawing. On the application, include your first and second choices of dates for a cabin.

ANNUAL EVENTS: Kodiak hosts a **golf tournament** every year on Pillar Mountain: one hole, par 70. Chainsaws not allowed, but you can use hacksaws to clear the brush around your ball. The tournament is held toward the end of March; check with the visitor center for dates. May brings the **Crab Festival**, while around the fourth of July you can enjoy the **Kodiak Heritage Festival**. One of the more unusual local events in Kodiak is the **pilgrimage to St. Herman's Monks Lagoon**. It celebrates the canonization of Father Herman by the Russian Orthodox Church with a trip out to his home site on Spruce Island. Contact the local church at ☎ 486-3524 for more information.

■ Scenic Drives

If you've got a car, there are plenty of pretty drives on Kodiak Island. Be aware, though, that it's very rare to see a bear on the road. For bear-viewing, you'll need to move farther afield. If you can't get a cabin or book one of the charters listed below, check the Kodiak visitor's guide for some last-ditch suggestions.

The north end of Kodiak's road network has a beach, lovely cliff views, and some gentle hills for hiking. To the south, the terrain is a little wilder, getting into progressively more muskeg, marsh, and steeper landscape. The road travels along the ridge of a steep cliff, which drops down into sentinel rocks and the ocean. Thirty miles south of town is the turn to Pasagshak Bay; at the end of that road is a huge fossil field where collecting is permitted. The roads out of town are dirt, but are in quite good shape and should present no problems for any car. For a short drive, head up Pillar Mountain: good views of St. Paul Harbor and the entire Kodiak area. All the drives give you a chance to get out into the incredibly dense green of the island. Wildflowers bloom in profusion in June and July, and there's good berry picking in the late summer.

■ Adventures

Hiking

Kodiak Island is thickly brushed, incredibly beautiful, and chock full of bears that you won't see until long after they've seen you. Be sure to take all bear precautions.

There's a quick, easy hike up **Pillar Mountain**, right behind town – a chance for good views, if there's clear sky the days you're there. Pick up the trail at the Tie Substation, out Chiniak Road; figure it's going to take the day to get up and back down. There's also an easier trail, which you can pick up by the TV satellite dish, that heads out along **Monashka Bay Road**, where you can also pick up the **Termination Point Trail**, a nice hike through the forest. The main trail is about five miles, and there are some branches you can take, if you feel like staying out longer..

The **Barometer Mountain Trail** is five miles long, and quite challenging, as you're heading straight up the mountain. You peak out at just under 2,500 feet. Pick up the trail by the Buskin River Campground, right past the airport runway. Killer views. Take plenty of water.

Charters

Kodiak has only a fraction of the charter outfits that Homer does. Prices here are usually a little higher – expect roughly $200 per person for a full-day charter. The scenery is lovely and there's great fishing. Many of the charter operators also work hunting trips; check when you call. Kodiak probably draws as many sport hunters as it does fishermen. Elk, deer and, of course, bear are the prizes. Check with Alaska State Fish and Game for hunting rules and regulations. You'll need to plan well in advance to get a tag. The easiest way to get hold of a charter operator is to go through the central service. The **Kodiak Charter Boat Association**, ☎ 486-6363, or 888-972-6363, is your best bet. Call them up, tell them what you want to do, let them hook you up with the right people. In summer, they also run an info desk inside the Kodiak Inn.

McNeil River & The Really Big Bears

To see the bears, you've got to get away from the city, because the grand irony is that, although the biggest bears in the world are on Kodiak Island, the island itself is not good for bear-watching. That means you're going to have to head out, and there are three quick ways: the Alaska Marine Highway to Port Lions, a flight to McNeil (check with the local charter companies), or you can hook up with one of the lodges that operates in the remote corners of the island. Accommodations range from rustic to deluxe. The lodges can take you fishing, but the reason to come here is bears – you can fish anywhere. These places keep in business on the strength of their bear-spotting skills.

McNeil is the bear locale of choice. Located on the Alaskan Peninsula, across Shelikof Strait from Kodiak, just north of Katmai, it's where all the incredible bear documentaries you see on PBS are filmed. The salmon have to jump the falls; the bears know that, know that the falls create a salmon jam, and they come running like it's an all-you-can-eat buffet – because for them it is.

The sheer number of bears that come to McNeil to take advantage of the salmon run has required that the Forest Service put regulations on visiting humans to keep interspecies interactions from getting dodgy. A permit system and user fees are now required at the McNeil River State Game Sanctuary by the Alaska Department of Fish & Game. This provides the public an opportunity to view and photograph bears, maintaining a concentration of undisturbed animals. Only 10 people a day are allowed in to see the bears, from June thrugh August. You get to stay for up to four days, and you remain under the supervision of park guides who are really keen to ensure that you're not eaten on their watch. From the camp, it's a two-mile hike to the viewing area; expect to see bears anywhere along the trail.

You've got to file an application by March 1 with Alaska Department of Fish and Game, Division of Wildlife Conservation, 333 Raspberry St. Anchorage, AK 99518-1599, ☎ 267-2180, or you can print a copy of the permit from their website: www.state.ak.us/adfg/adfghome.htm.

AUTHOR TIP

Request the application early: it has to be returned with a $5 processing fee by May 1. They then hold a lottery to determine who gets out to see the bears. Only 10 people a day are taken out to the falls. It's often possible to go standby, though, since not everyone shows up. Check at the office in Kodiak or Homer to see what the chances are.

King Salmon & Katmai

Since your odds of getting drawn for a spot at McNeil are fairly small, you'll need to have a backup plan in place. A more secure way of getting out to see some serious bears is to book one of Kodiak's charter fliers to **King Salmon**. Located on the edge of **Katmai National Park**, a volcanic area that makes Yellowstone Park look like a sputtering stove top, King Salmon's entire economy is based on getting people out to the bears. There isn't the density of bears here that McNeil enjoys, but the scenery can't be matched.

King Salmon is the gateway to Katmai National Park. There's a dirt road from King Salmon to Lake Camp, at the park's edge. After that, you're in a wilderness area, with only one other road for a couple of hundred square miles. It isn't the bears that set Katmai apart, though. It was here, in 1912, that **Novarupta Volcano** absolutely blew its stack – violently enough to make Mt. St. Helens look like a hiccup – forming the ash-filled "Valley of Ten Thousand Smokes," where steam rose from countless fumaroles. When the mountain blew, smoke and ash rose miles into the air, spreading out to cover an area larger than the state of Connecticut. It was totally dark in the daytime for a hundred miles from the volcano. A man named Ivan Orloff was nearby, fishing. He later wrote to his wife, "We are covered with ashes, in some places 10 feet and six feet deep.... It is terrible, and we are expecting death at any moment.... Here are darkness and hell, thunder and noise. The earth is trembling."

By the end of the eruption, more than 10,000 holes had been blown into the floor of the valley. All vegetation had been burned off over an estimated area of 53 square miles. An exploration team that went into the valley in 1915 found nothing to burn for fuel – plant life had not yet come back – and so they cooked their food in volcanic vents. How long for a moose steak at 1,200°?

Today only a few active vents remain, but they make for dramatic viewing. If volcanoes and destruction aren't enough for you, as an extra bonus, the park contains part of the **Alagnak Wild River**. The area was proclaimed as Katmai National Monument on Sept. 24, 1918; it was finally established as a national park and preserve on Dec. 2, 1980. Today, about 55,000 people a year come to the park to see the bears and the wreck of a landscape that can be brought about when nature decides to go bonkers.

In King Salmon, there's a **visitor center** next to the airport. The staff there will provide information on which operators can take you deeper into the park. You can also get bear-proof food containers from them, an absolute must if you're going to be hiking or spending the night in the bush.

In Katmai, the premier spots are **Brooks Camp** and **Brooks Lodge**, both right on the Brooks River, a kind of disco for bears. For either place, you're going to need reservations well in advance. Book through **Katmailand**, ☎ 800-544-0551 outside Alaska, or 800-478-5448 inside the state. Katmailand also has a store where you can pick up some very pricey supplies. You can get meals at Brooks Lodge, whether you're staying there or not.

There is one road going through Katmai, and you can pick up a day tour along its route from Brooks Camp. The road weaves 23 miles around through the volcanic area, and you end up on a nice hike up to Ukak Falls. Call Katmailand for reservations.

The Brooks Camp visitor center is open in the summer months. Go there for the "Brooks Camp Bear Etiquete School," to learn how to behave around bears. You can also pick up bear-proof containers here.

Seeing the Bears

Once you know what to do, it's time to go see the bears, and you'll find them on the Brooks River. There are two viewing platforms over the river; the lower platform is handicapped-accessible, although the Park Service warns that close encounters with bears are common, and you may have to be able to move "briskly" to get out of the bears' way.

 There are a lot of bears out here and, before you come, read pages 42-47 on how to act around bears. They're bigger than you. They have claws bigger than your face. They're not impressed by tourists wearing little bells to warn bears away. Don't mess with them.

As at McNeil, or Anan, or Pack Creek, the bears all come here for the salmon jamboree. The fish get slowed down in the river, get packed tight, and make for easy pickings. The bears are like little kids after a particularly successful Halloween night of trick or treating, with so much candy it gives you a stomachache to think about it.

You'll see a lot of fish parts about, bits the bears didn't want. This is particularly true by the end of the summer, when the bears are stuffed and have become pretty picky, going only for the fattiest parts of the fish – skin, brains, roe.

If you're going to go into the backcountry away from the more traveled areas, get a backcountry permit from the Park Service. You don't have to, but it's a good idea to let people know where you're going. There are two maintained trails. **Dumpling Mountain**, which starts at Brooks Camp and then climbs a total of four miles to the peak; and **Ukak Falls**, which starts at the Three Forks Cabin, at the far end of the valley road. It's 700 feet up to a great overlook.

When you're out and about, remember that you can't legally get within 50 yards of a bear or 100 yards of a group of bears. The bears can, of course, approach you. If you are planning to bring in bear spray for protection, remember that it's not allowed on airplanes; if you've got any on the flight in, tell the pilot, and it'll be carried on the plane floats.

Bear viewing at Brooks Camp is best in July and September. There are few bears in August, though they still are seen occasionally. July and September are crowded; expect waits and time limits when going to the Brooks Falls platform in July. Weather and bears are always a factor at Katmai, so plan extra time to work around delays. Contact **Katmai National Park**, P.O. Box 7, King Salmon, 99613, ☎ 246-3305.

From town, the easiest way to get out to the bears is to fly. Any of the air charters will take you out on a half-day trip (four or five hours) to see the bears. However, it's going to cost – figure a bit over $400 per person. If this is your only reason for coming to Kodiak, you could get the same trip from Homer – plus you save on the extra city travel.

■ More Bear-Watching: Port Lions & Larsen Bay

 Without leaving Kodiak Island, Port Lions and Larsen Bay make good bear-watching bases. Neither town is particularly designed for visitors, but there are basic services and the bears run close to town. It's not unusual for kids in Larsen Bay to grow up completely fearless of bears: they're toys to them, just like big squirrels. Not a wise attitude for visitors to take.

AUTHOR TIP *Both Port Lions and Larsen Bay are surrounded by land owned by Native Corporations. Larsen Bay charges $50 per day for camping or fishing on the Karluk River. Ask before heading out.*

There are quite a few remote lodges on Kodiak Island. Prices vary dramatically, depending on the season, the activities you're interested in, and what the charter flight companies are charging. Contact them well in advance for rates and reservations. Most lodges concentrate on fishing and hunting, but bear-watching is always a possibility. Ask how much bear activity there has been in the area when you call. As with so many places in Alaska, lodges tend to go in and out of business fairly quickly; check at the visitors bureau for a complete list.

Some of the places that have been around for a long time include **Larsen Bay Lodge**, Box 54, Larsen Bay, 99624, ☎ 847-2238. They can take you hunting, fishing, or sightseeing. Bear-watching on the Karluk during the salmon run is only 45 minutes away and they guarantee you'll see one. **Munsey Bear Camp** is quite a ways from town – you're going to have to charter a plane out to it. However, once you're there, you've got incredible scenery, you're farther out in the boonies than maybe you've ever been before, and the fishing will give you lies to tell for the rest of your life. Five nights runs $3,200 for a couple, including all meals. ☎ 847-2203.

Another good option is **Kodiak Wilderness Lodge**, Box 1593 Kodiak, ☎ 486-4232. Private cabins, hunting, fishing, animal watching, and kayaking, from $250 and up per day.

The **Katmai Wilderness Lodge** guarantees that you'll see bears. They run a four-day/three-night package that starts around $2,000. ☎ 486-8767 or write Box 4332, Kodiak, 99615.

■ Food

 Don't expect much in the way of gourmet dining in Kodiak. This is a working town. **Henry's Great Alaskan**, right by the Small Boat Harbor, is one of your better bets. They do lunch specials, and you can also get seafood, burgers and a cup of java juice there. Also good to satisfy your caffeine and sugar cravings is **Beryl's**, 202 Center Ave, which has luscious desserts to go along with your latte, or you can pick up a light sandwich here. A popular place for locals is **Harborside Coffee**, 216 Shelikof, with more baked goodies.

El Chicano Mexican Restaurant, 104 Center Ave., has very good south-of-the-border fare for the Far North, and at a good price. **King's Diner**, in Lilly Lake Plaza on Mill Bay Road, is good, reasonable, and filling.

Two of the hotels, **Buskin River Inn**, by the airport, and the **Shelikof Lodge** downtown, both offer pricier but good surf & turf fare, especially at dinnertime.

For chain food, there's a **McDonalds** (intersection of Center & E Reznakof); a **KFC** (next to Safeway on Mill Bay Rd.); a **Burger King** (on Mill Bay Rd); a **Subway** (by the ferry terminal); and a **Pizza Hut**.

■ Accommodations

 The City of Kodiak has a 6% sales tax and a 5% bed tax, so be sure to add that in to your budget calculations. The **Buskin River Inn** is next to the airport at 1395 Airport Way, ☎ 800-544-2202 or 487-2700. Doubles run from $140. The **Shelikof Lodge**, 211 Thorsheim, ☎ 486-4141, has a restaurant and lounge. It's clean and comfortable, with a convenient downtown location. Doubles from $85. A good choice for Kodiak, they'll also get you to or from the airport.

The **Kodiak Inn**, at 236 Rezanof, ☎ 800-544-0970 or 486-5712, has doubles from $130.

There are quite a few B&Bs in town – many offer a better deal than the hotels, as the average room rate is $70-80 and includes breakfast, and often a ride to/from the airport (ask when you make your reservation). **Kodiak B&B**, 308 Cope St., ☎ 486-5367, is close to town, with doubles around $80. **Shahafka Cove**, 1812 Mission Rd., ☎ 486-2409, also has water views and they'll pick you up at the airport or ferry terminal. Rates start at $65.

Inlet Guest Rooms, 1315 Mill Bay Road, is a little ways from downtown, but there are nice rooms, starting at only $55. ☎ 486-4004. Basic, but comfortable. Much more upscale is **Captain's Quarters**. They're close to Ft. Abercrombie, so it's only a decent option if you've got a car. A nice suite runs $125 a night. ☎ 486-6444.

Bear & Bay is convenient to downtown, and they have some nicely thought-out extras. Double with a private bath is $95; shared bath, $75. ☎ 486-6154.

AUTHOR TIP *The Kodiak Chamber of Commerce website (www. kodiak.org) lists dozens of B&Bs if you're in a jam and need more options.*

■ Camping

For campers, **Fort Abercrombie** has some of the most beautiful campsites in coastal Alaska. There are drive-in spots and some very private tent-only walk-in sites for $10. The other choice for camping is at **Buskin River**, by the Kodiak National Wildlife Refuge office. It's not as scenic or protected, but is okay if you can't get into Abercrombie. $10. If you've got transportation, time, and want privacy, there's free **camping** at Mile 45 out toward Pasagshak Bay.

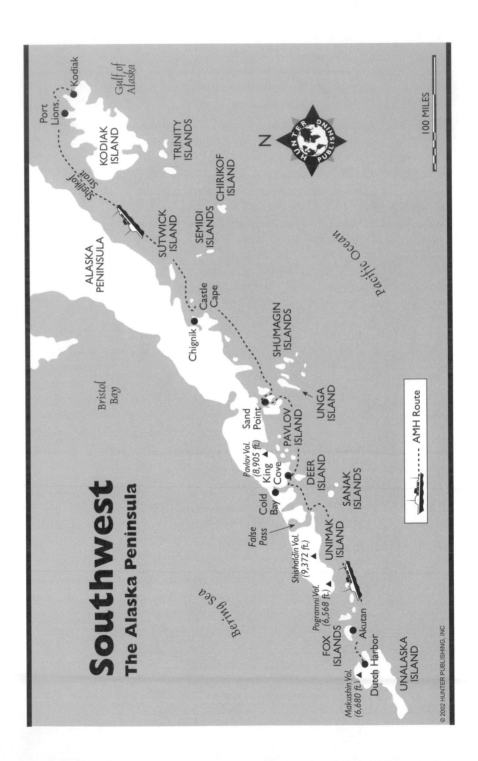

Southwest
The Alaska Peninsula

© 2002 HUNTER PUBLISHING, INC

Southwest

The Aleutians & the Alaska Peninsula

The M.V. *Tustumena* makes its bread-and-butter runs serving Homer, Kodiak, and Seward, but was designed for a trip it makes only seven or eight times a year: the run to Dutch Harbor, in the Aleutians.

Passengers who've come to the *Tusty* from the Southeast's fleet should look at a few of the ship's modifications – no life boats, just those life pods that look like they should be on *Star Trek*, the magnets holding doors open, the high steps to prevent water coming in, and the fact that everything, absolutely everything, is bolted down.

The weather in the Aleutians is considered to be the worst in the world by meteorologists. Fog, rain, wind. There's enough rough open water to turn the most experienced sailor green. If the *Tusty* gets two clear days on a five-day round-trip to Dutch Harbor and back, the crew feels divinely blessed. So is it worth the trip?

Absolutely.

The ship passes rafts of birds a mile long, half a mile wide. Most of the passengers on the *Tusty* (other than the locals headed home) are on the ship to birdwatch, and nobody goes home disappointed: puffins crashing back into waves because they've eaten so many fish that they're too heavy to take off, shearwaters, murres, kittiwakes, storm-petrels, almost the entire world population of emperor geese, and the ultimate prize, the whiskered auklet.

Not a birder? Fin whales 70 feet long, 1,200-pound Steller's sea lions, sea otters, harbor seals, and fur seals should keep you interested.

And if the wildlife isn't enough, the scenery when the clouds lift is astounding. Imagine the Rocky Mountains, but then turn each peak into a volcano – most of them active. The snow-capped and sometimes smoking ranges of volcanoes rise above sheer cliffs that drop into the water, or from rocky beaches that provide nesting habitat for the huge Aleutian bird colonies.

For the historian, the run is rich in World War II artifacts and memories. It's hard to walk around Dutch Harbor without tripping over a bunker and, when you get tired of the history of this century, just visit the Russian church, one of the finest in Alaska.

When you talk to the ferry crews in Alaska, almost every single crew member has stories to tell about the *Tusty*. The Aleutian run is a kind of prize on the AMH. Crews on the *Tusty* stay on board as long as six months at a time, instead of the week-on, week-off enjoyed by the crews of the other runs. But the *Tusty* is a serious ship and people line up to work on her. That makes her crew an eclectic and interesting bunch.

The run to Dutch Harbor happens only a few times a year. It's the jewel trip of the Alaska Marine Highway and five of the best days of traveling a person can have.

■ The Aleutians

The 279 islands that make up the 1,400-mile-long Aleutian chain are the tips of volcanoes, most of which were formed about 70 million years ago. However, the volcanoes are not quiet: 46 of them are active and 26 have blown their tops since the Russians first arrived in the islands. Volcanic activity 200 years ago created an entirely new island in the chain, Bogosloff.

VOLCANOES

Alaska contains over 100 volcanoes and volcanic fields that have been active within the last 1½ million years. Over 40 of these have been active within recorded history. Alaska's volcanoes make up about 80% of all active volcanoes in the United States and 8% of all active above-water volcanoes on earth. Most of them are located along the 1,550-mile-long Aleutian Arc, which extends westward to Kamchatka and forms the northern portion of the Pacific "rim of fire." Other volcanoes that have been active within the last few thousand years exist in southeastern Alaska and in the Wrangell Mountains. There are some smaller volcanoes, some active within the last 10,000 years, in interior Alaska and in western Alaska as far north as the Seward Peninsula, but the Aleutians are the place to go to watch mountains smoking.

Hardly a year goes by without a major eruption from a volcano in the Aleutian Arc. Those in the largely unpopulated western arc often go unremarked by all but volcanologists. The remote volcanoes are potentially hazardous, however – jet airplanes that enter eruption clouds often are severely damaged, and sometimes lose all engine power, albeit temporarily. There are nearly 50,000 large aircraft per year, and 10,000 people per day, in the skies over Aleutian volcanoes, mostly on the heavily traveled great-circle routes between Europe, North America, and Asia. Volcanoes in the eastern arc, especially those in the Alaska Peninsula, near Cook Inlet, can cause severe problems. The series of 1989-1990 eruptions from Mt. Redoubt was the second-most costly in the history of the United States, and had significant impact on the aviation and oil industries, as well as the people of the Kenai Peninsula. The three eruptions of Mt. Spurr's Crater Peak in 1992 deposited ash on Anchorage and surrounding communities, closing airports and making even ground transportation difficult, disrupting air traffic as far east as Cleveland, Ohio. The 1912 Katmai eruption, which formed the Valley of Ten Thousand Smokes on the Alaska Peninsula, was the largest 20th-century eruption on earth.

■ Geology

The Aleutians are not really a single chain of islands. They are actually a kind of super chain, made up of smaller groups: the Andreanof, Delarof, Fox, Four Mountain, Near Islands, Rat, Shumagin, and Sanak Islands. These rocky sub-chains are bordered by some of the deepest water on the planet. To the Pacific side, water depths commonly reach 25,000 feet; on the north side is the Bering Canyon, 249 miles long, 10,600 feet deep.

The Aleutian Islands and the Aleutian trench along which they lie are products of the Pacific plate to the south being gradually forced beneath the North American plate in the Bering Sea. Many earthquakes result as a consequence, including some of the largest that have ever been recorded.

Typically, great earthquakes of magnitude 8.0 or more occur on an average every 70 years within different segments of the arc. During each of these large earthquakes, the accumulated strain is released along a certain length of the arc system, generally on the order of a few hundred miles (the 1964 Prince William Sound earthquake of magnitude 8.4 released strain along a total distance of over 400 miles, from near Valdez to south of Kodiak Island).

One segment of the arc that is arousing the concern of seismologists is in the area of the Shumagin Islands, off the tip of the Alaska Peninsula. The last great earthquake known to have occurred there (according to Russian records) was in 1848. This nagging seismic silence along a 200-mile-long zone very probably portends a strong earthquake there in the foreseeable future.

According to seismologists working at universities inside and outside the state, a great earthquake (up to an 8.6 magnitude) is likely in the next 20 years. Scientists on a Columbia University team claim that there is a 16-90% chance for a great quake in the next 10 years, and a 30-99% likelihood that it will strike in the next 20 years. These figures are not predictions, but statistical probabilities based on the historical record, including accounts gathered by the Russians before they sold Alaska to the U.S. in 1867. Because the Aleutians are so sparsely populated, the primary hazard to population centers would probably be from tsunamis, or seismic sea waves that could be damaging as far away as Hawaii.

The islands themselves, churned by earthquakes, volcanoes, and climate, aren't exactly garden spots. There are no trees, only low brush (we know a boy who grew up in Dutch Harbor, moved to Ketchikan, and hated the place because it stank so much – what he was smelling was forest). Forget farming of any kind. Because of the inhospitable land, the natives turned toward the abundant sea for their livelihood. Historically, as many as 25,000 natives found a way to make a living here, fishing and hunting for marine mammals.

■ History

The first traces of material culture in the Aleutians date back about 8,000 years. It was not one single culture over the length of the island chain; several different language groups lived in the islands and each maintained its own traditions. For example, whales were hunted only in the eastern islands.

On the other hand, there were certain similarities. The languages were close enough to be mutually intelligible, and the material culture, developed by need, was largely similar. Baidarkas (kayaks) were the most important tool for the Aleut Indians, but they also had a complex array of bone and stone weaponry. Waterproof clothes were made of mammal gut, decorated with fur strips and embroidery. The best place to see examples of the Aleutian material culture – from dolls to fishhooks – is at Sheldon Jackson Museum in Sitka.

BIRDSKIN PARKAS

Birdskin parkas are made of murre, puffin, or cormorant skin, with the feathers removed. Cormorant parkas are considered the ones of the highest quality. For adventurous folk, here's how you make a parka: suck the fat out of the skin and smear the skin with fermented fish eggs. After a time, scrape off the eggs and squeeze skin until dry. Or you can soak the skins for two or three days, then wash them and squeeze dry.

As in Southeast, Aleutian villages actually consisted of two sites, a summer and winter home. Families had their own hunting and fishing grounds that were not used by other members of the community. Most villages averaged 50-60 inhabitants, though some had as many as 300. The buildings in the village were communal. Burial rites often involved mummification, burying the mummy in a cave with all the possessions needed for the next life.

The Arrival of the Russians

All this changed with the arrival of the Russians, who were looking for fur and riches. The Second Kamchatka Expedition, consisting of the ships S.V. *Petr* and S.V. *Pavel*, arrived in the Aleutians in 1741. The first landfall was probably in the Shumagin Islands (the ferry passes these islands on the second day out from Kodiak).

It took six years for the Russians to decide what to do with the Aleutians (which they called the Katarina Archipelago, naming it after Catherine the Great). The great idea they finally came up with was to kill anything that moved. Hunting parties got larger and larger as the wholesale slaughter of marine mammals began. But the marine life was not the only thing moving. In 1747, sailors from the S.V. *Evdokom* went on a binge and killed 15 natives. The human bloodbath was on. The Natives retaliated, and battles escalated to the point where the Russians started demanding hostages as insurance against their hunting parties getting raided.

Despite the risks, the Aleuts didn't take this sitting down. A steady resistance to the Russian occupation grew and, in 1763, nearly 200 Russian sailors were killed in altercations with the Aleuts. But the natives were outgunned by the Russians, who came up with a very effective method of quashing rebellion: they destroyed the Aleut war weapons. Tragically for the Aleuts, these were their survival weapons, as well. The Russians methodically destroyed all harpoons and baidarkas. Aleut population in the contact zone dropped from perhaps 3,000 at the time of the first Russian contact to fewer than 200. The seals and sea otters, which had brought the Russians to the islands in the first place, fared about the same. With lack of food and mistreatment came disease – TB ran rampant among the Aleuts.

Ironically, the Russians sent their first missionary to Unalaska in 1796. By then there was almost no one left to convert and the bulk of the Russian traders had moved to Southcentral and Southeast, decimating the native and wildlife population wherever they went.

Life improved little with the U.S. purchase of Alaska. While the Russians had – rather late, it's true – instituted some conservation measures, the U.S. began a full-bore slaughter of the few remaining animals. Between 1880 and 1890, the number of seal-hunting ships in the Pribilofs increased eight-fold.

The animals were hunted down to barely viable communities; the Aleuts almost disintegrated as a people. Luckily for both beast and man, a time of recuperation – largely bestowed upon the area for the simple reason there wasn't enough game left to make hunting economically viable – descended upon the Aleutians. From the turn of the century to 1942, the islands were nearly forgotten. The Aleuts and the animals they based their way of life upon started to make a very small comeback.

World War II

But that comeback was nipped in the bud. The area burst back onto the global stage when Japan and the United States chose these barren rocks as the site for a showdown between world powers. On June 3, 1942, the Japanese attacked Dutch Harbor, killing 35 people. According to propaganda, this attack was in retaliation for James Doolittle's raid on Tokyo. Doolittle was from Alaska. The propaganda ignored the fact that the Imperial Army had been running surveillance missions into the Aleutians – which stretch like a string of stepping stones straight to Alaska's heart – for nearly two years.

The Aleutians were the only U.S. territory that the Japanese managed to occupy. They were in control of all the islands west of Amchitka, more than 500 miles west of Dutch Harbor/Unalaska. The worst fighting of the Aleutians war took place another 50 miles or more beyond Amchitka, on the islands of Kiska and Attu. More than 2,500 Japanese soldiers were killed in the battles to control Attu.

On June 1, 1942, there were roughly 45,000 U.S. soldiers in Alaska; 13,000 of these were stationed in Cold Bay, just to keep the Japanese from getting their hands on these rocks in the middle of nowhere.

On June 2, 1942, a naval patrol plane spotted the approaching Japanese fleet – two aircraft carriers, five cruisers, six subs, and four troop transports, all under the command of Vice Admiral Boshiro Hosogaya – headed for Dutch Harbor.

The battle for Dutch Harbor was quick and confused. The Japanese came in, dropped some bombs, and fled. A total of 43 U.S. citizens were killed, and 10 Japanese aircraft shot down.

The Japanese backed off a bit, heading for less populated areas of the Aleutians, seeking to gain a foothold. It was a strategy that had worked for them all over the Pacific, but they didn't have much luck here. They occupied Kiska and Attu – uninhabited islands – and the Japanese press reported a great victory in the Americas. And in a way, it was a great victory. It had been a very long time since the U.S. had been attacked by a foreign power on its own soil. And as with the other occasions – take the War of 1812 or the destruction of the World Trade Center as examples – the nation was galvanized and sprang into action.

Over $100 million was spent on construction in the Aleutians during the war: harbors, docks, airports, houses, and forts were built with the single thought of keeping the Japanese off the mainland.

Reports that there were Japanese ships in the Bering Sea brought about the first massive airlift in U.S. history. Within two days of the supposed sightings, more than 2,300 soldiers were in Nome, ready to fight.

Meanwhile, in the Aleutians, a blockade was set up around the Japanese-occupied islands. On March 26, 1943, the largest single battle of the Aleutian war took place, the Battle of the Komandorski Islands. On the U.S. side, there were three battleships, an aircraft carrier, and a pack of cruisers, subs, and destroyers. The Air Force kicked in 54 bombers and 128 fighters. Like the battle for Dutch, the Komandorski campaign was over quickly, within about 3½ hours. The Japanese were handily defeated, and Attu was back in U.S. hands.

On the island, there were 2,351 dead Japanese soldiers found; it was assumed that there were another few hundred buried in the hills. A grand total of 28 Japanese surrendered. On the U.S. side, 549 men lost their lives in the fight over Attu. Another 1,148 were wounded. This makes the fight for Attu the most costly battle in the Pacific, in terms of numbers engaged/numbers lost, except for Iwo Jima.

As might be expected, as soon as the war was over, the soldiers pulled out and everything was left to rot. The very small Native population had been resettled during the war. As a result, the Aleutians were empty enough to allow Amchitka – so fiercely fought over during the war – to serve as a test site for nuclear bombs (a popular Alaskan joke says the A-bomb bombed the "chit" out of Amchitka).

■ The Aleutians Today

It has only been in the last 30 years, since the settlement of the Native Claims Act, that the Aleutians – and the Aleuts – have been allowed to develop on their own. Since the 1970s, the fishing industry has done nothing but grow, bringing prosperity to the most remote islands. Dutch Harbor is one of the richest fishing ports in the world, moving endless tons of fish. The tiny village of Sand Point has one of the highest per capita incomes in Alaska – the state with the highest per-capita income in the country.

However, over the past two or three years, there have been hints that the catches are declining and that, as in so many other places, the islands are going to have to turn to tourism for their bread and butter. Beyond their remote location and abysmal weather, the Aleutians particularly have a couple of problems for wholesale tourist development. First, the war left huge amounts of metal lying around that could explode at any moment.

The U.S. armed forces spent years trying to clean the islands, but they didn't get everything. Avoid suspicious looking bits of metal if you're walking outside the towns.

The Alaskan Peninsula and the Aleutians form the major part of the Alaska Maritime National Wildlife Refuge and are one of the prime birding habitats in the world. The birds are the major draw to the region for visitors and biologists fear the increasing ship traffic. Ships invariably carry rats; a single pair of rats making it to one of these remote islands, say after a shipwreck, could breed and take over the entire island, wiping out the nesting bird population. This kind of intrusion of small, imported predators already proved its deadly possibilities with the fox farms that dotted some of the islands in the early part of this century.

That said, if visitors treat the islands with respect – leave nothing, take nothing – there's no reason why this remote corner of the U.S. can't remain the lovely, fascinating place it is today.

■ Basics on the Run to Dutch

The *Tusty* runs once monthly from April through October (twice in September), leaving Kodiak on a Friday, returning the following Wednesday. You can continue on the return up to Seward and Valdez. The *Tusty* also usually makes one extra run per year, sometimes as late as December, although the weather rarely holds that long.

Staterooms book up early on the *Tusty* and the forward lounge and solarium are not nearly as comfortable for sleeping as those on the Southeast ships. The solarium is heated and protected from the wind. Booking a stateroom for the round-trip does not mean that you'll be in the same room on the outbound and return portions of the trip; usually you have to switch at Dutch Harbor.

Food on the *Tusty* is good and cheap as it is elsewhere on the ferry system, but more limited. The dining room is open only for an hour at meal times. Hot water is always available and there are some vending machines. You can pick up supplies in any of the stops along the way, but food is expensive in the villages.

 AUTHOR TIP *When making onward plans, keep in mind that the* Tusty *almost never arrives back in Kodiak on schedule. The weather keeps it running late, often by as much as 12 hours. Don't book any close connections.*

There is a Fish and Wildlife naturalist on board most of the *Tusty* runs. Besides providing expert animal-spotting skills, the naturalist runs films on Aleutian history and wildlife, gives lectures, and maintains a lending library of books on the region that you can check out for the voyage.

The alternative to five days on a ship is to fly in or out of Dutch Harbor. The outbound trip takes a day more as it has more stops than the return passage. They both pass all the same scenery, though. Check for flights with **Alaska Air**, ☎ 800-426-0333. You can fly between Dutch Harbor and Anchorage or Seattle.

The Trip

The communities that the ferry stops in can, with the possible exception of Dutch Harbor, be seen adequately in the time the *Tusty* is in dock. The smallest stop, **Akutan**, (a whistle stop; the ferry doesn't always come in here) takes less than five minutes to walk end-to-end. If you want to explore more territory during your time ashore, bring a mountain bike: the roads, which lace the islands away from the communities, are gravel but are well maintained. Only Dutch Harbor and Sand Point have taxis.

Chignik

C hignik, roughly 450 miles southwest of Anchorage, is on the Alaska Peninsula, not in the Aleutians. In fact, the first stop in the Aleutians proper – away from the islands dotting the peninsula's off-shore area – is either False Pass, Akutan or Cold Bay.

Geographically, the Alaska Peninsula greatly resembles the Aleutians. There are the same rocky beaches, the same towering volcanoes. The peninsula is every bit as cut off from Alaska's center, if not more so. It does, however, enjoy a larger variety of wildlife: moose and caribou are found in the mountains around Chignik and beyond.

Chignik Lagoon is located on the south shore of the Alaska Peninsula, bordering the Pacific Ocean. The village is approximately 280 miles east of Unimak Pass (the separation between Alaska Peninsula and the Aleutian Islands), 450 miles southwest of Kodiak Island.

WATCHABLE ... **WILDLIFE**

Chignik is an important birding area. Cormorants, puffins, auklets, loons, geese, harlequins, peregrine falcons, bald eagles, and more live or pass through the Chignik area. In winter, seabirds congregate here, enjoying the relatively warm water of the bay.

Chignik is set into a U-shaped bay bordered by a range of mountains that decrease in height from the dock side of town. These mountains are punctuated only by waterfalls as they curve around the bay and end in a series of half-caves and cutouts before petering into the sea.

The name, Chignik, is the Aleutian word for wind. The main portion of the village is compacted into an area about 600 feet long, connected by boardwalks. The mainstay of the economy in Chignik Bay is commercial fishing. Salmon, halibut, black cod, and tanner crab are harvested. Aleutian Dragon Fisheries and Chignik Pride Fisheries operate year-round fish processing plants.

■ History

A native village, Kaluak, once occupied the present location of Chignik, but the village was destroyed by Russian fur traders in the late 1700s. While the Chignik area was originally populated by Kanaiguit Eskimos, after Russian occupation, the intermarriage of the Kaniags and Aleuts produced the Koniags, who now reside in villages in the Chignik area. The people of this era were sea-dependent, living on otter, sea lion, seal, porpoise, and whale. During the Russian fur boom from 1767 to 1783, the wildlife population was decimated. Due to a combination of factors, including disease and warfare, the native population was reduced to less than half its former size.

Toward the end of the century, most of the area villages focused on fishing (Chignik now serves as a regional fishing center) – Chignik was established as a fishing village when a local cannery was constructed in the early 1900s. A four-masted sailing ship called the *Star of Alaska* transported cannery workers and supplies between Chignik and San Francisco.

Chignik is the oldest community of the five villages in the area. During the 19th century, several Koniag villages existed along the Pacific Coast of the Alaska Peninsula. They included Douglas, Katmai, Wrangell Point, Mitrofania, Kanatak, and Chignik. Today, descendants from these communities can be found in villages on both sides of the Alaska Peninsula and Kodiak Island.

■ Attractions

There's not a whole lot to do or see in town. The beach, the best walk in Chignik, is completely covered in bivalve shells. There's a small shipwreck on it, about five minutes from the ferry terminal. Chignik is a working town and almost everything is geared toward the cannery operations. The ferry actually docks at the tip of the cannery. Head right to reach the town's lone grocery store and restaurant, **Grandma's Kitchen** (the other restaurant, to the left of the cannery, is for workers only). There is a **souvenir store** next to the restaurant, but it's opening times are unpredictable. There are no accommodations in Chignik.

Western Pioneer and **Coastal Transportation** provide weekly barge service from Seattle during the summer and monthly during the winter. The **Alaska Marine Highway ferry system** provides scheduled service to nearby Chignik Bay three or four times a year beginning in May, with scheduled stops in June, September and occasionally October.

KAK ISLAND WILDLIFE

On the very rare occasions when the ferry is running ahead of schedule, the ship sometimes diverts from here to Kak Island on the return trip to Kodiak. Kak is one of the Semidi Islands, due east of Chignik. The Semidis are mostly cliff-faced, towering rock columns, topped by a little vegetation, and they are home to the world's largest horned puffin colony. Between Chignik and Sand Point you also enter an area with Cassin's auklets and rhino auklets. The Semidis are the easternmost breeding site for least auklets. The western tip of the Semidis is also the end of the range of the crested auklet, the birder's gold medal on the ferry run. Kak Island, typical of the Semidi group, also houses a large colony of Steller's sea lions on its north shore. There may be 40 or 50 sea lions here, dominated by a huge bull, estimated to weigh over 1,200 pounds.

Sand Point

Sand Point is on Popof Island, one of the Shumagin Islands. It was near here that the Russians first landed in the Aleutian/Alaska Peninsula area. The island group, 12 main islands and about 150 islets and rocks, are all gently hilly and of volcanic origin, but today there is no active volcanism. On **Little Koniuij Island**, on the eastern outliers of the group, is a group of sulfur lakes. The highest point in the island group is **Mt. Betton**, on Unga Island. An extinct volcano, it's 2,400 feet high. Most of the islands in the group are part of a nature reserve. Popof is one of the smaller islands in the chain, situated between the islands of Korovin and Unga, the largest of the group. There are several old abandoned settlements in the area, on Unga, Big Koniuij, Simeonof, and Korovin Islands.

The Shumagin Islands themselves were first visited, but not named by Alavarez de Castellozzo of Spain, in 1578. They were later "discovered" again in 1725 by Germans Tschirikov and Bastell, who were working as navigators of the German-Russian Bering Expedition, for the Czar. In 1790, Alexander Baranov founded a merchant post on Unga Island; a few years later, Russian monks founded a monastery on the islands.

With a population of around 1,000, Sand Point is one of the larger communities in the region. It is also one of the oldest settlements in the entire state, founded by Russian Governor Baranov in 1793, and it's currently the only permanently populated part of the Shumagins. The original Russian settlement was abandoned, and the current town was founded in 1898 by a San Francisco fishing company who used it as a trading post and cod fishing station. The town was used as a repair and supply center for gold mining during the early 1900s, but fish processing became the dominant activity in the 1930s. The city is fairly prosperous. Alaska's first cold storage plant was built here in 1946, and the city lives on commercial fishing.

It's a pleasantly rolling, green island, and the low hills give Sand Point a nice air. From the ferry terminal, walk toward town by passing through the ship repair yard. Just past the dry dock is a bridge, which leads to the Russian Orthodox Church, and beneath the bridge is an assortment of dead and dying ships – it looks like a maritime graveyard as the wooden boats return to the sea the hard way.

■ Attractions

St. Nicholas, the church, is closed and run down. It's not in much better shape than the boats rotting in the water below, but it is a lovely, tiny building, the smallest of the Russian Orthodox structures on the ferry route. It was built in 1933.

Sand Point has a store, the **Aleutian Commercial Company**, a couple of restaurants, **Aleutian China Restaurant**, ☎ 383-5676, on the main street, and **Popof Pizza**, ☎ 383-3333, and the vague possibility of rooms for temporary lodging. All are in the same building. Continue past the church to the main street and turn right – it's the largest building straight ahead.

The hotel is the **Anchor Inn Motel**, ☎ 383-3272, or you could try **Hodges B&B**, ☎ 383-5607.

There is even a taxicab service, **Sand Point City Cab**, ☎ 383-5252.

Leaving Sand Point, **Pavlov** and **Pavlov's Sister** come into view, twin volcanoes with almost perfectly conical shapes. Pavlov, the taller of the two, is 7,028 feet high. The volcanoes dominate the landscape to the west almost until the ship's arrival in King Cove. Coming around so the back of the cones are in view, on clear days there is a view of the Cathedral Ledge, a rock and ice formation that looks like a row of vicious teeth.

King Cove

King Cove sits on a narrow sand spit, under the shadow of Frosty Peak, a 5,784-foot dormant volcano 20 miles to the west. The town itself arcs around the cove, set on a spit of the Alaska Peninsula overlooking the Deer Passage, which separates Deer Island from the mainland.

King Cove's 800 or so residents make their living from commercial fishing and from the huge processing plant in town. The town was founded in 1911 by the Pacific American Fisheries Company, which built a salmon cannery here. Early settlers were Scandinavian, European, and Aleut fishermen.

■ Attractions

There isn't too much to see or do in King Cove. There is a restaurant at the end of the spit leading to the ferry terminal; to either side of it is a huge stack of crab pots and fish nets. Climb the hill above the restaurant for views of the town or to pick berries.

If you follow the road, you will pass a chandler, the fishing boat harbor, and then cross a small bridge. To the right is the school, the very basic store, and a rather large bar. Straight ahead is the **Russian Orthodox Church**, set right at the foot of the mountain that separates King Cove from the peninsula's interior and the **Alaska Peninsula National Wildlife Refuge**. The refuge is home to grizzlies, wolves, and caribou. And just outside King Cove is the **Illiasik Passage**, which has a large kittiwake colony. That's about it.

Most King Cove residents make their living from the fishing industry.

Cold Bay

C old Bay is only 40 miles from the tip of the Alaska Peninsula. Soon after leaving here, the ferry has truly entered the Aleutians. Unfortunately for those who want to see Cold Bay, the stops here are in the middle of the night and nothing is open or even visible.

Cold Bay was probably an important stopping point for Natives, perhaps as far back as the days of the Bering Land Bridge, which ended near here. There are extensive shell middens all around the town. The Russians left few traces of their brief stay in Cold Bay, and what most shaped the modern city was the war: Cold Bay was home to a large airbase whose construction led to the town's road network. The airstrip is still one of the largest in Alaska and is used as a hub for the Aleutian Islands and the Pribilofs. Cold Bay has one hotel and one restaurant. Since the ferry usually stops here in the dead of night, the town is only interesting to those looking for the **Izembek National Wildlife Refuge**, on the Bering Sea side of the peninsula. The refuge is, like most of the region, a birder's paradise, with nearly a million birds passing through during migration. It contains some of the largest beds of eelgrass in the world, which serves as an international crossroads to migrating birds. The world's population of Pacific brant, thousands of Canada geese, and other waterfowl congregate on the lagoon from late August through early November. Each spring and fall the entire population of emperor geese migrate through Izembek, with several thousand wintering here. The colorful Steller's eider, a threatened species that nests on the Arctic coast of Alaska and Siberia and molts on Izembek Lagoon in fall, is the most common wintering duck. Izembek Refuge provides the final opportunity for many migrating shorebirds to feed and rest before their long over-water flights to winter homes as far away as South America, the South Pacific, and New Zealand.

Numerous species of seabirds and marine mammals inhabit the surrounding area, including harbor seals, sea otters, and Steller's sea lions. Watch the surrounding waters for gray, killer, and minke whales that migrate along the coastline and make rare visits to bays and lagoons.

Once you're in Cold Bay, if you want to get out to Izembek, there is very limited access via 40 miles of gravel road. The rest of the refuge – more than three million acres – can only be reached by foot, boat, or plane. For more information, write Izembek National Wildlife Refuge, P.O. Box 127, Cold Bay, AK 99571, ☎ 532-2445.

■ Fun Things the Government Does with Your Money

Late in 1998, Congress decided to build a road in the absolute middle of nowhere. Maybe they were bored that day. The people of King Cove and Cold Bay have long complained that they have no access to the rest of the world. (This is what happens when you move into the middle of nowhere.) To make themselves feel better, for years they have whined for a road that would at least link them together, so they could get into one big group and whine that the nearest McDonalds is in Kodiak.

Actually, the official reason for the road is better access to medical facilities. The idea was that the road would enable citizens of Cold Bay to get to King Cove's medical facilities. The fact that, for decades, planes have been used to do just that, hadn't quite dawned on anybody. Neither had the fact that the road, called the Golden Gravel Road in Congress, was going to be impassable much of the time anyway because of ice.

Wisely, no one wanted to build the road, because it would have had to cut through the heart of Izembek, endangering waterfowl habitat, the staging grounds for the entire world population of Pacific black brant and emperor geese, the overwintering habitat for half the world's population of Steller's eiders, and a few hundred other bird species. Ah, but give a man a bulldozer and a spot on the map that he couldn't find again with his four closest aides, and the fact that the road bisects a major caribou migration route just doesn't matter. The fact that 56 Native villages depend on the region's wildlife for subsistence hunting and are strongly opposed to the road didn't really matter, either, did it?

Congress, still calling ketchup a vegetable in school lunches to save money, somehow found the cash to authorize between $30 and $40 million (depending on whose numbers you believe) to build this road. Luckily, after the intense political back-scratching ended in Washington D.C., Alaskans decided they really didn't need the road after all, and settled for a $37.5 million package that included a medical clinic, airport upgrades, and the possibility of a road and ferry system that does not cross into a wildlife refuge.

False Pass

False Pass is the first town west of the North American continent. The town was named False Pass because the Isantoski Strait, which separates the Alaska Peninsula from Unimak Island, and the Bering Sea from the Gulf of Alaska, was too narrow and too shallow for large ships to pass through. The ferry does not always stop at this community of under 100 (58, in 1998). It is located on the eastern tip of Unimak Island, with Ikatan Bay leading away to the south, Bechevin Bay to the north. The town is a whistle-stop for the ferry and usually you won't know until you're on board if a stop is planned.

The area was originally settled by a homesteader in the early 1900s, and grew with the establishment of a cannery in 1917. Natives immigrated from Morzhovoi, Sanak Island, and Ikatan when the cannery was built. A post office was established in 1921. The cannery, which operated continuously, except in the mid-1970s when two hard winters depleted the fish resources, was later purchased by Peter Pan Seafoods. It was destroyed by fire in 1984, and was not rebuilt. A few years ago, however, a cod processing plant was completed. False Pass is an important refueling stop for Bristol Bay and Bering Sea fishing fleets.

There's not much to see in False Pass. The town survives on its location as a refueling stop for ships headed into the Bering Sea. There are no restaurants and no lodging, unless the processing plant has some dorm rooms not being used by seasonal workers.

WATCHABLE

WILDLIFE

False Pass is rich in wildlife; the community is small enough so it does not scare away the bears that come right up into town, and in the sea there are a lot of harbor seals, sea lions, and the occasional walrus. The tip of the peninsula is part of the Alaska Maritime National Wildlife Refuge and is a haven for birds.

Akutan

The ferry made its first stop in Akutan in June 1993 and the entire town (at least those who weren't out fishing) – maybe 50 people – turned up to watch the ship pull in. The *Tusty* does not stop here on every run – it's a whistle-stop – but hope your ferry does pull into the small dock. A half-hour here shows the Alaska you've always dreamed of.

Akutan is on one of the Krenitzin Islands, a sub-section of the Fox Islands, approximately 750 miles southwest of Anchorage, 45 miles northeast of Dutch Harbor. The year-round population barely hits 100, but there are perhaps another 300 people employed nearby in the cannery.

The village was founded in 1878 as a trading port for the Western Fur and Trading Company. In that same year a church and school were built. The company's agent established a commercial cod fishing business, attracting Aleuts in nearby villages. The Pacific Whaling Company built a whale processing station across the bay from Akutan in 1912. It was the only station in the Aleutians, and it operated until 1939. After the Japanese attacked Unalaska in 1942, the U.S. government evacuated residents to the Ketchikan area. In 1944, Akutan was re-established, but many villagers didn't return.

The small, squat church is the sole real attraction. It's surrounded by a white picket fence and has graves covered with purple lupin and fireweed. The mountains form a backdrop, including the often-smoking Akutan Volcano, 4,272 feet high, its white sides smudged with black ash. It's postcard pretty.

Russian Orthodox Church graveyard, Akutan.

ZERO CAPTURE

Akutan figured prominently in the history of World War II. Near here, a Zero was brought down. It landed nearly intact. Until this point in the war, Japanese Zeros had been running circles around the U.S.-built fighter planes. The capture of the Zero allowed U.S. engineers to find out why the Japanese plane was so much better and modify the U.S. fighters accordingly. It was the turning point of the Pacific air war.

With World War II nothing more than ghosts in some abandoned bunkers, what makes Akutan such a charming place is its atmosphere. When the *Tusty* disgorges a horde of tourists who run off the ship to take pictures of the tiny, well-kept houses, the boardwalks, the salmon drying on lines next to the laundry, the people of Akutan are open and, frankly, happy for the distraction. The residents maintain a fairly traditional lifestyle, making their living in the still-rich cod, crab and pollack fisheries around the town, or at Trident Seafoods nearby. The population of the town can double during the fish processing months.

Akutan is a difficult place to describe. It's like stepping into a world that has managed to find the best of the past and the present. A visit here is a highlight of the *Tusty*'s run.

There is a small grocery store in Akutan, directly across from the ferry dock. The store can also help arrange accommodations (very limited) in town. However, other than the ferry, the only way out is through a charter plane to Cold Bay or Dutch Harbor, where you can connect with flights to the mainland.

Dutch Harbor/Unalaska

The largest community in the Aleutians, with a population of over 4,000, the twin cities of Dutch Harbor/Unalaska processed the most fish (by weight) in the U.S. during 1989 and 1990. Not much has changed since then. Over the past couple of years, the port has also become the highest for value of catch, rising from its usual position of second. In 1996, fishermen brought in 579 million pounds of fish to Dutch, with a wholesale value of around $119 million, making the community the port with the highest volume and dollar value of fish in the country. When you're in Dutch, you know: everything revolves around the fishing.

■ History

Russian fur hunters arrived on Unalaska Island, one of the Fox Islands, in 1758. At that time, more than 3,000 resident Unangas (known since the Russian era as Aleuts) lived in 24 settlements on Unalaska and Amaknak Islands. It took only 10 years for the Russians to develop a trading port for the fur seal trade and to start killing everything in sight. Once they burned out the region, they just packed up and moved on: in 1787, many seal hunters and their families were forced into virtual slavery and relocated by the Russian American Company to work in the extremely lucrative seal harvest in the Pribilofs.

The island was first mapped by the *Iulian* expedition, under the command of Stepen Glotov, who also discovered Fox Island.

With the Russians gone and the Native population sadly reduced, not a whole lot went on in Dutch for a hundred years or so. An 1898 U.S. expedition reported that "Twenty years ago many an Aleut hunter lived in affluence on the income derived from the sale of sea otter pelts; now the animal is very scarce and the industry has about disappeared." Still, there was a little life, because that same year, in 1898, the westernmost post office in the U.S. was built here – but that was because of the fishing, not because of any great service to the people who actually had made Dutch their home. Facing the usual problems caused by contact with outsiders, fewer than 300 Natives crowded into four settlements by 1910.

The U.S. did not take long after purchasing Alaska to recognize the cash value of the Aleutians and the Pribilofs. There was a boom in the fur trade, which nearly depleted the stock of animals yet again. Dutch Harbor served as a base for the fur ships, and also as a coaling and supply station for vessels headed into the Bering Sea. In 1940, the U.S. Navy "appropriated" Dutch Harbor. The town was bombed by the Japanese in 1942, and the Aleut population was sent, with many other Aleuts, to Southeast Alaska for wartime resettlement. The military went on a building spree, and bunkers and fallen quonset huts are a regular feature of the landscape today. When the military pulled out, only a fraction of the Aleuts chose to return. It was the advent of the rich king crab fisheries in the 1960s that brought Dutch Harbor back to life.

The rough Aleutian weather can be a nightmare for any ship coming to Dutch. When you're on the *Tusty* you'll see certificates of thanks from other ships the ferry has saved from mortal peril.

SHIPWRECKS & OIL SPILLS

Shipwrecks are almost common out here. One of the bigger ones happened on November 26, 1997, when the Japanese-owned freighter M/V *Kuroshima* ran aground at Summer Bay on Unalaska Island. For the Aleutians, the weather really wasn't that bad: the wreck happened during a storm, and the 100-mph winds blew the ship aground. Two crewmen were killed and 39,000 gallons of heavy fuel oil were spilled. The wind blew the oil upstream into Summer Lake, bordering Summer Bay; the rest strung along the shoreline of Summer Beach and Humpy and Morris Coves. This is just one of the little spills that you never hear about, but which, over the course of the year, add up to a much worse disaster than the spill in Prince William Sound.

There were some extra problems with the spill in Dutch. They could only work on stabilizing and cleaning the spill until freezing weather covered the oil with snow and ice late in December. While the ship was salvaged and taken to Magone Marine in Dutch Harbor for repairs, repairing the damage to the ecosystem wasn't so simple. Still, they tried. A winter maintenance program was implemented to check for wildlife activity, remove any tar that might get exposed during thaws, and to monitor the overall status of the spill area.

■ Basics

_i_ Dutch Harbor is the end of the Alaska Marine Highway's run. If on schedule, the ship arrives here in the early evening, when there is still enough light to see the sights. The other way onto the islands is by plane: **Alaska Air** will get you out here, but it's going to cost. ☎ 800-252-7522.

Both the airport and the ferry harbor (there is no terminal here) are a long way from town, and catching a cab is highly recommended. Plenty of cabs meet the ferry; there are more than 30 of them cruising the town and it's never difficult to flag one down. The cost of a taxi anywhere on the island is about $5 per person, no matter where you go. Tourism is becoming bigger here as a handful of cruise ships have started adding Dutch to their itineraries (five make stops here), so expect changes.

AUTHOR TIP *For orientation, keep in mind that the ferry and the airport are both on Amaknak Island at the town of Dutch Harbor; across the bridge, on Unalaska Island is the twin city of Unalaska. The whole place is usually called Dutch.*

If you're going to be in town for more than a few hours, you may want to rent a bike from **Aleutian Adventure Sports**, ☎ 581-4489. Car and truck rental is available, but you will pay for the convenience. If you're interested, call **B.C. Vehicle Rental**, ☎ 581-6777.

Tourist information is available at the **Convention and Visitor's Bureau**, located in the lobby of the Grand Aleutian Hotel (☎ 581-2612) and open 8-5 daily in the summer.

You can also get area info, along with a few maps and books, at the **Swanson Visitor Center** in Unalaska, on West Broadway and 3rd St., which is housed in the previous residence of Henry Swanson, a well-known local fisherman/hunter. The house is open only on Saturdays from 1-4, but it's worth calling to see if somebody's around and will let you in. ☎ 581-1297. You have a better chance of stocking up on books and maps at **Nicky's Place**, at the corner of 2nd and Broadway, a short walk from the Swanson House.

UniSea (if on foot, walk around the hill from Holy Ascension, cross the bridge, around the lagoon, and you're there) has a good selection of reading material and groceries for those taking the ferry back to Kodiak.

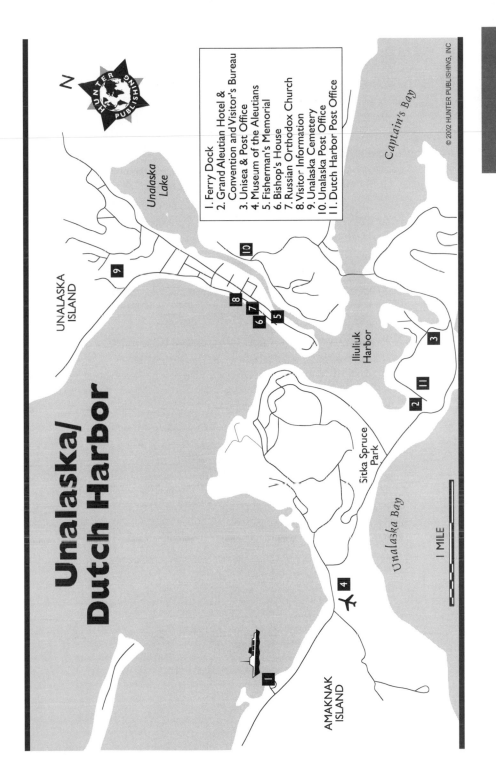

Unalaska/
Dutch Harbor

1. Ferry Dock
2. Grand Aleutian Hotel &
   Convention and Visitor's Bureau
3. Unisea & Post Office
4. Museum of the Aleutians
5. Fisherman's Memorial
6. Bishop's House
7. Russian Orthodox Church
8. Visitor Information
9. Unalaska Cemetery
10. Unalaska Post Office
11. Dutch Harbor Post Office

UNALASKA ISLAND

Unalaska Lake

AMAKNAK ISLAND

Sitka Spruce Park

Iliuliuk Harbor

Captain's Bay

Unalaska Bay

1 MILE

© 2002 HUNTER PUBLISHING, INC

Southwest

■ Museums & Attractions

The main reason to come out here is to just enjoy the stark and natural beauty of the place. This said, there are a few things to keep you amused while in town.

HOLY ASCENSION ORTHODOX CHURCH: Dutch Harbor has the single most beautiful Russian Orthodox church in Alaska. It is the oldest Russian Orthodox cruciform-style church in North America. The site was first sanctified in 1808; the church was replaced by Father John Veniaminoff (St. Innocent) in 1826, and that church in turn was replaced by another version in 1853. The current one was built in the 1890s.

The original structure remains and there is a lovely graveyard within the fenced compound. The church and the faith did a lot better here than in most of the rest of Russian Alaska, in part due to the wisdom of the founding priest, Veniaminoff, who, with local assistance, composed the first Aleut writing system and translated the scriptures into Aleut, instead of simply forcing the people to give up their language.

The church has been undergoing a long restoration (it was nearly destroyed by evacuating U.S. Army troops at the end of WWII). It was number one on the list of American Heritage's Most Endangered list for a while, but the repair and restoration have made a spot that was once stunning into something breathtaking.

The collection of icons and artworks inside is simply not to be missed. This is perhaps the best collection of Russian works in the Americas – certainly the best used collection. But like the church, the icons did not have an easy time of it during the war. When the government kicked everybody out of town, parishioners were given a week to pack up the icons. These they took with them to Southeast, where many were damaged by climate. Restoration is ongoing.

There are tours of the church available; a donation of $5 is requested.

BISHOP'S HOUSE: Next to Holy Ascension is the Bishop's House, also undergoing restoration. The house was built in 1882, but fell into disrepair during Dutch Harbor's bad years. The restoration will be on-going for many more years; every care is being taken, and it shows. Right now, most of the time, you can only look in the windows, but tours are beginning. Check with the visitor's bureau.

RUSSIAN HISTORY: Evidence of the Russian culture may be found elsewhere on the islands as well. If you rent a car or go on a historical tour, you may see some of the old Russian grave markers (many are topped with the double Russian-style crosses). The hillsides overlooking the beachfront of the town of Unalaska were used as the main graveyards for the public after use of the earlier graveyard surrounding the church was discontinued at the end of the 19th century. Sailors and other temporary visitors who died while here were buried on a separate part of the hill. The town has begun mapping and recording information on the 700+ markers (many wooden) and started a conservation and restoration effort. The Orthodox graves are oriented to face Holy Ascension. There are also graves for everybody from the Elk's Club to the Baha'is.

USS *NORTHWESTERN*: While over on this side of town, visit the memorial to the USS *Northwestern*, which was sunk in the bombing of Dutch Harbor. The propeller there was recovered by divers in 1992, as part a 50th anniversary commemoration.

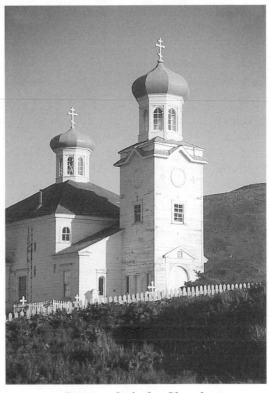

Russian Orthodox Church, Dutch Harbor.

MUSEUM OF THE ALEUTIANS: The Summer Bay dig got a big financial boost from the payoff following the Kuroshima oil spill. You can see the prehistoric artifacts the workers have dug up in the museum. ☎ 581-5150 for more info. It's open 10-4 daily, with an admission charge of $2. The museum is located on the remains of a WWII warehouse, which was once part of Fort Mears. There's an old sentry bunker that's been turned into a display, so you can go inside and find out how much fun it was for soldiers to sit in a concrete hole and stare at fog. The museum also has nice views of the old section of Unalaska and the Margaret Bay archeological sites. The museum combines displays of the town's history with its Russian and WWII heritage.

MILITARY REMAINS: There are still a lot of military remains in and around the towns. Notice on your ride in from the ferry or airport the round concrete structures. Just after you cross the bridge coming into Unalaska from the ferry, there is a gravel road leading up Bunker Hill. Up on the peak is a good view of the bay (if you're lucky enough to be there on a non-rainy day, that is) and you'll see remains of quonset huts, gun turrets, and other concrete structures.

ARCHEOLOGICAL DIGS

You may see archeological digs at Margaret or Summer Bay. Margaret Bay is the older of the digs, providing artifacts with links to other sites up to 8,000 years old. In Summer Bay, the archeologists, students, and volunteers have uncovered a variety of artifacts dating the area, which was probably used as a salmon run camp in the summer, from around 2,500 years ago. Local materials were chipped into skin scrapers, stemmed knives, projectile points, and adz blades. Grinding stones were used to pulverize the crimson mineral ocher into a powder that could be mixed with sea mammal oil and applied as paint on hides, artifacts, and used as face paint. Elaborately barbed harpoons, fish hooks, wedges, digging tools, artwork, and decorative pendants were carved from sea mammal bone and ivory.

ALEUTIAN WORLD WAR II NATIONAL HISTORIC AREA VISITOR CENTER: In the summer of 2001, the town's newest attraction opened. Located at the Unalaska Airport, the center is devoted to the memory of those who served here during the war, and it's the best chance you're going to have to see what it was like when there were more than 60,000 servicemen in town. There's a hilltop walk that has bunkers, gun mounts, and magazines, all looking out for Japanese ships. The park also includes the ruins of Fort Schwatka. Inside, there are exhibits on the war in the Aleutians, and displays of what it was like for farm boys to suddenly be shipped out to a place where the weather was enough to drive them insane. There are also plane exhibits, a radio bunker, and more. Call for hours and admission.

SITKA SPRUCE PARK: Hiking is also nice out by the airport: you can see a few of the only trees on the island at this park. These six trees were planted by some uncelebrated Russian in 1805 and are really the only thing larger than brush you're likely to see on the entire island. Most of the area has no developed trails, but the hike up the 1,600-foot Mt Ballyhoo is popular – there is a dirt road up the side, but most people wouldn't recognize it as such, or be comfortable driving it. For those who aren't radical mountain bike stylists, or haven't rented a 4WD, try the hike instead.

■ Adventures

 There are some tour operators in town. The **Grand Aleutian Hotel** runs a few packages, starting at $1,100 per person for three days (including transportation from Anchorage). Birding tours are a bit cheaper. **Extra Mile Tours**, ☎ 581-6171, runs two- and four-hour tours of the town, perfect for the time the ferry is docked. You can also try **A.L.E.U.T. Tours**, ☎ 581-6001.

Aleutian Adventure Sports, ☎ 581-4489 or 888-581-4489, will rent you gear, or take you out on day-trips or kayaking.

If you head out on your own to hike the backcountry in the Dutch Harbor region (or, for that matter, on any of the Aleutian islands) you'll need a permit from the local village corporation, **Ounalashka** (☎ 581-1276). Their office is near the Grand Aleutian Hotel. They can also fill you in on the local rules and regulations governing camping on the island.

Charters

The only reason this town is here is because there are so many fish around. Go out and get a few of your own with one of the town's charter operators. **AVI Charters**, ☎ 581-5960, or **Shuregood Adventures**, ☎ 581-2378 or 888-FHS4FUN. Either can also do sightseeing trips around the islands.

■ Food

There are two restaurants and a lounge in the **Grand Aleutian** hotel. The **Margaret Bay Café** has a nice soup and salad bar and is a good place for breakfast or lunch, while the **Chart Room** is a great place for a splurge, complete with linen and china.

The **Peking Chinese Restaurant** is out near UNISEAS, with good specialties in Chinese, Japanese, Korean and Vietnamese food. Most dishes are around $15. **Ziggy's**, on East Point Drive, has good burgers and Mexican food. **Stormy's**, at 2nd and Broadway, has a little bit of everything, and a location right near the church.

Get your coffee fix along with your books at **Nicky's**, on Front Street. For shopping, there's the **Eagle Food Supply** and the **New Alaska Commercial Company** stores, with huge selections.

■ Accommodations

Remember how far out on the farthest edges of the United States you are when you consider Dutch Harbor's hotel prices. Remember, too, that someone has to bring all these supplies out to the very edge of civilization. And, until quite recently, most of the accommodations were set up only for cannery and construction workers and fishermen.

UniSea had, until a few years ago, the only hotel in Dutch, the **UniSea Inn**, ☎ 581-1325. The inn offers basic, newly renovated rooms from $100.

But Dutch Harbor has been growing. The same company owns the premier hotel in town, the **Grand Aleutian**, ☎ 581-3844, 980 Salmon Way. Unexpected luxury at the end of the world, with doubles from $175. Another place to try for lodging is **Carl's Bayview Inn**, near the church. Some rooms have kitchenettes and the inn also has a steakhouse, ☎ 581-1230. Doubles from $125. Or check out the **Royal Dutch Inn**, on Captain's Bay, ☎ 581-1636. **Statewide Services**, at Mile 4 Captains's Road, ☎ 581-1515, and **Alaska Ship Supply Guesthouse**, 1640 Valleyhoo Road, ☎ 581-1640. Both offer good basic accommodation and the best prices in town – doubles from $80. There are no formal camping sites in Dutch, but check with the native corporation, **Ounalashka** (☎ 581-1276), if you're interested.

Connections

Once you've gone the distance on Alaska's coast, you have two options for getting deeper into the north. The first, the Alaska Highway and its sideroads, opens up the interiors of Alaska – from Anchorage to Denali Park to the Arctic Circle – as well as Yukon and British Columbia. The second, B.C. Ferries, can be picked up in southern Canada, taking you by ship from Prince Rupert to the famed Queen Charlotte Islands, and to lesser-known beauties such as Salt Spring Island. It's your choice: more coast, or the great northern interior.

The Alaska Highway

■ From Southeast

The Alaska Marine Highway connects to the Alaska Highway and its feeder routes in four places in Southeast Alaska and southern B.C.: at Prince Rupert, where you can get on the Yellowhead Highway in southern B.C. and follow it to either the Cassiar or the Alaska Highway; at Stewart/Hyder, which offers much the same options as Rupert; at Haines, where a stunningly beautiful 152-mile road leads to the Alaska Highway at Haines Junction; and at Skagway, where it's 99 miles to a point on the Alcan just south of Whitehorse.

The road connecting Skagway to the Alaska Highway parallels a trail that was once a nightmare for thousands of miners who had to drag a full year's supply of goods up the steep path. Snow conditions made it almost pointless to use ponies, since they tended to bog down and drop dead (it was called Dead Horse Trail for a reason). But it's easy getting up the pass from Skagway today; the road is smooth and good, and quite pretty. Emerald Lake shows deep blues and greens; the world's smallest desert (actually, an area of blown glacial silt) is right by the roadside; mountain goats are common in the hills; and Lake Bennett offers a glimpse of where hundreds of miners once built boats from the trees along the shore, hoping to be first to the Klondike.

From Haines, the road parallels the Chilkat River, passing through the bald eagle reserve before climbing at the Canadian border and entering a narrow pass between two mountain ranges. The road is rough in places to the border; afterwards, it is one of the smoothest, loveliest roads in North America. The views are staggering: high mountains covered with snow and boggy terrain in a thousand shades of lush green. The Haines Highway connects with the Alaska Highway at Haines Junction, the location of the Kluane National Park Visitor's Center.

■ From Southcentral

Virtually all of the towns in Southcentral (except for Kodiak) link up with Alaska's road system.

For ferry travelers, the monthly cross-Gulf runs of the *Kennicott* open up a vast array of possibilities. In the old days, when there was no ferry link between Southeast and Southcentral, you had to drive from Haines or Skagway to get quickly into the Interior, and from either of those towns, it was a long two-day drive to Anchorage and the Kenai. Now you can transfer your car from the Southeast line in Juneau, put it on the *Kennicott*, and unload in Seward, in the heart of Southcentral, or in Valdez, in Prince William Sound.

From Seward, you're mere hours from Anchorage or Homer, depending on which direction you want to drive; from Valdez, you're hours away from the massive Kluane/Wrangell-St. Elias wilderness, or a long day from Anchorage.

One caveat about this route: the *Kennicott* is an uncomfortable ship, and it's a long two or two and a half days across the Gulf of Alaska. The scenery can be worth it, though: if the weather allows, there are fantastic views of the Fairweather range. The water never gets all that rough, and for two days of sitting on a boat, you can cut out a day of driving. Book a stateroom, though. The *Kennicott* is torture if you're sleeping out on deck.

■ History of the Alaska Highway

The Alaska Highway (the Alcan) was built between March and September, 1942. The road construction was spurred by the threat of Japanese invasion, and the military crews that built the road worked like men possessed. They had to fight weather that dropped to 60 below, permafrost that melted when the overburden was stripped off – and then swallowed tractors whole – muskeg that could cause entire fleets of trucks to disappear in the watery depths, distance from home, low morale, and the ever-lurking mosquito. The construction of the road was a heroic task indeed. More than 200 bridges were built, many requiring divers to go beneath the frigid waters of the north-flowing rivers.

The first highway was a tenuous thing, filled with lots of corduroy road patches, mud bogs, and potholes bigger than some eastern states. The first truck to drive it averaged just 15 miles an hour. The highway today is paved in its entirety, despite persistent rumors to the contrary. There is usually some construction going on along the road; keeping it in shape is a year-round job though crews can work only during three or four months of the year. Frost heaves are common.

 There are some steep grades, so vehicles should be in good shape; carry spares of everything you know how to fix.

The Alaska Highway asks little, but rewards are great. Jagged blue peaks punctuate vast snowfields speckled with alpine ponds as the road crosses through the Yukon into Alaska. Moose and bear are often spotted by the roadside, and an abundant supply of pristine rivers and lakes offer a freshwater alternative to the coast's saltwater fishing.

■ Precautions

The main road is completely paved; at any given time, however, there may be extensive construction, which means some sections will be gravel-paved. Although the gravel is oiled and compacted, it still makes for rougher traveling than asphalt. It's a good road, but it can be demanding on vehicles, and once you get off the main road, conditions can deteriorate in dramatic fashion. For this reason, before you leave home, make absolutely sure your vehicle is in top shape. There are plenty of garages and service stations along the way, but they may not have the parts you need, or the services may be 100 miles down the road from where you have trouble. Here is a list of things you should do before your trip. Make sure you do them all.

- Before you leave home, take your vehicle to a trustworthy mechanic and have everything checked and repaired as needed. Don't leave home with a worn-out belt or hose, hoping it will hold another 10,000 miles. While a broken hose won't end a vacation, it will certainly slow you down.

- No matter what you are riding or driving, you should carry a **full-sized spare tire**, **jack**, **lug wrench**, and a **puncture repair kit**, *and know how to use them*. The half-sized spares now included with most passenger cars are not suitable for the Alaska Highway. No matter how much extra trunk room it takes, bring a full-sized spare. If you're planning extensive side-trips, bring two. Although blowouts are more common than punctures, a few cans of compressed air and puncture sealant can be useful, too. (Get the more expensive kind with nozzles that thread onto the valve of your tire.)

- You should also take along a **spare fan belt** and **radiator hose**. Since you've done all your repairs in advance, you probably won't need them; but if you do, you'll need them badly. Not all garages will have stock on hand, and having the appropriate belt or hose with you means you won't have to wait while one is ordered. There's really no such thing as overnight package delivery in most of these parts – delivery more likely will take three or four days.

- Also take along an **emergency kit:** jumper cables, flares, a flashlight, duct tape, a crescent wrench, a small socket wrench set (before buying your socket set, check to see if your car is on the metric or inch system), pliers, and a large knife. Most auto repair shops carry prepackaged repair kits. Take one of these as a base, and build it from there. If you don't know exactly what you need, find someone who does, and ask.

While you may not end up needing all this stuff, you're likely to meet up with someone who does. There is a strong sense of fraternity in traveling the Alaska Highway, and you'll frequently find people crawling under each others' cars to check for leaks at campgrounds. Carrying spares is good for you and for everyone around you.

Many people put screens over the front of their cars to protect them from flying gravel. Also, cheap plastic headlight covers can save you from buying new, expensive glass ones at the end of your trip. There are places where the gravel flies thick. The AAA tells you that, because of the gravel, you will break your windshield. That's not necessarily true, but there's a pretty good chance, so make sure your insurance covers the possibility. On our trips, we have ranged from zero to six cracks in the windshield (our record is five cracks in one day), and we never leave home without double-checking our insurance coverage.

AUTHOR TIP *Towing insurance could save you a fortune should something go wrong. Give your insurance agent a call to see what is covered and to make sure your policy is good in both countries. Get a proof of insurance card for traveling in Canada. It is mandatory to be insured in Canada, and they will ask about this at the border.*

- For those traveling in RVs or campers, before leaving home check all the **window screens**; make sure they are of the smallest mesh you can buy. Also outfit your vehicle with **mudflaps**, to help control the problem mentioned below.

- One side effect of the road construction is that, after awhile, the **taillights** of most cars are completely obscured. Always check when you stop for gas, to avoid having mud instead of brake lights.

- At each stop for gas, **check all the other fluids** in your car as well; it's easy to be complacent if you just checked the oil yesterday, but that might have been nearly 1,000 miles ago. Make it a habit at each stop.

- **Gas** is readily available all along the highway; the only long stretch of the Alaska Highway with no services in the summer is between Whitehorse and Haines Junction, about 100 miles. Gas prices are higher than in the continental U.S., and Canadian gas prices are considerably higher than those in Alaska. For those with political leanings one way or the other regarding the oil spill in Prince William Sound, Exxon is Esso in Canada.

- In the Yukon, the law says you must drive with your **headlights** on at all times. This is an excellent idea in Alaska – there are places on the Kenai that require headlights – and British Columbia as well. It's often difficult to see cars against the dark backdrop of trees, and headlights are a great help. Seatbelts, of course, are a must everywhere.

- Finally, take along a simple **repair manual** for your vehicle and a couple of blankets. These small precautions can prevent a lot of discomfort waiting by the roadside. Don't worry in advance. Just take all the proper precautions and use care.

Canadian Ports & the B.C. Ferries

The Alaska Marine Highway stops in only one port in Canada: **Prince Rupert**, near the mouth of the Skeena River on the Canadian mainland. Here, the AMH connects to the Interior of Canada via the **Yellowhead Highway** (east-west) or **Cassiar Highway** (north).

Prince Rupert is often used as an alternative to Bellingham: many of the AMH runs terminate at Rupert and so the town makes a convenient start/stop point for those looking to explore southern British Columbia as well as Alaska.

Prince Rupert is more than the AMH terminus, though. It's also the northernmost point for B.C. Ferries, the Canadian territory's equivalent of the Alaska Marine Highway.

B.C. Ferries overlap the AMH only in Rupert. For travelers coming from or going to the Inside Passage, the most useful ferry runs are to Port Hardy from Prince Rupert, and the many short-hop ships from Victoria and Vancouver. AMH Inside Passage travelers who don't want to get on in Bellingham can go to Victoria, one of Canada's most charming towns, drive the length of Vancouver Island, catch a B.C. Ferry at Port Hardy, and switch to the AMH in Prince Rupert. It's a good alternative if you don't want to be on the boats for the 2½-day trip from Bellingham to Ketchikan, or if you want to see some inland scenery.

■ The Ships

B.C. Ferry runs more than 40 ships. Many of them are open-air, so you just sit in your car. No reservations are taken or needed on the short trips. The ships get progressively nicer on the longer hauls, up to the pride of the fleet, *Queen of the North*, on the Rupert-Port Hardy run. On the longer runs reservations are a must, especially for people traveling with vehicles.

The B.C. Ferry runs considerably nicer ships than the Alaska Marine Highway: they're newer, renovated more often, cleaner, and in better shape. The B.C. government puts considerably more money into its ferry system than Alaska, which is forever hoping for more federal funds. However, the larger Canadian ships lack the relaxed, almost camp-out atmosphere of the AMH's working ships. The Canadian ferries seem to exist only for the tourists on its main runs, and you don't get the chance to mingle with residents as much. B.C. runs a high-quality, spotless ferry operation, but the Alaska Marine Highway is considerably more fun. On the other hand, B.C. Ferries are a lot more "civilized," with not nearly as many people sacked out on the benches and almost nobody shaving in the hallways.

■ Food

Food is available on the larger ships; the *Queen of the North* has a dining room, a cafeteria, and vending machines. The larger vessels also have excellent information stations, and can be of assistance with reservations, maps, and city touring plans.

■ Regulations

No smoking is allowed inside any of the ships, other than in a few designated areas. As with the AMH, pets have to stay in your car; there are car deck calls, but again, as with the AMH, these are few and far between, and you're going to have a very unhappy pet by the end of a longer voyage. For RVs, all propane cylinders must be off, and you're not allowed to bring more than two on the ship.

■ Information

For more information on B.C. Ferry, contact them at 1112 Fort St., Victoria, B.C., V8V 4V2. In Canada, ☎ 800-665-6414; in the U.S., 800-642-0066; in Washington State, 800-585-8445.

Legalities & Customs

There are a few things to keep in mind when crossing the border between the U.S. and Canada. You should double check all of this before you hit the border. Over the fall of 2001, things started to change quickly, with both countries requiring extra documentation.

- U.S. citizens entering Canada and Canadian citizens entering the U.S. need not have passports or visas, although showing a passport does speed up the border crossings. Without a passport, all travelers should carry some form of identification. Usually a driver's license suffices, but a birth certificate or voter's registration card are also acceptable. Permanent residents of either country who are not citizens should carry proof of residency. Again, check for current regulations.

- Although recently Canadian Customs have gotten more careful with searches (particularly looking for illegal animal products and guns), as a general rule Customs at both borders are quick and easy. If you look less than clean-cut and prosperous, Canadian Customs usually asks if you have adequate funds for your planned stay in the country. People have been turned away at the border for having less than $150.

- Fruits and vegetables may be inspected or confiscated. This is especially true when you enter Canada from Washington; remember this when you're driving past the fruit stands that line the highway in the miles before the border.

- Dogs and cats over three months old must be vaccinated for rabies; you must have a certificate from a licensed veterinarian that the shot has been given within the past three years.

- You cannot take pistols or any firearm with a barrel length of less than 18.5 inches into Canada. "Long guns" – rifles – are allowed, at least hunting rifles and shotguns. Semi-automatic weapons are forbidden. Canadian Customs will ask if you are carrying any weapons, and the penalty for bringing in an illegal firearm is stiff. Again, this is one to check. Canada has been changing its firearm laws over the past few years.

- Do not even think about bringing illegal drugs into either country. Carry copies of your prescriptions – this speeds matters up if they want to check the pill bottles, and it makes it easier if you lose your bottle and need a refill somewhere along the way.

- Both countries prohibit import of products made from endangered species. This becomes confusing, because there are products made from whale, walrus ivory, bear, seal, and wolf in gift shops all along the highway. However, if you buy one of these items in Canada, you will not be allowed to transport it into the U.S.; if you buy it in Alaska, you will not be allowed to transport it through Canada on the way home without a special permit. Avoid this hassle by not buying endangered species products in Canada. If you're a U.S. citizen, buy them in Alaska and mail them home. Same deal if you're Canadian: buy them in your home country, don't carry them across the border. Those from elsewhere, check your local regulations before you buy.

- You can buy fossilized ivory and whalebone, legally transporting it through either country. If you have any questions, contact the local Fish and Wildlife Office or its equivalent. (As for the ethical questions of buying products made from endangered species, see the section on *Shopping*, pages 91-93.)

- When you return to your home country, Customs officials will assess duty on items purchased abroad. For U.S. citizens who have been out of the country for less than 48 hours, the duty-free allowance is $25; after more than 48 hours, it's $400. Canadian citizens are allowed $20 after 24 hours, $100 after 48 hours, and $300 after seven days.

- People who are not residents or citizens of the U.S. or Canada should check with local embassies or consulates for current entry requirements. A multiple-entry visa is needed for both countries to complete a round-trip of the highway.

For the latest information on Customs, write to: **Department of the Treasury**, U.S. Customs Service, Washington, DC 20041, or your local Customs office. In Canada, write: **Customs Office**, 1001 W. Pender St. Vancouver, B.C. V6E 2M8, Canada.

A SHAMELESS PLUG

For complete information on driving in the north, pick up a copy of the third edition of *Adventure Guide to the Alaska Highway*, written by the same people as the book you're now holding. Same attitude, same attention to detail, and lots and lots of new territory to explore.

Connections

Index

Notes

Notes

Notes